RELUCTANT LIEUTENANT

D1557462

Joseph G. Dawson III, General Editor

Editorial Board:
Robert Doughty
Brian Linn
Craig Symonds
Robert Wooster

RELUCTANT LIEUTENANT

★ ★ ★ ★ ★ ★

FROM BASIC TO OCS IN THE SIXTIES

JERRY MORTON

INTRODUCTION BY G. KURT PIEHLER

TEXAS A&M UNIVERSITY PRESS
COLLEGE STATION

Library of Congress Cataloging-in-Publication Data

Morton, Jerry, 1942–
    Reluctant lieutenant : from basic to OCS in the sixties / Jerry Morton ;
introduction by G. Kurt Piehler.—1st ed.
        p.   cm. — (Texas A&M University military history series ; no. 94)
Includes index.
    ISBN 1-58544-328-x (cloth : alk. paper) — ISBN 1-58544-359-x (pbk.)
    1. Morton, Jerry, 1942– 2. United States. Army—Officers—Biography.
3. United States. Army—Officers—Training of. I. Title. II. Texas A&M
University military history series ; 94.
U53.M67A3   2004
355'.0092—dc22

                                                                2003019688

Photographs are from OCS Graduation Book, U.S. Army Infantry Officer
Candidate School, published by Columbus Office Supply Company under
the supervision of the Officer Candidate Operations Section, The Student
Brigade, Fort Benning, Georgia. Photographs by OC Manners, OC Class
17-67, Fort Dix, New Jersey.

Contents

Preface

THIS BOOK IS an account of my reluctant entrance into the U.S. Army in late August of 1966 and of the ten months and twenty-six days of training it provided me before I was commissioned as a second lieutenant in the infantry. The reader and I reexperience Basic Combat Training (BCT), Advanced Infantry Training (AIT) and the Infantry Officer Candidate School (OCS).

During the spring of 1966, the Vietnam War was a constant evening news item. There was talk of sending in more troops and there were shots of antiwar protesters pressed in between television commercials. I paid attention to the situation because I was concerned that I might become involved in it; my main focus, however, was on my graduate studies. I hoped that it would not affect me directly as I was married, in graduate school planning to get a master's degree at the end of August, and then to do a yearlong internship as a school psychologist in one of the school systems around Cincinnati, Ohio. After the internship I would work for a school system. All of these activities were draft exempt. I thus was surprised when I received an induction center notice in June saying that I had been reclassified 1-A. It meant that I could be drafted at any time. I immediately called my Pittsburgh, Pennsylvania, draft board. They put me at the end of their monthly draft list until September, which meant that on September 1 I would be the first one on the list and would be drafted into the army. It was too late for me to get into an officer candidate class in the navy or coast guard. I was going to be in the army.

After talking with the recruiting sergeant and taking the army's OCS examination, I learned I could go to any army OCS class I wanted to after basic training and AIT. I explained to the recruiter that I would like to work in an area of the army in which I could use my training as a master's-level school psychologist. He said that I wanted to be in the

Adjutant General Corps. Unfortunately, there was no OCS program for that branch. I would have to request a branch transfer after I got commissioned, he explained, and the army's infantry branch had the highest rate of branch transfers from it. With that in mind, I signed up for the infantry and went back to school intent on finishing my master's program. A few days after I completed the last exam for my M.A., I was in the army.

I grew up in a career coast guard family. My father was a chief boatswain's mate and we had moved frequently as he was transferred from lifeboat stations on the Great Lakes to the navigable waterways of the Ohio and Mississippi Rivers. The military was not a bad life to my way of thinking. Being in combat, on the other hand, was not something I wanted to do. I wanted to work on making things better for schoolchildren. Being in the army would interrupt all of that.

In basic training I learned that a lot of the men had just graduated from college or graduate school as I had. They had all suddenly lost their draft-exempt status and had signed up for OCS. Throughout basic training, AIT, and infantry OCS, the people in charge commented on what a highly educated group we were. The infantry OCS graduation book the army gave me states that the men in my OCS company had an average of 15.7 years of education. However, the vast majority of us were commissioned as second lieutenants in the army with about the same amount of army experience: ten months, twenty-six days.

I wrote this book for several reasons. First, many of the stories I relate are funny. I enjoy sharing them and have told them more times than I can count to relatives, friends, and acquaintances. Another reason for writing the book was to share with younger people what was really happening to me and hundreds of thousands of other men at that time. Too often I have encountered young adults who try to interpret that time in an overly romanticized or demonized way. I realize they do not know how it really was. I want them to understand how it actually was, at least for me. With that goal in mind, I have tried to avoid interpreting the things that happened to me other than the way I interpreted them at the time. I have also described the events as I remembered them in the order in which they occurred. As I progressed through the army's training program, some of the earlier events made more sense to me. Again, I did my best not to reinterpret what had happened to me earlier. I want the reader to experience army training in the same manner that I did. My third reason for writing this book is the fact that in the areas of education, business, and human services systems I see too many of the same faulty training assumptions and approaches to the institutional change process today that I experienced in the army in 1966. I hope that in reading this book the change agents in these organizations will see some of the practices that their organizations need to improve upon.

As I mentioned, I have tried to be as accurate as possible in telling my story. I am aware of the tricks that memory can play when one tries to recall events from the past. The belief systems that people possess cause them to interpret events in a specific manner. Thus, people with different beliefs interpret the same events in a completely different way. Those of us who have brothers or sisters often experience this phenomenon at family gatherings. My psychology training before, during, and after my time in the army has made me keenly aware of the problems inherent in eyewitness accounts, especially in stories told from memory that relate to emotionally traumatic events. While acknowledging the difficulty of achieving completely factual accuracy in writing this book, I believe it is a true account of the events in which I participated.

I can say with greater certainty that this book provides an accurate picture of my emotional response to the training I experienced. While it is probably true that there are some factual errors in my narrative, I am not aware of them. Where such errors may occur, they do not detract from the core truth of the book. I have been diligent in carefully recording everything exactly as I remembered it. The reader will note that there are places where I am vague on the exact number of days that we spent doing some things, such as living in tents in the field. I simply do not remember those details, so I omit them. Again, details like that are not important to conveying to the reader the cultural significance of events or the emotional impact they had on me. There are several facts that give me assurance that I have accurately related the overall experience described in the book.

In support of these facts are the positive responses I have received from Vietnam-era veterans who have read my narrative. I also rediscovered my infantry OCS graduation book, and it confirmed what I wrote. I found the original orders sending me from OCS to Fort Bragg, North Carolina, which verified my account of those events. I obtained confirmation about the cold weather I remembered at Fort Dix. Dale Patrick Kaiser of the Carbon Dioxide Information Analysis Center in the Environmental Sciences Division at Oak Ridge National Laboratory was able to review the temperature records for October and November, 1966. On several days the temperature in the region was below freezing. The coldest was October 31, when it got down to twenty-one degrees Fahrenheit.

It was reassuring to discover that my memory was fairly accurate in recalling such things as the manual of arms and the military terminology of the time. Dale Wilson, a retired army major and the copyeditor of this book, graciously corrected the errors I did make.

I have been meticulously careful to report exactly what I have remembered with one exception: I used pseudonyms for all of the people mentioned in the book except myself. In many cases I can remember only a person's nickname; for many others I have no memory of any name. I did, of course, have some close friends whose full names I still remember. However, I felt it best to be consistent and use pseudonyms for everyone.

As a literary device for conveying the immediacy of the moment we all felt during training, I frequently use dialogue. The vast majority of the dialogue is not literally what was said, but it does convey the meaning and its emotional color. In a few cases, the quotations are exactly as I remember them.

Throughout the book I mention rumors I heard. Rumors were always going around, and we were always acting on them. Some were later proven to be accurate, but most of them were not. When I report that the "rumor mill" said such and such, I am not saying that a rumor was true. I do not know if it was true; I had no way of verifying what was rumor and what was fact. We had to determine if we believed something and then act accordingly. The consequences of such actions took care of themselves. In the main, the army never tried to address the rumors one way or the other that I could tell. I thus have related rumors as I experienced them and the impact that they had on me and the other trainees when we heard them.

It is my desire that you find this book interesting and gain insight into the thinking of the young men caught up in the beginning of the military buildup in Vietnam. I hope you will better understand what these young people experienced during their initial contact with the army culture of 1966 and will reflect on how both people and institutions under stress deal with change.

This book is dedicated to Anna, my wife and enthusiastic resident editor, who supported me throughout my U.S. Army experiences and the other events of our thirty-nine years together. It is also dedicated to the men and women who went through the training that I describe. This is our collective story.

There is another important group of people to whom I wish to dedicate this book: all those who supported me in writing it. Foremost is Charlotte Duncan. It was Charlotte, a professional editor, who convinced me that the book needed to be written and would be well received. Charlotte edited all of the work before I sent it to the publisher. Her desire to read each chapter before it was written was a constant motivation. Scot Danforth is another person whose continued optimism inspired me to complete this book. Kurt Piehler's support of my efforts was also a significant encouragement. Jim Sadkovich's early recognition of the book's merits and support through the publishing process were greatly appreciated. There are many more whose names I do not list here to whom I wish to express my deep gratitude for their support of this project.

From the perspective of being an educational administrator and school psychologist during the thirty-two years since I was a student in the Infantry Officer Candidate School, I find that there is one individual from that military experience who has my sincerest admiration for his dedication to making positive changes in the training program. I wish to offer a belated thank you to Lieutenant Colonel Nick J. Nikas, my battalion commander at the Infantry Officer Candidate School in 1967.

RELUCTANT LIEUTENANT

Introduction

Until the First World War, the United States relied on volunteers to fill the ranks of the armed forces. In the nineteenth century, the U.S. Army generally had little difficulty finding enough immigrants, African Americans, and displaced workers to serve in the enlisted ranks.[1] When larger armies were needed in major conflicts, citizens spurred on by patriotic fervor flocked to join the locally raised U.S. Volunteers. When the initial euphoria slackened, bounties and other inducements often succeeded in prodding young men to fight. Only during the Civil War, after the casualty rolls mounted, did conscription become necessary to raise an army. Both the Confederate States of America and the U.S. government adopted a draft with mixed success. In the case of the Confederacy, conscription served primarily to ensure that those who had enlisted voluntarily earlier in the war remained in uniform. The Union army raised few new recruits through conscription and succeeded in provoking the worst riot in American history. In July, 1863, it took Union troops fresh from their victory at the Battle of Gettysburg to fully suppress the New York City draft riot.[2]

In the twentieth century, America relied on conscripts to fight the world wars and "limited" wars of the Cold War era. During the First World War, Pres. Woodrow Wilson and the U.S. Congress abandoned the traditional reliance upon the U.S. Volunteers system for raising a wartime army and the Congress, after considerable debate, adopted a selective service system. Opponents of conscription questioned whether compulsory military service remained constitutionally permissible or militarily necessary. Wilson and other advocates of conscription countered by insisting all male citizens of a republic were obligated to serve their country in time of war, although not necessarily on the battlefield. They insisted that a "selective service" system offered a more equitable and rational way to allocate the manpower necessary to wage total war. At the same time, the Wilson administration supported conscription in order to prevent such political opponents as former president Theodore Roosevelt from raising volunteer regiments.[3]

The United States raised a large army to fight in America's first major overseas war, but there remained a significant amount of draft resistance, especially in the rural South. All-white draft boards in the South often discriminated against African Americans. In many communities, blacks were disproportionately drafted into the army to fill quotas. Many business owners believed the federal government should use the threat of the draft to foster labor peace and prevent wartime strikes. Not surprisingly, organized labor vehemently opposed efforts to use conscription to curb the right of workers to organize and bargain collectively.[4]

After the Armistice in November, 1918, the United States returned to a volunteer army. However, the precedents established regarding the draft would shape how Franklin D. Roosevelt's administration raised an army to fight against Nazi Germany and Imperial Japan. Even before the United States entered the Second World War, Roosevelt prodded Congress to enact peacetime conscription in 1940. During the war, over ten million men would be drafted into the military, with another six million joining voluntarily. The Japanese attack on Pearl Harbor and the German declaration of war had served to unite the country. Although national conscription had much broader support than in either the Civil War or the First World War, there still remained differences over how it should be administered. Who should be exempted from military service? Despite the pleas of educators, few blanket exemptions were granted to college or graduate students. In contrast, there remained substantial public support to offer exemptions to farmers, essential war workers, and fathers with young children (especially pre–Pearl Harbor fathers).

Victory against Germany and Japan in 1945 did not lead to an end of conscription, except for a brief interruption from 1947 to 1948. Even when in the late 1940s Pres. Harry S. Truman pruned defense spending and relied on atomic weapons for national security, the draft remained the principal means by which the military filled the ranks, especially in the case of the army. Conscription not only fed draftees to the military, it also provided a major incentive by encouraging "voluntary" enlistments. Several Defense Department studies conducted in the early 1960s show that just over a third of new enlisted men indicated that the prospect of being drafted had spurred them to sign up.[5] By enlisting, a young man could better determine his fate by picking a more desirable service, which for many was either the navy or air force. In the case of physicians, the possibility of conscription into the enlisted ranks served as an inducement to encourage these and other vital medical personnel to apply for commissioning and thus enjoy the benefits of "officer status" while practicing their profession.

From its inception, supporters of conscription believed it should be used to channel manpower to vital defense occupations. The total wars of the twentieth century required the mobilization of the entire economy and, as a result, key defense workers during the world wars and the Cold War received draft exemptions. During the late 1940s and 1950s there remained significant support both among educators and the general public for exempting college and graduate students from the draft. A widespread consensus developed among federal officials, the business community, and academe that the United States must produce more scientists, engineers, and educators to prevail against the Soviet Union technologically. The successful launch of *Sputnik* in 1957 only heightened concerns among policy makers of the need to strengthen the country's educational infrastructure.

As America's longest war, the war in Vietnam required a substantial number of men to fight it. Our first involvement in Indochina dated back to the Second World War, when the Office of Strategic Services (OSS) provided limited logistical assistance to Ho Chi Minh and his forces in their fight against the Japanese, who had occupied Vietnam with the permission of the Vichy French government in 1941. Although initially reluctant to endorse French efforts to retain Indochina as a colony immediately after World War II, by 1950 the United States was committed to support France's military campaign to defeat Ho Chi Minh. Not only did the United States underwrite the French effort financially in the early 1950s, it also began to send military advisers to the war. When the French decided to pull out of Vietnam after being defeated at Dien Bien Phu in 1954, the United States decided to support the creation of a viable noncommunist regime in South Vietnam. Although the administrations of Dwight D. Eisenhower and John F. Kennedy initially hoped to confine their support of South Vietnam to military hardware and economic aid, the number of military advisers steadily increased, especially during the early 1960s.[6]

American involvement in the Vietnam War must be seen in the context of the larger Cold War. When John F. Kennedy assumed the presidency in January, 1961, he embarked on a major buildup of both nuclear and conventional military forces. In the view of many of his defense advisers, a substantial conventional capability remained essential to make nuclear deterrence credible, especially in Europe. Even after the United

States escalated its involvement in Vietnam, it still maintained massive commitments outside of Indochina. To support the North Atlantic Treaty Organization (NATO), the United States deployed over a half-million troops on the European continent. The U.S. Navy maintained a global naval presence, as well as substantial strategic nuclear capability through a fleet of Polaris submarines. The U.S. Air Force devoted substantial personnel and resources for a high level of readiness for the Strategic Air Command and its force of land-based strategic weapons. During the Vietnam War era, 8.7 million men, the majority of those in the armed forces, never saw service in Indochina. Only slightly more than a third, 2.7 million men, served in country and another six hundred thousand were stationed at air bases in Thailand or Guam or on naval vessels off the coast of Vietnam.[7]

Many myths surround the Vietnam War. Without trying to minimize the impact or significance of the antiwar movement, there remained significant political and public support for American intervention in Indochina, especially in the early 1960s. Many Americans shared Kennedy's vision that the United States must fight the spread of communism throughout the world. The United States during the early part of the Cold War provided military and economic aid to countless Third World nations seeking to suppress communist insurgencies. In the Western Hemisphere, the Kennedy administration in 1961 sought to overthrow the government of Fidel Castro in a Central Intelligence Agency (CIA)–sponsored invasion by Cuban exiles. A year later, President Kennedy compelled the Soviet Union to remove nuclear weapons from Cuba through diplomatic pressure and the enforcement of a naval quarantine around the island.

When Lyndon B. Johnson escalated American involvement in Vietnam in 1964 and 1965 in order to prevent the collapse of the South Vietnamese government, few major public figures publicly dissented. For example, in 1964, the Gulf of Tonkin Resolution authorizing the Johnson administration to intervene in Vietnam to repel North Vietnamese "aggression" unanimously passed in the House of Representatives. Only two members of the Senate voted against this wide-ranging resolution. Many in Congress and the wider public accepted the arguments advanced by the Johnson administration and its supporters concerning the threat posed by the collapse of South Vietnam and how it could lead to a domino effect with emboldened communists going on to seize Cambodia, Thailand, Malaysia, and the rest of Asia.

In retrospect, we know a significant amount of dissent remained within the Johnson administration, Congress, and the military regarding the wisdom of escalating American involvement.[8] Why so little open dissent? The legacy of McCarthyism cannot be discounted. Johnson and many in Congress remembered how Sen. Joseph McCarthy (R-Wisconsin) and other right-wing critics had taken Truman to task for losing China in the late 1940s. Historians even disagree over Johnson's own commitment to the war. Although some have portrayed his decision to escalate U.S. involvement as inevitable, others are less certain. Most biographers of this complex president agree that the Great Society was LBJ's first love and that he remained strongly committed to building a domestic reform agenda that would rival Franklin Roosevelt's New Deal. His critics—both at the time and since—have faulted Johnson for trying to have both "guns and butter" because of the damaging consequences for the economy. Moreover, LBJ is criticized in many quarters for not having fully mobilized American society for the Vietnam War. For example, he only reluctantly agreed to raise taxes to pay for the war's costs. Moreover, there remained only a limited mobilization of reserve and National Guard units.[9]

Jerry Morton's memoir says little about ideology or patriotism as a motivation for joining the military. This was not unique to the Vietnam War era. During the Second World War, social scientists surveying American troops found that small-group loyalty served as the essential force that motivated men to fight. For most combatants, an unwillingness to "let their buddies down" proved more important than patriotism, support of democratic principles, or even hatred of the enemy. Those who read soldiers' memoirs, letters, and oral histories from the Second World War, Korea, or Vietnam will often find that most servicemen and women focused the majority of their daily attention on such mundane matters as food, weather, access to creature comforts, relationships with friends and comrades, and personal survival.[10]

During the period in which Jerry Morton served in the army, there was still significant support for the war, even on many college campuses. As George Flynn has observed, the majority of college students between 1964 and 1970 told pollsters they agreed with the U.S. decision to intervene in Vietnam.[11] Not until after the Tet Offensive in the spring of 1968 did support for the war begin to wane among national elites and the general public. Even after Tet, the majority of Americans were reluctant to leave Indochina unilaterally. In 1968, Richard M. Nixon won election to the presidency pledging that he would achieve "peace with honor." Not until the early 1970s did lack of support for the war prod Congress to begin placing restrictions on U.S. involvement in the war, most notably limiting the use of American ground troops in Cambodia.

Even then, most Americans wanted out of Vietnam not because they viewed it as an immoral war, but because it was not working.[12]

The war in Vietnam was a long war, and when Jerry Morton entered the service in 1966, the armed forces were expanding rapidly, growing from 2.6 million in 1965 to 3.5 million by 1968.[13] Moreover, manpower policies required the continuous influx of new personnel. In contrast to the Second World War, U.S. Army troops during the Vietnam War rotated home after a fixed tour of duty for either reassignment or discharge, just as they had during the Korean War. Volunteers served in the army for three years, but draftees only had to remain in the service for two years. Not only did the military—especially the army—need enlisted men, they also had to train scores of new junior officers. Jerry Morton's memoir suggests that this rapid buildup was not without problems. The army, especially at basic training facilities, groaned under the weight of processing so many new recruits.

The baby boom of the post–World War II era had ensured a large draft pool. In 1955, the draft pool numbered 21,641,000, but by 1964 it had grown to 29,519,000.[14] Proportionally fewer men of draft age were required to perform military service compared to either the Korean War or during the late 1950s. Although a smaller percentage of the eligible male population was drafted, conscription provoked considerable public debate in the late 1960s and early 1970s. Many questioned the fairness and effectiveness of the Selective Service process. Many claimed that conscription imposed an unfair burden on the poor, the working class, and minority groups. In the aftermath of the Vietnam War, both intellectuals and politicians on both the left and right have argued that America's cultural elites did not have to share the burden of this conflict.[15]

Jerry Morton reminds us that there remained a significant number of college-educated men who served during the Vietnam era as a result of conscription. In his accounts of basic training at Fort Dix, New Jersey, and Advanced Infantry Training at Fort Anniston, Alabama, Morton describes the divisions that existed between those with college degrees and those with only a high school education or less. Statistically, Morton was not unique for his level of education. As George Flynn observed in *The Draft*, large numbers of college age men did serve in the Vietnam era: "In 1964, for males aged 27 to 34, only 41 percent of those with an eighth grade or lower education served in the military. High school dropouts served at a 70 percent rate; high school graduates at a 74 percent. College dropouts at a 68 percent rate, and college graduates at a 71 percent rate. By late 1967 the relative proportions were as follows:

60 percent of high school graduates, 50 percent of non–high school graduates, and 40 percent of college graduates saw duty." [16]

Morton's memoir is an invaluable reminder to the nonveteran that army service requires a number of skills and abilities. During the Vietnam War era, the military continued to reject a substantial number of men as unfit for military service. For example, Flynn writes that in 1964 slightly over half of all draftees inducted into the armed forces were rejected as unsuitable for military service.[17] The poor and those without high school diplomas had a higher rejection rate for military service than did inductees who had completed high school or attended some college. Moreover, the army that fought in Vietnam was better educated on average than the one that fought in the Second World War. In Vietnam, 80 percent of all soldiers possessed a high school diploma, but in the "Good War" only 45 percent of men possessed that credential.[18]

Morton is also conscious that there were those with political connections who escaped the draft and were able to join the National Guard. In his memoir, he recalls the disdain he and his fellow soldiers had for members of the guard contingent at Fort Anniston. Although a significant number of middle- and upper-class Americans avoided service in Vietnam, many did not. As in the world wars and Korea, the officer corps during the Vietnam War remained disproportionately the preserve of men holding college degrees and of middle-class backgrounds. Many young officers never made it back home. In the case of the army, they represented 13.5 percent of those killed in Vietnam.[19]

There remained inequities. In contrast to both the Second World War and the Korean War, the majority of Vietnam-era veterans were volunteers. But during the height of American involvement in the war, draftees bore a disproportionate share of the fighting.[20] As Jerry Morton recalls with great honesty, he, like many young men of his generation, volunteered for military service in order to avoid being drafted into the army and assigned to an infantry unit. Although Morton volunteered with the expectation that the army would use his skills as a psychologist in the Adjutant General Corps, when he arrived at boot camp he learned that things would not go according to his original plan.

Most soldiers during the Second World War and the Korean and Vietnam Wars never experienced combat. Modern warfare is dependent upon a vast network of support personnel. For example, during the Second World War, less than a third of army personnel were assigned to the combat arms. During the Vietnam War era, the percentage of troops in combat specialties had declined to 14 percent by 1971.[21] In popular culture, we tend to focus on the experiences of those who serve on the front lines.

During the war itself, the role of the Green Beret gripped the popular imagination. Several novels, a popular song, and even a Hollywood movie starring John Wayne featured the exploits of the army's Special Forces. As Charles Moskos observed in *The American Enlisted Man,* the Green Berets deployed in Vietnam never numbered more than four thousand.[22] Except for the Green Berets, it would not be until the aftermath of the Vietnam War that novelists and Hollywood would grapple with the experiences of the average U.S. serviceman and woman who served in Indochina. In the late 1970s and 1980s, novels and motion pictures focused on the alienation and mistreatment of the average "grunt."

Most Vietnam-era veterans were not grunts. Moreover, as B.G. Burkett notes in his book *Stolen Valor,* the majority of Vietnam veterans were more like Jerry Morton than the shattered wrecks of men depicted in such films as *The Deer Hunter* and *Rambo.* Morton's memoir also reminds the reader that the senior leaders in Vietnam were men who had fought in the Second World War and Korea. Both the senior noncommissioned officers and the colonels and generals of this conflict were men whose military careers had begun in what has commonly been perceived as a "good war."

Since America's withdrawal from the war in 1973 and the collapse of the South Vietnamese regime in 1975, Vietnam has continued to evoke significant debate. Morton's tone is remarkably free of rancor or ideological clichés. His memoir does, however, raise some important issues for both historians and the general public about the war and its aftermath. Did the army adequately train the men who fought in Vietnam as officers and enlisted men? Morton also recounts an army that has not existed since 1973. A generation has passed since the last draftees reported for basic training. Morton offers an unsentimental look at how the conscript army worked. Those who advocate abandoning the "all-volunteer" military and resuming conscription should carefully consider his memoir.

G. Kurt Piehler
Center for the Study of War and Society
University of Tennessee

NOTES

1. Edward M. Coffman, *The Old Army: A Portrait of the American Army in Peacetime, 1784–1898* (New York: Oxford University Press, 1986).

2. Iver Bernstein, *The New York City Draft Riots: Their Significance in Ameri-*

can Society and Politics in the Age of the Civil War (New York: Oxford University Press, 1990).

3. John Whiteclay Chambers II, *To Raise an Army: The Draft Comes to Modern America* (New York: Free Press, 1987).

4. Chambers, *Raise an Army,* passim. Jeanette Keith, "The Politics of Southern Draft Resistance, 1917–1918: Class, Race, and Conscription in the Rural South," *Journal of American History* 87 (Mar., 2001): 1335–61.

5. Charles C. Moskos Jr., *The American Enlisted Man: The Rank and File in Today's Military* (New York: Russell Sage, 1970), 49.

6. For the best introductory text on the Vietnam War, see George Herring, *America's Longest War: The United States and Vietnam, 1950–1975,* 4th ed. (New York: McGraw-Hill, 2001). For an anthology offering a diverse range of historical interpretations of American involvement in the Vietnam War, see Andrew J. Rotter, ed., *Light at the End of the Tunnel: A Vietnam War Anthology* (Wilmington, Del.: Scholarly Resources, 1999). For two excellent historiographic essays, see Gary R. Hess, "The Unending Debate: Historians and the Vietnam War," *Diplomatic History* 18 (spring, 1994): 239–64; and Lorenzo M. Crowell, "Thinking about the Vietnam War," *Journal of Military History* 60 (Apr., 1996): 339–57.

7. B. G. Burkett and Glenna Whitley, *Stolen Valor: How the Vietnam Generation Was Robbed of its Heroes and its History* (Dallas: Verity Press, 1998), 51.

8. For two recent studies that document the misgiving within the U.S. military toward American involvement in Vietnam, see Robert Buzzanco, *Masters of War: Military Dissent and Politics in the Vietnam Era* (New York: Cambridge University Press, 1996); and H. R. McMaster, *Dereliction of Duty: Lyndon Johnson, Robert McNamara, the Joint Chiefs of Staff, and the Lies that Led to Vietnam* (New York: HarperCollins, 1997).

9. There is a vast and growing literature on the Johnson administration's decision to escalate American involvement in the war. See, e.g., Robert Dallek, *Flawed Giant: Lyndon Johnson and His Times, 1961–1973* (New York: Oxford University Press, 1998); Lloyd Gardner, *Pay Any Price: Lyndon Johnson and the Wars for Vietnam* (Chicago: Ivan Dee, 1995); and Fredrik Logevall, *Choosing War: The Lost Chance for Peace and the Escalation of War in Vietnam* (Berkeley: University of California Press, 1999). For an excellent study of the relationship between the press and the American war effort in Vietnam, see William M. Hammond, *Reporting Vietnam: Media and Military at War* (Manhattan: University Press of Kansas, 1998).

10. See Samuel A. Stouffer et al, *The American Soldier,* 4 vols. (Princeton, N.J.: Princeton University Press, 1949), for a classic sociological study of the American soldier in World War II. For more recent scholarship on combat motivation, see Gerald F. Linderman, *The World Within War: America's Combat Experience in World War II* (New York: Free Press, 1997).

11. George Q. Flynn, *The Draft, 1940–1973* (Manhattan: University Press of Kansas, 1993), 185.

12. For an early analysis of the ambivalence of the American public toward the war, especially after the Tet Offensive, see Godfrey Hodgson, *America in Our Time* (New York: Random House/Vintage, 1976), 384–98.

13. Flynn, *Draft,* 170.

14. Ibid., 169.

15. For two sophisticated arguments on the equity of Vietnam-era conscription,

see D. Michael Shafer, "The Vietnam-Era Draft: Who Went, Who Didn't, and Why It Matters," in *The Legacy: The Vietnam War in the American Imagination*, ed. D. Michael Shafer (Boston: Beacon Press, 1990); and Christian G. Appy, *Working-Class War: American Combat Soldiers and Vietnam* (Chapel Hill: University of North Carolina Press, 1993). For a differing interpretation, see Burkett, *Stolen Valor*, passim.

16. Flynn, *Draft*, 194.
17. Ibid., 207.
18. Burkett, *Stolen Valor*, 55.
19. Ibid., 48.
20. Flynn, *Draft*, 234–35.
21. Ibid., 227.
22. Moskos, *American Enlisted Man*, 23–24.

CHAPTER 1

Zero Week

IT DID NOT START as it always does in the movies when new recruits arrive. In the movies, as soon as they start getting off the bus, drill instructors begin shouting at everyone. The scared recruits in turn try to do everything demanded of them at once, without success. In contrast, my arrival at Fort Dix for basic training that night had a surreal quality. There were no shouting drill instructors or scared recruits. It was just a bunch of guys who got on a bus with me at the Newark, New Jersey, bus station late that night. It was the middle of August, 1966. No doubt, the nightly TV news had reported on the expanding Vietnam conflict, Lyndon Johnson's resolve to send more troops, and protests from those opposed to the draft—the typical news you saw on a slow-news night.

The bus stopped. In a subdued voice the driver said, "Fort Dix." There was a little mumble from some of the passengers as we rose from our seats. Picking up small suitcases and parcels, we slowly descended the steps onto military ground.

It was dark. A large wooden building stood alone about fifty yards or so ahead of us. Lights blazed from it. Nothing looked familiar. The darkness and the open space surrounding the building seemed to go on for a great distance. The lit building was the only place to go. No one was there to tell us what to do. As if we were a species of herding animals, our group assumed a subtle movement. It had established its own momentum. I moved with it.

Inside was a long, linoleum-topped counter with a host of active clerks behind it. One group of civilians was just exiting the building at the far end as we entered. "What's your shirt size?" a clerk said to me as another handed me an army-green duffel bag. "Medium," I replied as he pushed a pile of green fatigue shirts my way. From observing some of the men in front of me, I knew to put my shirts into the duffel bag. Progressing down the line, I also received pants, underwear, shoes, and socks. Then I was outside in the dark again. No one had shouted at me. No one had cursed. The whole operation seemed to function on its own without anyone being in charge.

As our group grew in size, an army bus drove up. The herding instinct again took over and we filled it up. The bus pulled out and smoothly accelerated. We traveled down a road for several minutes and then approached the fringes of a large area crammed with buildings. They were long, two-story wooden structures. The streetlights were intense. The buildings seemed to go on in endless rows into the illuminated darkness.

The bus stopped and the door opened. A building that stood between the lights on the street and the darkness behind it was before us. Struggling to carry the fully stuffed duffel bags, we filed off. Someone began moving toward the building. The rest of us followed. I was tired. It had been a long day and it had extended into the late night. Boarding the plane in Cincinnati that morning had been hard. As we pulled away from the terminal I could see my wife inside the glass-walled boarding area, waving and struggling not to cry.

New York was my first stop. After figuring out how to get to a commuter airport, I arrived with a long layover to endure. The army had meticulously arranged my journey and provided the tickets. The commuter plane flew me to Newark in the evening. I waited until midnight to catch the bus to Fort Dix. While sitting there in the dingy, trash-scattered bus station I fully understood: The army was not giving me any special treatment. The comfort of the commercial airline flight had seduced me into thinking otherwise.

Inside the building was a large room with two rows of steel-frame bunk beds. A mattress was neatly folded at the end of each bed. Folded sheets and a mattress cover sat on each of them. As the men filed into the room they moved toward a bunk, dropped their gear, pulled down the mattress, and lay down. No one bothered to put on the mattress covers, sheets, or pillowcases. It reminded me of arriving at Boy Scout camp in the summer. You claimed a bunk and that was it. For me, sleep came instantly.

The morning light woke me. There was quiet talk inside the building. Most of the beds had been slept in, but many were now empty. My bunk was centered on a window facing a four-lane street. In the distance were identical buildings similar to the one that housed us. The main activities for my building had to be on the opposite side—the side that had the unending rows of my building replicated innumerable times.

The latrine was at the end of the building. A long row of urinals, commodes, and washbasins with accompanying mirrors greeted me. After taking care of my basic needs, I realized I was hungry. I dressed in my civilian clothes. That was what most of the others had done. While I was brushing my teeth, I started talking to a guy who had arrived a little earlier than I. He asked me what I thought about the killing last night. Killing? What killing? Nothing had awakened me. He asked where my bunk was. I told him. It was outside my window that the MP was killed, he said.

Vietnam returnees awaiting discharge from the army were housed in buildings located far across the four-lane road. Some of them came over to prey on the new inductees, who did not know what was going on. They would sneak into the barracks and steal their valuables, my new companion explained. He said two military policemen had been chasing one of them behind our building. The trailing MP had shouted for the man to stop or he would shoot. He meant to fire a warning shot in the air. His gun hand came down as a natural part of his running motion when he pulled the trigger. The back of the head of the first MP was blown off. My informant could not believe that I had slept through it. When I got back to my bunk I looked out the window. Traces of blood were in the grass.

Well, I thought, so this is the army. Accidents happen everywhere. However, this one was close. The strangeness of it all kept me from having a deep emotional reaction to the incident.

Outside, I asked someone where the mess hall was. He said he thought the mess hall was about four buildings over and nine down, but he was not sure. I thanked him and began walking. The farther I went into the maze of buildings, the fewer people I saw dressed in civilian clothes. The level of military dress was not the same. Some men wore civilian shirts with fatigue pants. Others had the reverse. Military shoes and boots were intermingled with a variety of civilian footwear. Most of the men lounging around the area wore army boots, fatigue pants, and a T-shirt. It was hot. That would become my uniform when I returned from breakfast. I would blend in.

Moving through the chow line, I got scrambled eggs, bacon, coffee, and toast. It looked good. The servers seemed uninterested in their jobs, but they performed adequately and spoke pleasantly enough when spoken to.

Tray in hand, I surveyed the hundreds of men eating throughout the dining hall in search of someone to sit with. I needed to find out what was happening, so I chose to sit with a group of guys dressed in the uniform of the day. They did not know what was going on. They had been there two days and no one had told them anything. This was "zero week," they said. It did not count as part of basic training. Somehow you were were assigned to a basic training company, but they did not know how or when that took place.

It was a relief to return to my building. I was having difficulty remembering which building it was. The fact that it faced away from the four-lane street helped. My gear was still under my bunk. Meanwhile, someone else had put his stuff on the top bunk. A few guys were scattered around the building reading or sleeping. A couple of guys were talking. I put on my army clothes. They fit fairly well. I liked the boots. They were made of black leather and had uppers that fit comfortably above the ankles—good hiking boots. In fact, they were my first leather boots ever.

The day passed slowly. We waited around for someone to come and tell us what to do, afraid that if we went too far from the building we would miss something. When some empty army buses showed up early in the afternoon, expressions of relief and dread were intermixed on the faces of the new inductees.

A T-shirt-clad guy wearing combat boots walked into the barracks and started yelling at us. At first it was difficult to make out what he was saying. He talked fast and kept turning his head this way and that. Whatever he said, people were getting on the buses. I followed. As my bus pulled out, someone explained that we were going to get haircuts. I looked around. Almost everyone's hair was relatively short. Overall, we looked like conservative college guys. There were a few outstanding exceptions. One guy took the prize. His hair hung well below his shoulders. Why would someone want to come into the army that way, I thought? Surely he must have known that it would be a real magnet for drawing comments. It was.

The hippie-hairstyle guy was the focus of attention as we filed into a large hall outfitted with barber chairs and barbers. A horde of T-shirted army guys pushed huge piles of hair into even larger piles by the walls. Laughter and catcalls filled the building. There was no need for chairs along the barren walls. The line moved continuously toward the busy barbers.

A roar of laughter spilled out when the hippie sat in a barber's chair. He laughed, too. The clippers moved through his hair like a snow shovel. At first it just mounded up; then it toppled over, falling off to one side. The grayish-white skull showed through the thick hair like a dirty sidewalk. The laughter increased. Quickly he was shorn of his stringy, oily, brown-and-black locks. It made him look naked. He appeared to be much thinner. Obviously he had come in with several friends who knew him well. His name was Louis. He left the chair in good humor and kidded his buddies as they, too, lost their hair.

When my turn in the chair came it was no big deal. The barber nodded to me and I climbed through the four-inch-thick mat of hair surrounding his workstation and sat down. He whipped a sheet around me. The cutting began. It took him about eight sweeps of my head and it was over. When he finished, I paid him the obligatory dollar. It seems the barbers were real civilians.

We reboarded the buses and went back to the barracks. The cause for the excitement seemed small, but it provided such a boost after the boredom of the morning that it magnified itself. We all had something to joke about and to break the ice when talking to each other. The bald heads gave us a sense of commonality.

The next morning, everyone woke up when he felt like it. We started dressing the same. After breakfast, several of us were sitting outside the barracks when we spotted someone wearing a single stripe on his uniform sleeves walking toward us. We concluded that he must have been around a little while or he would not have had time to get the stripes sewn on his uniform. He explained that he was a private E-2 and was just walking through. We asked him if anyone was coming by soon. He laughed and assured us that the army would not let us miss much. All we had to do was be patient. About an hour later, three guys wearing fatigues came into the barracks and started yelling for everyone to get outside in a line. A few men ran out the door but most of us walked. Admittedly, we walked briskly, but we did walk.

Outside, the three army guys told us that our barracks had to send two guys to work in the mess hall, eight guys to clean up some compound somewhere, and fifteen guys to go on a truck to do something else. Then they went down the line and started counting people out: fifteen for the truck, eight for the compound, and two for the mess hall. I was in the select group going to the mess hall.

It was about 11 A.M. when the two of us arrived at the eating factory. A guy dressed in white and wearing an apron told me to get into the kitchen and start cleaning pots. There were two other fellows there. They were soaked with sweat. Leftover food decorated their arms, faces, and all of their clothing. Pots were everywhere. It seemed as though every one of them had burned stuff clinging to their bottoms. I walked to the sink, grabbed a scouring pad, and began scrubbing. It was nice to have something to do. I had worked in my college's dining hall throughout my undergraduate years. Scrubbing pots was nothing new. Just as it seemed we were getting ahead of the clutter, new pots would come in. It never stopped. One of my partners seemed to disappear at around 2 P.M. I was feeling pretty tired.

A member of the kitchen staff came by and said we could stop and rest awhile. I asked him if we could have something to eat. He seemed surprised that we had not eaten lunch. After he showed us where we could get some food, we loaded up our trays and rested for about half an hour.

My partner was from a small town nearby. He was housed in a barracks deeper inside the maze of buildings. This was his third day in the army. He did not know any more about what was going on than I did. Washing pots and pans was the hardest detail he had been assigned to, though. He said picking up around the barracks the day before had not been all that hard. New people were coming in day and night. He reported that the place was getting pretty crowded.

"Okay, break's over," the mess-hall person said. Sure enough, there was a huge pile of dirty pans waiting for us. Around six in the evening, my partner went to get something to eat. He never came back. About 10 P.M., a different mess-hall guy came back and told me I could leave the few remaining pots in the sink. He added that I was to come back at eight the next morning. He said I was a good worker.

Eight o'clock in the morning came early. I awoke at 7:30 A.M. To my amazement, I got to the mess hall in time to get a bite to eat before eight rolled around. The same mess-hall guy I had seen the morning before was there. He was pleased to see me. Around nine or 9:30, three other guys joined me. They, too, had been assigned to the pots-and-pans detail. After I had our crew organized and an assembly-line type of system going, the mess-hall guy called me over. He said I did not need to work so hard. He told me to take an hour or so to sweep out the mess hall. After a cup of coffee, I went to my task. It did not take long. I worked at a brisk pace and within an hour had the whole floor swept.

When I returned to the pot-scrubbing crew, one of them had gone. I took up his duties. By two in the afternoon I was tired. I asked one of the crew how he knew when the detail was over. He said he did not know. He figured they would work you to death if you let them. The last couple of days, whenever he got tired he would just drift off from the detail to which he had been assigned and go back to his barracks. No one seemed to care.

By 4 P.M., both of my remaining crewmembers had disappeared.

Three new guys were working with me. Around five, I left the kitchen to go to the latrine. Everyone was working hard. Placing my dirty apron on a chair, I calmly walked out the door. Returning to my barracks, I talked with some of the other guys. They said an acting sergeant had come. He would be our assistant drill instructor (DI) in our basic training company. The training company had just graduated a group of new soldiers and they would be going over our paperwork in a day or two. He would be by at that time to answer some of our questions. The group decided to go to chow. It was almost 6:30. I decided to go with them, hoping to hide myself in the crowd.

There was a long line of men waiting to go through the chow line. I was anxious. None of the regular kitchen staff were recognizable to me. The cooks were all back at the stoves.

In the morning, I made it a point to be on the lookout for people who looked like they were collecting recruits to go on a detail. I avoided them all. Breakfast went smoothly. Several guys were picking up trash around the place, so I joined them just for something to do. They were from all parts of the Northeast. None of them seemed to be from the Cincinnati area. I was alone. The guy in charge of the detail was not very interested in how well we did the job. The day passed pleasantly.

On the fifth day at Fort Dix, I decided to go exploring. It was mid-afternoon. An army truck had brought our work detail back early. We had spent the morning in a warehouse putting mattress covers on new mattresses. It took two men to do the job efficiently. One guy held the mattress up so that the midpoint rested on his head and pulled the sides down so that it formed an elongated inverted V. Meanwhile, the other guy slipped the mattress cover onto the end he was facing and worked it up as the head-holder jiggled it down. If it had not been so hot, the work would not have been all that bad. It sure beat sitting around waiting for something to happen.

Leaving our barracks, I began to walk back into the maze of buildings. The walk started out all right. The sweltering heat caused you to start sweating that sticky kind of sweat that just hangs on you. It was never enough to roll nicely down your face. It just sat there and added to your discomfort. At first there were not many people around. They must all have been inside the buildings or away on details. You did not want to go inside any of them for fear of being jumped as a thief.

About fifteen buildings into the maze, more and more half-civilians-half-soldiers began to appear. Another five buildings into it and I was astounded. People were everywhere. The streets were impassable. People were swarming like confused ants. You had to watch where you put your foot down at almost every step. If you did not watch you would step on a person, a mattress, or someone's personal belongings. As far as I could see, the streets were crowded with a buzzing mass of men in civilian clothes or a mix of civilian and army clothing. No one was as fully army dressed as I in my T-shirt, fatigue pants, and combat boots.

My appearance prompted several of the civilian-army guys to approach me. They wanted to know what they should do and what it was like to be in the army. How the hell did I know? There was a shared humor in the recognition that I did not know much more than they did.

Gradually, I began to understand part of their story. There was no room at the inn. More precisely, all of the barracks were full of inductees. My bus had dropped us off at one of the last, if not *the* last, empty barracks designated for new arrivals. Everyone after that was given a mattress, a mattress cover, a sheet, and bits and pieces of whatever army clothing the issue point still had in stock. It looked as if they had run out of combat boots and black leather shoes first. The next item to go was T-shirts. Then it was fatigue pants.

These guys were miserable. There were only a couple of trees to sit under for shade. No one came to tell them what was going on. Some of them had been there for several days. Others arrived as I watched. What would happen if it rained? The overall scene was depressing. I never returned during my remaining days of zero week.

Zero week ended up lasting ten days for those of us in my barracks. It did not count as part of our eight weeks of basic training. The recruiting sergeant who signed me up had said that I would go to basic training for eight weeks and then to Infantry Officer Candidate School for six months. After that I could get a branch transfer to the Adjutant General Corps. My entrance test scores were so high that he was sure I would score high in my OCS classes, making me eligible for a transfer out of the infantry to any branch I wanted. After two years as an officer, I would be a civilian again. Zero week was just lost time to me. What a frustration it all was.

The acting sergeant who had visited our barracks earlier, Sergeant Nickels, returned as promised. He made a nice impression. The brown campaign hat the DIs wore was imposing. It looked like a Canadian Mountie's hat you see in the movies. His highly starched fatigue pants and shirt were wrinkle free. Both had precise, sharp creases in them. That was something, given the day's heat. He was tan and lean. His nose was large, but not obnoxiously so. There was a fine edge to it in the classic Roman style. It was his most outstanding physical characteristic.

The sergeant carefully explained that his three yellow chevrons sewn on each sleeve indicated that he was a buck sergeant, the lowest grade of sergeant. He added that he was really a specialist fourth class, but they had made him an acting buck sergeant. A buck sergeant is an E-5, whereas a specialist four is an E-4. The big difference was that E-5s made more money and sergeants had command authority. Sergeant Nickels wanted us to clearly understand that he was only an acting sergeant. That fact seemed very important to him. He said he would be our assistant DI. The DI for our basic training platoon was Staff Sergeant Boone. Sergeant Nickels said we would all like him because he was extremely knowledgeable and fair. Sergeant Nickels said that Staff Sergeant Boone had already taught him a lot.

When we reported to our basic training unit, we would be the third platoon in Charlie Company. We would be given an opportunity to send our clothes to the post laundry. It would cost a couple of dollars per load, depending on how much we sent out. This was good news to me as my pot-cleaning clothes were quickly ripening. The army had issued us white cloth bags that were closed with a drawstring. We were all using them as our laundry bags. Mine was stuffed full. Before we sent anything out, we needed to get our names stenciled on all of our clothes. We were to buy our own marking pens, but Sergeant Nickels had some old ones we could start using now so we would have a head start on the project. The base store, known as the post exchange (PX), was about two miles from our barracks. There we could get things like permanent ink pens, stencils, shoe polish, toothpaste, and various other items. The sergeant told us to stock up before we started basic training. Because the training was so intense, we would have little time to visit the PX once it began. Several of us thanked him. He was very personable.

As we waited to be sent to Charlie Company to start our basic training, I began to learn more about some of the guys who were going to be in my platoon. A little over half of them had graduated from college in June and been drafted. Several had signed up for officer candidate school. Most of those were going to Transportation Corps OCS or Signal Corps OCS. A couple of them were going to Field Artillery OCS. I could find only one other guy who was going to Infantry OCS. He was a big, quiet guy who came from a farm in central Ohio. Most of the college guys and all of the noncollege guys were from New Jersey. It seemed that the only ones from outside the New Jersey area were those who had signed up for OCS before entering the army. There was only one other guy beside myself who had a master's degree. His was in English. He seemed a little strange and stayed to himself. He read a lot.

It took a while to find the PX. Like everything else, it was in a converted barracks building. They seemed to have a little bit of everything except someone to help you find what you needed. The PX was filled with newly inducted civilians in partial military dress. The nice thing was, we were all in the same boat. If you wanted to know where the shoe polish was, you just asked the guy next to you. If he did not know, the guy next to him remembered seeing it a few aisles back. And so it went. I decided to get an extra razor and can of shaving cream. In my discussions with some of the guys, they had said that in OCS you always had to have a spare of everything—a spare that you never used. You would set them out for inspections and hide the stuff you actually did use. If you did not do that, you could never get the stuff you used clean enough to pass inspections. With that in mind, I got an extra toothbrush and toothpaste. After all, I reasoned, in just eight weeks I would be in OCS. For all I knew, this might be my last chance to get my supplies.

I wrote a letter to my wife every day. She was unable to mail her daily letters to me because we were not assigned a mailing address until we got to our basic training company.

At last the buses came for us. We were going to start being in the real army. For the most part, we joked and laughed as we boarded the bus. Some of the guys remained quiet. Groups of friends stayed together. People who had known each other before joining the army stayed together; the OCS guys tended to clump together on the basis of the branch school they were going to attend; and so on. I did not feel particularly close to any one group, but I tended to gravitate toward the college graduates.

CHAPTER 2

The Beginning

T HEY WERE there waiting for us, the sergeants.

"Move. *Move!* MOVE!"

"Get out of there!"

"Form up in a line!"

"Quick, quick!"

"You're in the army now!"

They were screaming at us from everywhere. It was chaos. Rushing off the bus as fast as the crowd would let me while dragging the duffel bag on the floor with the laundry bag and little civilian tote bag over my shoulder, I squeezed out of the narrow doorway onto the sidewalk and bumped into a screaming sergeant.

"Third Platoon over here!" Sergeant Nickels shouted as other sergeants called out for the 1st, 2d, and 4th Platoons. We tried to form up quickly by platoons. Stragglers were wandering everywhere. Some looked dazed; others had an angry look. Some just looked put out.

"Which platoon am I in?"

"How in hell should I know?"

"Form up in four ranks!"

"Get in any platoon!"

"That's my duffel bag, idiot."

I could hear and understand only a few random statements out of the swirl of shouting that filled the air. There were a lot of sergeants. Too many to sort out.

Sergeant Nickels was standing next to another sergeant. The rank insignia on his sleeves consisted of three arrow-shaped chevrons pointing upward like Nickels's and a rounded, upside-down one underneath it called a "rocker." Staff Sergeant Boone stood with his lower lip slightly extended, surveying the platoon. He stood about five feet, ten inches tall. He was of stocky build with an observable potbelly. It was not overly large. It just looked out of sync with the rest of him. He wore dark-rimmed glasses.

This was our platoon sergeant. Without emotion he began barking out names. "Anderson, William!" was first. Down the alphabet he went. The other platoons were going through the same process. Those in the wrong platoon were sent to the one that had them on its roster. In short order, it appeared that most people were finding their little place in the army's grand plan.

"Third Platoon, you're on the third floor!" Sergeant Boone shouted. "When I tell you you're dismissed, you are to go as quickly as you can to the third floor! You will select a bunk! You will make up the bunk with the mattress cover, sheets, and blanket that are on the bunk! You will take possession of the wall locker to the right of your bunk! You will prepare for an inspection of your bunk, your wall locker, and your gear! The inspection will begin shortly after you enter your platoon bay. The company commander, Lieutenant Brown, will conduct the inspection! Are there any questions!" The barking sergeant's words were more statement than question.

All kinds of sergeants were walking around, glaring at various ones of us as we stood at attention. Periodically, they would seem to converge to mumble something and then scatter for more glaring.

A thin black guy in the platoon to my right seemed to draw a lot of attention. His face was covered with a short, curly stubble and myriad little bumps. One sergeant got up close to his face and screamed something about his sloppy appearance. The guy screamed back at the sergeant—something about not being able to shave. We were stunned that he had shouted at the sergeant. So was the sergeant. He got red in the face, his fists were clenched at his sides, and he spoke in a loud, rapid voice. It was too garbled to understand. He was definitely pissed. Others were also attracting the various sergeants' attention. They seemed to be particularly irritated by people smiling or coughing. There seemed to be an ample supply of both. I was determined to remain anonymous, if that were at all possible.

An Asian-looking sergeant with two rockers under his three chevrons centered himself in front of the four platoons and shouted out something that brought the platoon sergeants to the front of their platoons. They stood at attention, facing him. It was clear that the Asian sergeant was a warrior. He had deep lines in his face and a lot of patches of one kind or another on his uniform. There appeared to be no fat on his body. He could have started out in a slow trot and kept it up for the rest of the day. It was clear from everything about him that you did not want him on your case.

"Bring your platoons to attention!" shouted the Asian sergeant.

The platoon sergeants looked over their right shoulders and shouted in unison, "Platoon! Atten-*shun!*"

Silence mostly fell over the group. A few of the new recruits kept talking. They had made a mistake. Their respective assistant platoon sergeants ran to them and hoarsely whispered things that caused them to be silent.

When silence was present, the warrior, Sergeant Soto, spoke. Without the slightest hint of a smile, he welcomed us to Charlie Company of the Nth Battalion of the Nth Brigade of the Something-or-Other Army. He said he was Sergeant First Class Soto, the company's senior drill instructor. We could talk to him about our problems any time he was not too busy to hear them. He had a slight Asian accent. I doubt that anyone wanted to point it out to him. After his brief introduction he uttered a few sharp, barking words that were unintelligible to most of us but caused the platoon sergeants to turn and order us up to the platoon bays at a run.

When we got to the double doors in the center of the three-story cinderblock building the real chaos began. People fell down. Duffel bags got separated from their owners. The owners tried to fight the tide with marginal success. Behind the mob were the sergeants. "Move! *Move!* MOVE!" they screamed.

The next hurdle was the stairwell. It was a sea of cursing people that rippled like the kicked sides of a snake whose only goal is to escape the pain.

Steel-framed cots with spring-supported metal webbing holding thin, folded mattresses were in neat rows against both sides of the long walls. Everything was neat and clean as we burst into the 3d Platoon's bay. Immediately beds were claimed. Duffel bags and the like piled up around them. I unfurled my mattress and began making up the bed. Someone seemed to know the army way of making it and was showing a friend. Several of us gathered around and watched. Someone else seemed to know how to put your stuff in the locker the army way. In short order, the 3d Platoon's bay began to look neat in what we thought was the army way.

A routine was thus quickly established. Someone would have a way of putting up something that seemed impressive and the rest of us copied it. Another person would say that he had a friend who was in the army and he said that the sergeants wanted your shaving gear to be really clean. Guys started to clean out their safety razors with their tooth-brushes.

My shaving gear was in bad shape. You know you never pay attention to such things until someone else points them out to you. I guess I had been using my razor for six years or more. I mean, it was a perfectly good razor. All you had to do was rinse the shaving cream off of it and change the blade every so often. As I looked at it for the first time with a critical eye, I was shocked. There was no way I was ever going to get it looking clean before the sergeants came up to inspect us. Part of it had turned into a sickly green crust that would not come off. Other parts had a soap film layered over them so many times that they had the lacquered look of old furniture left out in the sun too long and then rained on. The rain dried as flies got their wings stuck in the sticky mess. In their haste to escape, the insects had left parts of their wings behind. These had become part of the lacquered finish as well.

The toothbrush situation was little better. Anyone could look at my toothbrush and know that something must be alive in it. The caked-and-dried residue of thousands of applications of toothpaste had to be protecting some blissful creature, unaware that it was in the army now. Even the ends of the bristles were frayed with use.

Thank heaven the accumulated crud in the nozzle of my can of shaving cream could be removed with a borrowed toothpick. The yellow stain flecked with suspicious material was another matter.

Most of the men seemed equally concerned about the lack of cleanliness of their toilet articles. They were vigorously scrubbing on them. Once I realized it was impossible to clean up my stuff, it was a simple decision to substitute it with the brand-new gear. I would simply bury my regular razor and toothbrush in the laundry bag. Part of me shuddered at the thought of my toothbrush touching all of those filthy clothes. What the hell! I would clean the toothbrush before I put it in my mouth again.

Simply opening up my laundry bag was an unpleasant task. It smelled bad just to be within a hand's reach of it. Opening it allowed the smell of stale sweat, rotten kitchen food, and other unpleasant but unidentifiable odors to rush into your nostrils in one big *whoosh*. Bad business, indeed. Part of me felt a little guilty about hiding the stuff. It was what they routinely did in OCS because everyone knew it and the army condoned it or it would not be what was done went my reasoning. I just had not known that I would have to do it in basic training, too.

Word went through the bay that the sergeants and Lieutenant Brown had started inspecting 1st Platoon down on the first floor. We could hear them yelling and screaming and throwing stuff. It was bad. Apparently people had a lot of stuff that the lieutenant did not want them to have. Candy was a definite no-no. God; I had a couple of candy bars and some chewing gum in my locker. Into the laundry bag they went—along with several other items of possible contraband or dubious cleanliness. The laundry bag was stretched to near bursting. Boy, did that bag stink! I doubted that I would eat anything that had been in there. I just had to get it out of sight. One thing seemed certain: No one but me would voluntarily put his hands into that laundry bag.

We all had our laundry bags tied to the end of our bunks in basically the same manner. Rumor had it that that was the army way. Any other way would get you in trouble.

"Attention!" barked Sergeant Soto. We all froze in place. The room was filled with bodies as still as ice. The lieutenant walked in. Eyeballs rolled to the door. He was not much to look at: about five-foot-five and slender of build. He was not skinny, just wiry. Dark-rimmed glasses, just a little too big for his face, sat on the bridge of his nose. Bright, white front teeth were his most prominent physical feature. Their white tips peeked through his closed mouth. His head was topped with coal-black hair that stood up on its short stubble like a 1950s' crew cut. If his skin had not been white he could have been a model for the *Sgt. Fury and His Howling Commandos* comic book. No, he would not have been Sergeant Fury. He would have been one of the North Korean commies that Sergeant Fury routinely blew away with a machine gun tucked under one arm and a long belt of ammo supported by the other as he screamed in bold type: "AAAAAAAAAAAAAAAAAAA!"

"Stand in front of your lockers for inspection now!" boomed Sergeant Soto. "Stand at attention in front of your locker, Soldier!" he screamed at the unlucky man whose locker was closest to the door. We all flinched. A few coughed. My locker was about two-thirds of the way from the door where they started inspecting. The inspection began with the first guy in my row.

"This shaving gear is filthy. It's gross!" Lieutenant Brown said flatly, his voice tinged with disgust. He slammed down the razor. It seemed to echo in the silence of the room. The coughing started again.

The next man's principal sin seemed to be his filthy clothes. He started to explain. A quick look from the lieutenant's black eyes shut him up. Disgust was then layered upon the young man for lacking any pride or common sense for his personal hygiene. And so it went until they got to the man beside me.

The lieutenant lost it. In one quick motion he swept everything out of the top shelf of the man's wall locker. Items scattered throughout the bay—skimming over the floor and ricocheting off bed legs before finally coming to rest in both obvious and hidden places.

"I just left the Korean DMZ! People are ready to kill or be killed at a moment's notice and this is the shit they are bringing in to be combat troops? I just can't believe it!" he screamed to no one and everyone.

He was in my face. I braced at attention. He was close. If I had not been so bothered, I probably could have smelled his breath. Sergeant Soto stood behind him. His arms were behind his back as he stood crisply at parade rest, his straight-ahead stare boring into nowhere.

Slowly the lieutenant looked into my wall locker. Reaching over my shoulder, he gently picked up my safety razor. Turning the handle, he opened the blade holder. He held it close to his glasses and then lowered it to his side as he moved directly in front of the open locker. He moved the few clothes I had hanging in it and picked up the army dress shoes I had just finished shining. In his methodical way, he turned them in several directions before gently returning them to their original spot.

Moving the razor to within an inch of my nose he loudly stated: "This is the cleanest razor I've seen all day. This is the way it should look. Good job, Soldier!" He gently replaced it in its original position. He turned to go to the next man. I felt relief. I had made it through my first encounter with the real army in fine style.

Sergeant Soto reached into my locker and retrieved my razor from its resting place. Just as Lieutenant Brown was squaring up in front of the next man, Sergeant Soto whispered something in his ear. The lieutenant stopped, turned, and took the razor from him. Instantly he was in my face.

"Have you ever shaved with this razor?" he shouted.

This was going to be bad was the message that raced through my mind. "No, Sir!" I replied.

"You tried to deceive an officer!" he hissed at me, spraying my face with spittle. His white face had turned red. His fists were clenched at his sides.

"No, Sir," I said with less confidence. This was *really* bad.

"Why did you try to deceive me?" he said, glaring.

Sputtering through my semihyperventilating, constricted throat, I explained: "They told me that you need two sets of shaving gear in OCS, Sir: One to get you through inspections and one that you really use. So I got a set for inspection and figured that this was just the beginning of using it."

"Where's the stuff you use?" he demanded.

"In my laundry bag," I said with a nod of my head in its direction.

"Get it, get it! Pour everything out of it onto your bed now! Move, *move!*" he screamed.

I jumped into motion.

Oh, this was bad. Even without opening the bag anyone without the severest of head colds could smell the stink. Oh, this was very bad. Like vultures, the lieutenant and Sergeant Soto hovered over me as I untied the bag. I turned it upside down and everything came out: Filthy underwear, dirty socks, the rotten-food-drenched KP T-shirt. Lieutenant Brown did not touch anything.

Hovering over the mess, he slowly surveyed the scene. Pointing to the razor, he hissed, "Pick it up!"

God, it was filthy. I was truly embarrassed by the previously unnoticed filth on my razor. The lieutenant shook his head. His eyes locked on mine. He was not angry. I was stunned. His clenched fist, locked arms, and tight neck muscles all said he was angry. His eyes were calm. Reaching into the pile on the bunk he pulled out the shaving-cream can. "There's no lid on this!" he shouted. "There's no protective lid on the top of this can! What happens when you're carrying the bag and something pushes on the top?" he shouted as he pointed the can at my face and placed his finger on the top of the can. "Everything gets soaked with soap!" he said, answering his own question as he tossed the can on the bunk.

He was right, though. I had never thought of that.

My interrogation was over. The inspection continued. I was so upset by the encounter that I could not follow what was said to the others. There was shouting and things were knocked on the floor. It was much the same as it began. And then he was gone.

Morning began as it was scripted in the movies. At 5 A.M., Sergeant Boone turned on the lights in the platoon bay. He yelled for everyone to get up because at 5:30 we had to be in formation in front of the building with the rest of Charlie Company. It was a mad rush. Everyone went to the latrine to relieve themselves, shave, and so forth. A lot of guys were going to the showers. Why they had not showered the night before was a mystery to me. Thirty minutes is not much time to get into your army clothes, make your bunk, and have all of your toiletries placed back in the right spot for surprise inspections during the day. Some guys were still lying in their bunks when I got back from shaving. The guy directly across from me really seemed to be sawing logs. Everyone was moving so fast that no one had time to spend on someone else. The guy could pay the price for his extra sleep if that was what he wanted.

"Everyone out!" came the order.

We rushed for the stairwell. I was dressed and ready to go. Just a few of the others had preplanned as I had. They had laid their morning clothes out to jump into at the first wake-up call. Socks stashed in their combat boots to make them easy to find and slip on and black web belt already inserted into the loops of the pants. Anyone who had not done those things was in trouble. As we joined the mob from the other platoons rushing down the stairs, people were tripping over their own or someone else's untied shoelaces. Some dud had dropped his belt in the middle of the stairwell while he was trying to put it on. He had the bad judgment to stop and try to reach for it. The uncontrollable momentum of a couple of hundred men flowing down the steps bowled him over. He tumbled backward, partially supported by the legs of the people he fell into. Several others fell in the process, but the herd of men could not be slowed.

By the time I reached the double glass doors on the first-floor landing, the glass in both of them was vibrating from the constant slamming against the walls. It was a miracle no one was pushed through the glass. Over the roar of combat boots stomping down the stairs could be heard the voices of various sergeants ordering people to move faster.

Dashing from the lights of the building into the darkness of the night left most of us blinded. It did not, however, stop us from running. It was a bizarre obstacle course. You could not quite tell if you were moving into an object or the object was coming toward you. Only the voice of your platoon sergeant guided you to the right spot.

"Company, atten-*shun!*" Sergeant Soto barked.

It became mostly silent. A few individuals kept talking. They were sweet flypaper, and the sergeants were the flies. "Don't you understand English?" "Why are *you* so privileged to talk when no one else can?" "Shut your mouth, Stupid!" were some of the biting comments the talkers received.

"Company!" shouted Sergeant Soto.

Each of the four platoon sergeants called out in almost perfect unison, "Platoon!"

"Left!" Sergeant Soto said.

"Left!" came the vibrating echo from the platoon sergeants.

"Face!" Sergeant Soto screamed, the echo from the platoon sergeants almost drowning him out.

It was not too bad for the first time that a bunch of civilians had responded to a military order as an organized group. About 10 percent of the men turned to their right or stayed motionless until they realized their obvious error. Many of them got immediate coaching from the sergeants, but there were more error makers than sergeants to go around.

"For-ward, *march!*" came the order as the company moved out in fairly good order. When we got onto the street the order was to go to double time. It was not quite a real double time, though, as we could not pick up our knees and run. The men in front were too close. Instead, there was a rapid movement of picking up and putting down of your feet without raising them too high. We picked up on the proper way to do it by watching the sergeants as they ran alongside the formation. They kept their arms down at their sides with a slight bend to them rather than the typical elbow-and-forearm-parallel-to-the-ground running position. We later learned that this was called an "airborne shuffle." Someone said they used this technique at paratrooper school because it was the best way to run without damaging your knees.

It was not all that hard to do at first. We had no idea how far we were going or where we were going. We were just going. The lieutenant was with us, as was Sergeant Soto. Of course, all the platoon sergeants and their assistants were running along beside us. They focused on those who could not keep in step or started to allow a gap to form between themselves and the man in front of them.

After the first five blocks of airborne shuffling it stopped being easy. I was breathing through my mouth. People in front of me began to lose their place in line. You could not help bumping into them, but you kept going. The blistering tongues of the sergeants upon the slower shufflers became increasingly sharp. I was determined to keep up. Sweat was building up on my face despite the brisk morning air. It was still pitch-dark. There was no moon, but the streetlights were strong enough to give you night blindness. Eyes could not penetrate the dark, although no one had time to focus on this fact.

Sweat poured freely down my face. My armpits were soaked. My feet hurt. On we went. Trying to figure out where we were was no longer an issue. Fighting the muscle ache and keeping up was all that was on my mind. Then someone up front fell. A couple more guys fell or stumbled over him. I was in the middle of the formation, hopping, shoving, and dodging my way through. "Close up the ranks!" Sergeant Boone demanded without a pause in his steady breathing. Behind us you could hear a chorus of shouting at the stragglers. It was not good to be a straggler.

I was beginning to wonder if I could keep going. Others were, and as long as they could endure, so could I. Around the corner we went. It seemed that everyone was hurting, yet on we went. My world had shrunk to the four men who surrounded me in this sea of motion. Others surrounded them, but it took too much energy to look at them and try to figure out what was going on. My four companions were both my support and my prison as we moved together. No one spoke. Everyone was in pain.

"Quick time, *march!*" shouted Sergeant Soto. The platoon sergeants echoed his order. We did and we sucked air. The company's barracks were just behind us. That was a lot of energy to get back where we had started. It was the army way. Our reward for staying with the formation was to be marched to the mess hall for breakfast. We were first in line. That would have been a nice reward before the run. Now I was too physically tired to eat much of anything. After a few bites, I had no desire to eat more.

When we returned to the barracks, they had been turned upside down. There were just a few bunks that were still made. The blankets and sheets had been pulled or twisted off the rest of them. They had not been made the army way. Mine was okay. As a kid, my parents, both with Coast Guard backgrounds, had seen to it that I knew how to make a tight bed with hospital corners.

At the next formation they marched us to the obstacle course. From the looks of it, it just might be fun. There were ropes to swing on over mud pits, a big gully to jump over, and a number of other different things to climb on or over. The problem was, you did not know what to do when. It was all confusion: Sergeants constantly yelling and telling you what to do and never speaking so that you could understand what they said. Men were running here and running there. No matter where they ran, it seemed to be the wrong place or they were doing the wrong thing. My group had just completed the rope swing across the mud. A few guys landed on the edge of it, but we all managed to get across the obstacle. Some of the men were laughing and enjoying parts of the process. This seemed to irritate several sergeants, who converged on them.

Railroad ties held up the banks of a trench we were to jump across. The trench was about as deep as a man is tall plus four feet. If you fell into it, you would have a hard time getting out. It was wide enough that you had to run up to it to jump across. No one would be foolish enough to try jumping across from a standing position. At first glance, it looked easy enough. Upon greater reflection it was quite possible that I might

not make it. In order to make the jump, I would have to get a good running start. Surging toward it at a brisk run, I could see a few unfortu-
nates in it, struggling to get out. You could not stop. The push of the
group running behind you could cause you to fall and be trampled. Just
before my leap I realized that I was a little short of the speed needed to
get over it. The trench was wider than I had thought. Too late to build
up more speed, I tried to compensate with extra effort in a springing
jump. My right foot hit firm ground, allowing my body's momentum to
carry me across. Then, *Bam!* My left foot slammed into the side of the
trench, solidly smacking my big toenail squarely into a railroad tie. God,
it hurt! There was no stopping or I would be run over. I immediately began limping. No one seemed to notice. No one cared. Damn. *Damn!* I
knew I could not let my body be hurt here. It was going to be bad
enough with a whole body. I would just have to go on. My toe throbbed
all day. There was never any time to take off my boot and look at it until we returned to the barracks.

Our next task was going through the army physical fitness test. Each
soldier had to score at least three hundred out of a possible five hundred
points in order to graduate from basic training. This first run-through
was just to see what kind of score we got in the beginning.

You were awarded a hundred points for each task that you maxed
out on. A score of five hundred was perfect. What perfect in the eyes of
the army meant was not clear. Sixty points on a task meant that you had
achieved the minimum passing score. Running a mile in eight minutes
earned you sixty points. That was no small task. You wore your combat
boots. They are heavy. Running the mile was the last of the five tasks to
be completed. Most people were worn out from completing the other
four tasks.

Like everywhere else in the army, you had to line up and wait for your
turn. No one told you what to do, but they all told you *when* to do it.

By now my big toe really hurt. I was limping. No one asked me if I
had a problem. Interrupting one of the screaming sergeants did not seem
to be an option. A cloud of dust masked my first PT testing ground. The
sergeants called physical training "PT." Everything in the army had an
acronym or an abbreviation. My first event was the "Forty-Yard Low
Crawl."

"Get your butt down!" bellowed a sergeant as he poised his foot over
the soldier's pelvis. The crawler stopped momentarily, his face hidden in
the dust. "You'll get it shot off in Vietnam! Go to the end of the line and
do it over!"

Using our elbows and the insides of our thighs and pushing off with

Waiting your turn.

The one-mile run.

The monkey bars.

the arched sides of our feet propelled us forward. Using your knees raised your stomach off the ground and exposed your butt above the rest of your body. That got you sent to the end of the line. To hell with Vietnam. The end of the line was a more immediate threat.

My turn came. Stopwatch in hand, the sergeant shouted, "Go!"

From a crouch, I launched my stomach into the layer of powdered earth. It knocked the breath out of me. I sucked in dust. Chaos filled my ears. I was moving—fast. Nothing mattered but moving. The turn for the trip back and no boot yet. Loud words, scurrying bodies, dust, out of breath, grass, made it! Eighty points were mine. So were the black rings around my nostrils, the grit in my mouth, and the mud tears on my cheeks. Then my big toe remembered to hurt.

Monkey bars ahead. I hated the monkey bars in school. They always made blisters that immediately tore open. The skin on the callused part of my palm just seemed to roll off. You know what I mean, the place where each finger joins the palm. They would seep that clear fluid and be sore. The army's name for the event was "horizontal ladder." You had to negotiate something like forty-eight rungs to get the minimum passing score of sixty.

Lane was a little way ahead of me in the monkey-bar line. I knew his name was Lane because that was what his buddies were calling him.

"Show them, Lane!"

"Yeah, man! Don't stop."

"Just swing on back to Bayonne!" came the laughing calls from his admirers and friends.

His shoulders were massive. The biceps he carried were a ninety-six-pound weakling's dream. In all my life I had never seen anyone with as broad a chest and as narrow a waist. How could one person be so physically perfect? What did he do to get into such shape? Was he a professional athlete? I would say not. His friends were definitely rough folks. They were not college bound. Could he be a construction worker? What kind of a job would build muscles like those? I had worked as a deckhand on ocean-going dredges during two summers of undergraduate work. It was hard work. You sweated all day. There were some really strong men on the crews who lived hard all of their lives. None of them had developed a body like Lane's. He was a mystery. The fact that he was black seemed irrelevant to his black and white cheering friends.

Lane sprang to the bars like a feather kicked by a light breeze. His movement down the bars appeared to be effortless. It was musical. The pivot at the end for the return trip was a ballet dancer's delight. A big smile was on his face. He talked to the cheering section as he glided toward them. Twisting completely around on one hand, he started back with the same ease with which he had started. Midway to the end, he stopped. Hanging by one hand, he brought his feet up to his armpits. Scratching them with his feet brought hoots and howls from his friends, me, and others watching. The sergeants glared. Quickly, Lane swung to the end and returned to begin again. The sergeants called him down. As he descended, we all cheered. Lane was something.

I jumped up and almost fell. After three bars I was in a rhythm. By six bars, my palms hurt. At the tenth bar, I did not know if I would make it to the end. The pivot for the return trip caused deep pain. Three bars into the return trip I fell. Both of my palms were bleeding. I always hated the monkey bars.

The grenade throw was incongruent with the other tests. It seemed to me to be more of a skills test than a physical fitness test. You were required to throw a defused grenade at a bull's-eye target stretched out flat on the ground. You had to be on your knees or lower when you tossed it. I threw it as though I were throwing a baseball. Greater vigor was required to reach the target. I put more strength into the second toss. It landed considerably to the left of the bull's-eye and was still short. This was perplexing. My shoulder muscles were hurting. I had always prided myself on my throwing ability. Why was I having such difficulty? Surely, I had not gotten that badly out of shape during my two years of graduate school. Yes, I had put on forty pounds; 180 pounds on a six-foot frame hardly fit my idea of fat. After the third and final toss, I was depressed. The twenty points the sergeant awarded me did not help.

I was out of breath and physically shaking after putting all I had into the mile run, for which I earned sixty points. I had a total of three hundred. Being minimally competent physically bothered me. My toe hurt and clear fluid was seeping from my palms. I was going to have to do much better. The march back to the barracks was a time of deep reflection. So far, my first day in the army with sergeants directing my activities had not been pleasant.

Again bedding was ripped off the mattresses. Some of the mattresses were on the floor. Wall lockers were empty, their contents scattered around the bay. No one was spared from the destruction. No one had prepared everything the army way.

One exception did exist: The bunk across from mine had been put back to its original condition when we had first gotten off the buses. The mattress cover had been removed and the mattress was folded over itself, leaving the cot's springs exposed. A new mattress cover was neatly folded and placed on top of the mattress along with sheets, blanket, pillowcase, and pillow. The wall locker was completely empty. The late sleeper never returned. Rumor had it that he had died during the night. Somebody said that Sergeant Zarconi had told him the guy died of pneumonia.

We had to get ready for the next day's inspection or face the same chaos. There was no time to talk about the empty bunk. I do not think anyone knew the guy's name.

Mandatory lights out came before we were ready. My bruised and bloody toenail was going to fall off. There was nothing to be done about it. I knew the process. I had lost a few toenails and fingernails in my time. You just went on.

CHAPTER 3

Testing

"Up! up! Formation in thirty minutes!" Sergeant Zarconi announced as the lights flicked on and off several times.

We moved fast. Even though it was just the second morning, the beginning of a pattern was forming. Shave, brush your teeth, get dressed, make your bunk, set the wall locker straight, square away the footlocker, and tie down the laundry bag at the end of the bunk. Everything was done the army way. After a mad dash down the stairwell through the slamming glass doors to stand at your spot the rest of your twelve-man squad forms around you, as do the other squad members in the four-squad platoon. All four platoons form up quickly and the company is ready to go on its two-mile jog before breakfast. Well, almost ready.

There were always stragglers. Right beside them were the sergeants. All around both was noise punctuated by coughing. One or two guys would be singled out for special attention. The sergeants would converge on them for some unknown reason, unknown except for the black guy with the funny beard. They were always on him for not shaving close enough. This morning was no different. He stood at attention and shouted in his crisp, British-sounding accent, "You're ignorant."

"You calling me stupid?" one of the noncoms screamed.

"No, you are ignorant," he repeated in a loud, crisp voice.

"Then you *are* calling me stupid!" the sergeant shouted as he danced around the target of his wrath like a barracuda moving in for the kill.

"You do not understand the facts," the black guy loudly replied. He was jerked out of formation. The whole company was ordered to make a left face. The black guy was left behind. In my opinion, he had good initiative but seemed to suffer in the area of judgment. I soon learned that the army had an apt phrase for that condition: "Good initiative—poor judgment."

We stepped off in quick time and were quickly ordered to double time, which meant more of the airborne shuffle. Arms straight down at the sides, leading foot about one and one-half inches off the ground, and a half-pace stride that made the shuffle easy to do for a city block or two. After that you began to breathe hard. A half-mile into it, the stragglers had begun to make their move.

Stragglers make a two-mile run more difficult than it ought to be. They are spread throughout the formation. At first they start to slow down. If one of them is in front of you, you have to slow down, which makes the guy behind you slow down. It takes great skill to avoid stepping on the heels of the guy in front of you. Most people lacked such skill. The sergeants seemed to sense where the stragglers would appear. One always materialized to urge them on in an unfatherly manner.

When a sergeant's words failed to motivate a straggler, the sergeant would turn on those around the guy and demand that they pull, push, drag, or do whatever else was necessary to keep the guy in formation. Even this assistance was not enough for some stragglers, who would gradually fall behind the company. Such behavior seemed to be intolerable to the sergeants. They would pull a panting trooper from the formation and make him stay with the straggler to urge the poor fellow on. This meant that the two of them would be late to wherever they were going.

In the case of the morning trot, it meant they would be last in line for breakfast. Being last in line meant that you probably would not have time to eat all your food before the company formed up again outside to begin the day's activities. Stragglers were not a happy group—nor were those who had to deal with them.

Breakfast was good. Lots of good food. Unfortunately, few of us had much of an appetite right after a two-mile run. This was not good. We had been warned that there would be no snacking. We were not allowed to have candy bars or to receive "care packages" full of goodies from home. They said it brought out cockroaches.

The army did not allow you many options for making personal choices. You only ate when the army told you to eat, which was three times a day—unless a straggler, extra duty, or a screaming sergeant delayed you beyond the point of no return.

After chow, they marched us to the dental clinic. Long lines greeted us. You quickly get used to standing in line waiting for something to happen. It is a great opportunity to get caught up on the rumors. In the army, no one officially tells you anything. Rumors keep you informed. Someone told me that with a master's degree in psychology, I was eligible for a direct commission as a first lieutenant in the Medical Service Corps. That was news to me. Why had my recruiter not told me that?

Someone else said there were guys in their third week of basic training who still had not been issued combat boots. They were doing all of their marching in civilian shoes. God, I thought, that had to hurt. The army seemed to be short of everything or just have too many men. Several were willing to volunteer to leave the army just to help out.

I was surprised at the large number of men who said they had been told to return to the dentist to have teeth removed. Some had teeth pulled on the spot. Others were given appointments for extractions that afternoon or the next day. Guys were bragging about how many teeth they had pulled. Five was the largest number I heard that day. They must have had a lot of Novocain, for they were all smiles and laughs as they reported their totals.

Next came the eye doctor. The optometrist I saw told me that I really did not need glasses, but they could clear up the fuzziness I experienced when I was reading. I was unaware that I was having trouble reading. He asked me if I wanted a pair ordered. What the heck, I thought, they *are* free. I accepted his offer.

More marching. And no one ever tells you where you are going or what you are going to do when you get there. Another long line out in the sun. This line is taking a long time to get to where we are supposed to do something. The people in charge at the end of this line are particularly nasty. They are shouting. People near the front are often ordered to drop and knock out ten, twenty, sometimes fifty push-ups at a time. Some guys were on their backs with their arms and legs scratching at the air. The "dying-cockroach position" becomes extremely painful to maintain for all but the shortest time.

The closer I got to the table with two sergeants sitting at it, the more intense the harassment got. I tried my best not to "eyeball" the non-sergeant soldiers assisting the sergeants at the table. Eyeballing happens when you look to the left or right when you are supposed to be looking straight ahead at nothing. The assistants bore no rank on their arms. They probably were privates or new arrivals like us. It had already become clear that the army liked to give temporary status to people who did not know what they were doing—so they could tell others what to do. I think they thought it was good training. The guy in front of me was ordered to knock out twenty push-ups. Because they were caught talking, two guys behind me were ordered to assume the dying-cockroach position.

No one spoke to me. I worked hard to keep myself under control. I did exactly what I was told when I was told. There was no eyeballing on my part. As a result, I had no peripheral knowledge as to what would happen when I reached the end of the line. The sergeant's voice came as a surprise to me. I knew that I would be the next up. My compliant behavior had kept me from gleaning enough information to understand what was about to happen. I had no idea what I would be asked to do when I reached the head of the line.

When the man who had been in front of me finished whatever he had been doing at the table with the two sergeants behind it, one of them motioned for me to step forward. I quickly complied.

"Look inside this and tell me exactly what you see," the sergeant grumbled as he pointed to a binocular-like device sitting on the table. He pointed at my left hand, in which I held a card I had been given to fill out earlier, and said, "Give me the card."

I handed it to him and then leaned over the machine on the table and rested my eyes over the two eyepieces. I had no idea what I would see. Whatever it was, I had better tell him exactly what I saw or it was clear I would be in a world of hurt.

"I see a dog on the left side and a ball on the right, Sergeant," I stated as honestly as I could, raising my head from the instrument.

"Don't get smart with me. I'll send you to the end of the line, and you can try again if you want to be an asshole, Asshole," he snarled.

I was stunned. I had done exactly as he had asked. What had I done wrong?

"Look again, and this time you'd better not be a smart Alec about it, Dipshit," he said. Both the speaker and the other sergeant leaned forward as if they were about to spring out of their chairs and hit me.

I was undone. It made no sense. Again I looked in the two eyepieces. "Oh," I said in surprise, "the dog is jumping over the ball."

"Okay, get out of here," came the response.

Up to that point, I had not known that fear could significantly alter the way we see three-dimensionally. I had thought the mind's ability to put the separate images it receives from the eyes into one three-dimensional picture was an automatic brain function. I had always believed that only seriously brain-damaged people were deprived of this ability. It had never occurred to me that it could be triggered by emotions. I must have missed that in the college textbooks on the psychology of perception. Maybe researchers had not yet discovered that fact. I was to learn a lot from the army about how fear and stress affected human behavior—my behavior.

After lunch, they marched us a long way. The sun was hot. Soon we were all dripping with sweat. I was tired, as was everyone else. When we finally got where we were going, they put us into a large open room with little school desks in it. This was the paper-and-pencil testing area.

As testing goes, many of the items were interesting. Having just finished two years of studying about testing people with the Stanford-Binet IQ Intelligence Test and the like, this was educational to me. There were few written instructions, but a lot of diagrams. Many of the sub-tests made clear what they wanted to know about what we knew. For example, one test required us to match pictures of certain hand and power tools with pieces of equipment to be repaired. Anyone who had worked on cars would have done well on this one. I had never worked on cars. Instead, I had to use logical deductions. That was hard work. It was made even harder because we were tired, stinking with sweat, and thirsty. Test after test after test was given. They even gave us a test that was pretty much like a typical driver's license test.

The last test was the OCS qualification test. That's what it said on the cover. Like the one I had taken in early July, it had a lot of questions I could not answer. That was just two months ago. I had to use logic to make educated guesses. The questions were not derived from my every-day life experiences. The muzzle velocity of a bullet fired from a .30-.30 rifle was something I had not learned in college or graduate school. School psychologists did not study such stuff. However, I did know the speed of light and the speed of sound. The bullet could not be traveling at the speed of light but it was traveling faster than the speed of sound. That was a start to figuring out the most probable answer from the choices presented. The exam was pretty much like that, except for the railroad-schedule questions.

I had taken the OCS exam in July in a completely different environment. My Pittsburgh, Pennsylvania, draft board had classified me 1-A early in June. Until that time I had thought I was immune to the draft. I was under the impression that being married, in graduate school, and having a year to go on a school psychologist internship in a Cincinnati-area school system exempted me from military service. I had thought wrong. When I called the draft board and explained that I would not finish my master's program until the first week of August and that I then had a one-year internship to do, I thought they would change my status. The best they could do, the voice on the other end of the line stated, was put me at the end of the list of eligible men to be drafted in June, July, and August. Then, on September 1, I would be the first one on the draft list. This did not mean that I would not be drafted before then. If the army told them they needed to call up everyone on the June, July, or August list, then I would be called up, she said. That was the best they could do, she repeated.

My wife and I had briefly considered leaving the country. My thinking was that I had enjoyed the benefits of being a U.S. citizen without many demands being made upon me. Now I was being asked to fulfill an obligation of citizenship. The fact that others might not have to serve in the military was not a big issue. My country had called upon me to pay my dues. It was all right with me if I never paid them, but that was not my choice now. Having consumed many privileges—including a public education, government loans for higher education, police protection, good roads, and so forth—my obligation to repay the country when asked to do so was clear. That was how we reasoned it out for ourselves. We had not followed news of the escalation in Vietnam very closely. I spent all of my time studying in graduate school and Anna spent her time teaching high school English or preparing her lessons in the evening for the next day. There just was no time for national affairs. We both knew I could get killed in Vietnam.

During those deliberations, I remembered a dream I had had. It was when the Cuban missile crisis was at its peak. The campus Navy Reserve Officer Training Corps (NROTC) building was located behind my college dorm. Late at night I could faintly hear the sound of dots and dashes emanating from its large radio tower. I figured it was Morse code and often would fall asleep with that sound in my ears. I was aware of its presence. Part of me wondered if I was being foolish by not signing up for NROTC in order to get my military obligation out of the way. At the time, I thought there was a serious possibility America might get involved in a full-scale third world war. The Cuban missile crisis was hot news.

Anyway, I had this dream in which I was pinned down behind a rock that was slightly bigger than my head. An enemy machine gun was zeroed in on my rock. Bullets were hitting it in a steady stream. I dared not move. Several other soldiers were in the same position as I was, with one exception. I could see a lieutenant standing up, fully protected by a huge boulder. He was a classmate of mine. Unlike me, he was enrolled in the NROTC program on campus. Unfortunately, I had always considered him to be both obnoxious and out to lunch. Over the chatter of the machine-gun bullets pinging off my rock, making it smaller and smaller, the lieutenant yelled at us, "On the count of three you will get up and charge!"

As he slowly counted, I thought: Like hell I will, you stupid fool. You'll get me killed instantly without even exposing yourself.

For the first time in my life, I was faced with the reality that I would not be a hero. All of my adolescent life I had read about heroes. Horatio Hornblower, Ivanhoe, Robin Hood, John Wayne in the movie *She Wore a Yellow Ribbon*, and scads of others who did brave things against impossible odds while being morally impeccable were my idols. I wanted to be just like them. I loved westerns. *Shane*, starring Alan Ladd, was a real favorite. Randolph Scott cowboy movies had been a staple for me as a kid. The heroes always stood up and did what needed to be done. In my dream, I realized that war could kill you. Stupid people could get you killed. I was not going to do something that would get me killed just because a stupid, silly, uncaring authority figure told me to do it when I knew it was wrong.

When I awoke from the dream, it was with several stark realizations. If I had to be in the military, I needed to obtain as much authority over myself as I could. Officers routinely got their men killed by accident. A lot of people were becoming officers who would not make good decisions. That was their nature. They were not about to change just because they took some ROTC courses or the like. Most important, I realized that I was not going to be a storybook hero. Those stories do not match up to reality.

I knew I did not want to be in the army. I would have to do whatever it took to get into the Coast Guard or the navy. My father was a career Coast Guardsman, my grandfather was a career Coast Guardsman, and my mother had been raised on Coast Guard stations. Family tradition had it that only stupid people went into the army. My experience at the Cincinnati Armed Forces Entrance and Examination Station (AFEES) in May had confirmed that mind-set. When we were all herded together to take the army exams, it was clear from the questions that some of the prospective draftees asked that several of them could not read. Yes, sir, stupid people went into the army. Stupid people got themselves and others killed in the army.

In between exams and paper assignments at Miami University of Ohio, I contacted the Coast Guard and navy recruiting offices. I wanted to take their OCS exams. You cannot just walk in and take their exams, however. Appointments have to be made because they only give the tests at specific times. The Coast Guard exam was first. I knew it would be heavy in math, which was my weakest academic area. I could never remember formulas for things like the volume of a cylinder. My algebra was also very rusty. Since that stuff was difficult for me, I would have to get the right books and study. I had a heavy schedule at the university, so you can guess what happened: I never did get around to studying. A couple of weeks after taking the Coast Guard OCS exam I went back to the recruiting office to learn how I had done. They had both good and bad news. The good news was that I had passed the exam. The bad news was that all of the Coast Guard OCS classes were filled until January. I thus would not enter the Coast Guard until January, 1967. That was four months too late. Come September 1, I would be a private in the army, marching off to war.

My score on the navy's exam was below the cutoff for their OCS program. Again, math was my low area. This time two of us entered the recruiter's office to get the word on our scores. The other guy was in the clinical psychology master's program at Miami. Fate had brought us together at the same interview time. We had been in a couple of classes together. He had another semester to go before graduation. I could not remember his name, but we struck up a friendly conversation as we waited for the recruiter. The recruiter was seated at his desk talking to somebody on the phone. Our conversation was pleasant. There was a degree of controversy at the university over the clinical and school psychology master's programs. The two groups of students had very little interaction. In the course of our conversation, the clinical psych guy told me that a lot of his peers really admired my answers in the projective testing class. Whenever we were asked to speculate about the underlying meaning of a client's response to a Thematic Apperception Test card or other projective test item, my responses were always on the mark. He said they were in awe of my ability to understand the client from such little information. I was both stunned and flattered by his praise. I had had no previous feedback from the instructor or from the students concerning my responses in the classroom. That was why I had stopped making any input in class as of late.

Addressing my classmate, the recruiter congratulated him on passing the test. He told him he had made good scores across the board. I was embarrassed to learn that my scores were just below the cutoff point. Having my classmate there, particularly after he had just told me how much other graduate students valued my in-class responses, was tough.

The recruiter must have been listening in on our conversation while he held the phone to his ear. After giving me the bad news, he told me to wait a minute. He dialed a number, waited a moment, and then said: "Yes, Sir, about the other one: I know his scores are a little low, but I think he has other qualities that make him a good candidate."

After a brief pause, he said, "Aye, aye, Sir," and hung up.

Looking directly at me, he smiled and said: "You're both in. You'll be in the January OCS class."

Good news and bad news, all at the same time. It was bleak news that I had to give my wife that night. Here it was early July and I could not get into either the navy or the Coast Guard in time to avoid being drafted into the army. I would have had to spend four years in either service, but that was better than two years as a grunt in the army. People got killed in the army. The stupid people in the army got people killed that did not have to be killed. This was not good. I would have to go to the army recruiting office as soon as possible. Maybe I could get some special training or something that would help me stay alive. I was going into the army, that was for sure. How I was going to make the best out of this bad situation was the only unanswered question left.

I explained my situation to the recruiting sergeant. He was most understanding. The first thing I needed to do, he explained, was take the army's OCS exam. That was fine with me; I was ready to set up an appointment with him to do just that. He smiled and said no appointment was necessary. I could take it right then if I wanted. Wait just a minute, I thought. I need to study and prepare for the exam. Remember, I do poorly in math. Wait just a minute: This is the army. Its OCS exam cannot be that hard. They have the lowest average IQ of all the services. People must pass their tests who cannot read, I reasoned, remembering the questions asked at the induction center.

The sergeant escorted me to a little room. It had a small table and a chair in it. He explained that the test would be timed. He would give it to me and return when the time was up. I would have to stop the moment he reentered the room. The examination began.

It was much like the one I was taking in basic training. If I had been raised in a hunting and farming community with lots of hands-on experience with practical problems, I think I would have clearly known the answers to many of the questions. As it was, I had to rely on logical deduction to figure out the answers. Things were humming along fine until I hit the section about the railroad schedule. God Almighty it was complicated! There was a big section full of train schedules from one city to another at different times to many different locations. Under it was a long series of questions like, "If you left Detroit at 8 A.M., what would be the earliest you could arrive in Seattle?" Well, if there were a direct train from Detroit to Seattle, the answer would be fairly simple. However, instead of going straight to Seattle, it looked as if you would have to make at least three transfers, maybe more. As I studied the complex schedule, my first impulse was to just skip those questions and go on to the rest of the exam. They were just too hard to work out. No, no, I reasoned. Remember: this is the army. They make tests stupid people can pass. I knew I was not stupid, so surely I could figure it out. By the time I completed that series of questions, I was certain I had correctly answered all but one of them. Time, however, had to be getting short. I could always go back to it at the end if there was any time left. Now it was a race to get through the easier questions. I had no idea how much time was left, but I knew I had to rush. I had spent a lot of time on the railroad questions. Just as I completed the last question, the sergeant entered the room and said, "Stop." It was a relief to be done. The railroad questions were really hard.

"When should I come back to find out how I did?" I asked the sergeant.

"We're going to score it right now," he said cordially. "You just wait here. It'll only take a few minutes." He took the exam book and my answer sheet and left.

I overheard two people talking in the hallway outside my door. They entered the room in front of mine and continued their conversation. The wall was thin, and I recognized one of the voices as that of the recruiting sergeant.

"He's doing pretty well," the sergeant said, his voice muted by the wall. There was a brief period of silence.

"My God, he's figured out the railroad schedule!" the second speaker exclaimed. "No one's ever done that. He must have cheated."

"No, Sir, Captain," replied the sergeant. "I watched through the window as he took it. He didn't bring anything into the room. He just sat down and did it."

"Well, that's the best score I've ever seen," the captain stated.

"It might be the highest score anyone's ever gotten. I'll go check up front, Sir." There was the sound of a chair sliding on the floor, then a door opened and I heard the sound of footsteps traveling down the hall. A few minutes later the sergeant was back. "We only have records for our region, Sir," he said. "He clearly has the highest score anyone who took the test here ever had."

"Sign him up," said the captain.

Doors opened and closed. I felt pretty good. Hell, I felt damn good.

"You really did well on this test," the sergeant said, his face beaming as he entered the room. "Let's go to my office and talk."

He told me that because my test score was so high I could enroll in any OCS program I wanted. I explained that with my M.S. degree in school psychology, my training could best be used in a position in which I helped soldiers determine their aptitudes for different career paths in the army.

"Oh, that's the Adjutant General Corps," he explained. "There isn't an OCS for that. You'll have to get a branch transfer from some other branch of the army that has an OCS."

"Well, what branch is the easiest to get a branch transfer out of?" I replied.

"More people transfer out of the infantry than any other branch," he responded without hesitation. "With your high scores, you'll do very well in Infantry OCS. The top ten percent of each Infantry OCS class can get a branch transfer upon graduation. You should have no problem being in that category. That's when you can transfer over to the Adjutant General Corps."

"Oh," I said, in complete confidence that things would work out fine.

We agreed that I would start in early August, six days after I finished the last of my courses at Miami of Ohio. As I remember it, the sergeant said that I would have to go through eight weeks of basic training before going to OCS. I would take basic training at Fort Dix, New Jersey, and then go to Fort Benning, Georgia, for Infantry OCS. It would last six months, after which I would have just two years to serve. This was working out better than I had ever hoped. The army would put me in a working situation that related to my education and I would only be in the army for two years and eight months. The other services would have had me doing things unrelated to my training for four years. I was pleased with my good fortune. What had seemed to be a bad situation was turning out well.

When I got home that evening, my wife and I celebrated the nice turn of events and began planning what we would do. There was not much time for me. Being a full-time graduate student was consuming most of my waking moments. I could not afford to do poorly in my courses. If you got two C grades in the master's program they dropped you from graduate school, regardless of your grade point average.

Anna wanted to move closer to her relatives in Kentucky while I was at Forts Dix and Benning because she would not be allowed to live with me during my training. That meant she would have to find a teaching job in Kentucky, we would have to find a place for her to live, and then we would have to move. That left us with a lot to do from early July to the end of the first week in August. We managed to do it all while coping with life's little unexpected adventures—like blowing a rod through the engine block of the car just before final exam week. It was a relief to get on the plane in Cincinnati. I was really tired.

All of these thoughts were in my mind as I stared at the railroad schedule in the OCS exam. It could not be the identical OCS test I had taken in Cincinnati. It had to be a different form. I scanned the schedule and read the first few questions. I thought that it required too much concentration. It was too hard. I was too tired. It was the end of the day. I just could not concentrate. I took a few educated guesses, but I just could not bring myself to weave through all those possible train transfers to be certain my answers were right. Besides, what difference did it make? I was already accepted for Infantry OCS.

Two days later, we got our test results. They provided a surprisingly detailed computerized analysis of our scores. My overall score placed me in the 93d percentile. The quiet guy in the bunk next to mine was in the 99th percentile. I had received a passing score on the OCS exam. It was a lot lower than my first score. I wished I had concentrated on the railroad schedule. Obviously there were people in the army a lot smarter than me. I was embarrassed at my ignorance. The quiet guy was from a farm family. He did not want to go to OCS. I thought that was a mistake. He said his family needed him to come back home as quickly as possible so he could help make ends meet. Extra time spent in special training programs meant more time away from the farm for him.

On the day we got our test scores about twenty other guys and I were called out of the company formation. We had been selected for the hands-on portion of the truck-driving test. If you passed the test, you would be assigned as a truck driver for details. The word was that being a truck driver was the best detail assignment you could get. Almost all of the others were hard, boring tasks. On detail assignments you were the janitors of the base, the hard laborers on construction jobs, and the grunges in the kitchen clean-up process. Truck drivers just drove trucks. They did not load them. They did not unload them. They were never assigned to any duty but driving the truck. Nice work if you could get it.

They took us to the driver-testing area in a truck. It did not make sense to me. I could not remember anything on any of the army tests that suggested I was truck-driver material. Oh, yeah, there had been the driving exam, but it was simply rules-of-the-road stuff. Everyone in the company should have passed that. I had never driven a truck in my life. I had no experience with a manual transmission. The car we used in high school driver's education was an automatic. My parents had always had cars with automatic transmissions. In my entire life, I had never even tried to shift gears in a car with a stick shift. I just did not know how to do it.

"You're next," said a salt-and-pepper-haired sergeant, his clipboard in his left hand and his assistant at his side.

"There's no point in having me get in the truck, Sergeant," I said sadly. "I've never driven a stick shift before. I don't know how."

He looked at me with a kindly smile and said: "You passed the written portion of the examination. You know more than you think."

"I'll wreck the truck," I said, trying not to be disrespectful. "I really have no idea what to do. Besides, passing a written exam has nothing to do with knowing how to shift gears."

"Son, the army says you'll take this test, so I guess you will." He spoke in a consoling manner, much like a father talking to his own son. "Besides," he said with a beaming smile, "it isn't all that hard to learn. I'll teach you."

"Okay, Sergeant." I shrugged with a smile of sad resignation.

The sergeant, his assistant, and I climbed into the cab. Clipboards in hand, the sergeant sat next to me with his assistant riding shotgun. I was in the driver's seat. The two-and-a-half-ton truck (soldiers call them "deuce and a halfs") was big and had a cab that was high off the ground. First he showed me where first, second, third, and reverse gears were. Then he had me practice pushing in the clutch and putting the floor-to-steering-wheel-high gearshift through the series of gears. You started out in first and, once it got going, shifted into second. Then, when the engine seemed to be straining, you went to third. He told me to always push in the clutch when starting the engine or changing gears. It was also important to come to a complete stop before trying to put it in reverse. If there was any forward motion you could strip a gear. Finally, after moving the gearshift, he told me to slowly let the clutch out to engage the gear.

"You got all that?" he asked after about five minutes.

"No," I said laughing. "I can't remember all that."

"Not to worry. Start 'er up and I'll tell you what to do as we go," he said a little more seriously.

I reached for the dash panel and moved the ignition toggle switch to the "on" position. The sergeant nodded and I depressed the gas pedal slightly and stepped on the starter button. The truck lurched forward. My foot automatically hit the brake, forcing the truck to momentarily stop. Since I had failed to step on the clutch, the truck continued to jump violently forward in short rabbit hops. It only took a second or two, but we had jumped ahead several yards before I remembered and stomped down on the clutch pedal.

Pushing himself away from the dashboard and reaching for his clipboard on the floor, the sergeant patiently said, "Remember to push in the clutch before you start it."

With a sheepish grin, I nodded. This time I pushed in the clutch before turning the toggle switch on. It started just fine and began to roll forward. Another truck was pulling out from the parking area and was about to pass in front of me. I took my foot off the clutch and put it on the brake. The truck stopped instantly and the engine stalled.

Once again, my two passengers pushed themselves away from the dashboard and picked up their clipboards. "You want to push in the clutch as you put on the brake so it won't stall out," the saintly man said quietly. "That means using your right foot on the brake instead of your left."

This time I got it started and moving in first. I made a right turn to get out of the parking area. As I approached the stop sign at the motor pool gate, I remembered to push in the clutch before taking my other foot off the gas. Before I got my right foot off the gas, the engine roared into racetrack form. Quickly, I remembered to ease off on the gas. Unfortunately, I pulled back more on my clutch-pedal foot than on my gas foot. The truck shot through the intersection. My quick reaction time in turning the steering wheel no doubt saved us from hitting the stop sign on the other side of the road. It did not keep the truck from stalling.

Appearing a little more wide-eyed than when I had first met him, the sergeant dryly commented, "Let's give reverse a try."

The truck was predisposed to jerk. No matter how hard I tried to prevent it, the thing jerked and stalled, jerked and stalled. I was pleased that I got it into third gear twice. The grinding of the gears whenever I shifted was so profound that every head in the testing area instinctively turned our way. All three of us were perspiring. The sergeant said he would park the truck for me. He agreed that I needed a little more practice before I could qualify as a driver. A lot of people watched me get down from the cab. It was embarrassing. I had blown my chance to get easy detail duty. When I told the story to the guys at supper, their laughter helped.

CHAPTER 4

Your Weapon

"T HIS IS your weapon. It will keep you alive. You must treat it with respect. You must take care of it so that it can take care of you," Sergeant Boone said to our platoon.

We were standing at attention with our weapons pressed against our right legs with their butts on the ground in a position known as "order arms." You held the rifle parallel to your body by grasping the upper part of the stock just right with your fingers. Holding your right arm down straight at your side and cocking your wrist up put your fingers in the perfect position.

"You will learn the manual of arms. You will learn to clean and maintain your weapon. You will learn to fire your weapon. Do . . . you . . . understand?" he demanded.

"Yes, Sergeant!" we shouted in unison.

This was just like they did it in the movies, I thought, feeling a slight sense of comfort in that realization.

Sergeant Boone demonstrated a position he called "port arms." After drawing himself to attention he said: "On my command, you will pull the rifle up with your right hand while moving your left hand to your chest in preparation to receive it from your right hand"—as he talked he slowly executed the movement, keeping in sync with his words. "As you bring the rifle up to your chest area, you grasp the receiver with your left hand while shifting your right hand from the upper hand guard below the muzzle to the small of the stock near the butt. At this time you are holding the rifle with both hands at a forty-five-degree angle to your head so that it bisects your body from your right hip across your chest to your left shoulder. Are there any questions?" Sergeant Boone's glare openly dared anyone to ask a question.

He returned the rifle to order arms and then demonstrated the move-

M14 rifle being inspected in   Breaking down and cleaning the M14 rifle.
ranks.

ment at normal cadence. It was smooth, quick, efficient, and simple. When he finished he looked from one side of the formation to the other and asked, "Everybody got that?"

"Yes, Sergeant!" we roared in unison.

"Platoon!" he shouted, "Atten-*shun!*" He paused while we snapped into position and then hollered, "Port . . . *arms!*"

I hauled my rifle briskly to my chest with my right hand. It felt heavier than I expected. Just before I completely lost my grip, I caught the barrel with my left hand and moved the thing into position. I was at port arms! My concentration had been so intense that not until I had achieved my goal did it become apparent that several men had been unable to complete the maneuver. They were either picking up their weapons from the pavement or still fumbling with getting their rifles across their chests. I had the feeling it was going to be a long morning.

"Shoulder arms" means putting the rifle on your shoulder so you can march with it the way they do in parades. "Right shoulder arms" and "Left shoulder arms" are the commands for which shoulder to put it on.

In a maneuver called "inspection arms" you went to port arms and then exposed the inside of the receiver so that the sergeant could check to see if you had a bullet seated in the chamber. He did not want to see a bullet in the barrel. That, presumably, was why he had you open it. He wanted to be sure that you had remembered to take all of the bullets out before you left the firing range. This significantly reduced the possibility of accidentally shooting someone. The movement was executed by sliding the palm of your right hand down the side of the rifle so that the edge of it caught the protruding piece of metal attached to the bolt and forced it back so you could then stick your thumb inside, push down on the piece of metal in there, and lock the bolt open with a satisfying click. This required coordination, strength, and speed. It was a difficult maneuver to do in one fluid motion. If you did not hit the lever just right, the thing would pull back only to slip off the edge of your palm and slide back shut with a sharp clapping sound. Those who failed to execute the movement properly were immediately identified by the sound. Our platoon sounded like an appreciative audience at a bad high school play. Fortunately, no one had gotten his thumb caught inside the receiver. If you did, they said it usually meant you would lose the nail. Sergeants Boone and Zarconi did their best to get us to execute this drill so that our rifles clicked rather than clapped. They never fully succeeded.

The two finesse moves in the manual of arms are stacking arms and fixing bayonets. It takes three men to stack arms. The middle guy leans his rifle forward while standing at attention without moving from that position in any other way. The guys on either side of him step toward him with their nearest foot and insert their rifle barrels into the tightened sling of his rifle. They then lower the heels of the butts of their rifles to the ground and move back to the position of attention. Miraculously, the three rifles form a tripod and stand. The order given before stacking arms is "prepare to stack arms." When it is given, everybody adjusts their rifle slings so they are nice and taut.

Hearing the command "Fix bayonets!" always gave me chills. It is one thing to be shooting at a bull's-eye target or a green silhouette of a man's upper torso. Somehow it just does not seem real. Being told to "Fix bayonets!" puts it in your face. You might hear it given just before an enemy attack, in which case you will most likely have someone try to jump on you and bite your face off, stab you, stomp on your head, or some such. Your bullets will have failed to keep this killer off of you. Or maybe you simply run out of bullets. Perhaps there are more of them than you and the others can shoot before they are on top you. In any event, something has either gone wrong or is about to go wrong if you are given the order to fix bayonets. If you have to fix bayonets in battle, you are probably going to die. You will die in pain. Certainly more slowly than if you are shot to death. Ugh! I do not like to think about it. Mostly, I do not. However, whenever I hear the order "Fix bayonets!" I think about it.

When the order "fix" is shouted, you move your right hand up the barrel of the rifle to the muzzle and lean the barrel forward with the stock still beside your right foot. On the next word, "bayonets," you move your left hand over and grasp the barrel while releasing your right hand. You then move your right hand smoothly across your stomach to your left hip, where your bayonet hangs from your belt in its scabbard. After unsnapping the cover over the handle of the bayonet, you grasp it firmly in your right hand and pull it out of the scabbard while making a smooth circular motion with your hand until the blade is pointing skyward. You then slip the large ring at the base of the handle over the muzzle and slide it down the barrel until the second, smaller, ring at the front of the handle slides over the muzzle and then seats itself firmly when the little clips at the base of the handle clamp down on the stud below the muzzle. This strongly affixes the bayonet to the weapon, creating a solid bond between the rifle and the blade. They are one. When that move is complete, you return to the position of attention with your rifle at order arms. It is a very efficient maneuver. No motion is wasted. You are then ready to bring your weapon to port arms, from which you can either defend yourself or launch an attack of your own.

We marched and marched with our weapons. When we were not marching, we were drilling on the manual of arms. Then it was time to return the weapons to the arms room. That was where the company stored our weapons. We had to open the breech so the sergeants could verify that we had no rounds in the chambers. Of course, we did not. All we did was drill and march in formation. No one gave us any ammo. Next, you filed into the storage area and placed your rifle in the rifle rack with your rifle's serial number on it. That serial number was important. The rifles all looked the same. That one rifle was your responsibility. No one messed with your rifle. After you left, someone ran a chain through all of the trigger guards and put a padlock on the chain. The process was repeated in reverse order the next morning.

Of course, we did our morning airborne shuffle before breakfast. Then we got our weapons. The M14 rifle is a solid weapon. Its wooden stock is solid. The whole piece has weight to it. When you are carrying it at high port, you know you have something strong to hang onto. If you had to use it as a club, it would do a good job. No one wants to be hit in the head with it.

The only time I had ever fired a rifle was one summer at Boy Scout camp. It was a lightweight .22-caliber weapon. They would not let you carry it around with you. You got it at the firing range, paid for your six bullets, and then shot at the target. I did not have much money to waste on bullets. Other than that, I had fired someone else's shotgun a few times. That was the extent of my firearms experience.

The M14 felt the way a rifle ought to feel, as you would imagine a deer rifle, a .30-30 hunting rifle felt. You know, the kind the mountain men carried around. The kind of weapon John Wayne's movie characters used: a man's weapon.

After we had all drawn our weapons, Sergeant Soto had the company form up. He began shouting manual-of-arms commands. As soon as he would give an order, the platoon sergeants would repeat that command to their respective platoons. When Sergeant Boone spoke, we moved. Collectively, we were pitiful. The platoon sergeants and their assistants were scurrying through the ranks singling out the most pitiful and telling them exactly how pitiful they were. It was all redundant. Fortunately, my pitiful efforts were less pitiful than some of the more pitiful others. No one got into my face.

Sergeant Soto called us all to attention. Silence reigned, except for the continuous coughing. I had kind of gotten used to it. Everybody was supposed to be silent when we were at attention, but the coughing never stopped. There was never a point when it could not be heard. I had begun to get a runny nose. Clearing my throat threatened to become a habit of necessity.

Sergeant Soto glared at us. He strode back and forth in front of the formation. We stood at attention, holding our collective breath. Something was about to happen. Abruptly, he stopped in front of a man in second platoon and screamed, "Port . . . *arms!*"

There was a collective sucking in of air. The lone soldier snapped his weapon smartly into position. It was perfect. "Left shoulder . . . *arms!*" demanded Sergeant Soto. The guy moved swiftly and correctly. "Right shoulder . . . *arms!*" was the quick follow-up order. The targeted man moved like a finely crafted watch. Soto barked out order after order and he moved briskly through the movements without error. Who was this guy? Thank God that I had not been singled out like that. How did he learn to do all those maneuvers so fast?

No smile creased Sergeant Soto's face. He slowly turned away and gave the order to march us off to begin the day's activities. We were ordered into trucks. They took us to a cleared area in the woods. After forming up and stacking arms, we were ushered into bleachers facing a clearing surfaced with packed mud. Several sergeants were moving around in front of us and two of them lugged a frame holding a large flip chart with a picture of an M14 on the first page and set it down roughly centered on the bleachers. We were about to receive our first in a never-ending series of military training lectures.

"This is the M14. It is your weapon," began the primary instructor, pointing at the picture. "You will learn the nomenclature of all its parts. You will disassemble and assemble your weapon until you can do it with your eyes closed while someone is shouting in your face. You will learn to clean your weapon and keep it operational under all kinds of conditions so that it can keep you alive in Vietnam. Do . . . you . . . understand?" he demanded.

He was right. We learned how to disassemble and assemble it. After the lecture we were formed into small groups. The other instructors came out and sat with us. They were all very patient and soft-spoken. You could get help anytime you asked and they were quite pleasant about it. I learned the basics quickly. Every fifty minutes we got a ten-minute break.

During one of the breaks, we began discussing the amazing control the guy in 2d Platoon displayed under Sergeant Soto's demanding eye. Someone said the guy had gone to the Coast Guard Academy the previous year and decided to quit. He got sucked into the army right after that. I had heard that during the first year at the service academies you were constantly harassed by upperclassmen. Sergeant Soto was not going to rattle this guy. I had a long way to go to achieve that degree of skill. In the process, I did not want to draw attention to myself. Doing so would not be good.

Cleaning your weapon is a tedious process. When the inside of the barrel is perfectly clean, it shines. To check it, you put your thumb inside the firing chamber. With your thumbnail reflecting light up the barrel, you can look down it and see both the shining metal and the grooves of the rifling. Unfortunately, you can also see any dirt that may be in it. I am not sure that the dirt is dirt. When a bullet passes through the barrel, hot gases from the exploding gunpowder follow it up. That is why you see the muzzle flash as the bullet leaves. The gasses burst into flame as they come out of the muzzle because they finally get enough oxygen to flame up. Meanwhile, the hot gasses passing through the barrel leave carbon deposits. Firing your weapon dirties the barrel. The more rounds you fire, the dirtier your weapon gets—which means you will have to spend more time running your cleaning rod through the barrel. There is a cotton patch that you put through a hole in the tip of the cleaning rod. It looks like a huge needle. Rather than running your patch all the way through the needle, you leave it there with half of it sticking out either side of the eye at the tip of the cleaning rod. First, however, you douse the patch in cleaning solvent. Then you keep running the rod up and

down the inside of the barrel, changing patches repeatedly. It takes forever and never seems to do the job perfectly, although that is how your
sergeant wants it done. If it does not please him, he will keep you at it
while others do more pleasant things. When your rifle finally passes inspection, you can sometimes get privileges. For example, the cleanliness
of your rifle seemed to be a key factor in being selected to serve as the
orderly for the officer of the day (OD). That was privileged duty, indeed!

Being an orderly was the same as being a "gofer." You ran errands
for the OD whenever he wanted you to get something. Usually, the only
thing he asked for was coffee. At least that is what those selected always
said. I do not really know, having never served my country in that way.

Lieutenant Brown displayed a bad habit during the classes on breaking down our weapons. Whenever he found someone not paying attention to the instructors or making a significant mistake, he would hit
them on their helmet liner with his little swagger stick. Our helmet liners were made of some sort of plastic. They fit inside our steel pots and
had straps around the inside rim that you could adjust so it fit fairly
snugly on your head. Painted army green, it looked just like the regular
steel helmet, but it sure was a lot lighter. When we had to wear the steel
pots—like when we went to the rifle ranges or participated in field exercises—we just put them over the helmet liner. They made a good fit.
Happily, we were not required to wear the steel pots much of the time.
When the bullet-casing tip of the lieutenant's swagger stick struck someone's helmet liner, it made a loud clicking sound to those standing near
the impact. To the one wearing the impacted helmet liner, the sound
must have been greatly intensified—or so it seemed, judging from the
wearer's startled reactions. Accentuating the startled response was the
recipient's total unawareness that he was about to be struck. Lieutenant
Brown had developed a keen ability to approach from his intended victim's rear or blind side. One moment the hapless soldier was enjoying
the numbness of mind disconnect, and the next he was immersed in jar-
ring sound. The startled reaction was always the same: an instantaneous
straightening of the back with a quick jerk of the head toward the point
of impact of the swagger stick, with the rest of the upper body following the turn of the head as the mind struggled to grasp the situation.

The trucks brought us to the rifle range. We clambered out of the
backs of them and formed up in front of the ammo point, where we were
issued ammo and magazines before we entered the range. Crisp instructions had been given on how to load our twenty rounds into a magazine.
These were followed with instructions on how to insert the magazines

into our weapons. The sergeant explained that we only needed to pull the bolt back once to lock and load. After you fired your first round, the weapon automatically ejected the shell casing and shoved the next round in the magazine into the firing chamber. This all happened because the M14 is gas operated. That is, some of the gas from the exploding gunpowder in the shell casing that pushes the bullet through the barrel at such a high rate of speed bleeds off through a small port and pushes a rod connected to the bolt to the rear. Of course, a lot can go wrong—and when it does, you need to know how to fix it in a hurry. They did a good job of teaching us how.

The M14 is a semiautomatic weapon. That means you have to pull the trigger every time you want to fire a round. Of course, because it is gas operated, you can pull the trigger very fast. The weapon can also be fired in the automatic mode: One pull of the trigger and it just keeps firing until your magazine is empty. There is a little thing on the side of the rifle by the receiver that you adjust to put it into automatic-firing mode. We were told not to attempt to set it for automatic firing on our own. Someone else would take care of that for us at the proper time. A few of the guys immediately started fooling with mechanism when it was brought to our attention. The rapid clicks of helmet liners being struck by Lieutenant Brown's swagger stick attested to that fact.

Having a hang fire out on the range was a bad thing. It meant that you had pulled the trigger and the firing pin struck the end of the bullet but nothing happened. A dangerous situation. Your bullet could be cooking off, meaning that the gunpowder inside the casing is burning slowly. If that is the case, it will eventually fire the round. We were taught never to eject a round that hang fired because it could go off as it flew through the air or on the ground. They told us to keep our rifles pointed down range and not swing them around because the bullet could fire at any moment and someone might get hit. We were to immediately call out, "Hang fire!" and wait for someone to come and assist. The important thing was to remain very still with your rifle pointed down range.

Everything was very precise on the firing range. It is a place where people can get killed. There were always lots of sergeants and lieutenants around. A guy in a tower overlooking the firing line issued instructions over a PA system, telling us exactly what to do. The sergeants moved quickly to anyone not following the instructions or who raised a hand for help. It is a serious place.

Once everyone was in place, the guy in the tower told the occupants of the foxholes facing the bull's-eye targets down range with their rifles pointed in the same direction, "Lock and load!" Knowing that their

An M14 rifle being fired on automatic.

magazines held live ammo, the firers silently went about their deadly business.

"Ready on the right?" asks the man in the tower.

"Ready on the right!" shouts back the sergeant in charge of the right section of the line.

"Ready on the left?" the tower questions.

"Ready on the left!" comes the reply.

"All ready on the firing line. Commence firing!" The order is complete.

Noise dominates the scene. The smell of cordite burns your eyes and stings the inside of your nostrils. No one firing notices these things until the tower orders, "Cease-fire! Cease-fire! Cease-fire!"

The first phase is intended simply to get us used to firing our weapons. The second phase is to get us to zero the sights. Each person has unique firing characteristics. It might be due to the slightest of variations with eyesight or thousands of other unidentifiable quirks. In turn, each weapon has its own little nuances. Zeroing your weapon means that you make slight adjustments to the sighting mechanisms on your rifle until you and your rifle are in sync. You know this is the case when you have a tight shot group, meaning you have put three rounds through the bull's-eye of the target in a tight cluster. Well, at least close to the bull's-eye, anyway—and hopefully close enough together to form a visible group. For some, the concept of a "shot group" was very broadly defined. The tighter your shot group is, the greater the probability you will hit what you are aiming at. This becomes more dramatically true as the distance between you and your target increases. If you correctly zeroed your weapon, you knew you could hit what you were aiming at as long as you held it in your sights. Without a properly zeroed weapon, the likelihood of you hitting what you aimed at was low.

Time after time we went through the firing-range ritual. It was getting to be old hat. The tension lessened as we waited for the tower operator and his assistants on the firing line to go through their rituals. Hair-Cut Louie was fidgeting around with his weapon as his group waited for the ritual to begin. They were given the order to lock and load, but Louie continued to fidget. The lieutenant was walking quickly toward him.

"Ready on the right?" blared the tower.

Lieutenant Brown raised his swagger stick as he approached Louie, who was still messing with his weapon. The sergeant replied, "Ready on the right!"

One more step and the lieutenant would be there. "Ready on the left?" the tower operator asked in his dull, boring manner as the lieutenant's swagger stick came down.

"Clank," rang Louie's helmet as his head turned back and his torso followed, swinging the M14's muzzle from down range to flank the firing line.

"Crack, crack, crack, crack, crack!" Bullets spat out from the rifle. Geysers of dirt shot up. Sergeants dove into the ground. Everyone in the foxholes intuitively ducked down. Louie had sprayed the firing line with live fire. No one was hit. A hush fell over the range. Slowly, people began to move. Then it was a mad rush of sergeants converging on Louie. He was removed from his foxhole and the lieutenant left.

We never saw Lieutenant Brown on the firing line after that. For that matter, we never saw his swagger stick again, either.

After we finished cleaning our weapons and had returned them to the arms room, we were addressed by a sergeant who had more stripes on each sleeve than I had ever seen before. He was the company first sergeant, and a dapper man, he was. His neat, pencil-thin mustache had just a fleck of gray in it. His thin frame was lean and fit so that his small stature was an asset to his personal appearance. No doubt about it, he was a diminutive David Niven. One got the impression that he would be retiring soon. He had the look of having been around a long, long time. Calling us to gather around him, he spoke softly and kindly. After explaining a few details about his role as first sergeant, he asked us how we liked the army. There were a few chuckles, but the men seemed to murmur agreement that it was all right under the circumstances. It was obvious this guy had real power. He told us that we could ask him anything we wanted.

One fellow asked if we would be able to go to church on Sunday. Of course we could, the first sergeant replied. There would be time off in the morning for everyone. You either stayed in the barracks or you went to church. It was your choice. Someone asked when he could use the phone to call his wife. He told us that we would be able to use the one pay phone in the barracks at the end of the following week whenever we got some free time. The next questioner wanted to know when we would get a weekend pass. He dodged that question a little, saying that we could receive visitors on Sunday of our fourth week. Family members, wives, sweethearts, and friends would then be welcome to come and visit. Why, we could even have a picnic with them at a designated spot. As a further incentive, the three soldiers who received the top scores on the rifle qualification test would be awarded a weekend pass the following weekend. Since we took the test around the fifth week, it meant the sharpshooters would probably be able to go off post during the sixth weekend. Well, that was that. Anna and I would not be able to be with each other until sometime after basic training. It just would not be worth it for her to fly up for a Sunday-afternoon visit. Moreover, there was not a chance in hell that I would be among the three best shots in the company. Zeroing my weapon had been harder than I had imagined it would be. Almost everyone else succeeded. I always had one bullet that strayed from the shot group. I just hoped I would be able to make the minimum qualifying score when the time came. Without that score, I would have to take basic training over again. That would just be lost time for me. It would delay my getting to OCS. No matter how long it took me to get to OCS, I would still have two years of time to serve. Just getting to OCS had the potential of being a long, frustrating process.

There would be a one-week to two-week leave time after graduation from basic training. We would know how long as soon as we got our orders for our next assignments at the graduation ceremony. Some would be sent to specialty schools and others would go to Advanced Infantry Training. I asked if that meant going directly to OCS. No, everyone going to OCS would first have to go through the eight-week-long AIT program, he explained. That was news to me. I was sure—well, pretty sure —the Cincinnati recruiting sergeant had told me that I would go to basic training and then to OCS. No mention was made of Advanced Infantry Training. This was bad. I was depressed and mad.

"First Sergeant!" I yelled out from the back of the pack. "Someone told me that I'm eligible for a direct commission as a first lieutenant in the Medical Service Corps because I have a masters degree in psychology." It was true that one of the college guys had told me that, but I had doubted the truthfulness of it. Besides, after basic training, I would be going to OCS, and with the high scores I was sure to get, I would be in the Adjutant General Corps in no time. Well, now I was not so sure what was true and not true.

"What's your name soldier?" he asked gently. I told him and he wrote it on a piece of paper. "I'll check into it for you and let you know," came his fatherly response.

I hated for everyone to see me stand out like that. I did not want anyone thinking I thought I was better than everyone else. That had already happened to a few guys. They were paying the price with isolation and pulling shit details handed out by the pretend squad leaders and other temporary trainee officeholders. More significantly, the core group of trainees was made up of rough-edged guys who had the clear markings of tough street fighters. They were not people I wanted to have irritated at me.

Thus far I had interacted well enough with everyone. I fit in with whatever social grouping I found myself. Having been the only Caucasian deckhand on an ocean-going dredge boat during college summer breaks had taught me to value and respect those who worked all their lives with their muscles, knowing that they would probably never get the chance to do otherwise. Mostly, it never occurred to them that they might get a better break in life. They liked getting drunk on Friday and Saturday nights. There were a lot of laughs to be had at the drinking fests. They liked being strong and kicking butt every once in a while. I understood that feeling. There were some real good times to be had living that way. It was not, however, the way I wanted to live my life; I had other alternatives. They mostly did not. I had seen more than one horse's behind get his clock cleaned during my time. It was usually from a sucker punch the guy never saw coming. If he was lucky, he went down and out right then. Being conscious enough to try to get up was bad. He was at the mercy of his attacker. That is not the time for mercy. A barrage of kicks to the head and body would follow. The horse's behind was definitely better off getting knocked unconscious by the first blow. Kindness could be shown to him later, after he had regained consciousness and acknowledged the victor's superiority. The pecking order would be set.

No more asshole behavior toward the strongest. The matter was then settled. All was right with the world. Everyone could get drunk together and share some laughs.

My letter to Anna that night was a joyous one. I told her I would be able to spend a week or two with her after basic.

CHAPTER 5

Soldier Skills

MARCHING AND RUNNING in formation are highly valued skills for any soldier to have. Why else would we spend so much time at them? Every morning we had our jogging together. No matter how often we did it, there were stragglers. Wherever there were stragglers, there were sergeants pulling other soldiers out of line to grab a straggler. Stragglers could not be left behind.

Everyone had his spot in the marching formation. My place was just about in the middle. The biggest, strongest guy in the platoon was at the front. He carried the platoon's flag as well as whatever equipment the rest of us were carrying. Hawk's position was in the front third of our moving block of men. He had been a track star in college. There was no doubt that he was fast. A base record was almost broken when he ran the mile in the first PT test we took. He had the lean, hollow-cheeked look of a distance runner. His blond hair and blue eyes made you think of the movie star Alan Ladd. The image Alan Ladd conveyed on the screen of a quiet but intense person with a good heart fit Hawk perfectly. People seemed to gravitate to him. You hardly noticed his small stature because his presence was so large. He was kind to everyone. I liked him, and so did a lot of other people. Two years was all he wanted to spend in the army. He planned to serve his time and get out.

The sergeants quickly paired Hawk up with a straggler. Jim was a pasty-skinned fellow who looked like he had never even *walked* hurriedly in his life. His pudgy frame spoke of a sedentary lifestyle. He seemed nice enough. Walking, jogging, and running were not part of his repertoire. When Jim called out that he could not make it at some point during a run, Hawk and one or two others would grab Jim's arms and pull him along. He would protest that he simply could not make it and ask them to please let him go. It was a scene that repeated itself like a badly scratched record. Jim would be pulled and pushed along until we finally got to wherever it was we were going. Many were the times when I was so tired and exhausted that I would consider dropping out. But if the others could keep going, so could I. Everyone had to be tired, but they kept going. I kept going. There was, however, no energy left in me to be pushing or pulling a straggler like Jim. Hawk had grit—and he was always so nice to everyone.

One night we were returning late to the barracks from a long march. All 250 of us were dog tired. We had layers of sweat marks in our armpits. Some activities they had us doing that day would get us all sweated up, and then we would stop for more instruction. The sweat would sweat us up again. The next activity would get us sweating and then we would stop again. The sweat rings just kept building. Anyway, as we were heading back to the barracks that night, Sergeant Soto ordered us to start double timing. We groaned in unison. That really made him mad. He shouted at anyone he spotted talking in ranks—which meant that he was shouting all of the time. Sergeants Boone and Zarconi were jogging along beside our platoon, barking out orders to keep up, shut up, and stay in step. The weight of the field packs, half-empty canteens, and our weapons added to our misery. People kept tripping over unseen objects under their feet, which in turn broke their rhythm. The result was that you either stepped on the heels of the guy in front of you or the guy behind you stepped on your heels. Both things often happened at the same time. The heaviness of your feet and weariness of your whole body dominated your thoughts. Keep going; do not embarrass yourself; the others are doing it; they are as tired as you are. Just keep going, you tell yourself. Somehow I managed to keep moving. Gaps began appearing in the ranks. Some of the men began falling behind. The dust from our feet clogged our noses. Coughing increased at a rapid rate.

Breaking out of the trees, we could see our cluster of barracks in the distance. Just one more mile or so. Our goal was in sight. I felt relieved. I could make it. As we moved onto the level surface of a paved street, the double timing got a little easier. We were all breathing heavily through our mouths. Everything we did was punctuated with coughing, and this run was no exception. My own coughs added to the chorus.

Something was happening. It was dark, but I was able to see that something was going on three or four rows in front of me. Then suddenly Jim began crying out: "I can't make it. I can't go on. Let me go. Let me go."

Through the darkness and bobbing bodies, I could see Jim pulling back as Hawk and another guy tugged on Jim's arms. Damn, it made me mad. There they were, just as tired as I was, yet they had to pull this guy along so that he would stay with them. Meanwhile, Jim was planting his feet on the street just like a puppy whose owner is dragging him by his leash at an obedience class. Jim's cries of protest and Hawk's voice telling Jim that he could make it were too much.

I hunkered down into a semisquatting position and ran between the two or three guys to my right without tripping them as they jogged forward. As soon as I was clear of them, I squirted up the side of the formation. I passed Sergeant Boone and darted into the moving mass right behind the struggling group. Grabbing Jim by the shoulder, I pushed him to the ground. Soldiers immediately began tripping over him. Some stepped on him and fell to the ground. As he went down, Hawk and the other guy turned to reach for Jim. The moving formation and their own forward momentum kept them in place as I screamed at them to let him go and keep moving. They turned and did as they were told.

It did not take long to reach the barracks. As we were being dismissed from the formation to go inside, my anger at Jim had changed to shame. I wanted to help people. At least that was what I thought. That was why I had chosen to become a school psychologist. So what is a helping person doing pushing a fellow down to be trampled on by a couple hundred men in the middle of the night? As I was walking to the barracks doors, I came within hearing distance of Sergeants Boone and Zarconi.

"Did you see him zip out of the formation like that?" Sergeant Zarconi laughingly asked.

"Yeah, where did he get the energy to move that fast?" Boone replied. They both chuckled.

Inside, Hawk approached me and asked, "Why did you do that?"

"It made me mad, Hawk," I said. "You were exhausted. He couldn't go on. You couldn't have pulled him the rest of the way. It was time to stop. He has to start pulling his own weight. If he can't, then he can't. All the same, I'm sorry that I did it." Hawk told me it was all right. He said he knew that the situation could not continue as it had been. It was okay.

The next morning at breakfast, I sought Jim out. He was seated alone, not talking to anyone. I sheepishly approached him. When he saw me he smiled and motioned for me to sit down. "Thanks for making them stop pulling me last night," he said. "I just couldn't go on. My feet were hurting me so badly I couldn't stand the pain anymore."

I was stunned. After feeling so rotten for having pushed him to the ground, here he was thanking me. I sat down beside him and told him that I would try to help him and encourage him, but that I would not drag him or let other people drag him in formations. He knew what he was capable of doing and the consequences of not keeping up. We all needed to value his decisions. I felt real compassion for him. From then on, we were often together in various training situations. I liked him and felt sorry because his feet hurt so much. He never was able to keep up with us on the long marches or while double timing. The sergeants gave him a lot of hell over it, too. Jim just accepted it and maintained his pleasant demeanor with the guys. His limitations were an ever-present reality. We just kept on going.

The instruction we received on throwing a hand grenade was helpful. You have to keep your body close to the ground and lob the grenade over your head. It then makes a nice high arc as it approaches the target. The trick is to hold onto it for a second or so after releasing the fuse lever before throwing it. That way it is likely to explode in the air just above the place for which you are aiming. An airburst has a larger killing zone than one that lands on the ground before detonating. The instructor coaching us in the art of tossing a hand grenade was really good. From that time on, I always got a high score on the hand-grenade toss event on the PT test. A guy in the company from Australia never was able to get the hang of it, though. Hawk explained that, as kids, they just did not throw things over there like we did. This guy just could not master the technique of throwing it the way we were taught. They learned to throw the way we throw softballs. Their ball games did not have them throwing over the shoulder as we do in baseball or football, Hawk said. The sergeants would not let him throw it the way he wanted. The guy was doing well in all of the other physical activities required of us. We were all understanding of his problem and sympathetic about it.

It was news to me that an Australian could be drafted into the U.S. Army in the first place. He explained that one of the conditions of being allowed to enter the United States on a work visa was that you were eligible for the draft. He had been working in New York City for a couple of months when he got his draft notice. Rather than being mad about it, he saw it as an opportunity to get to know the country better. It also might help him get an extension to stay after he got out of the army, he speculated.

Tossing a live grenade was more anxiety provoking than I thought it would be. A story was going around about a recruit in the grenade-tossing pit with one of the instructors. The guy had dropped his grenade right after pulling the pin. Once the pin is pulled, the only thing keeping the grenade from "cooking off" is the lever-like handle you keep pressed down in the palm of your hand. As soon as you release it, the chemical reaction inside the grenade's fuse starts. There is no stopping it. Four seconds later the grenade explodes. Dropping a grenade after pulling the pin is *not* good. The story we heard was that the recruit panicked when he dropped a live grenade. While thrashing around trying to get out of the pit, he kicked both the grenade and the sergeant several times. The sergeant finally grabbed hold of the kid and pushed him down to the bottom of the pit with one hand while picking up the grenade with his other and rolling it over the top just as it went off. Neither one of them was hurt. Thank God for sergeants with cool heads.

My turn came. It was no big deal until the grenade was in my hand. This was dangerous. I did not want to make a mistake. The sergeant was calm. He said everything would be all right. He would not let anything happen. Following his instructions, I pulled the pin and stretched my throwing arm back while reaching forward with the other. Then I flung the grenade in a high arc and we both ducked. The boom was not as loud as I thought it would be. Since we had both ducked before it exploded, I could not tell if it hit the target. The sergeant told me I had done a good job. That was the first and last time I threw a live grenade in training.

Karate-like training was the key for hand-to-hand combat. You stood sideways to your opponent, legs comfortably spread apart for balance so you looked a little like a person in an ancient Egyptian wall painting. Extending your left arm straight out, parallel to the ground, you held your two lead fingers rigidly pointing at your enemy with the other fingers curled into your palm. This way you could easily poke your counterpart in the eyes, nose, or throat. You kept your right hand above your extended left arm with its two lead fingers held rigid but your elbow bent for the same basic purpose. Obviously, your attacker thought you were inching up on him in this exaggerated posture to poke his eyes out. That was just the time you needed to fool him by dropping both of your hands to cover your testicles while simultaneously swinging your right leg around to kick him in the testicles. It was a very clever move. The reason for protecting your testicles was a precautionary one. Just a split second before you decided to kick the other guy's groin he might decide to kick yours.

The first of the native New Jersey guys to sneak off post got a chance to use the move in real life. The story I heard goes like this: He went out to get a couple of beers that night and came back the next morning with both his eyes black and purple with a series of unique blends of the two colors that defied description. It seems that he was very proud of his hand-to-hand combat skills and had leaned on some dude at the bar. The two of them squared off. Just as our soldier switched from the finger-pointing move to cover his crotch with both hands and raise one leg off the ground to do in the villain, the villain punched him right between the eyes. He went down on the floor, out cold. Some of his high school buddies brought him back to the post. The guys said he was still a little groggy when he arrived.

I had always thought that going absent without leave (AWOL) was a real bad thing. In the movies, guys got shot for going AWOL. At Fort Dix, several of the guys went AWOL on a frequent basis during the night. The main four-lane highway was within sight of the barracks. Just a mile or so down the road was the civilian world. It was a temptation. How these guys found the strength at the end of a day's training to slip out at night and drink was a mystery to me. The sergeants put you in a world of hurt in the morning if your boots were not shined and your belt buckle did not gleam from extensive rubbing with a special polishing compound in a can called Brasso. The only time we had to do that was at night, just before lights out. Of course, you also had to have your personal area perfect to pass morning inspection or you would find your stuff tossed all over creation when you got back from training. In addition to all of that, there were group work details to be accomplished, such as cleaning the latrine or polishing the floors. There was just a lot to do. Plus, there were things to study, like the chain of command from Sergeant Zarconi to President Johnson and the military code of conduct. It was all I could do to get these things done. There was no way I could then slip out until the wee hours just to drink.

Lamar was reportedly one of the worst when it came to going AWOL. When he was not around, you noticed it. He was such a dramatic physical specimen. He could do anything that required strength so much better than anyone else. We always looked for him. He would unerringly demonstrate what none of the rest of us would ever be able to accomplish. On top of that, he was joyously happy about doing whatever he was doing. You just wanted to share in that happiness by watching him. They kept us pretty much with our own platoon, so we did not see people from the other platoons except at a distance or while standing in line to practice some training activity. Our platoon had to strain to look over to Lamar's platoon during training, but strain we would—just to see him perform. The story was that the sergeants would counsel Lamar, but nothing ever happened to him. After a while, Lamar just was not around. No one knew what had happened to him. The sergeants, of course, said nothing.

At the beginning of the second week of training, the honey-bun truck started showing up wherever we were. We could have been marching way out in the woods for several hours, and suddenly the sergeants would announce that we had honey-bun privileges. There would be a small truck with its side panels up revealing candy bars, peanuts, honey buns, and the like. If we messed up on some training session, fell asleep in the bleachers, or talked too much while marching, we were threatened with the loss of our honey-bun privileges. I did not like honey buns. That did not matter. What mattered was being able to get a little treat that you usually were denied.

"Is the spirit of the bayonet in your heart?" shouted the sergeant.

"Yes!" we screamed back in unison. Our vigorous reply pleased the sergeants conducting the training. We were full of smiles as we looked at each other. Hell no, the spirit of the bayonet was not in our hearts. You have got to be kidding, I thought. No one I knew in the crowd of trainees around me wanted to be in the army in general and none of us wanted to be in a bayonet fight in particular. It was a joke. The sergeants took our maniacal screams as a sign of our enthusiasm when we knew they were screams of frustration over this stupidity.

"High port! Horizontal butt stroke! Slash and stab! HO!" came the order. Twenty or so crude dummies hanging on posts were stretched out in a line in front of us. Standing about twenty yards from each dummy was a line of about a dozen soldiers. On the command, "High port," the first man in each line pulled his bayonet-fixed rifle across his chest. When the sergeant shouted "Ho," he ran toward the dummy while screaming wildly in chorus with the other charging grunts. As the men in the first rank came within a pace of the crosslike post with the straw-stuffed dummy tied to it, they tried to plant both feet squarely in front of the inanimate figure. Not quite accomplishing the stance, they would swing the butt of their rifle toward the side of the dummy's head. Then, pretending that their "opponent" was falling backward onto the ground, they brought down the bayonet's blade as if they were viciously slashing their falling enemy across the chest. Having smashed the rifle butt into the imaginary foe's face, slashed him across the chest in the downward sweep of the rifle as he fell, they were standing naturally over the victim with the knife blade in a convenient position to neatly stab him. Exit

Is the "spirit of the bayonet" in *your* heart?

imaginary enemy number one. High port, butt stroke, slash, and stab was a nifty ballet move for the Chinese opera. The problem was that a real-life enemy would not stand there waiting for you to do your little dance of death in front of him. It was not going to be like that in Vietnam. We all knew it. From the way we viewed the situation, bayonet drill was just another waste of time. What was important was getting back to the barracks and cleaning up the latrine so that we could get some free time on Sunday afternoon. At the very least, we would get the platoon bay's floor spit-shined or our shoes spit-shined and thus avoid having to do punishment push-ups.

We had spent most of the day learning to execute various bayonet moves. The army obviously thought they were important. We had already spent several training periods on them and no doubt would spend many more in the days to come. Properly executing the bayonet moves we learned was part of the proficiency test we would have to take at the end of basic. Each soldier would stand on a platform before a dummy. A sergeant would call out some bayonet drill, such as the butt stroke, slash, and stab. You would then assault the dummy and be graded on how well you carried out the attack. From there you moved on to the next platform and waited for the sergeant at that station to issue another bayonet assault order. In all, you had to perform three successful bayonet attacks. If you failed the proficiency test, you had to repeat all or part of basic training. No one wanted to repeat basic training. It just was not all that much fun.

The continuous criticism of our bayonet work was related to our apparent failure to be aggressive enough. We screamed and yelled as we ran up to the dummy, but it never seemed to satisfy them. All I wanted was to be able to remember the moves well enough to pass the test. My wish pretty much reflected the desires of my associates as well. The sergeants told us that we could get a good score on the proficiency test simply by being aggressive. He said they were less concerned with the precision with which we executed the moves than they were with the degree of aggression we showed.

One more afternoon of bayonet drill. This was getting old. We had gone through all of the maneuvers except one. When we finished learning this one, we could take a long break. Just standing in line gets old. My throat had been sore all day, I coughed a lot, and my damn big toe hurt. Moreover, you were never allowed to sit down while waiting in line. The only time we were allowed to sit was during breaks. I was at the end of the line, joking around with some of the guys, when I suddenly had a great idea. The heat of the glaring sun coming from the cloudless sky probably brought it on. There were still about ten guys in front of me, so I still had a long wait before it would be my turn. In the meantime, Hawk, Ben, Jim, and a few others of us had been laughing about funny scenes in movies we had seen.

"Watch this," I said spontaneously. "This will be good for a laugh." Turning to the guys waiting patiently in front of me for their turn to do the new bayonet drill, I shouted: "Make a hole! I'm coming through! Give me room! The spirit of the bayonet is in my heart!" Pushing people aside as I rushed to the head of the line, I screamed: "I'm ready! I'm ready! Let me kill! I have to kill now! The spirit's in my heart!" I tried to act as crazed as possible as I rushed to the front. No one resisted my advance. Puzzled looks whizzed in and out of my vision as I went forward. It was all I could do to keep from laughing. What a spectacle I must be: a soldier gone mad. It was truly funny. They were taking it all so seriously. At last I reached the front of the line. The men in the front rank were waiting for the sergeant to announce the bayonet move they were to execute along with the command to start.

"I'm sorry," I sputtered between growls and grunts to the guy at the head of my line. "Let me go now! I have to go *now!*"

He nodded with widened eyes fixed upon me and stepped a pace or two back. Hunched down with my rifle at high port, I stomped my feet, snorted, growled, and grunted as if I were a Spanish bull in the fighting ring about to begin my charge of rage and death upon the frail matador. Oh, how I wished I could have seen myself. It had to have been funny to the onlookers.

"I've got it! I've got it!" I shouted. There was a mixture of hoarse-throat coughing in my voice that accentuated the strangeness of the scene. "It's in my heart. The spirit of the bayonet is there! I have to *KILL!*" Out of the corner of my eye I could see the lead men in the other lines begin to turn and look at me, their mouths open.

"High port. Parry left, stab, withdraw, and charge, HO!" barked the sergeant.

I lunged forward in a semibounding motion, my legs spread wide apart, and made the most god-awful sound from deep within my chest that I could pull up into my throat and out of my mouth. Moving as fast as I could in this exaggerated manner caused my feet to scrape up a trailing cloud of dust. Again, my peripheral vision communicated to me. The other attackers had fallen behind, their attention riveted on my shenanigans rather than on their own targets. This spurred me into even faster movements accentuated with jerks, screams, and hops as the dummy moved into the center of my vision.

Swinging the rifle from high port to the assault stabbing position while at a fully animated dead run was more than I had bargained for. I lost my grip on the upper portion of the rifle. The blade began falling to the ground. I fumbled to catch it as my momentum carried me forward. The blade caught the ground, causing the entire rifle to serve as an impromptu pole-vaulting tool that lifted my feet off the ground as my chest crashed into the dummy. It vibrated as I wrapped my arms around the dummy to keep from ricocheting off of it and falling on my back. Stunned and disoriented, I twisted and fought the dummy with my left hand while dragging my rifle up to my chest with my right. I fell back. At the last second, my feet stabilized on the ground, saving me from falling over backward. Swinging the rifle up, I slammed it into the dummy, catching my fingers between the hard four-by-four pole and my rifle. The pain was instantaneous. Bouncing back from the impact put me into a crouching stance with my rifle at high port as I stared into the dummy's featureless face.

Standing there, facing the dummy, I realized that I was surrounded with silence. The others had stopped their attack. Everyone was looking at me. I was in trouble. It was a joke, but no one was laughing. All I wanted was to make a joke out of it and take an early break. This was not good. With my weapon still at high port, I slowly started walking toward the rest area.

"That's what I mean by being aggressive, men," the sergeant's voice boomed over the silent field. "Let the spirit of the bayonet *lead* you. Good job, Soldier!" Turning to the lines of men yet to attack the dummies, he barked out orders for the next group to assault the dummies. When I reached the rest area, it struck me that the noncom thought I had been serious. I could not believe it. It was a joke.

Good soldiers know how to put their gas masks on quickly. Their training has taught them this skill. Our training on the matter was fairly straightforward. You adjust the straps so the mask fits snugly over your head. You check to be sure you have a good seal by placing your hand over the snoutlike breathing thing in the front and sucking in until you feel it tighten on your face because of the suction. If you feel air coming in from the edges, the straps need to be adjusted. You keep adjusting the straps until you get a good seal. After that, it is just a matter of responding correctly to the cry of "Gas!"

As soon as someone yells "Gas!" you hold your breath and jerk open the bag carrying your mask. It is conveniently hanging from your shoulder. Having opened your gasbag, you quickly slip on your mask, check the seal, adjust the straps as needed, and then start breathing normally. Well, almost normally. You are sucking air in through a filtered snout. It does not just come in. There is a little work involved. On top of that, you cannot see very well with the mask on. You look out through two eyepieces that greatly limit your field of vision. There is a tendency to bump into or trip over things while wearing your mask. The sergeants have you repeat the drill for putting on your mask over and over and over. Then they will call out "Gas!" in the middle of some other activity, like when you are waiting in line to buy a honey bun or some other treat. All in all, people become fairly skilled at quickly putting on their gas masks.

The big test of your gas-mask skill is going into the gas chamber. A couple of sergeants who are already masked walk you and a few others into the chamber. Your mask is still in its case, hanging at your side. Once everyone is inside and the door to the little building has been closed, someone opens a small hole in one of the walls and tosses in a tear-gas canister. The sergeants' muffled cry of "Gas!" can be heard. Immediately, you stop breathing and put on your mask. My testing went just fine. Several of the others had serious difficulty, though. One guy never did get his mask on. The biggest problem for most was getting a good seal. Those who could not began coughing and fumbling around for the door. Someone opened it fairly quickly and they emerged from the chamber in a rush with mucus streaming from their noses and a flood of tears running down their cheeks. Their condition, as observed by the unaffected, was a stern warning always to be ready to put your mask on and get a good seal. No one had bad enough enemies to want to be up close and personal with them as they suffered from exposure to tear gas. The only thing worse than being confronted by a gasping, mucus-flowing-nosed person with eyes involuntarily shut and tears streaming from the red, swollen slits was having that person be you.

Along with the regular gas attack response drills were the nerve gas attack drills. Again, when the cry was given, you stopped everything and began taking protective action. The nerve gas drill was somewhat more abstract. We simulated it. Part of the protective action involved taking a small piece of specially treated cloth and pretending to blot off blobs of the persistent form of the nerve agent that wind up on your outer garments or exposed skin. Like the bayonet and hand-to-hand combat moves, we would have to demonstrate these skills at the end of basic training during the final proficiency test.

Not getting lost was another skill the army valued in its soldiers. To prove it to us, the army had us use a compass to find our way to lots of stakes in the ground. They call this dead reckoning and it was one of the easier tasks for me. I had always prided myself on being able to use a compass, one of many skills I had learned in the Boy Scouts.

In the main, the sergeants doing the instructing were very patient. A lot of guys had never seen a compass before. The army compass I was issued was more complicated than the Boy Scout compass I had used, but the principle was the same. It could not be any different. We spent a lot of time on compass courses.

Fort Dix had been a basic-training complex for a long time. Every compass course we went on had a trail beat into the underbrush that was totally free of vegetation. So many feet had walked down each compass trail that the ground was worn down below the level of the surrounding topsoil. Using the compass was only necessary to get you started on the right path. At least, that was how it appeared at first glance.

During the day, you could locate landmarks and fix your compass bearings on them. Once a landmark was fixed, you just walked up to it and took another fix. Say, for example, that from your starting point, a numbered stake beside the gravel roadbed, you are to find a stake in the woods that is on a compass reading of thirty-six degrees from your stake. All you have to do is point the compass's spinning North-seeking arrow to zero degrees and then twist the moveable top to thirty-six degrees. Next, you pop up this nifty sighting device on the moveable top and look through it. Spotting a prominent landmark through the aiming slit aligned with the thirty-six-degree mark, you just walk up to it. A thin wire running down the middle of the aiming slit makes the selection of a landmark much easier. In addition, there is a neat little magnifying glass attached to the sight finder that you look through to see the small degree markings on the compass. I could never see any of the numbers easily with it. In a pinch, you could also use the magnifying glass to start a fire. You just let the sun shine through it and focus the rays on a piece of paper. That was another tip I got from the Boy Scout handbook that I thought would be helpful someday. You could set your compass bearing on a dead tree, a big rock, the trunk of a big tree, a hilltop, or a building. Whatever it is, you walk straight to it. As you walk, you look for the stake in the ground. Your compass-course card tells you that the stake you are looking for is so many hundred yards from the starting stake. That is not much help, though, because the rough terrain makes it impossible to accurately judge distances. If you should walk past that stake, you are in for a long day. Looking for something that is not there is tedious. Your nerves get on edge as you begin to suspect that you have made a mistake. Since you start your compass training with four or five other trainees, you quickly find the flaws inherent in committee work.

You begin to realize at the very beginning that there are many things that can go wrong with your compass reading. Perhaps some of the metal attached to your fatigues caused the magnetized needle to stray from magnetic north. Your web belt buckle is made of iron. It could be the culprit. Or maybe your steel pot caused the needle to stray by a few degrees. Being five degrees off is no big deal if you only have to walk thirty yards—unless you are looking for buried treasure. It *is* a big deal if you have to walk three thousand yards. A two-foot high, one-inch-by-one-inch wooden stake painted red is hard to see when you are a hundred feet from it in dense underbrush—even if the ground has been trampled to dust within a ten-foot radius of it. Another problem could have been that your hands were shaking when you were sighting in on your landmark, making the needle jump around a lot. In that case, the best you could do was estimate where thirty-six degrees was. Estimates have a tendency to be wrong, particularly when you are tired, irritable, and know that you could have been done several hours before if earlier mistakes had been avoided.

Once you found your stake, you pulled out your course card, read the instructions for finding the next point, and took your reading. Relieved, you and your happy companions set off once again. Usually, each team was given five or six stakes to find and then it was over. Those who completed the course first sat around smoking and joking while they waited for the less fortunate to find their way to the final point.

Smoking and joking was a big deal. Whenever you were being instructed or performing a training task, everyone wanted you to be quiet. Even when you were marching, they expected you to have your canteen, ammo magazines, rifle sling, backpack, and all the other items you were carrying anchored down so that you did not sound like a tinker's truck bumping down the road—you know, the old truck with pots and pans hanging on its sides. The western movies had the same thing with the old chuck wagon jolting down the trail behind the herd of cattle. Making noise was a sure way to get some sergeant to jump your case. No matter how hard you tried, however, you just could not keep from making noise. Sergeants were always riding you about it. If you were not the specific target of their wrath, it was because someone else had the bad judgment to make more noise than you did. Taking a ten-minute or longer break from the whole game meant you could talk, sit down, and smoke.

All of our packaged C-ration meals came with a complimentary pack of four cigarettes. All of the major brands were represented. One package of C rations would contain Winstons and another would have Camels or some other brand. Guys were always trading. I usually gave mine away. Smoking a pipe was my thing. Never having mastered the art of inhaling was no deterrent to my smoking. Smoking the pipe gave me something to do. Some of the sergeants could not understand that you needed to rest just because you were physically tired. All of them understood the need to stop to have a smoke: No smokie, no needie to have a restie. I smoked my pipe a lot. Sometimes it is the subtle things in life that ease the basic burdens.

A few guys just never could find their stakes on the compass course. I was grateful to them. They provided us with nice, long rest periods. After a while, they would wander across a stake in the woods. Any stake in a storm will do. The voices of the more successful soldiers smoking and joking guided them to the end of the course. Naturally, the last stake they chose to call their own was wrong. The sergeants always went out of their way to help them understand they had made significant errors in judgment.

As our compass-reading skills improved we started going out in two-man crews. Having just one partner sure made decision making easier. If he was sharp, the two of you could zip on through.

Traversing the compass course at night was a lot more difficult. The very first thing we were told was never to use a flashlight. There was a rush to the PX to buy flashlights. Since you could not see a lot of landmarks at night, you used your partner as one. After establishing the correct course for your compass reading, your partner walked in that direction until you could just barely see him. You whispered for him to stop. Logically, you would yell at him to stop, but that was a violation of what the sergeants called "noise discipline." It took a little practice to get so you could whisper loud enough for him to hear but not loud enough to attract a sergeant's attention. Sometimes your partner did not hear you. He would disappear into the darkness. With both of you looking for each other, the night had the potential of being very long. When the two of you lost sight of each other there was a degree of confusion about how to get back together. Shouts in the darkness usually brought you together, but the risk of bringing a sergeant to your rendezvous point was always present.

Once your partner stopped at the edge of your field of vision, you directed him to move to the left or right until he was standing exactly on the correct compass heading. This frequently resulted in some dramatic falls. With both of you concentrating on achieving the correct alignment, no one was focused on the ground. Hidden logs, holes in the ground, stones, and other obstacles were often found by unsuspecting feet. The crash of a falling body in the dead of night is quite dramatic. Such sounds were always followed by muttered curses—as well as laughter from those who did not fall. Of course, you could never be sure that you had gotten an accurate compass reading in the dark. Thus, your risk of getting lost was significantly higher at night. In the best of situations, night compass courses meant little sleep.

Having a flashlight significantly reduced your time on the course if you used it properly. The biggest advantage was that the guy serving as the landmark could go deeper into the woods. He held his fingers over the lens before turning the light on. Little peeps of light were all that made it out from between his pressed fingers. They were enough for you to sight in on him and give him directions to move to the correct spot for the reading. This was always risky business. A sergeant might see the light and give you hell. If the light was too bright, it could ruin your night vision. That was the pits. You started stumbling all over the place.

Without your natural night vision, moving in the woods is a terrible experience. If Charlie (the Vietcong or VC) was out there hiding in the bush, you were dead. There was no way you could keep from sounding like an elephant crashing through a glass factory. Of course, you were probably dead anyway. He just shot wherever the light appeared in the air. You stopped his round. Becoming dependent upon a flashlight for taking compass readings at night was definitely a bad thing. On the other hand, there were no VC at Fort Dix. There were only sergeants. With the assistance of the flashlight, your partner could move farther away from you in the darkness. This meant that you had to stop fewer times and take fewer sightings. You saved time. Without the flashlight, you would lose sleep. Lost sleep meant being irritable and tired the next day. That meant making mistakes that could get you hurt. Getting hurt could set you back in basic training. A lot of people chose the lesser of the evils. Flashlights were definitely "in." Fortunately, I had good night vision. Except in extreme cases, my partners and I did not have to use them. "Extreme cases" meant it was a very, very dark night or we were short on time. Even then, we never seemed to make up much on the time side of things.

Late one night, we were on a long march back to the barracks after completing a compass course. Over all, I was feeling pretty good, as were many of the other guys. A dozen or so trainees had gotten seriously lost out on the course. That meant the rest of us got to lie down and relax. Some guys slept. Others talked. Everyone smoked. Finding lost campers in the dark woods does not make Boy Scout leaders or sergeants happy.

Sergeant Soto was in a particularly foul mood. He kept telling people to stop talking and coughing. Since he could not see more than ten or twenty soldiers at a time in the dimness, his words had little impact.

Finally, he gave the order for the company to form up. He marched us at a brisk pace toward our destination. Sergeants Boone and Zarconi were moving up and down the platoon, trying to catch people talking. As soon as one soldier was reprimanded, the murmuring voices of a few others could be heard somewhere else in the ranks.

"Company . . . *halt!*" Sergeant Soto's high-pitched scream pierced our ears. "You want to talk do you? I'll show you who wants to talk. Put on your gas masks."

A collective groan from all 250 of us rose in the night air as we pulled them out and adjusted them onto our faces. The damn things were hot. They always made it hard to breathe.

"Forward . . . *march!*" came the order.

We leaned into it, the muffled voices taking on an eerie sound as complaints ruffled through the ranks.

"That's it. That's it you assholes!" Sergeant Soto was pissed. "Double time . . . *march!*" he ordered.

My breathing immediately became labored. Straining to get air and never getting enough is bad. It is seriously bad. Then the damn eyepiece lenses began to fog over. Everyone's lenses were fogged. People were falling down. Others fell over them, but the sergeants ordered us on. The fallen would bungle their way up and rejoin the formation only to fall again. It was hard. Guys pulled their masks from their faces and rested them on top of their heads, only to be confronted by shouting sergeants. Using the fingers of my nonrifle-carrying hand, I broke the seal of my mask. The night air rushing over my face felt cool. It was good. Sergeant Boone screamed at me to remove my hand. I did so immediately. However, the seal of my mask had been broken. A slight nudge set it a little more askew. This allowed enough fresh air to enter the mask that I could breathe properly. Not only that, but my lenses began to clear. It was still unpleasant, but it was bearable. With the lenses fairly clear, it was easy to dodge those who kept tripping and falling. I wondered why more of them did not catch on to this small but important adjustment to their gas masks. From the continual dropping of bodies around me, it was obvious that a whole lot of guys missed the point: Sometimes *not* having a good seal was better.

Standing guard duty at night was another important skill the army wanted us to have. There was a stylized ritual to the task. From my perspective, the important thing was not getting jumped by a crook or being made a fool of by an officer. The probability of encountering a crook was low, but having an officer on your case was high. We would be marched off to some isolated spot as a squad. One by one, the sergeant of the guard would take the man at the front of the line and tell him to guard a spot. The old guard became the last man in the line. Then the sergeant marched the remainder of the squad off into the darkness.

There you were. All alone with your M14 on your shoulder. It did not have a magazine in it. Your ammo magazines were in pouches hooked to your web belt. The magazines were full of blanks. They were good for making a lot of noise. They would inflict damage only if the supposed attacker got very close to you. Instead of firing a bullet from the round, it shot out a wad of paper stuffing that sealed the gunpowder in the crimped shell casing. We had been repeatedly warned not to aim our weapons at anyone close to us when firing our blank rounds because the paper wad could strike someone in the eye and penetrate through to the brain. If that happened, the poor guy was dead. You could kill someone or seriously injure him with that paper wad.

Should you be unlucky enough to have an officer test you on your knowledge of guard duty protocol, you had better do it right—or else. I was never sure what "or else" meant except that it did not sound good.

When someone approaches your guard post, you are to shout out the password. If the shadowy figure is one of the good guys, he shouts back the countersign. This simple procedure seemed to pose several problems. If there were bad guys around, they would hear the two of you shouting back and forth. Should they decide to attack, they now knew exactly where you were, which meant that you would be killed in the first few moments of the assault. Another problem was that a loud exchange of the sign and countersign would clue bad guys in on the code words so that they could trick you into letting them get real close to you. Logic says it is very bad to let someone intent on killing you get too close. Thus, you wanted to shout out the password just loud enough for the approaching person to hear it—but no one else. It was a tricky maneuver. Too soft a yell and he did not hear you. Too strong a yell and everyone knew you were there.

Anyway, you were supposed to shout out the password. If the guy shouted back the countersign, you kept on marching back and forth and let him pass through. Things got complicated if the guy was a good guy but did not know the countersign. You order him to halt. If he does not, you shoot him. It is a pretty simple process once you get the basics down. Fortunately or unfortunately, depending on your perspective, the approaching person almost always stops. When this happens, you order him to place his military ID on the ground in front of him, take fifteen steps backward and then stop. Oh, I forgot to mention that you have your rifle trained on him all this time. Somewhere in this process you have slipped a magazine into it. Cautiously, you approach the ID card and inspect it. If the guy's picture matches his face, you let him through. The darkness makes this process work better on paper than in reality. It does not make any difference if he is an officer or not. We were told that this was the way it was done.

I spent a lot of night hours walking alone in the dark on guard duty. Once I actually had someone wander into the area I was guarding. I could hear him approaching in the darkness. The place I was protecting for democracy was a fenced-in supply area. There was gravel all around it. The crunch of footsteps approaching me sent chills up my neck.

A shadowy figure took form. "Halt!" I ordered. The steps stopped. The figure just stood there.

Swinging my M14 into high port just in case I needed to use it as a club, I barked out the password: "Bear!"

Silence met my demand. The figure just stood there. "Bear!" I shouted out with an edge of real concern. The guy needed to say "Track" to show everything was all right.

"BEAR!" I loudly demanded. No one had told me what to do if someone just stood there. Hell, we might wind up standing there all night.

"It's all right, Son," a soft voice stated from the shadows. "I'm the officer of the day."

"Place your ID card on the ground at your feet and take fifteen paces backward, Sir." I demanded.

Calmly, slowly, the figure reached back and pulled his wallet from his back pocket, laid something at his feet, and walked backward until he stopped. Cautiously, I approached the object on the ground. Bending down slowly, without taking my eyes off the potential attacker, I picked up the ID card. It was definitely a military ID card. That was all I could make out in the dark. The guy was too far back for me to see his face clearly and it was too dark for me to see any distinguishing features in the photo on the card. Nothing in the army ever seemed to go according to the book. It is very frustrating. What to do now was the big question.

"Come forward please, Sir," I said in a subdued tone. The shadow became a real person with lieutenant's bars. Fumbling the ID card to my left hand while trying to juggle my rifle with it as well, I raised my right hand and saluted.

He returned my salute saying, "Good job, Soldier."

"Thank you, Sir." I replied dropping my salute.

"Anyone else been by?" he asked, holding out his hand for his ID card.

"No, Sir," came my brisk reply as I gave him the card back.

"Carry on," he ordered as his hand started up to salute again.

Quickly, my hand shot up to salute him as I replied, "Yes, Sir." He left. When the sergeant of the guard came up with the rest of the squad to relieve me, no one said a word. I went to the end of the line and marched off to the barracks. A few hours of sleep were better than none.

Interacting with officers was something our company commander, First Lieutenant Brown, seemed to think was a good skill. He passed out our pay to us. We got paid at the end of each month. We were given cash in an envelope. Married men got more than single men. They called it an allotment. The money went straight to your wife. There was some flexibility in how much went to her and how much you got on payday. I had the full allotment sent to Anna. The rest of my pay, about $97, was in the envelope Lieutenant Brown handed me each month.

The entire company lined up in alphabetical order to be paid. When we got to the table where Lieutenant Brown was sitting, we were to salute. While holding the salute, we were to say "Sir," state our rank and full name—last name first—and say we were reporting for pay. The lieutenant would return the salute, hand you your pay envelope, and you would move to the left, to the table beside him. There stood Sergeant Soto. You were expected to give him a donation for the United Way. Sergeant Soto had already told us that the lieutenant wanted every man to contribute to the United Way. The company would get a ribbon to hang over our unit flag signifying 100 percent of us had given donations. We were sternly warned that no man had better mess up that record.

"Sir, Private Morton, Jerome H., reporting for pay," I crisply announced with my right hand locked in a sharp salute. Without looking up, the lieutenant returned my salute and handed me the envelope. I took it and slid over to Sergeant Soto's table. Taking out my money, I handed him a five-dollar bill. I resented having to do it, but it was the army way. In my mind I resolved that once I got out of the army I would never again allow myself to be forced to give money to a charitable organization. Until then, I had never understood the implications of an organization having a record of 100 percent employee contributions. It meant that coercion was taking place.

The second time I went to get paid by the lieutenant, I felt like I was an old army guy. There was not the tension that I had experienced in our first encounter. I had not continuously rehearsed in my mind what I was supposed to say to the lieutenant, as I had done the first time.

"Sir, Private Mor—Morton," I said, stuttering my last name. Oh, my God! I'm messing up. With my salute stuck to my head, I finally got out, "Sir, Private Morton, Jerome H., reports."

Raising his head, the lieutenant smiled at me and said, "Reports for what, Soldier?"

My hand still glued to my forehead, I rapidly blurted out, "Sir, Private Morton reports for pay."

The lieutenant laughed, returned my salute, handed me my pay envelope, and shook his head as he said, "And you want to be an officer, Morton. Knock out fifty push-ups here beside my table."

"Yes, Sir," I responded as I moved to the side and began pumping out

the push-ups in perfect form. It was not hard to do them. In fact, it was
a piece of cake. What was hard was the humiliation. As I knocked them
out, he continued to hand out pay envelopes to the other guys. How had
he known I was going to OCS? It did not seem possible that he could
have remembered our first encounter with the shaving-cream disaster on
day one. This was just the third time the lieutenant and I had interacted.
I wanted to do well and I had not done so. That was what was embarrassing. The mistake was *so* stupid. I would try to avoid being intimidated by an officer again, I thought.

CHAPTER 6

Misunderstandings

A PATTERN was beginning to evolve. We automatically woke up in the morning before the sergeants turned on the lights. Most of us were able to finish our morning chores before we were ordered to rush downstairs and through the glass doorway. We would straggle down and stand at our spot in the dark, cold morning air minutes before the sergeants began yelling.

On one such morning, a hundred or so of the guys and I were awaiting the arrival of the rest of the company. The morning runs in the pre-dawn hours were no longer a strain for me. They were just something that had to be endured. Well, that is not exactly true. I was beginning to enjoy feeling fit and strong. I had scored 360 points on the last PT test. I knew I would be able to pass the PT exam at the end of basic without a problem. My palms, however, still seeped fluid from the damage done to them by the monkey bars. It was just one of those things. The same was true for my big toenail. It was dead. The black, congealed-blood bruise beneath it still throbbed. Pus came out from around its edges. Overall, it was just one more endurable thing. I would be glad when it finally fell off. What was irritating was my inability to stop coughing. Other than those few inconveniences, I was feeling pretty good.

Suddenly a hush fell over the group. Several guys were looking up. I instinctively looked up as well. High in the night sky and directly overhead was a rapidly expanding whitish ring of light that left a glowing mist in its inner circle. In less than an eye blink, it expanded to cover a huge area of sky while changing color to a glowing purple. The stars shone through the purple veil like bangles on a prom dress. Then the color began to fade. It was like a giant skyrocket suddenly bursting forth with its beautiful colors at a Fourth of July celebration, but there was absolutely no sound, only silence and this unearthly purple color bathing the night sky.

A hushed voice broke the silence. "Do you think it was a nuclear explosion?"

Murmurs and nervous laughter followed the statement. "We're all dead then," someone said.

I felt at a slight loss. If it were an attack, should I not be diving for cover? Standing there in the middle of the parade ground did not seem to me a good thing to be doing in the middle of an attack. That was stupid, though. If it really was an attack, I thought, then it was an air war. There was nothing for an infantryman to do. Time enough for the infantry in due course. No, this was something else that had a logical explanation. I did not know what it was. Maybe I never would. The army does not tell you everything. The beauty of it caused me to reflect. To my way of thinking, this was one of those once-in-a-lifetime moments. I was glad the army had me up in the wee hours of the morning to witness it.

A few days later some guy said he had read a newspaper report about the light in the sky. There was some kind of upper atmosphere testing taking place. Gas was released from a rocket to measure something or other in the stratosphere. The government had not told anyone about the test in advance because no one thought anyone would be up that early in the morning to see it, the guy stated. That explanation seemed a little weak. Something was wrong with it. Nothing else was ever mentioned about it as far as I know. Besides, I had sergeants filling my day and not much time for anything else.

My one connection with the civilian world was writing my evening letters to my wife and reading her daily ones. It was hard to find the time to write, though. Sometimes I would write them in the dark, lying in my bunk with the streetlights outside providing the only illumination. They were important to her. Hers were important to me. I had been able to call her once or twice. There was just the one pay phone and 250 men. Standing in line to use it took so long. Then, when it was finally your turn, you could feel the pressure of all the others waiting to use it. Nothing very intimate could be said. So much had happened. How could you explain it all over the phone in a couple of hurried minutes? You could not. We stayed with our letters.

Various subgroups were forming among the men. The college graduates tended to gravitate together, as did the recent high school graduates. Then there were the hard-working, hard-living blue-collar types. Of course, each of these groups had their own subgroups. Some of the college guys were obnoxious. They had an air of superiority about them that was just plain irritating. No matter how they interacted with others, they sent out subtle and not so subtle messages that they knew they were better than almost everyone else.

Word ran through the company that one of the college guys, a fellow named Gary, had pushed one of the workingmen's buttons once too often. Mike was one of those heavily muscled types who obviously had never done well in grammar when he was in school. He had a thick New Jersey accent and his speech was riddled with tense errors and double negatives. It was plain he was no scholar. He was, however, a leader in his circle of work-hardened friends. I had found him to be friendly enough. It was true that he had a habit of cutting into the chow line. He and his friends had the ability to zoom in on someone who would be intimidated enough by them to not protest their stepping into the line in front of him. Sometimes they jumped in front of a friend, but mostly they barged in front of someone they sensed would be too afraid to tell them no. There were always guys who grumbled about it. Their protests had no effect at the time. I had seen it before at the various public schools I attended. Fortunately, Mike and his crew never pressed me. They did not cut in front of me. There were others that they did not challenge as well. You did not want to put yourself in a compromising situation with Mike. He respected that. From time to time we would get paired up for some training activity. Mike and I got along when that happened. He had his own integrity and his own way of living. That is how it is when different cultures come together. As long as you did not press them, they did not press you.

Gary, in his apparent arrogance, did not understand these subtleties. Mike was damned mad about something Gary had done or said. He was going to fight Gary that night. Hawk and a couple of others asked me what I thought about it. I said I thought Gary would get his clock thoroughly cleaned. He probably deserved it. The fight ought to happen. Once it took place, they could work it out in a subtle peace that would require few words. Let it happen, was my opinion. Gary needed to learn. So it was decided that we would not try to stop it.

After chow that night, a crowd began gathering in our platoon bay. Neither Gary nor Mike was in our platoon. Nonetheless, the fight was to be here. Bunks and chairs were moved to clear out enough space. This was a big deal. I had not realized that so many people were aware of the fight or were interested in its outcome. A number of college guys were hovering around Gary. Their conversations were hushed. He did not have many close friends. It was interesting that some of his critics were now there with him. This had the makings of a real confrontation between people living on opposite sides of the tracks. I had not thought that it would evolve in just this way. The press of people in the space and the cigarette smoke in the harsh, overhead barracks lighting created a 1930s atmosphere of a backroom beer hall. It fit the moment. The semi-professional fighters would complete the scene.

A wave of new faces pushed into the large bay area. It was Mike's vanguard. This was the first time I had looked at them as a group. God, they were tough. If that group had rushed the college guys, they would have beaten them to a pulp. These college boys were in over their heads. They were staring into the eyes of hardened street fighters. Luck was sit-ting on the shoulders of the college boys simply because of the restraint shown by their confronters. They had just a glint of understanding in their eyes, as was reflected in the wide-eyed stares they gave the street guys. At that moment I think they were suddenly glad they were not in Gary's shoes. The tough guys could have ended it right then and there. If they had feigned a charge, Gary's worried trainers would have pooped in their pants. The street guys were the kings of the ring. The group parted and Mike strode forward and stood tall like the champion he was. His supporters hollered catcalls at Gary, tormenting him with their shouts. Bets were being made.

As Mike moved into the open space in the center of the bay, Gary emerged from his corner as the college guys around him pulled back from him. He had not moved. The noise and tension were equally high. The two antagonists' eyes met. Gary was still wearing his fatigue shirt. Mike was stripped down to his T-shirt. His powerful arm and shoulder muscles rippled with tension.

Gary turned his lean frame to the side and began removing his col-lege graduation ring from his finger in a slow and methodical manner, his shoulders sloping in sadness or fear. It was hard to know which was the case.

POW! Mike stepped forward and sucker-punched Gary on the side of his jaw. The crack of knuckle on chinbone was so loud and sudden it stopped all talk. Gary's ring flew clear across the room, making a loud smacking sound as it struck the far wall. Gary crumpled to the floor like a dropped rag. He was out cold. The college guys murmured. All eyes turned to the crumpled form on the floor except mine.

Mike hesitated for just a second and then stepped forward, pulling his foot back to deliver a powerful kick to the pile of flesh. Knowing what was about to happen, I sprang in front of Gary's still form without thinking.

Confronting Mike in a deep crouch, ready to spring at him, I hissed through my teeth: "You've beat him, Mike. You won. There's nothing more to prove. You've done it."

He paused in midkick. Lowering his foot, he looked at me. His muscles were tense. My mind started to race. God Almighty, I thought, he is so much stronger than I am! He could do me great harm. If we start fighting, I must avoid thinking. If I think, I will surely freeze up. This has to be spontaneous and violent. My legs were too far apart to give me solid balance. My arms were too far from my body to throw a hard punch. I did not have a good platform of attack and I could not move. If he kept coming, it would be all over for me. I did not dare move unless he came at me. Any movement on my part would be perceived as attack. I was stuck in that awkward position. Our eyes locked. I knew it was going to be bad. His supporters were beginning to mutter. Other than that, the room remained silent. It seemed like minutes. It was only a few seconds.

"You've won, Mike. You've made your point. It's over," I said in a less intense voice without relaxing my stance.

Mike stepped back. His crowd cheered. They swarmed around him, clapping him on the back and messing his hair. Out the door and down the hallway the jubilant crowd moved en masse as they celebrated their victory.

Several guys were helping Gary to his feet. He was groggy. My heart suddenly went out to him. He had been doing the noble and fair thing by removing his ring from his finger. Having that ring on his fist would have given him an unfair advantage. It would have been a natural brass knuckle. Gary had thought that he was going to be in a boxing match of some kind governed by neat rules and the like. He had just encountered the hard realities of street fighting. It was dangerous stuff. Gary was lucky. The college guys were just beginning to understand how lucky Gary was and to realize their own precarious position in the scheme of things.

No one said anything to me concerning my actions. I went to my bunk and started spit-shining my shoes. After that night, I was kinder to Gary. He seemed to be less of an ass. Actually, he ended up being an okay guy. Meanwhile, Mike and his crew did not cut into line whenever I was around after that. There were never any repercussions from the incident. I did not trust him, but we got along okay and cooperated on a friendly enough level whenever fate brought us together.

The promised Sunday visitors' day the first sergeant had told us we would get was about to happen. I was looking forward to the time off. I would go to the PX and get some floor wax, shoe polish, and other items. Then I would write Anna some long letters.

One of the guys in the platoon asked me if anyone was coming to visit me. When I told him that my wife was too far away, he expressed regret and asked how I dealt with the loneliness. I told him it was not so bad. I was busy. There was little time to be lonely. He refused to let the matter rest. He said his wife was bringing a picnic basket. They lived just a few miles from post. The two of them had grown up together. The separation was hard for them.

A day or two later, he told me that he and his wife wanted me to join them on their picnic. Such an offer was a great honor. It would be an insult to turn them down. I tried to be gracious in accepting the offer even though I did not understand why they were going out of their way like this. If it had been Anna and me, we would have wanted to be by ourselves. This was truly a great kindness these people were extending to me.

The wife was very pleasant. Her fried chicken was good. They wanted to know how the army had snared me, so I told them my story. He said he was in the army by mistake. Bleeding hemorrhoids had been plaguing him for years. They had gotten so bad during the previous year that his wife used cotton swabs to soak up the blood from them when he came home at night. The army should have rejected him at the induction center, he said, but somebody messed up. They had written his congressman and included a doctor's letter saying he was unfit for military service. He expected to be released from the army soon. As it was, the seat of his army-issue boxer shorts was wet with blood by noon every day. She had baked a great apple pie. It was clear that they loved each other and were glad for his hemorrhoids.

Their hemorrhoid story brought to mind my day at the army induction center the previous May in Cincinnati. It was just five months ago, but it seemed like a lifetime. We had been rushed into a large room with hooks on the walls and instructed to strip down to our underpants, hang our clothes on the hooks, and turn in our valuables to be retrieved later. Sergeants were hustling us along. One guy among the several hundred in my group was wearing ladies' underwear. As he took off his pants, several of the men began whooping and howling in delight. Two sergeants rushed past me. One of them was saying that he would take care of the son-of-a-bitching draft dodger. They grabbed the guy by the arms and hustled him out of the room. That was the last we saw of him.

We were lined up in three long rows. A physician told us to turn around and then instructed those of us in the first row to drop our underwear to our ankles, bend over, and spread our cheeks. We did as we were told. He and a couple of other assistants quickly walked down the line looking at our anuses. It must have been quite a sight. They were checking for hemorrhoids. Apparently we all passed. After walking past all three lines of exposed butt holes, the doctor told us to turn around and face back to the front.

Next he announced that he was going to check for hernias. He told us that when he stood in front of us we were to turn our heads to the left. He would insert his finger into the man's right scrotum. We would be told when to cough. The process would then be repeated for the left side. Turning our heads to the left, we would cough when he told us to do so. Quickly, he moved down the line, the coughs becoming louder as he came closer.

Suddenly, he stood up and shouted in the face of one man as he spoke to us all: "Damn it! You turn your face when you cough. Do you think I want five thousand men coughing in my face all day long, showering me with their shitty germs?" He stared into the eyes of the man in front of him and snapped, "Now turn your damn head." After a short pause by the man's scrotum, which caused the guy to make a brief, involuntary sound of pain, the physician shouted loudly, "Cough!" The man did. The physician moved on. I remembered to turn my head when he stopped in front of me.

At the end of the day a sergeant said we would be notified by mail as to our draft status. My notice stated that I was 1-A. It came as a shock. I did not know then that it was the beginning of my army experience, but the fear had already started to creep in.

There was reason to suspect that my picnic companion's story was true. The physician at the induction center could easily have overlooked his hemorrhoids. Then again, they might not have been bad enough to get him a medical exemption. Since I did not need to make a decision one way or the other on the matter, I simply agreed with them. He would probably be dismissed from the army. I was sorry that he had to endure so much at the moment.

Fortunately, there was time that afternoon to get the floor wax and other items. Floor wax was forbidden, of course. It had been explained to us that we were not to spend our time or money on floor wax, spit-shining our shoes, or engaging in any other unusual cleaning activities beyond what was necessary to maintain normal neatness. We quickly learned that those people who *did* use floor wax, spit-shined their shoes, and took other extreme measures to clean their areas got the highest marks during inspections. Those with the highest ratings were then granted special privileges. To be more accurate, they were hassled less, did fewer punitive push-ups, and were not ordered to redo their cleaning details. The vast majority of us were not stupid. We did what was necessary. Every so often someone's hiding spot would be discovered and the guy would have to do extra push-ups for having floor wax. One guy was ordered to use up all of his floor wax while the rest of us looked on. Such inconveniences were regrettable but minor. The advantages for violating the rules far outweighed the consequences. Besides, the sergeants were careful not to look in specific areas for contraband during their inspections. We had a mutual conspiracy.

Our week in the field arrived just as a cold front passed through. We were trucked a long way into the woods. Each of us had been issued half of a pup tent—along with the necessary pins, poles, and rope—a sleeping bag, and an air mattress for the occasion. I could not believe the luxury. All of my campouts with the Boy Scouts had been without an air mattress. It was hard sleeping. Only sissies, girls, and the rich slept on air mattresses. Here I was going to war with an air mattress. This was luxury camping and people were complaining. I liked it.

Setting up a pup tent was duck soup. Camping out was play. I was good at it. So many of the guys lacked the basic skills necessary for cold-weather camping. I was glad to help out wherever I could. It rained constantly for the first couple of days. Then at night it would stop and any standing water would freeze over. Army ponchos are great rain gear. I had never had any rain gear like it. The hood pulled over your head and extended beyond your face. You could carry your rifle under it and keep it nicely protected. Even with your rifle and pack on underneath the poncho, there was enough of a spread that it allowed the rain to fall straight to the ground without getting your lower legs or feet wet—that is, as long as there was no wind and you were not marching. We were always marching. In the mornings, the concentric ice rings from the night's standing rain puddles would be the only mud-free item in view. During the day, it got just warm enough to melt the ice. We were miserably cold, wet, and dirty.

Early on the second night, Sergeant Soto informed us that army field jackets had arrived. They were piled up inside the large command tent. We were to go into the command tent in a single file and pick up a jacket. We were not to stop inside the tent. Once we were outside, we could try our jacket on. If it did not fit, we were to trade around until we found one that did.

The once longhaired Louie was in front of me as we entered the command tent. Good old Louie had acquired a reputation as a "ten percenter." Ten percent of the guys never get the word. They always manage to end up doing the wrong thing or being in the wrong place at the wrong time. No matter how many times you tell a group of soldiers something, 10 percent of them never seem to get the word.

The command tent was big. It was more like a small circus tent. Its sides hung straight down like walls and were about six feet high. The tent had a high, sloping roof and there were portable heaters inside. Electric light bulbs powered by a gasoline generator hung from the center posts. It was a welcome relief from the cold just to be inside it.

Louie picked up a field jacket right in front of Sergeant Soto. Instead of following the man in front of him on out of the tent, Louie stepped to the side and began to put it on. Soto just stood there in disbelief. Not only did this guy disobey an order, he did it right in the face of the very man who had issued it. The expression on Soto's face held everyone except Louie in limbo. It was as if a group of mice suddenly saw the bold black eyes of a coiled rattlesnake inches from their faces. Louie was the lone exception. He was in a different world. As he finished putting his arms through the sleeves, he turned to Soto and said, "Hey, fuck you man, this thing's too small."

"Fuck me? Fuck *you*, fuck me!" screamed Soto in rage and disbelief.

The intensity and immediacy of Soto's response managed to catch Louie's attention. For the briefest of moments the world stood still. Louie looked at Soto. Soto looked at Louie. Then Louie broke the spell. In a brilliant display of intuitive intelligence, he leaped to the tent's exit flap. Soto, standing with his fists clenched at his sides, turned to say something. With a great display of willpower, he turned back to the line and motioned for the next man to move on through. From that point on, our motto became, "Fuck me, fuck you, fuck me."

Wearing our ponchos as we sat in the training bleachers on those cold wet days was a real blessing. You could sink your head deep into the hood so that your face was almost hidden. Then, by slightly tilting your head down, your breath became trapped inside the hood and seeped down your neck onto your chest. The warmth was intoxicating. You could then gently close your eyes and drift off to sleep. Not until a few of the guys fell off the bleachers did the sergeants catch on that most of us were dozing during the lectures.

Once they understood the situation, they quickly adjusted. Two or three sergeants were always hovering around trying to catch someone sleeping. Once they spotted a sleeper, they would charge through the seated mass to confront the evildoer. Of course, the commotion of the charge and the vibration of the plank-type seating was enough to wake even the hardest sleeper. By the time the sergeants reached their victim, he was wide awake and protesting that he had been falsely accused. It got to be a real game. I mastered the art of sleeping with my eyes partly open. It was a skill that kept me out of a lot of trouble.

The principal difference between army training in the field and training back in the garrison complex appeared to be the camping out. We still did live firing at the rifle range. There were still gas-attack drills, and we still marched. Inspections never ceased. We had to clean our rifles and do clean-up details. Even the designated truck drivers continued to be awakened in the middle of the night and told to go drive trucks. I was learning to feel grateful that I had failed the driving portion of the truck driver's exam. It is funny how doing the wrong thing is sometimes the right thing.

There was a slight difference at the rifle range. They were having us fire at silhouettes instead of the traditional bull's-eye target. A pop-up, head-and-torso target would appear down range. After you fired your designated rounds at it, they would pull it down into the trenches. Within a minute or so it would reappear with little white circles drawn on it showing you where you had hit it. The sergeants said to aim low because if you aimed at the head and shot high, you would miss the target altogether. Hitting the ground in front of someone might still bring him down. The bullet would cause rocks and debris to fly up. Getting hit by a high-velocity piece of flying gravel was just as bad as being hit by a bullet. Most of us aimed for the heart. Some shot at the head. I was still having problems with my shot group. Two bullets would hit right where I wanted them. The third round would be off by two or three inches.

A new training activity was to have all of us look across an open field at a tree line. We would be told that there were camouflaged soldiers out there. Our task was to find them. It was difficult. Guys would yell out that they could see someone over there by such-and-such a clump of something. Then a few other guys would say, "Oh, yeah, you're right." Before long, everybody was seeing something. At least, that was what they said. Sometimes the sergeants doing the instructing would yell at the camouflaged guys to move. It was easier to spot them when they moved, but it still was not easy. All in all, everyone agreed that they could see the hidden soldiers when just about all of us were unable to see a thing. It made the sergeants feel good and we got an early break. Honey-bun trucks were our sweet rewards.

It finally stopped raining in the middle of the week. Mud was everywhere and on everything. Because the foxholes were full of water we were instructed not to jump in them when we practiced one type of gas-attack drill. Normally, you would approach a large foxhole at high port and in a trot. Meanwhile a sergeant, conveniently seated on a little folding chair, would shout "Gas!" or "Nerve gas!" In both cases you were supposed to jump into the foxhole. If the cry was "Nerve gas!" you would pull out your little piece of cloth and simulate pinching off bits of congealed nerve gas. The cry of "Gas!" prompted the gas-mask drill. After completing your preventive measures you would then lie on the edge of the foxhole with your rifle at the ready, waiting to repel the enemy.

Since the bottom of the hole held about six inches of muddy water, Sergeant Boone said that we should stop at the edge of the foxhole and pretend that we had jumped into it as we went through the drill.

My turn finally came. Sergeant Boone was beginning to realize that I enjoyed pushing his buttons a little every once in a while. On long marches, I would hum under my breath ever so slightly when he was near. He would cock his head and look into the ranks, never certain enough that someone was humming to call out a guy's name and confront him, but certain enough to make him listen just a little harder. He never asked anyone about the humming, and no one ever told.

Charging the foxhole at full speed with my best killer scream—*AHHHAAAAAAHHHHAAAAA!*—in my throat, I anticipated Sergeant Boone's shout. It did not come until I was on the lip of the mud hole.

"Gas," he half-whispered.

Instinctively reaching for my mask while suddenly realizing that I was going into the hole, I tried to stop. After putting my body through some near superhuman contortions, I paused on the edge, tottering violently. At last the momentum won. Both feet landed in the mud and burrowed into the ooze until they were deep enough that the cold, chocolate-colored water poured over the rim of my combat boots. The shock of the cold water on my feet and ankles took my breath away.

Rising from his chair, Sergeant Boone shook his head in disgust. "Get out and stand on the rim," he ordered with just the hint of a smile. I did as ordered. "Now jump in and shout, 'Gas!'" he said. I did. "Do it again." I did. "Keep it up. I'll tell you when to stop," he said, unable to hide the pleasure he was deriving from my situation.

There I was jumping in and out of a mud hole and shouting, "Gas!" as soldier after soldier ran up to the rim, received his gas or nerve gas alert and practiced the appropriate drill. A few of us made eye contact during this display and exchanged smiles at the sheer stupidity of it all. I could not conceal my grin from Boone, nor could he hide his. After twenty minutes or so, he told me to stop and move out.

The next morning, my cough was much worse. A couple of the guys insisted that I go ask Sergeant Boone for permission to go to sickbay. To my surprise, he agreed without protest. The supply truck took me to the main section of the post. I was instructed to catch it at three that afternoon for the trip back to the company bivouac site. If I missed it, I would have to wait there until someone decided to look for me. It was best to be sure I was there at three.

"Stick out your tongue," the white-smocked doctor ordered without displaying any signs of a bedside manner. Next he stuck one of those ear-viewing things into my ear and peered inside.

"Don't you ever clean your ears?" he asked gruffly. The guy did not look much older than I was. One thing was certain, though, he did not know much about what happens to soldiers in basic training.

Between coughs I responded in self-defense, "They don't give you time to do that or much of anything else."

He got a big syringe and hosed out my ears. A lot of lumpy stuff came out. No doubt about it, I was able to hear much better.

Like all good doctors, he wrote out a prescription. I was to take it to the hospital pharmacy. I glanced at the square piece of paper he handed me. It said I should take a couple of pills every so many hours for so many days. I had to walk about five miles to get to the hospital pharmacy. Still, it was easy duty as far as I was concerned.

It was about one in the afternoon by the time I finally got my medicine. I had an hour or so to kill before going to the pickup point. The thought occurred to me to ask someone in the Medical Corps about my being eligible for a direct commission as a first lieutenant.

There was a colonel who was a psychiatrist listed in the hospital directory on the wall next to the elevator. I figured he would most likely be knowledgeable about the rules for someone with a master's degree in psychology.

Riding up on the elevator, I began to have second thoughts about what I was doing. Maybe I should go back and see the company first sergeant about it, since I had already asked him about it. He might get irritated that I had broken the chain of command. They had drilled us heavily on the proper use of the chain of command right from the start. If I wanted or needed anything I was to go to my platoon sergeant. If he had problems assisting me, he would go to the senior drill instructor. The senior drill instructor would go to—this was where it started getting confusing to me. Did the senior drill instructor go to the first sergeant or did he go to the company commander? In our case, that was

Lieutenant Brown. Somewhere the lieutenant gets asked, and if *he* cannot come up with a solution then he asks a captain, who asks a major, who asks a lieutenant colonel, who asks a colonel, who—sheesh! Eventually the president of these great United States of America will be asked your question. That is, of course, assuming it is a tough question. This is ridiculous. Nobody is going to care if I go outside the chain of command on this, I reasoned. Anyway, who will ever know? The elevator door opened and I got out. My heart was pounding. Something told me that I was going to find myself in a world of hurt over this. Reason be damned! A private does not casually walk into a colonel's office to have a little chat. Hell, this is my life! If I can get a direct commission, then I should not have to complete the rest of basic training, eight weeks of AIT, and six months of OCS. I have already done all of the push-ups that a person should have to do in one lifetime. I do not need to be in this world of hurt, I reasoned. Logic prevailed.

Entering the reception area to the colonel's office, I walked up to the receptionist.

"Yes?" she said, flashing me a bright smile. For the briefest of seconds I wondered if she knew that I had clean ears. At that same moment it dawned on me that my fatigues were damp, dirty, and had the smell of having been in the field for several days. Since that was where they had come from, it was logical that they would communicate a consistent message. Unfortunately, I was the only one present who had just come from the field. Damned garrison soldiers always being pretty. They needed to be in the field where the action was. I laughed at myself. I was thinking like a combat infantryman. Before long I would be acting like someone in the regular army, an "RA," as opposed to the "US" guys. Those guys who were drafted into the army and were only in for the mandatory two years were the "US" guys. They just wanted to serve their time and get out. That was me. Sure, the army had me listed as RA because I had technically volunteered to join. I had volunteered to go to Infantry OCS, the army said. I was RA. No, I was US. I did not want to be in the army. If there had been no draft, I would not be here. I was US!

The receptionist delicately cleared her throat and asked, "May I help you, Soldier?"

"I'd like to see the Colonel, please," came my halting response.

"I'm sorry, he's out for the day," the Ipana toothpaste girl pleasantly replied.

Bad day at Black Rock, I thought. The phrase was the title of one of my favorite movies. Spencer Tracy starred in it. The one-armed combat veteran rides a train into this dusty town. Anyway, things just did not go right for Spencer or me. No matter what he did, it only seemed to get worse. As in all heroic movies, Spencer was forced to fight the bad guys and make things right.

I dutifully thanked the young lady and left to take the elevator to the ground floor. When the door opened, I found myself staring the first sergeant in the face. I was stunned. My jaw dropped. He took a step toward me so I stepped back.

My thin-mustached first sergeant, the nice grandfatherly guy, had found me breaking the chain of command.

"What floor, Soldier?" he asked in that brisk manner of his.

"It's okay," came my weak reply. I stepped inside.

"What floor?" he asked again, reaching to push a number as the door closed behind us.

"I'm in Charlie Company's Third Platoon, First Sergeant," I said.

"Yes," he said, looking first at the ceiling and then at me. "Are you ill?"

Remembering to cough first, I replied, "Yes, First Sergeant."

"Aren't you a little far from the sickbay?" he inquired, his voice sounding bored.

"Well, they sent me here to get some medicine and then I went to this colonel's office to see if I qualified for a direct commission in the Medical Corps, but he wasn't in. I'm supposed to catch the truck back to the field at three," I blurted out. Guilt sometimes makes you do foolish things.

In a wonderfully supportive tone he said, "Third Platoon, yes. Well, I hope you get better, Son." The elevator door opened. He nodded and left.

Worry hovered over my head as I rode the truck back to the bivouac site. Anyway, I thought, the first sergeant really was not interested in me. He was kind of bored and when he had ended the conversation he was so pleasant. Everything was going to be okay.

It was chow time. The army's hot chow in the field is excellent. It smells good, tastes good, and is good, in my opinion. I felt better after I had eaten.

As usual, the next morning we were called to attention in front of our pup tents to hear the orders of the day. Sergeant Boone walked right up to my face.

"You broke the chain of command," he said through clenched teeth, his eyes squinting.

I was stunned. I had been found out. "Yes, Sergeant," I replied crisply.

I looked straight ahead at nothing and unfocused my eyes. This was no time to be eyeballing.

Spitting words into my face, he said: "Get your entrenching tool. Go over by First Platoon's area and start helping them dig a field latrine." He pointed in the general direction he wanted me to go.

"Yes, Sergeant," I replied. With a sharp military about-face, I turned to the tent and pulled out my army shovel. Boone had walked away. This was not fair. This was the army. Hawk asked me what was up. I told him I had screwed up at the hospital, but not to worry, they were making no big deal of it. He was genuinely concerned, which warmed my heart. Joining the other six or seven guys already in the large, half-dug pit, I unfolded my entrenching tool.

Some excellent engineering went into the entrenching tool's design. It was issued to us folded up in a neat pouch that could be hung from your web belt. When you took it out of the pouch, it was compactly packaged. The blade folded back on the handle so as to not take up a lot of space. Folded over in that way, it was about two feet long. Backing off a screw at the base of the shovel blade enabled it to unfold easily. To secure the blade into position was a simple process. You simply re-screwed the screw on the handle. An added advantage to the tool was the stabilizing bar that protruded from the base of the shovel. If you did not fully extend the shovel blade to the open position but left it at a ninety-degree angle to the handle, the stabilizing bar became a pick. When the shovel blade was fully extended, the pick-like stabilizing bar rested neatly against the wooden handle, providing a solid tool. It was shaped to form around the handle and served as a brace for the shovel's head.

Back at the barracks, we used our entrenching tools a lot. We were always losing the keys to the padlocks on our wall and footlockers. The pick end of the entrenching tool efficiently broke the lock. However, it took two entrenching tools to get the job done. One would be rigged to be a pick and the other was used as a hammer. Setting the end of the pick extension underneath the shiny loop of the lock and on the base of the square locking mechanism while holding it steady was the tricky part. Once that was accomplished, your partner smashed his entrenching tool down onto the pointed end of the shovel blade. The lock busted open. The force of the impact broke the little tip of the round metal loop inserted into the lock. You did not have to smash the entire lock. The TV commercials that showed a lock getting shot and still staying locked were misleading. The strength of the lock was on the inside, not in the outer casing.

We were all very familiar with our entrenching tool. Up to this point, I had never used it as a shovel. Everyone was too busy to have us spend a lot of time digging foxholes whenever we played war games. As a basic shovel, the entrenching tool fell short. Digging with it is a real pain. It hurts your back because you never get to stand up fully when you are using it.

My comrades-in-shovel never revealed why they had been selected to serve on this digging detail. We just accepted one another, no questions asked. The hole was knee deep, about thirty feet long, and maybe six feet wide. It could handle a lot of behinds at one time. Imagining all of those bare bottoms lined up around the perimeter struck me as particularly funny. I began sharing my vision with our crew. Before long we had come up with a whole string of one-liners and fantasy situations that kept us laughing. Curious onlookers began coming by to find out what was so funny. The morning passed pleasantly enough, although I wound up with several blisters on my hands. No problem. Those monkey bars would make quick work of them.

At lunchtime, Sergeant Boone came over to the trench. We stopped laughing and talking as he approached. You always stayed on task when a sergeant was around. He surveyed the scene for a few moments without comment. We had moved a lot of earth. Happy hearts make hard work easy or something like that was said or should have been said by Confucius. Boone called me out of the trench. He said I had dug enough and told me to rejoin the platoon and eat some lunch.

When I got back I found the platoon cleaning weapons. They had already eaten and were getting ready to have them inspected. Hell. I had not cleaned mine in two days. We had fired them on the range three days ago. Yesterday had been sick day and today was ditch day. Usually, I cleaned my weapon as soon as possible after firing it because they were always pulling surprise weapons inspections. It just had not worked out for me this time. If your rifle did not meet the sergeant's approval, you caught hell. Push-ups, a shit detail or two, and verbal abuse were the standard consequences for having a dirty weapon. I was hungry. After considering my options, I decided to go and wolf down some of the leftover food the field kitchen crew was in the process of scraping into an open pit. After I had gotten down about four swallows, I heard Sergeant Boone call for the platoon to form up for rifle inspection.

This was really bad. Once you started sliding downhill, you just couldn't stop. No telling what Boone would do to me when he looked down my rifle barrel. Oh, how I wanted this all to go away. I felt sick at my stomach.

Sergeant Boone snatched the rifle out of the hands of the guy standing next to me and inspected it in great detail. He spun the barrel end
down so that the wooden stock was in his face. It was a masterful move,
efficient in motion and very military. Boone knew his stuff; you had to
give him credit for that. He pried open the butt plate at the end of the
stock and squinted as he looked for dirt in the hinges. Spinning the rifle
back to its proper position with made-for-TV precision, he inserted his
thumb into the breech and lowered the rifle so that he could look directly down the barrel. Returning the rifle to port arms, he thrust it back
at the private standing beside me. Not a word was spoken.

Boone sidestepped in front of me and snatched the weapon from my
hands with real force. One second it was in my hands and then it was in
his. A blink of an eye would have concealed the exchange. This was serious. He spun the rifle to present the butt plate to him at eye level. Not
once did he remove his steely stare from my eyes. I was caught. Looking
into his eyes, I was determined not to reveal any emotion. He closed the
butt plate without breaking his hold on me with those cold eyes. The
weapon spun to its rightful position. He lowered the barrel and looked
down the muzzle. Efficiently returning it to port arms and locking his
gaze on mine, he firmly but carefully thrust the weapon into my chest. I
held it.

He spoke clearly and loudly, "Good job, Soldier. That's the cleanest
barrel I've seen in several days." All the while he held my eyes in his
emotionless gaze.

Abruptly he turned to confront the next man. After we had all been
inspected and dismissed, Hawk came up to congratulate me. He said
that Boone had not given anyone a positive comment for several days.
I told him that the weapon was dirty. He did not believe me until he
looked down the barrel himself. We agreed Boone had told me that I had
taken my medicine and that all was right with the world. I could go on
being in the army without any ill will held against me.

CHAPTER 7

Rifle Qualification

RUMORS WERE RAMPANT. The cadre who scored our hits were really hardnosed. Most of them were specialists fourth class—soldiers in pay grade E-4, which is one rank below a buck sergeant. Those guys have been around awhile. One story had it that someone had attempted to bribe them. The attempt had failed, or so said the rumor, with major repercussions falling on the culprits. When you climbed into the deep foxhole facing the firing line, the scorers did not talk to you. They did not care how you did. The fact that you might have to repeat basic training if you did not hit enough of your targets was of zero concern to them. You shot; they scored.

Anxiety was high for all of us. Anyone who scored expert would get a three-day pass the next weekend. Since I could not even get a tight shot group, I did not waste time on such details. My goal was to achieve the minimum score. I needed to get out of basic training. It would be a waste of my time to have to repeat it.

We would be issued only the number of rounds necessary to hit all the targets. I think that number was seventy-five. Since there was no possibility of my being that good a shot, I did not consume any memory space for it. The same was true for the number of hits you needed to qualify for expert marksman. They said that maybe no one in the company would hit enough targets to achieve that honor. Other companies had failed to produce an expert marksman, the rumor mill told us. There were some really good shots in our company. I had seen their shot groups. At a hundred yards, they not only hit the bull's eye, but their shot groups were so tight that a quarter could cover all three holes made by the bullets they shot. Several of them had been shooting all their lives. They came into basic knowing how to fieldstrip a rifle. I was no competition to anyone. I just hoped I passed.

Several days before the qualification test, our time on the rifle range increased. Sometimes we shot both in the morning and in the afternoon. The sergeants running the range hovered over us like bees, constantly giving us tips.

"Breathe halfway in and hold it."

"Squeeze the trigger slowly as you hold your breath."

"Don't pull the rifle with your trigger finger when you put pressure on the trigger."

"You don't want to guess when it will fire."

"Stay steady and squeeze slowly."

"Let the rifle tell you when it's going to fire; don't you tell it."

The advice was nonstop, but it did not seem to help. I almost always had one round hit outside of my shot group. Worse yet, my shots rarely hit the bull's-eye. When they did, I was very pleased. Other guys would go around showing off their paper targets when the range people chose to give them to us. No doubt about it: we had some good shots in our company.

One of the guys said he had heard that each target would only be shown to us for a couple of seconds. If you did not hit it with your first round, you probably would not get a second chance. Some guys left the range with ten to twenty rounds unexpended. Others fired off all of their rounds before they had seen half of their targets. There were so many ways to mess up that the imagination boggled trying to deal with it all.

The night before the test, I had difficulty sleeping. This rarely happened. As soon as the lights were out I would quickly fall asleep. My body was tired; my mind was tired, and I had been under pressure to perform some training effort throughout the day. Getting to sleep was a simple process. I was surprised to wake up and discover it was morning. The nights seemed so short. I had gotten all of the sleep allotted to me by the army almost every night. The night before the rifle qualification test was different. I was consumed with fear. If I failed to get the minimum qualifying score, it would be bad. I would not get to see Anna during the break between basic and AIT. There would be no break for me. I would be immediately reassigned to a new basic training company and have to start all over again. It had already been announced that most of us would get two weeks off before having to report for AIT. Only those going to schools that started right after we graduated would miss out on the two-week leave. I had already written Anna about it. We were looking forward to being together. I would fly down to Lexington, Kentucky. She would pick me up at the airport. We would then go straight to the apartment in Danville. Naturally, she would still have to teach at the high school, but we would be together in the evenings and throughout the weekends. It would be wonderful.

They had told us that we could invite our families to the graduation ceremony. In fact, they had encouraged us to do so. Several of the guys were having their parents, grandparents, wives, and friends come to see it. Some of them were traveling a long way and had already made their travel arrangements. Anna and I decided that it would be best for her to stay in Kentucky. We would be together the next day. Besides, attending the basic training graduation ceremony seemed a little juvenile. I did not comment to anyone about the silliness of attending an event of such little importance as this. It was good that I had kept my mouth shut on the matter as it became apparent that many of the guys, particularly those who had not gone to college, thought it was important. I would not have wanted to have inadvertently offended someone. Of course, this all was based on the assumption that I would qualify with the M14 in the morning.

Two-mile run and the day is started. It is hard to eat anything right after the two-mile run. This morning the tension made it even harder. I could only eat a slice of toast. Coffee and juice were my main stomach fillers.

We got our weapons from the arms room. The tension was mounting. No one talked much; the quiet made it worse. Quickly, we loaded onto the deuce-and-a-half trucks. It was cold. The tarp over the top of the cargo area kept the wind off all but the last two or three guys seated on each side of the truck bed.

"Move! Move! Form up by platoons," shouted Sergeant Sato. The sergeants were strictly business. As soon as we formed up we were ordered to open the breeches of our weapons. Sergeants Boone and Zarconi whizzed by making sure there was no ammo in the chambers. This seemed like a foolish check. We had not been issued any ammo yet. We did not even have our ammo magazines. The out-of-place inspection added to the tension. As Boone walked by me, he looked me square in the eyes. He must have known I was tense. God, I hoped I would not mess up.

One of the range sergeants took over the platoon. This sergeant was new to me. I had not seen him on the firing range or anywhere else. The army seemed to have an endless supply of sergeants. He marched us to a high, artificially made ridge that seemed to go on forever. It had no trees or brush on it. It looked like a levee wall on the Mississippi River. We were given four loaded magazines and instructed not to lock one in our weapons until we were instructed to do so at our firing points on top of the hill. We would be individually told which firing point to go to and when. Once so instructed, there would be someone at the top of the hill to direct us into the foxhole from which we would fire. We were to keep our weapons pointed down range at all times. The instructor in the range tower would tell us when to lock and load. If we should lock and load before we were told to do so, we would be removed from the firing line and disciplined accordingly.

I could see little trails that had been worn into the hillside at widely spaced intervals. There was little question of getting lost. Sometimes you could see a helmeted head moving around up there. Rifle fire came from the left and right of the hill. The shooting had begun.

When my turn came to go up the hill, my heart skipped a beat. This was it. I briskly climbed up the steep bank. The spec four sat on a folding chair. He was leaning back on two of its legs and rocking it. He pointed to the foxhole beneath. I understood his direction and jumped inside. It was a little less than chest high, just right for resting my elbows on the ground at the top to make a stable platform for my weapon. Looking down range, I was stunned. There were no lines of trenches for the bull's-eye targets to be hauled up from. It was just a tangle of underbrush and trees as far as the eye could see. Panic hit me. What was this?

"I don't understand. Nobody told me what to expect," I blurted out to the spec four.

"Green silhouettes will pop up. You have to spot them and shoot them down. When you hit one, it will fall backward. Then another one will pop up somewhere else out there," he answered in a soft voice.

"Assume the firing position," he ordered.

I wrapped the rifle sling around my right arm and leaned into the firing position, using my free hand to place my four loaded magazines on the edge of the foxhole within easy reach.

"Firers! Lock and load one eighteen-round magazine!" came the order from the tower.

I did as I was instructed. Peering through the sights waiting for something to happen, I was totally focused.

"Get ready," said the spec four.

Fifty yards in front of me the leaves on a bush shook. I blinked and saw the green silhouette of a man's upper torso such as we had shot at a few times on the regular rifle range.

I squeezed the trigger. *Crack—ting.* An empty shell casing flew out and hit the dirt. The silhouette immediately disappeared into the ground. Seventy-five yards out and off to the left, the corner of my eye picked up a brief movement. Swinging my rifle to point at it and quickly aiming low, I saw part of the green silhouette. *Crack—ting.* It too went down. Then nothing. I could not see anything. My eyes darted around as fast as I could move them. To the right, nothing; to the left, nothing. Then I spotted it. The silhouette was down range about a hundred yards in the center of my lane. It was just standing there between two trees. I needed to squeeze a shot off quickly before it retracted on its own. Aim low; aim low, I kept telling myself. If I hit the ground in front of it, flying debris would take it out. *Crack—ting.* A puff of dust flew up just in front of the target and it went down.

Crack—ting . . . crack—ting . . . crack—ting . . . crack—ting . . . crack—ting . . . crack—ting. Target after target swam into view and went down. Then I heard a different sound: *Thunnng.* About twenty-five yards in front of me and a couple to the left a target sprang up. I did not even have to aim to blow this one down. Then nothing again. I could see nothing.

"What's happening?" I shouted at the spec four. "Is it up?"

"Hell, yes!" he replied, his voice tinged with excitement. "It's right in front of you!"

Nothing. I could not see it. God, I knew it was there and I just could not see it.

I sensed new movement and suddenly saw it going down. It had jiggled a bush about fifty yards out to the left center of my lane. Damn, damn, damn. I could have gotten it if I had just seen it sooner.

The next one popped up way down range to my far left. *Crack—ting.* It was mine. I was into it. It was fun. Just aim low. Aim low and it will go down every time.

Another pause. I knew another target was up, but I could not see it. Movement, it was going down. I squeezed out a round. Maybe I hit it. It was hard to tell. More targets, fire, replace the magazine, and keep on firing.

Damn. Another one was up and I could not see it. So far I had hit everything I had seen.

"You're on a roll," said the spec four. Right after I hit one way down range, he spontaneously called out, "Great shot!"

Pause. One was up, one was up and I did not see it. My eyes darted left and right trying to find it.

"It's up. It's up. It's right in front," blurted the specialist. "It's up! Can't you see it?"

Heck, I thought, this guy is pulling for me. I was starting to like this.

I saw it about seventy-five yards out and to the right. *Crack—ting.* I missed it. What to do? It was still up. I fired again. I had some extra rounds from targets I never fired at. It went down.

Crack—ting . . . crack—ting. A couple more targets go down and then there are no more.

"That's it," announced the spec four. "That's the last one. Nice shooting. Real nice shooting." He was smiling.

I was pleased. I had hit every target I saw. There were some that I could not find, but it did not matter. I hit a lot of them. I was sure that I had qualified. Damn, if they had told us during the target camouflage identification training how it would help on the live-fire qualification range, I would have paid more attention. Oh, well, there were only a few targets that I had not seen. There was no question in my mind that I had qualified. I was going to get out of basic.

"You qualified expert," the spec four said as he handed me my official scorecard. "Good shooting." He shook my hand.

I get a weekend pass! I had sixty-eight hits. This is unbelievable. This is wonderful. As soon as we get dismissed this evening I will get in the telephone line. Anna and I can meet somewhere. We can have next weekend together. Oh, I am so thankful, I thought. This is just plain outstanding.

After going through the "no brass, no ammo" inspection with Sergeant Boone as he looked into each of our open rifle breeches, we turned in our scorecards. Boone and Nickels looked at them as we turned them in. I was in Nickels's line. He just took the card. I walked away. Nothing was said.

Anna was so pleased. It was totally unexpected. We figured that the closest airport at which we could meet was Philadelphia. She made the airline ticket arrangements and hotel reservations. Her plane got in before mine early Saturday morning. We would meet at the airline's ticket counter. She would be there waiting for me. Oh, how wonderful. This was just fantastic.

The army never gave us any time to think. Thinking was the army's job; doing was the soldier's job, the sergeants had told us. Nonetheless, I puzzled over the fact that the army had trained us to shoot at stationary targets. We mostly shot at traditional bull's-eye targets that were posted at known distances. The few silhouettes that we had fired at were also stationary targets. None of our targets had ever been camouflaged. Why had the army trained us to shoot under one set of conditions and then tested us in a totally different setting? It did not make a whole lot of sense to me. Then again, what did I know? I was just a citizen soldier, not a

professional. Besides, I was pretty happy: I was going to spend the weekend with my lover.

The rumor was that four guys in our company had qualified as expert riflemen. That was it. I was truly lucky. This was so good.

The plane arrived on time. I was in my army dress greens. This was the
first time I had officially worn them. I had gotten the army shoulder patch
sewn on and learned how to attach the brass. The U.S. and crossed-rifles
buttons went on the lapels. The dress uniform was a lot like a two-piece
single-breasted business suit. You had a thin black tie and a tan-colored
shirt. The jacket and pants were of suit quality. From the feel of them,
they were solid wool. There was no doubt about it: the fabric was of a
higher quality than any suit I had ever owned. Then again, I had only
owned one suit. I had gotten it for my high school graduation and had
worn it so often since then that the seat of the pants had gotten shiny. A
sport coat and polyester slacks met my needs in graduate school. Because of the coming graduation ceremony, Sergeant Boone had seen to
it that we all sent our dress greens to the cleaners for a nice pressing. I
felt sharp in those greens. Before we left post we were instructed not to
hitchhike while in uniform. The fact that I was flying failed to deter them
from issuing me that set of instructions.

To tell the truth, I felt a little proud to be in such good physical condition. Except for my periodic coughing, tender palms, and pus-filled
big toenail, I figured I was close to being as fit as I had ever been. I was
definitely stronger than when I had worked on the dredge boats. I remembered the times Anna flew to the Texas coast to be with me. They
were good times, but not as good as this time. We were not married then,
so she had stayed with my folks. It was awkward, but far better than being apart—even if it was just for the summer breaks during our college
years. My fingertips had been rougher back then, covered with cuts and
bruises that made them scratchy on her skin. They were rough enough
now, but not nearly as bad as in those days. I hoped they would not
hurt her.

The airport was bigger than I had expected. It was a long walk from
the gate to the ticket counter. Most of the people rushing around were
in the military. I saw army uniforms everywhere. With this many people
in such rapid movement, it might be hard to find Anna. Wouldn't that
be the pits? I thought.

Then I saw her. There she was. Oh, she took my breath away. She had
not seen me, although she was looking in my general direction. I quick-

ened my pace. She still did not see me. I was so happy. Just as I came within touching distance of her she looked off in a different direction.

"Anna," I called, reaching out to hold her.

Turning toward the sound of my voice, she looked up in surprise. As I wrapped her in my arms, she began crying.

"What have they done to you?" she sobbed. It was a deep, breath-shaking sob.

I guess it was because she was not used to seeing me in a uniform. That was why she had failed to recognize me from a distance, I reasoned.

"They've starved you," she managed to say between sobs, kisses, and hugs. "You look like a POW from Germany! My poor baby."

Well, I *had* lost a lot of weight since she had last seen me. That had been five or so weeks ago. I knew I had lost at least forty pounds since then. In college I had weighed about 140 pounds. Three days after we graduated, we got married. In the three months that followed I had soared to 180. Married life was a good life for us. I knew I weighed less now than I had in my undergraduate days, but I was in the best physical shape of my life. I was physically fit and thought I looked good. The uniforms had been loose fitting when they issued them to us. With my weight reduction since then, they did kind of slip around on my frame with some added freedom.

My appearance clearly distressed her. We spent most of that weekend in a downtown hotel room. Anna had booked us into an upscale hotel. It was just wonderful to be with her, even though she cried a good deal of the time.

Once she started pointing them out to me, I realized that I had a lot of deep bruises and bumps on different parts of my body. I had not thought much about them. Training did that. My toe, raw palms, and coughing were the only things that really bothered me. They interfered with my performance. If you are hurt, it tends to increase the likelihood of getting more seriously hurt. We had already had guys break bones and the like. It put them back in their training schedule. They would have to do some—if not all—of basic over, according to the rumor mill. Heaven knew I did not want to be in the army any longer than necessary.

Late Saturday afternoon, Anna and I went out for a walk in downtown Philadelphia. The lady selling tickets to view the Liberty Bell said that we did not have to pay since I was in uniform. I think she was just being generous to two people so obviously in love. Everyone we met was extraordinarily kind to us. I felt a little awkward being among civilians in uniform. They did not seem to mind.

I was proud to be wearing my expert rifleman's badge. The army had even issued all of us a ribbon for being in the military at that time. They called it the National Defense Service Medal. I always wondered how those old generals got all their medals. Apparently they needed only to live long enough to have a lot of them issued. Once you understood what the medals, patches, and other attachments on a soldier's uniform meant, you could read a guy's military history in a glance. The stuff had never meant much to me in my civilian days. Soldiers do not wear their uniforms to impress civilians. They wear it with pride to let other soldiers know what they have been through and accomplished.

Anna and I had to part all too soon. Her plane left first. My heart hurt. She cried. She struggled not to, but the tears welled up from somewhere deep inside and slowly rolled down her cheeks, one after another. It was hard. We knew we would have that week or two break when I finished basic training. We would be together again in a couple of weeks. We had that to hold on to.

CHAPTER 8

Graduation

Two weeks to go. We were getting to be short-timers. In addition to drilling us on the things we needed to know to pass the proficiency tests, they started marching us in a formation with a sixteen-man front. That is a long line. It stretches all the way across a wide street.

The first stage of building the big marching formation was to have the men in each company line up by height. The tallest were in the front row and the shortest in the last one. They did this for each company in the battalion. That way, when we passed in review, the first men in the formation to arrive would give the impression of a massive group of big men moving by as one imposing force. Theoretically, few would pay attention to the end of the block of men as eyes shifted to the next company to pass in review. Each company was led by the biggest of the big carrying the company banners with various ribbons hanging from them. Even from my limited view of the process, it was impressive.

Marching in a straight line with sixteen other men is not all that easy. The goal is to keep the line perfectly straight at all times. The task becomes more and more difficult the farther you are behind the front row. I was about a third of the way back and four men in from the left side of the company's formation. If the guy directly in front of me slowed down for any reason, I had to slow down or step on his heels. In either case, I ended up out of perfect alignment with the other fifteen guys to my right. Of course, when I slowed down, the guy behind me had to slow down or step on my heels. The farther back in the ranks this ripple effect went, the harder it was for the last rank to maintain its alignment. I wish I could have seen the struggle the guys in the last couple of lines had to endure in order to create the illusion of a straight line. One thing was certain: I was glad I was not one of them.

We did all right until we got to the turns. What a mess. The guys on the inside of the turn have to take little, tiny steps while the guys on the outside have to take large, giant steps or the whole thing looks like a sick snake.

That first turn was bad. We were going to the right, which meant everybody on my side had to take giant steps. Immediately, the guy in front of me began slowing down. It took all of my concentration to keep from stepping on his heels. Unfortunately, the guy behind me apparently lacked the mental capacity to avoid doing the same thing to me. He stepped on my heels so dramatically and so often that I could not resist turning my head to see who was doing it. I made eye contact with him and he grinned sheepishly. It was the black guy with the British accent, the one the sergeants had given so much hell at the beginning of basic for not shaving close enough. I had seen him every so often during the various training activities. He was in 2d Platoon. Fate had not brought us together much, but he was pleasant enough when it did. I had admired the way he had stuck up for his rights when the sergeants were really on his case. He had not been singled out too much since then as far as I could tell.

Assuming that he could not help it, I endured the pain. The first couple of sessions of this parade practice were rough. My heels began to get red. Everyone had trouble with the turns. My trailing companion just could not keep off the backs of my feet.

Fortunately, the group began to catch on as the days went by. We were actually doing a good job. We all wanted to look sharp. Many of the guys had family coming to the graduation ceremony and we wanted to look good for them. However, we were not perfect. The turns were still causing problems. They were not nearly as bad as they had been in the beginning. The guy in front of me continued to slow down slightly, which in turn forced me to slow down or risk stepping on his heels. Then the black guy behind me would chomp up mine again. He just could not seem to adjust.

One evening after an afternoon of sixteen-man-front marching, my heels were particularly sore. It hurt just to take my boots off. The heels of both feet were bright red with flecks of blood oozing to the surface in a few spots. This was not good. I had to talk to the guy.

It felt strange going into another platoon's area. You knew it was identical to your own, but everyone was a stranger. In your own platoon you knew who slept in each bunk, what they were usually doing at any given time, and why. As I moved through 2d Platoon's bay nothing seemed to fit. I was an intruder. People looked up at me and knew I did not belong. Oh, sure, I recognized most of them. At one time or another we had been in line together or alongside one another during some training session or clean-up detail, but I did not know them the way I did the guys in my own platoon. I was a trespasser. Everyone knew it.

Finally I saw the black guy. He was sitting on his bunk polishing his shoes at the far end of the bay. Looking up with polishing rag in hand, he greeted me: "Hey, what brings you here?"

"We need to talk," I replied as I strode up in front of him.

"Sure thing," Rick replied. "Here, pull up a chair. What's on your mind?" He queried in his crisp, British-like accent.

"My heels are really starting to bother me. Look," I said, pulling down one sock to expose the deep red heel.

"Oooh, that looks painful," he said. Deep wrinkles furrowed his brow. "Looks like you need to put some ointment on that."

"Thank you. Is there any way you can stop stepping on me when we're marching?" I asked.

"Well, you see, Jerry, you keep slowing down on the turns. You fall back into my way. You need to walk faster on the turns, Jerry. I don't want you to get hurt, but you keep slowing down," he said as he buffed a shoe.

"I can't help it. The guy in front of me slows down, too. If I don't back off, I'll have to step on *his* heels," I explained in a reasonable tone.

"Well, there you have it, my good man. You need to speak to that chap. Tell him he needs to keep up and the whole problem will be solved." He flashed a knowing smile.

This was getting nowhere. "Look, Rick," I pleaded, "all I'm asking is that you please try to avoid stepping on my heels."

"I don't want to hurt you, Jerry. You're a nice fellow. You need to follow my advice and go talk to the chap in front of you and it will be all right. You'll see. I have to go now," he said, getting up from his bunk.

I think he understood. The conversation had been slightly strange, though. There was no point in tracking down the guy who marched in front of me. I did not even know what platoon he was in. He could not help slowing down any more than I could. Talking to him was pointless. At least Rick had said he would try to be more careful about stepping on my heels. He had seemed sympathetic enough. Part of me did not totally accept the logic of my thinking. I did not want this guy stepping on my heels much longer. You could understand it happening every once in a while, but this had been going on far too long. He seemed so nice.

Surely he would try harder to avoid stepping on me—or so went my reasoning. If I was wrong, I had a serious problem.

Hawk announced that he had decided to go for the post's record time in the one-mile PT test run. Our final PT test was coming up soon. He was trying to work out in the evenings. Sergeants Boone and Nickels were pulling for him. The whole platoon took on extra tasks—such as shining Hawk's shoes, polishing his belt buckle, cleaning up his area, and the other little time-consuming tasks that must be done to pass the various inspections we had to endure—in an effort to help. I wanted him to get the record and assumed, at an emotional level, that he would. Intellectually, however, I had deduced that Hawk was really tired. He was making some mental errors and seemed edgy. These behaviors suggested that he might not be at his top physical performance level when test day arrived.

Late one night Hawk woke me. "Hey, wake up! Wake up!" he whispered.

"Wha—what is it? What do you need Hawk?" I muttered in the darkness.

"Shhhh. Keep it quiet. Boone wants to know if you want to play some poker," he quietly spoke into my ear.

I sat up, rubbing my eyes. "Yeah, sure," I replied. "When?"

"Right now, in the Sergeant's office. We've been playing fairly regularly for a couple of weeks," he informed me as I dressed.

We walked down the hall in our stocking feet so as not to wake anyone. My mind was waking up. This was the inner circle. No wonder Hawk had been looking so tired. He was not getting enough sleep. I felt honored by the trust they were showing in me. Boone could get into a lot of trouble if word ever got out that he was playing poker with trainees. They were risking a lot to invite me. I was honored.

"Come on in and pull up a chair," Boone whispered as Hawk and I entered the room.

There were three other trainees present. Hawk and I made it six players. Three raises, a quarter to ante, no limit on betting, and no wildcards or weird games seemed to be the basic rules. It was a big bet if someone put up a dollar. I had played like this out on the dredge boats. Sometimes the pot got to be real money. One time I had come in second on a pot that had more than fifteen hundred dollars in it. I still came out ahead for the night. Not knowing how these people played poker was a disadvantage since they already knew each other's betting styles. One thing was certain: I did not want to wind up being the big loser. That would be a real status downer. Conservative poker had to be my strategy. Just play the odds without any dramatics. After two hours, I was about three dollars ahead. It was time to exit. My sleep was more important than maintaining my image or picking up a dollar or two. After thanking them for inviting me to play, I left.

Final PT test time was here. Some of the guys were really sweating it. If they got below 300, it was recycle time back into basic training. For once, I was not worried. My score of 360 on the last test told me that I could make it. There would have to be a serious effort, but I could make it. A score of 400 or better was considered outstanding. The highest score I had heard of was a 470—except for Lamar's perfect score that first time. Lamar had simply disappeared. No one knew where he was, and no one talked about him. I guess we were all just too busy.

The mile run is the last event on the PT test. As usual, my highest scores were in the low crawl and the grenade toss. There was some satisfaction in knowing that I was among the best in the two unequivocal combat-skill areas of the PT test. It was reassuring to know that I had a better than average chance of keeping my butt from getting shot off if I ever found myself trying to get out of the line of fire.

Finally, the mile run was at hand for Hawk. Most of us stopped what we were doing to watch and cheer him on. Word had spread through the battalion that he was going to go for the record. Someone said that Sergeant Boone had tried to get permission for Hawk to make the run in tennis shoes, but the powers that be had said no. He would have to run it in combat boots, fatigue pants, and T-shirt just like everyone else. He lapped the rest of his group at least once, and as he made the last turn on his final lap around the quarter-mile track you could see the strain in his face. He clearly was giving it all he had. When he crossed the finish line, we let out a loud cheer and ran up to congratulate him. They tell you your time immediately. Hawk had missed the record by several seconds. Of course, he had maxed the run. He got the full one hundred points for the event. A stranger would have thought he had failed it if the sad look on his face had been the only indicator of his performance.

I finished the run in seven minutes and twelve seconds. You had to make it in eight minutes or less to get the sixty points needed to pass. To my surprise, the extra points I had earned for finishing in less than eight minutes gave me a total score of four hundred. As we were leaving the PT area, Sergeant Boone walked up to the truck into which I was climbing.

Looking right at me, he asked, "What did you score, Morton?"

"Four hundred, Sergeant," I replied as I began climbing into the back of the truck.

"Well, I'll be. We might make a soldier out of you yet," he said with a slight smile. I grinned.

We had a little less than a week to go until graduation. Word came down that there would be no leave after the ceremony. We were all getting orders that would require us to report to our next assignment immediately. Some of the guys would have to catch trains or planes within an hour or two of the graduation ceremony. Everyone would be gone within a day or two—en route to their next training school or actual duty assignment. Some guys could expect to get orders to ship out to Vietnam and be in country within a week, the story went.

What a foul-up! There were going to be a lot of relatives at the ceremony. Everyone had plans. Now, none of it mattered. The army had changed its mind. What was the point of complaining? I felt sorry for the guys who had family coming. As for me, it was okay. The quicker I got to OCS, the better. It shortened my time in the army. Anna would be disappointed. We had no firm plans for the break between basic and AIT. That was a blessing.

When I called Anna to tell her that there would be no leave at the end of basic, she had sad news of her own to relate. They had been trying to call me or get a message through to me for more than a week. My step-grandmother had died. She, my grandfather, and I had been very close. They were childhood sweethearts who had been separated by social class. Her family had been highly educated. Grandfather's kin were a collection of bright, hard-working people living on the land in southern Ohio. Emma had gone on to get a doctorate in romance languages. When she and my grandfather finally married, they were already well into their fifties. She was on the faculty at the small Kentucky college I attended. I was the child she never had. Originally, she had planned to retire at the end of my junior year. However, because I was at the same school, she decided to stay on one more year. That spring she had developed breast cancer and was in and out of hospitals for the rest of the year. She seemed to be recovering during the two years I spent in graduate school. I had not expected her to die.

Anna said she had tried to call me at Fort Dix. The army would not let her contact me by phone or deliver a message. Next, she tried to get the Red Cross to contact me. The Red Cross refused because a step-grandmother was not considered immediate family. I was sad to hear the news. Realistically, it would not have been good to leave basic training to attend her funeral. I was just as glad not to be notified. Nonetheless, if she had called and I could have gotten off, it would have been a tough decision to make. It was a relief to have the army make the decision for me, I reasoned. Everyone could be mad at the army. They usually were anyway.

The sixteen-man-front parade line practice greeted us. Damn if Rick did not step all over my heels on the turns again. I was pissed. Giving him dirty looks while we were in ranks failed to diminish his torture of my heels. He just shrugged his shoulders, smiled, and pointed at the guy directly in front of me as if to tell me it was that guy's fault. Rick and I needed to do some serious communicating that evening.

The 2d Platoon's bay still felt like alien territory to me as I walked briskly to Rick's bunk. "Rick, you can't walk on my heels anymore. They're bleeding and I'm starting to walk with a limp. It has to stop," I stated with concern in my voice.

"Then *you* must tell the chap in front of you not to slow down and step on his heels if he does," came Rick's leveled response.

"Rick, I am *not* going to step on his heels," I stated.

"Yes, you are Jerry. The pain in your heels will force you to step on his," Rick logically replied.

I could not believe this guy. "My stepping on his heels won't help anything," I responded with exasperation in my voice. "He's slowing down because the guy in front of *him* is slowing down."

"When you step on his heels, he will step on the heels of the chap in front of him. That chap will step on the heels on the fellow in front of him and so on until the lines stay straight," the smiling Rick told me.

"There is nothing you can do to me to force me to step on the heels of the guy in front of me," I declared. "If you step on my heels again, I'm going to do something to you that you won't like."

"No, you won't Jerry," he said. "You are too nice a person to do anything to me. You know I'm right. Think about it. You'll decide to step on the chap's heels. You will see that I am right." He had a serious but kindly expression on his face.

I got up to leave. "I will *not* step on the heels of the man in front of me. I *will* do something if you step on my heels again," I said and left.

Just what the hell *would* I do? I could not risk my body being seriously injured. If he stepped on me again, I would have to do something. This could not go on. I just could not believe that this guy cared so much about the stupid line being straight. What the hell, the army had been unjustly on his case for a long time. Why should he care if the line was straight? This was stupid. Surely, I reasoned, Rick understood that I was not going to step on someone's heels just to keep a line straight. He should know that I would do something to him if he stepped on mine one more time. What *would* I do? That was the question in my mind as I went to sleep that night.

Fortunately, we did not have parade practice the next day. We spent it getting ready for the proficiency exams we had to take in two days. Rick would have some time to think about the situation. Maybe he would change his mind. I had been reasonable and forthright with him. I meant every word I said.

My big toenail was ready to come off. It was loose. The way it just slid around when I put pressure on it convinced me it was time to pull it off. Only a corner of it was still attached to some skin on the left side. The thing had not hurt me for several days, but it still had pus oozing from it. What hurt me were my heels. I decided to just pull it off. I felt a sting when it came loose. It started bleeding. A new toenail had grown to about two-thirds the size of the original. It was thin, but it was there. That night I wrapped a strip of an old-but-clean T-shirt around it. In the morning, all of the pus and blood were gone. As far as the big toenail department went, I was about as good as new.

Tension was high at the proficiency test area. People were rushing here and there. We were assigned to various stations and then rotated through the course under the direction of the many sergeants who were running the show. The bayonet station was the most confusing. Like everything in the army, before you did it you had to stand in line and wait. There were about ten lines. The men in each line were to go through the bayonet course on the lane directly in front of them. It was obvious when your turn came: there was no one ahead of you in the line. A sergeant took your scorecard and directed you to the first cement platform. Standing at high port on the platform, you waited for the sergeant to yell out an assault command such as "Butt stroke, slash, and stab, ho!" On that command, you would run at the dummy directly in front of you and execute the maneuver. You were graded on how well you did the moves and how aggressive you were. Then you went to the next cement platform and stood at high port. The sergeant would come up to you and give you another command that ended in a "ho!" After assaulting the second dummy you repeated the entire process a third time. That was it.

What made the process so complicated was figuring out which cement platform you were supposed to stand on and which of the sergeants was shouting your orders. The three cement platforms and subsequent three dummies were not in a straight line. They kind of zigged and zagged. That would have been okay if there were only your three dummies to worry about. However, each of the ten lanes had its own three dummies, which meant there were thirty dummies in the area with none of them in a nice, neat line. Actually, it looked as if there were a lot more extra platforms and dummies than there were lines for as far as you could see. The way they were all out of alignment made it hard to tell how many of them there were or which ones you were to assault. The whole course was picturesquely laid out among medium-sized trees. This made it harder to focus on exactly where everything ought to be. Further complicating the picture were the soldiers in the middle of the course. They were being screamed and shouted at by sergeants giving orders as they rushed at dummies or stood at high port. In order to get us all through, they did not keep the course clear for one man to go through all of the stations before starting the next one. Standing there at the beginning of the course amidst the chaos was unnerving. It was bad enough trying to remember all of the bayonet moves they could ask you to perform in this stressful environment when you could hardly figure out where you were supposed to do them. It was more than I wanted to endure, but that was not a choice for me.

After getting through the first dummy with just a few mess-ups, I stood at high port on what I hoped was the second cement platform in my predesignated lane. I waited for the lane sergeant to catch up with me. There was a lot of commotion behind me. Several sergeants seemed to be converging on a point to my rear. It seemed like forever before my sergeant appeared and gave me the second assault order. I charged the dummy and got through it.

There was a slight break at the end of the bayonet course. During any break, you would group up with your friends and shoot the breeze. Tom had been behind me in the line I was in on the bayonet course. He was a nice guy. Coming straight out of high school, the training had not upset him all that much. He stayed pleasant and levelheaded. I enjoyed sharing time with him. We were in line together whenever we had to form up alphabetically because our last names started with the same letter. Even though we were in different platoons, we got to spend a fair amount of time together. I appreciated his gentleness and good judgment. We had shared our anxieties about getting through the proficiency tests. I was looking forward to hearing how he had done. He never showed. I waited as long as I could before going to the gas station for the gas mask test. It was puzzling. Hopefully, I would see him back at the barracks.

Some of the guys were starting to get their orders. Rumor had it that some had already left for their new duty stations or were on orders to leave before the graduation ceremony. I hoped that had not happened to Tom. He could have been hurt on the course and taken away. No one would tell you such things. There was no time to check into it. The army consumed all of your time with their busy work. You had to do the busy work or they would take more of your time with greater unpleasantness.

Since they gave your scorecard back to you at the end of each proficiency test station, you knew how you were doing. I had passed. I was getting out of basic.

Two more days and a wake-up until graduation. The morning drill was the sixteen-man-front parade formation. What was I going to do if Rick stepped on my heels? I still had not figured it out. I knew I had to do something. The situation was intolerable. I simply had to do something.

The marching began. Rick was behind me as usual. I could see the intersection up ahead. We would be turning to the right. That meant that the guy in front of me would probably slow down, putting himself and then me out of perfect alignment. If Rick stepped on my heels, I would have to do something.

Tension was building within me. Why did this kind of situation inevitably seem to happen to me? Every time my family moved and I entered a new school system there would always be someone who wanted to push me around. One guy said I was stealing his girl and told me to leave her alone. I had no idea who his girl was. I had no interest in any girls at the time and hardly knew anyone's name. He just walked up to me in a friendly manner one day and tried to sucker punch me. Why did I end up being forced to stand up for myself like this in most new settings?

Three more paces and the turn starts, I thought. Now we're into it. The guy to my front is falling back. I am *not* going to step on his heels. Pain enters my mind. Chomp, chomp—he's walking on my heels. This is it. I do not care. I am mad. I am *pissed*.

Without thinking, I swing my right leg forward as far as I can and then swing it back with all of the force I can to hit Rick on some part of his body as hard as I can. In the middle of my kick I start to pivot on my left foot. After I kick him, he will charge. I'll be ready to punch him in the face as hard as I can.

As my foot swings back he sees it coming. He pulls back. The heel of my boot grazes his shin, brushes his shirt, and just misses his chin. My rank of men leaves me. My hands are up in a boxer's stance, ready to fend off his first punch and to punch him as hard and as fast as I can. He puts up his fists and pulls back as he teeters to regain his balance. His

rank of men is abreast of me moving on. The men on either side move
out of our way as they march past me. It is as if the sea has parted, except that the lines of men behind Rick cannot stop. Hundreds of men
press forward. The back row bumps into Rick. All of this happens in the
blink of an eye. The bump knocks him off balance. He falls. The men
behind him start to fall over and around him. He is struggling to get up
and at me. The growing pile of men keeps pinning him to the spot. I am
backpedaling furiously to partially keep up with my receding line. I am
isolated in the growing open space between the rank of marching men
to my rear and the growing pile of men falling in front of me. It is not
good to be isolated like this. I am thinking I need to turn and rejoin my
rank. Three or four sergeants seem to come from different directions
and rush into the widening space between me and the growing pile of
men. Rick is half-standing in the midst of the mob, struggling to get free
and come at me. His fists are up. He clearly wants to fight. The sergeants
grab at him and collectively jerk him out of the line. He is screaming in
the struggle and pointing at me.

   I am standing alone in this mess. Ahead of me is the receding line of
marching men. Behind me is the pile of soldiers, Rick, and the sergeants
pulling Rick away from the pile as more men fall over each other. They
are unable to stop.

   I pivot sharply. Instantly I turn. Three giant running steps put me in
my proper position. I am marching with the others. No one seems to notice the confusion behind us. We march on and the ranks behind us close
up. It is as if nothing ever happened. No one says a word to me. Nothing is mentioned about it at the break. Back in the barracks, no one comments. It is as if it never happened. I never saw Rick again. I do not know
if he ever returned to 2d Platoon or what took place. It was as if he had
disappeared. I have no idea what happened to him. No sergeant ever
spoke to me about it. For that matter, no one commented to me about
the entire incident. It was best that I not inquire or bring the matter up
in any way. That was the way it ended. Nothing was ever said. Rick had
disappeared.

The first sergeant called the company together to say good-bye. We all
stood around the front of the little building that contained his office. In
that rich grandfatherly voice of his, he told us that he hoped we had found
basic training to be helpful and offered to answer any questions that we
had. A couple of guys asked about the canceled leave. The first sergeant
said that they had no control over decisions like that. It had to do with
policies at a much higher level.

"First Sergeant," I shouted out from the back of the pack. "What have you found out about my direct commission in the Medical Corps?"

"What are you talking about, Son?" he replied, looking over the tops of the heads of the men in front in an effort to see me.

"The direct commission because I have a master's in psychology," I shouted back, barely concealing my irritation.

"I wish you had brought this to my attention earlier. It's too late for me to do anything about it now. Bring it up at your next duty station. Are there any other questions?" he asked, refocusing his attention on the men closer to him.

Graduation day had arrived. We were all in our dress greens. Sergeants Boone and Nickels were passing out orders as fast as they came in. Hawk was going to be assigned as a clerk-typist somewhere. He was not going to have to go to AIT after all. It looked as if he would be able to put his two years in stateside. He was really pleased. All of the guys slated to go to OCS had to go to AIT first. People were being sent all over the country for AIT and other specialty schools. A few guys were getting orders to go directly to Vietnam. If you pass go, do not collect $200, said the go-to-jail card in the Monopoly game. They were definitely not going to collect $200. This was disturbing news to everyone. I did not know anyone with those orders, but the word was they were given to some of the guys.

Reading army orders is complicated. There are so many acronyms and numbers. As best as I could understand it, I was supposed to catch a train the next day to go to Fort McClellan, Alabama. It was near Anniston. I had no idea where Anniston, Alabama, was. I would be there for eight weeks and then get two weeks off for Christmas. Early in January I was to report to Fort Benning, Georgia, for Infantry OCS. The time schedule of events was all there in black and white. I would be safe in training programs until the end of June, 1967. I hoped the army would not change its mind about my orders, I would not flunk out, and I would ultimately get a branch transfer or a direct commission in the Medical Service Corps.

The parade we had practiced for went well enough. The music from the army band made marching easier. Our four companies marched right into a big gymnasium-like building. There were bleachers for us to sit in as if we were about to attend a basketball game. Several hundred civilians were already seated. They were the relatives and loved ones. The marching feet inside the building made an awesome sound.

A full-bird colonel made our graduation speech. I was unable to focus on what he said other than that all of the platoons had 100 percent participation in the United Way campaign. He said he was proud of us. They gave a big trophy to the guy who was the best shot on the rifle-qualification test. He had a score of seventy-two.

The colonel apologized for the shortness of the graduation ceremony, but many of the men had trains or planes to catch and he wanted to give them what little time was available to be with the friends and relatives who had come to see this proud event. Several guys threw their hats in the air. It all seemed a little melodramatic. Clearly, graduating from basic training was an important event to some of the guys.

After the ceremony, it was pretty much mill-around time. You were on your own. Sergeants were telling people where they needed to go to catch a train, plane, or bus. The army had given some guys tickets with their orders, and others were instructed to go to the transportation site and await further instructions. I was one of those ordered to go to the train station. They would provide trucks to take hundreds of us to the station the next day. Some sergeant would meet us there and tell us what to do next. We had to stuff all of our clothing and other gear into our duffel bags and carry it with us. If it did not fit in the duffel bag, it was to be thrown away. I had one night left at Fort Dix.

CHAPTER 9

Here to There

Less than a third of the men in our platoon were left to spend the night in the barracks. Hawk and I were among the lucky few. The barracks seemed barren and strange. Most of the bunks had been stripped of their bedding and the mattresses rolled back. Sounds echoed in the huge room. Trash was scattered on the floor. Even the overhead lighting seemed harsh. There had been so much intensity in this place. It seemed as if every corner had a memory attached to it. I felt lonely in my space. It no longer belonged to me, yet I seemed to belong to it. I was still here.

Hawk said that we ought to stay up all night and spit-shine the floor.

"Why would we want to do that?" I asked in disbelief. He seemed to be serious about it.

"When the new recruits come in and see the way the floor shines they'll say, 'Who do you reckon did this?' They'll figure that the guys before them took pride in what they did and try to live up to the standard we set," he said with conviction in his voice.

I thought about it for a moment. The idea appealed to me. Besides, it would make Hawk happy. There was nothing else to do except finish stuffing things in our duffel bags. In the morning we would eat, say goodbye, and catch our separate trains. Why not spend the night creating a mystery? I agreed. Hawk convinced two other guys to join us.

Stuffing the duffel bags was a complicated process. It took at least two guys and sometimes three to get it done. Folding or rolling your shirts and pants to fit the space was the first step. After the bag was about a third full, you stood inside it to compress the clothes even more. Your partners held you and the sides of the bag up. Without them, you would constantly be falling over. With help, you only fell a couple of times. The process would be continuously repeated until all of your belongings were inside the bag. It is absolutely astounding how much you can get into a duffel bag. Just when you were certain that you could not put one more thing into it, one of your partners would find a soft spot on the side of the bag. A soft spot meant that some of your clothes, shoes, or other items had not completely compressed. This meant that there was more space in the bag. Sadly, the soft spots always seemed to be deep down inside. Unpacking and then repacking the bag more than three or four times tended to try the patience of many. If you took more times than that you would surely hear curses and shouts and see infantrymen looking like they were about to cry. The process was humbling. Despite the frustration, no matter how much you put into your duffel bag, there was always room for one more thing. I never saw anyone leave something behind because it would not fit in his duffel bag.

We started on the floors at about eight in the evening. It was fun. We told jokes. We laughed over the funny things we had witnessed during basic. The time went pretty fast until it got on toward midnight.

Clear shoe polish, water, and cotton balls were our tools. First, you get a cotton ball and rub it in the shoe polish. Next, you cover about a half-square-foot area with the wax. Then, you polish it up and cover it with a lighter coat of wax. You next dip a cotton ball in water you put in the lid of the shoe polish can for this purpose and use it to polish the wax into a reflective shine that enables you to begin to see your reflection in it. Another light coat of wax and further rubbing with the wet cotton ball brings it to an even higher level of glossiness. If there is any hint of a dim spot in the shined area you repeat the process.

By midnight we had a third of the platoon bay sparkling so brightly you might think it was covered with a thin layer of ice. This was going to be a long night. We still had two-thirds of the floor to do. The fingers on my right hand were starting to cramp. I had to stop and straighten them out with my other hand. The same thing was happening to the other guys. Even if we kept up this pace, I doubted that we could get it all done before we had to leave in the morning.

As 1 A.M. rolled in and out, our conversation was less frequent. We kept at it. Every so often someone's arm would slip. *Smack,* they would hit the floor. It was worth a few laughs. Some of the squares of linoleum that I was working on were getting smeared because I was not keeping my cotton balls wet enough. By two, we were getting giddy. Our jokes were not making sense, so they were pretty funny. I kept falling. My arms were not holding my face up. When we moved furniture, we would forget and move it over just-shined areas and scratch up the shine. That area had to be done over. No one complained. We just kept on. By 2:30

it was clear to me that we were starting to make a mess. I had made a mistake. I could not keep this up. I needed sleep.

"Hawk, we're not going to make it," I said with resignation.

"Yes, we are," he replied. "We just have to work faster."

"Hawk, we're just making too many mistakes. We're too tired," I responded.

"*I'm* not too tired. *I* can keep going. What about you guys?" he asked, looking at the other two.

"We can keep going if you can, Hawk," they agreed.

"Okay, but I can't. I'm sorry, guys, but I've got to sleep. I'm going to have to go to bed," I said with sadness but resolve in my voice.

"It's okay, Jerry," Hawk said kindly.

"Yeah," agreed the other two.

I hated to let them down. I had said that I would stay up all night and help. I had meant it at the time, but I was wrong. This was stupid. It would never get done. We were making things worse at this point. They could not see it. I was making my area worse. I should have had enough sense to know that I could not stay up all night doing this.

"I'm sorry, guys, I just have to get some sleep," I said, slowly getting up.

"It's okay," Hawk repeated softly.

Not bothering to take off my clothes, I climbed into my bunk. They kept working. Their muffled voices soothed me into sleep.

"Why are these lights on!" demanded a loud, commanding voice. "What are you men doing here?" It was the duty officer.

Hawk and the other two guys sprang to attention. I rolled over to get a view of the officer while pretending to be asleep.

Hawk responded with a mixture of surprise and pride in his voice, "Spit-shining the floor, Sir."

"This is ludicrous," said the officer. "Who ordered you to do this?" I could see he was wearing the silver bar of a first lieutenant.

"No one ordered us to do it, Sir," Hawk crisply responded. "We just wanted to do it."

"Well, I want you to stop it. This isn't right. Turn out the lights and go to bed. *Now!*" he ordered.

"Yes, Sir," the three of them responded in unison.

The officer left. Hawk turned off the lights. They went to bed without saying another word.

After breakfast the word came down that everyone going to Fort Mc-Clellan was to form up out front by the trucks. It took real skill to hoist the duffel bag onto your shoulder. The shoulder strap made it a little easier to carry. No matter how you did it, the damned thing was hard to manage. Some of the smaller guys just dragged it out.

There were about two hundred men lined up beside the long line of deuce-and-a-half trucks. Most of them were not from our company. I do not know where they came from, but they were here. No one from my platoon that I knew of was going to Fort McClellan.

Three sergeants had set up a folding table near the trucks. They started yelling out names from a long list. Like everyone else, when my name was called I responded with, "Here, Sergeant."

After identifying yourself, you went to the table and picked up your personnel file. Then you returned to the ranks. We were told not to open our personnel files. When we arrived at Fort McClellan, someone would take them. The confidential files were inside large manila envelopes. The metal clasps had been fastened to keep the envelopes shut, but the flaps' glue seals had not been dampened. They were not sealed.

As the seated sergeant handed me my personnel file he said, "Morton, you're in charge of getting every man on the train and to Fort McClellan. Here's the roster of men on your train."

He handed me a long list of names as my mouth fell open.

"How do I do that?" I asked in disbelief.

"That's your problem, isn't it?" he stated flatly. "The trucks will load up and leave for the train station in about fifteen minutes. While they're in formation, you'd better tell them your plan. Once they get on the trucks, it will be harder to communicate. That's all." He motioned for me to move on as there were several guys standing behind me waiting to get their personnel files.

I walked toward the formation, my mind racing. There were twelve trucks. About twenty guys could fit on a packed truck. Most people had a friend or an acquaintance with whom they had chosen to stand in the ranks. That had been my intention. I had seen several men that I knew. We had stood in line together while waiting to participate in some kind of drill, test, or training exercise during basic. Some of them had level heads; others tended to hack people off or foul up in some way.

By the time I had covered the thirty paces back to the formation, I had a plan. While the men were in formation, they were at ease. They were not at attention. Everyone was talking to everyone else. I picked out twelve guys I thought were okay. We huddled together in front of the formation.

"They've put me in charge of getting everyone to Fort McClellan," I said. "I need your help keeping track of people."

Everyone agreed to help. I explained the plan. Each man was to have a buddy. He was to select his own buddy. No one was to go anywhere on or off the train without his buddy. The twelve guys I had selected would each be responsible for a truckload of men. There would be roughly twenty men on each truck or ten buddy teams. Each of the truck leaders was to be in charge of that group for the whole trip. They were to keep track of the ten or so buddy teams that boarded their truck until we arrived at Fort McClellan. Since the train trip was to take about a day and a half, there would be unexpected stops, layovers, and other problems. We would get a head count after every stop. The trip ticket the sergeant had given me along with the roster of names said that we would have a four-hour layover in Atlanta. We would also be changing trains there. That would be just one of many headaches with which we would have to deal. We would need to keep meeting as a group to anticipate and deal with problems. Since I had never done anything like this before, I assured them that I did not know what I was doing. We would have to work together in order to pull this off successfully.

One of the buddy-team leaders asked if they could pick the guys who got on their trucks. I said it was fine with me, but told them I did not think they would have time to pull it off. I said I did not want anyone trying to prevent a buddy team from getting on their truck just because they did not know the guys personally. We agreed to adopt my basic plan.

I did not want to call the whole formation to attention and give them a series of instructions as if I were a lieutenant or a sergeant. I was a private, just as they were. During basic training the sergeants selected various people to take turns serving as acting squad leaders. I had never been selected to hold a leadership position. They gave the acting squad leaders buck sergeant stripes to pin on their sleeves to signify their leadership role. On this trip I had nothing but the responsibility. I had no authority. There were no stripes to wear on my arm. I would surely catch hell if we lost half of the men on the trip. I decided to use the rumor mill to get the word out on what people were supposed to do on the trip. We had about five minutes to go before the sergeants announced that we were to load up. I directed the twelve truck leaders to go back in the ranks and tell as many men as they could that they would have to pick a buddy and stay with that buddy for the whole trip. They would have to have a buddy to get on the trucks. Maybe everyone would get the word. Everyone except for the 10 percenters. There were always the 10 percent who never get the word. Once the men had boarded the trucks, each truck leader would let his group know that he would be responsible for keeping track of their buddy teams for the whole trip. I instructed them to make a list of the names of the men in their truck for accountability purposes and to advise the men in their group that they would have to get approval from them to leave the train at anytime. I added that requests for anything unusual should be cleared through me. That would give all of us some time to figure out how to deal with any unexpected situations.

It worked. Within the five-minute interval, all two hundred or so men got the word. By the time the trucks arrived at the train station, everything was in order. No one objected. I was amazed. The organizational structure handled the loading of duffel bags and men without a hitch. I had learned the effectiveness of the buddy system while pulling lifeguard duty as a counselor at a Boy Scout summer camp outside of Kenosha, Wisconsin, during my high school years. It was easy to lose track of one kid in the water, but the likelihood of losing two at the same time was just about zero. If a buddy team got separated, it showed up immediately when they were checking out of the water. We would know who was missing immediately and begin calling out the kid's name. The missing person was quickly found. If the kid was not found, we had to assume that he had drowned. That meant a massive search for the body and then applying artificial resuscitation until some camp official declared the victim to be alive or dead. We never lost anyone during my stay at the camp.

To my surprise, there were a lot of civilians on the train. It was not just a troop train. The soldiers sat anywhere they wanted as long as they were with their buddy and their team leader knew where they were. This seemed to be natural enough. The fact that their buddy was a chosen companion was a big plus. Since most of them knew and liked their team leader, the whole process worked well. People were staying together by choice rather than because of orders.

Once we were aboard the train we settled into a routine. It was clear that almost everyone was opening his personnel file. The metal clasps were all that kept the envelopes shut. There was no way the army would know if they had been opened since you did not have to tear the envelope to open it. You just pulled up the two wings of the metal clasp and it was open. Curiosity got the better of me. After all, I reasoned, everyone else was looking. The scores from the battery of tests that we took during the first week were recorded in it, as were our rifle qualification and proficiency test scores. Background information was also there: education, age, religion, and other identifying items. What I found most interesting was Sergeant Boone's comments about me. One section of a set of forms included a written evaluation of the soldier's performance in basic training by the platoon sergeant. Boone had written of me in that section: "seemed disoriented at the beginning of basic . . . did not interact as a team member often . . . by middle of basic became oriented to the program . . . was a strong contributor to the progress of the group from then on . . . was considered to be a leader." I did not agree with the first part of his evaluation. I liked the way it ended.

The frequent short stops at little stations along our route began to pose a problem. The team leaders were reporting that the men wanted to get off the train so they could stretch. "Okay," I said, "as long as they get off with their buddy and stay within sight of the train so they know when it's ready to leave." I figured they were going to do whatever they wanted to do and that it was best we not be too rigid. This way, when the conductors called out "Board," we would know who needed to get back on and could see them at all times. It worked. I worried about the longer stops. Those tended to last just long enough for someone to go inside the terminal, walk around awhile, and then be out of earshot of the conductor's call to board the train. We took a head count using the buddy system after each stop. Everyone was present.

Atlanta was tough. We had that blasted four-hour layover. I saw no point in trying to restrict anyone from going anywhere. They were going to go where they wanted to no matter what we said. Rather than create a big conflict, I thought we should let the men exercise their own good judgment. They knew the consequences of missing the train as well as I did. The only rule I imposed was that they had to have their buddy with them.

We took a head count minutes before the train was to pull out of the station. One man was missing and his team leader was in a panic.

"What shall we do?" he asked.

"Was his buddy with him?"

"They started out together," he explained. "The missing man is from Atlanta. He decided he wanted to see a girlfriend. His buddy was afraid they would miss the train so they decided to separate. The buddy came back to the train and said his friend told him he would be back on time."

"Well, there's nothing for us to do. If he misses the train, we'll simply report it to the Fort McClellan people. It's not our fault. Try not to worry about it," I told him. The poor guy was really stressed out. He was taking this responsibility thing a little too seriously. If anyone got into trouble, it would be me, not him.

Since leaving Fort Dix I had given serious thought to this whole situation. Any responsibility I had on this trip was an illusion. All I really had to do was tell someone at Fort McClellan who had gotten on the train at Fort Dix and who got off at Fort McClellan. We had no control over anyone. The guys could do whatever they pleased. It was surprising to me that they had done everything we had asked of them. This just proved, as far as I was concerned, what a responsible bunch of men these soldiers were. We had not had one unpleasant incident on the train. Everyone got along well together. We were in the same boat. No one wanted to make trouble for anyone else. We were all just trying to get through this experience and get on with our lives.

Part of me wondered why I had been selected to bear the responsibility for getting everybody to Fort McClellan. The sergeants had never selected me to serve as an acting squad leader. Sergeant Boone's assessment of me did not appear to mark me for an assignment like this. I could not figure out their rationale for putting me in charge.

Just as the train started to roll slowly forward, our missing man came running through the station doors and jumped aboard. It was a relief to see him.

No one on the train knew anything about Fort McClellan. We just assumed that it would be a copy of Fort Dix.

"Fort McClellan, next stop," announced the porter. "Good luck, men," he said with a nod and a smile.

Several of the guys shook hands with the porters. We had shared a long trip together. New friendships had been formed. All of the civilians who had gotten on and off the train were kind to us. Outside of having to sleep in a sitting position during the night and having to eat sandwiches sold by vendors on the train or at the stations, the trip had been pleasant.

Sergeants were waiting as the train pulled alongside the platform.

"Form up, people! Form up! Columns of four, let's go, form up in columns of four," came the shouted orders as we disembarked.

Trucks were waiting for us in front of the station. I approached the sergeant with the most stripes on his sleeves.

"Sergeant, here's the roster of men on the train," I said, handing him the list of names.

"How many men are missing?" he queried, looking over my shoulder at the men forming up behind me.

"None, Sergeant," I replied. "They're all here,"

"Okay," he said, taking the sheets of paper. "Go ahead and fall in with the others."

I did as I was told.

CHAPTER 10

Settling In

W E GOT OFF the trucks and walked into a huge barrack. There were rows and rows of steel-frame bunk beds. A row was against each long wall. In the center were two rows of bunks with their ends pushed together. This arrangement resulted in two long pathways for walking from one end of the barracks to the other. Each of us had a wall locker and a footlocker for our personal use. The barracks were made of wood and seemed quite old. They probably had been constructed for use in the Second World War. Our entire company of two hundred or so men was bunking in it. If you had a tendency toward claustrophobia, you wanted to be somewhere else. The latrine was filthy. The commodes and urinals had been flushed, but the chrome on the water faucets had turned green and was covered with crud. The same was true for exposed pipes, except that they had large rust-flecked areas all over them.

Noticeably absent were screaming sergeants. There were a few noncoms around. They just gave brief general directions like, "Go on in and pick out a bunk," or "Chow is from eighteen hundred to nineteen hundred hours." I still had to take a moment to translate that to civilian time: 6 to 7 P.M. The first morning formation would be at 0600 hours.

Late that afternoon, a slightly pudgy infantry captain addressed the company. He wore glasses. His fatigues were too big for him, were badly wrinkled, and in need of cleaning. His shirt had sweat stains around the armpits.

"Welcome to Fort McClellan, men," he began. His voice was so quiet that you had to strain to hear him. "Fort McClellan is the home of the Chemical Warfare School, the home of the WACs, and now the home of your Advanced Infantry Training. For the next eight weeks we will do our best to prepare you for combat. You will spend a lot of time training in the field. We will try to give you time off on the weekends as often as we can. Your performance in the field will determine how much time off you will be given. I hope to arrange for at least two weekends that you can go off post. One of them will be a three-day pass. Listen carefully to the training staff. The things they tell you can save your life in Vietnam. If you have any problems, talk to your sergeants. If they can't solve them, they'll speak to me. I will do my best to make your training here valuable for you."

The rumor mill had already told us that this was where the army trained all of its women soldiers. They were called "WACs," which was the acronym for Women's Army Corps. This was supposedly the only place where they trained them. Another fact generated by the rumor mill was that ours was just the second battalion's worth of soldiers to undergo AIT here. The "field" was a jungle. There were no well-worn paths in the woods. It was hard to move through the underbrush. Lots of people had gotten lost during the previous eight-week training cycle.

Most of the training sergeants had seen combat in Cuba during the Bay of Pigs invasion, or so the rumor mill said. I thought that was strange. From my recollection of the newspaper stories I had read about the Bay of Pigs, almost everyone involved had been killed or captured. Rumor had it that the soldiers who fought at the Bay of Pigs were all exiled Cubans who had been shipped over there by the CIA. I did not see any Latino-looking sergeants. There were a lot of black noncoms, but not a single Latino-looking sergeant had passed my way. They were real short on sergeants with any Vietnam experience. Most of the sergeants with that experience seemed to still be in Vietnam getting it. We were hungry to talk to anyone who had been to "the 'Nam." We had a pretty good idea of where we were going and what we would be doing about eight weeks from now. Either we were going to some other very select training, like OCS, or we were going directly to Vietnam. Those of us who went on to specialized training knew it was most probable that we would ultimately end up in 'Nam. I was beginning to realize that 'Nam might be my ultimate destination along with everyone else. I still had hope that I could get a branch transfer out of infantry, but the army tests were proving to be no piece of cake. I might not do as well on them as I had been led to believe I would. Then again, there was hope for the branch transfer to the Medical Service Corps. I was having trouble finding out the truth about that. Once an infantryman, always an infantryman seemed to be the unspoken motto.

In the morning, trainees began appearing with those strap-on sergeant stripes. They started giving orders left and right. One guy in particular was actually dropping soldiers to do push-ups for not doing what he said or not doing it right. I was amazed. Rumor had it that he had gotten into an argument with one of the college guys over his belief that Chicago was a state. Unfortunately, this trainee sergeant was in charge of the platoon to which I was assigned. The first few times I came into the guy's presence, he just stared at me. I would look back at him with a blank expression. After a few seconds that lasted a long time, I would finally nod. He would nod back and go on with whatever he was doing. He never spoke directly to me, nor did he ever hassle me. It was one of those situations that you could never understand.

As always, the platoons were broken down into squads. There were four squads per platoon and four platoons to a company. I assumed it took four companies to make a battalion, but that was just a guess. There were at least five identical barracks lined up with ours. We were in the second to last one on the left. The last one, the one next to ours, was different. It was up on the hillside. All of the others were at the bottom of the hill on level ground. The hillside one was not filled up until the next day. It was full of army reservists. We all knew what that meant. They were play soldiers. They were the ones with enough political pull to avoid the draft. After they completed their eight weeks of training, they would go back to Jody, Sister Sue, smoking and joking, school, or a job. Oh, yeah, they would also go to once-a-month army reserve training in their hometown. The one place they would not go was Vietnam. They were a joke as far as we were concerned. Of course, if there were ever a general mobilization, they would be called up and expected to fight, just like the rest of us. In that case, none of us would want to be with them. Since their training was a joke, none of us would want to be anywhere near them. They would wind up getting people killed because of their ineptitude. The general opinion of the rank and file was that if you were going to war, it was best to be well trained.

The squad system broke down when we were in the barracks. Squad members were spread out all over the barracks. Since we had randomly picked our bunks, there was no organization as to who slept above you, on either side, or across the aisle. I had selected a bottom bunk two-thirds of the way down from the main entrance and against the left-hand wall. When it came time to hand out barracks cleanup details, I volunteered along with several other guys to do the bathroom. When we got together to subdivide the latrine cleaning tasks, I volunteered to clean the urinals and sinks. This included polishing the chrome plumbing attached to same. All of the faucets, urinal handles, and chrome pipes underneath the sinks, as well as anything else made of chrome related to those two pieces of prized American porcelain were mine to clean. My thinking went like this: It looks so bad now that anything I do will be such an improvement that I will never be hassled during inspections. In addition, everyone hated the urinals. No one in my brief experience in the army ever hung around the urinals or sinks. You did your business and left. Thus, once everyone was done in the morning, the place would be all mine. No one would hassle me as long as my stuff passed inspection. When cleanup detail time came, I would be left to my job. If I got it done early, I could stay there or go to my bunk and do other things, important things—like polishing my shoes and belt buckle or cleaning my rifle, the things that kept you out of trouble.

The armory for our company and the reserve company was just a few hundred yards from the barracks. Right off we were issued our rifles, the solid M14. I had grown to really like that weapon. It was powerful, accurate, and felt good in your hands whether you held it on your shoulder while standing at attention or at high port while jogging down the road. We intermingled with the reserve guys when we picked up and returned our weapons. It was my first interaction with them. They seemed to be a nice enough group of guys.

My weapon was filthy. Obviously, the last guy who had fired it had not cleaned it afterward. We were immediately put to the task of breaking our M14s down and cleaning all of the parts. It took hours and hours of work to get the weapons back up to the well-cared-for condition of our basic-training-issued rifles. To help pass the time spent rubbing the damn barrel, I began making sounds. They were a mix of American Indian chanting, Buddhist "ommmming," and the random sounds emitted by the totally insane. I thought it fit the situation nicely. I thought that the way I allowed a little drool to flow out of the corner of my mouth and down my chin was an appropriate touch as I moaned in my soft, guttural way.

After a few hours of this, a guy with a master's in English came up to my bunk. Earlier, he had identified himself to me by saying that he had a master's degree in English. He had heard that I had a master's degree in psychology. After I had confirmed that fact, he told me how refreshing it was to meet someone else who was an intellectual. He thought that almost everyone he had encountered thus far was pretty stupid. That just struck me the wrong way. I did not rise to the bait. I shook his outstretched hand, determined to have little to do with him.

Several days passed during which we spent a significant amount of time cleaning our rifles. My mindless sound making was developing into a fine art. It really relaxed me.

"I can't stand it. I can't deal with that noise you're making. Please, please, *please* stop!" the obviously distressed English major pleaded as he stood in front of me. Hell, wouldn't you know it? I thought. This horse's behind would be the one to complain. Damn! His bunk was at least eight or nine bunks away from mine. None of the guys immediately around me had complained. I was being purposefully soft in my chanting so as not to disturb anyone. Besides, the chanting actually made this tediously boring task tolerable.

"It can't be all that bad," I blandly stated as I wiped spittle from my chin.

"I, I can hear it all the way through my bones. It sets my nerves on end. I just can't deal with it anymore," he blurted out in a panicky, whiny tone.

The guy is a neurotic, I thought. He's a pain in the butt. This was not bothering anybody else. If it had been, someone surely would have said something to me after all this time, went my thoughts in a flash of a second.

"Tell you what," I said, remaining outwardly calm. "If you can get two other guys to say that it's irritating them and they want me to stop, I will."

"Okay, I'll be back shortly," he said backing away from my bunk.

Takes all kinds of people to make up this world, I reflected. If he did find two other guys to complain, I would stop. Hell, he would never find two to complain. What if he found just one? What would I do? If it bothered him so much that he would go to the trouble of convincing someone to come forth, I would stop. I did not want to drive someone up the wall, but the chanting really did seem to make the time go easier.

"Here they are," he said with real concern etched into his wrinkled brow.

"Are you here to complain about my noise?" I asked the two of them.

They both looked sheepish, their heads hanging down, and shifted from one foot to the other as they stood there in front of me.

"Yeah," the one closest to me finally said. The other guy nodded in agreement.

With resignation in my voice I inquired, "Do you want me to stop?"

"Yes," the first guy said, without looking me directly in the eye.

Turning to the English major, I said, "Okay. I'll be quiet. Sorry it bothered you."

He smiled slightly and left with his two companions. Nothing else was said.

I got a letter from Anna. It had a newspaper clipping in it with a picture of me in my army uniform. It was the head shot from the basic training book they gave us at graduation. The book was laid out like a high school yearbook. Instead of photos of the track team, the cheerleaders, and the student body president, there were shots of soldiers stabbing dummies with bayonets, throwing hand grenades, and crawling under live machine-gun fire. Oh, look! Here's my high school class going to the pool, and here's my basic training unit getting gassed. Give me a break. The army was pushing it, in my opinion.

The article was from the little Danville, Kentucky, newspaper. Anna was teaching high school there and living in an apartment above a garage. The army must have thought I was from there since that was our mailing address. The college we had attended was in Danville. I had lived on campus for four years, but Danville was not my home. The only people there who knew me were either on the college faculty and or had been my classmates. I had graduated two years earlier. Not many people would remember me. The article was a little embarrassing for me. The army had thought to impress the home folks. For me, it was not a status piece.

It said that I had been promoted to private first class under the army's new rapid promotion system. No one here told me anything about it. Maybe I would get a couple of extra dollars a month pay. I would have to check when they gave out the next pay envelope. In the meantime, I could imagine some of my college professors reading the article and wondering what I was doing as a private in the army. Another graduate gone bad; a failure in life. He was only an average student, so what did we expect?

In my letter to Anna, I told her about the three-day pass we would probably get around the middle of the course. Most of the guys said that the best place for us to meet was Atlanta. We started to plan for our next time together. I had learned not to trust the army. No matter what they told you, it could change at the last minute. I could not be certain that they would give me any leave time at Christmas. My orders said they would, but other things change, and this could, too. If Anna and I had a chance to be together, we would take it whenever it came.

CHAPTER 11

Advanced Infantry Training Begins

Right off they had us wearing our steel pots and carrying gas masks. We carried our weapons on almost all training activities. This was true even if we were not going to fire them. We often would stack arms and go on with the training activity. Once that training was over, we would pick up our weapons and march. It was always a long march back to the barracks.

One of the first training exercises was reading the compass. We spent the first week doing compass courses and firing our M14s. We shot at bull's-eye targets to zero-in our weapons. None of the sergeants were particularly interested in your being a good shot. If you asked, someone would come over and give you some brief assistance, but that was about all the instruction you got. Zeroing your weapon and target practice took up the week's live fire. Most of the other time was spent with your compass.

Unlike at Fort Dix, the compass course at Fort McClellan was over rough terrain and through wild underbrush. Few feet had walked these compass courses. No one had trampled down the underbrush. Alabama's underbrush was different from New Jersey's. Most of it still had green leaves on it. There were vines everywhere. They weaved a loose net that never wanted to yield as you pushed through it. A lot of the vines had thorns that stuck into your hands and face. Every time we came back from the bush we had streaks of blood on our necks, faces, arms, and hands. One time, as I was walking backward away from my partner who was sighting on me, I tripped and fell. The "wait-a-minute vines" and sticker bushes held me in a tangled mass in midair. Pushing through the stuff was not pleasant.

The third night there they sent us out on a night compass course. It was so far out from anywhere that they had to truck us out rather than march us there. We picked our partners. The sergeants led us to stakes alongside a narrow dirt road. The course was so huge that you could not see where they had dropped off the teams to your left or right. At Fort Dix the other teams' starting stakes had been less than twenty-five yards from your own. We had five different compass headings to follow that night in order to complete the course. We were to cover about three miles through the woods and end up a long way from where we started. At Fort Dix we knew the compass course would take us in a circle so that we would end up pretty close to where we started. Not so here. We were going to a new spot. If we missed one stake, we would be lost. The sergeants said that they expected about a fourth of us would be lost all night. I did not want to be pushing through this underbrush all night.

My partner had a small flashlight. The sergeants said that we were not to use flashlights. They would be out in the bush looking for people using lights. If they caught you, there would be hell to pay. I did not like to use a light at night. Once you turned it on, even if you held your hand over the lens, it ruined your night vision. In this place, your night vision was crucial. If your eyes went into shock from overexposure to light, everything was black in the dark. You could not see the vines, trees, or bushes. You just walked blindly into them and got all scratched up.

Another instruction was to be as quiet as possible. For example, we were not to shout out directions to each other about moving farther back for a more distant sighting or about moving to the right or left to be on the correct compass reading. If you made too much noise, it would serve as a magnet for the sergeants to home in on you. They promised to make our lives miserable if we attracted their attention. That did not appear to be too difficult a task for them, I thought, as I remembered the compass course we had been on the day before. It had been an all-day struggle with wait-a-minute vines, thorns, and multiple branches pulling at my face, pants legs, and ankles. It was miserable enough just being there. You did not need some gung-ho sergeant springing from the darkness with the sole purpose of making new miseries just for you.

We started the course. Don, my partner, held the compass. Our first heading was thirty-seven degrees for twelve hundred yards. Don held his arm up and pointed in the direction I was to travel. I counted my paces carefully, estimating each pace was a yard. I stopped after taking twenty-five paces and turned around. I could still see Don's dark body, but not his arm. The brush was waist high. Hidden vines pulled at my ankles. To any lurking enemy I must have sounded like a lost pig frantically thrashing in the brush in hope of escaping the butcher's wife who had just taken a swing at him with a meat cleaver.

"More to the left," came Don's strained, whispering voice. I stopped and faced him. Then I took two sidesteps to the left and bumped into a low-lying bush. "More," he hissed. "You've got to move more to the left." I walked around the bush and moved three more paces to the left. "A little back to the right." He was beginning to sound irritated. Irritation comes quickly when you lack sleep and are faced with a task that can be easy or difficult, depending on how other people perform, and is rapidly becoming difficult.

"That's it," he ordered. "That's it. Hold it, I'm coming to you."

He pushed through the underbrush as if he were walking through heavy surf with a strong undertow pulling him to the right.

"Damn! This is going to take all night," he lamented. I agreed. We were not going to make good time, even if we stayed on course.

"You're better at sighting than I am," Don said, "and I've got my little flashlight. Why don't you let me get to the limit of your night vision the regular way and then I'll use the light for you to guide me farther out. That way, we'll get done in half the time. At that distance, the light won't hurt your night vision. We'll be okay."

"I don't know. If we get caught, they'll make us pay," I cautioned.

"Not to worry," Don replied. "I'll keep my fingers pressed together over the lens and just let the smallest amount of white light peek through. Come on, we want to get this over with as soon as we can."

"Okay, but if you suspect a sergeant is coming at us, toss the light deep into the woods," I warned.

"Sure thing," Don said, with a smile.

"Oh, and Don, be sure to turn the light off before you toss it," I joked.

We laughed. Don was brave. He kept going farther and farther out. Every once in a while he and the light would disappear amidst crashing and thrashing sounds as he tripped on hidden obstacles and fell to the ground. It was spooky when he would disappear. One second he was there in the shadows, backing up, and the next he was gone. The sound of breaking branches and his body falling through thick brush would abruptly stop when he landed. The silence after the fall was the strange part. So much noise and then silence. It was as if Don had disappeared from the face of the earth. In the darkness, I could not even be sure of the spot from which he had disappeared. Don's muttered curses would finally fill the void of silence. For those brief moments of silence you became aware of how alone you were. You needed your partner, even if you were lost. Your partner was your connection to civilization. That was important out here. The silence and isolation punctuated the point.

Three hours in the brush and we were at the second stake. Three more to go. This was taking far too long. Both Don and I had stopped making jokes. We were sweating even though the night was cold. Our canteens were just about empty. It took a lot of energy to push through the thick underbrush. I had bruised myself several times in multiple falls over hidden objects.

Adding to the overall misery was the distant grinding sound of an overstressed vehicle engine. It kept grinding and straining. At times it would slow to an idle, but mostly it just strained and sent a sense of urgency through the night into your bones. As we tediously moved toward our third stake, we seemed to get closer to the sound. It was hard to tell if we were getting closer or if the engine was just working harder. There was a hint of lights off to my right toward the sound. Sometimes I thought the sound was moving. Other times it seemed to be stationary. I was not sure if it was just one vehicle. It could have been two or three, maybe even more. Then again, it might just have been one, what with sounds playing tricks as they bounce off low-lying hills, banks of foliage, and the like. Whatever was going on was the army's business. I was glad I did not have to deal with it. Pushing through the underbrush was bad enough. If I had to do real heavy work like the operators of those vehicles were doing out here this late at night, I would be under a lot more strain.

Don had backed so far away from me that I was having trouble spotting the peeks of light passing through his fingers. What with the distance and the brush between the two of us, as well as the constant grinding of that damned engine, I was in danger of losing Don's position all together.

"Where in the hell are you?" I demanded into the darkness, a little louder than usual.

Suddenly there was a huge rushing rustling of moving underbrush to my left. The abruptness of it froze me to the spot. The sound and movement came directly toward me so quickly that I did not have time to lower my compass from my face before I was grabbed. An arm shot forth from the bushes and grasped my shoulder. A body rapidly followed it. Before I could react, I was twisted by the arm and confronted with a shadowy face heavily breathing into mine.

"Where's the well the soldier fell through?" the face demanded of me in a roaring voice.

It made me mad. Anger, frustration, and released fear provoked me to shout back into the face: "How in the hell should I know? Damn it to hell, I'm out here trying to get through a damn compass course so I can get some sleep and you, you asshole, jump out of the woods, grab me, and ask me a dumb-ass question."

We were frozen in time for a split second as we stared at each other. The silence was broken by a voice calling out from thrashing bushes to the right: "Over here, General. They're over here."

"Okay, I'm coming," my captor responded.

The guy released my shoulders and rushed off to follow the voice. His form disappeared into the night, to be followed by the receding sound of other bodies pushing through the underbrush toward the straining engines.

I was stunned. I had just cursed at an army general. The confusion of the moment had saved me. Don and I speculated that the fallen soldier must have been walking backward as instructed by his partner with the compass and stepped into an old well that no one knew about. What a shock that must have been! You are walking backward and then you are falling straight down, not knowing when—or if—you will ever stop. The poor compass sighter suddenly loses sight of his partner, not knowing what happened. Strange stuff in the middle of the night! I hoped the guy had not been killed or seriously injured.

Given the fact that I had just cussed out a general, Don and I figured that it was best not to mention the incident. If we talked about it, the general would know I was the one with the foul mouth. He could make big trouble for a private first class.

Completing the compass course was anticlimactic. We did it. Then we got onto the back of a truck and were driven to our barracks. Two hours of sleep and then up to start another day of training. No one ever mentioned anything about someone falling into a well. It was as if it never happened. The army only tells you what it thinks you need to know. Apparently we did not need to know that the army did not know a whole lot about the land on which we were playing soldier. Such knowledge might inhibit our zest for training.

Preparing for an assault was interesting work. About fifty of us lined up in one nice, long horizontal line. There was about three feet between each man. Our rifles had blank adapters affixed to the muzzles. We had four magazines of blank rounds per man. Once again we were cautioned not to point our weapons at anyone unless we intended to kill them. Blanks shoot out a wad of paper that could maim or kill someone if it hit them in the right spot. Someone must have gotten injured in this manner or they would not be telling us this so often. Sergeants were at both ends of the line and behind us. When they gave the command, we began walking forward in a straight line with our barrels pointed forward, holding our rifles at hip level, firing at will. It was important for everyone to stay in line during an assault. If someone got ahead of the line, the soldiers behind him would shoot him in the back when real bullets were used. That seemed pretty logical to me. Never get ahead of everyone else when they are shooting straight ahead or you will get shot. In turn, if you failed to keep up with everyone else, you would be the one accidentally shooting your buddies in the back. Everyone should stay in line during an assault. It was good advice. Yet, no matter how many times we practiced it, there were always guys who got way out in front and guys who fell way behind. Frontal assaults on enemy positions are dangerous—even if the enemy is not home.

After a couple of half-days of drilling on walking frontal assaults, they had us practice frontal assaults while running. They lined a hundred or so of us up at the top of a hill. We were to run down the hill, through the trees and brush, chasing an imaginary foe. At the bottom of the hill we would cross a dry creek bed and run up the side of the next hill. When we got to the top of the other hill we would stop, having been victorious in successfully routing the enemy.

When one of the sergeants gave the command, we all charged down the hill. It was great. We were all shouting together in a big roar without even thinking. *Pow, pow, pow* went our M14s. The assault line was going to pot. Fortunately, we were spread out enough to avoid simulating shooting some of our comrades in the back.

I was loving it. Sprinting down the hill, keeping my balance, firing my weapon every once in a while was fun. This was grown-ups replaying their childhood days of cowboys and Indians. As I approached the dry creek bed, I could see that, near the bottom, it had steep banks on both sides. Once you committed to it, you could not stop. If you tried to stop, you would fall, roll, tumble, or slide into the rocky creek bed. Commit to it, and your momentum would carry you down, across, and then up the far bank in a smooth, swift motion. Without hesitation, I committed.

Just as my lead foot entered the steep decline and I passed the point of no return, a casually dressed soldier appeared from nowhere, all hunkered down. Scurrying from my left, he threw a gas grenade into my path. Just as quickly, the sneaky little devil scurried out of sight as I careened down the bank. There was no stopping. There was no time to pull out my gas mask and get a good seal around my face before running through the gas rising out of the creek bed. I could hear other gas grenades being tossed. They were not my concern. My momentum would carry me up the hill and away from them. Only the cloud of gas directly in front of me was my concern. I was going through it. Holding my breath was the only defense I could use.

Plop! Both feet landed squarely in the creek bed. I could not see the other bank through the cloud of gas. Running downhill had made me short of breath. I needed air. Tear gas covered my face. My eyes were burning. God, how they hurt. Blindly slamming my body into the other side of the bank, I grabbed tree roots, sapling trunks, and chunks of grass to pull myself up. The forward momentum of my body was still assisting me. It was too much; I was totally out of breath. I sucked in air. Immediately, I began gagging and dry heaving. A huge volume of gas had entered my airways. This was bad. Quick peeks of scenic woods passed between teary blinks of my eyes as I frantically climbed upward in blind, clawing movements. Up the hill I scrambled amidst huge coughs and strained gargling of uncontrollable dry heaves. I was near the top of the hill. The gas cloud stayed in the creek bottom. There was no wind to move it out. No point in putting on my gas mask now, I thought as I moved up to join others in as bad a shape or worse than I was.

After that incident, none of us had any difficulty pulling out our gas masks instantaneously when someone shouted "Gas!" We were gassed several more times while on maneuvers. The Chemical Warfare School students liked to practice on the infantry. It seemed to make them happy and there seemed to be no shortage of tear gas. They had plenty, judging by the frequency they used it.

On another frontal assault exercise we had to go through a simulated field of fire. Several hundred of us lined up in a long-stretching row. In front of us we saw a lot of sandbagged, barbed-wire circles. Inside them were explosive charges. They would go off as our line moved through the large, treeless field toward our objective. We have to cover a large area of rolling hills. All of it seemed to be strewn with the barbed-wire circles. No matter what happened, we were not to go into any of the barbed-wire circles. The consequences of failing to follow those instructions could be fatal.

The order to move out was issued. It is impressive to be one of hundreds of armed men moving out in a single assault line. There is a sense of power you feel just being a part of it. You feel as if nothing could stop this force. The sergeants could be heard telling various men to keep up or slow down. That was the only noise that broke the silence.

We pass the first series of explosive pits. None of them have gone off. Our line is pretty. The line stays straight as we pass through the second series of explosives holes.

BOOM! BOOM! BOOM! KA-BOOM! On and on go the explosions. Immediately, the line goes to pot. There is no order. Some of the guys are walking in circles. In the distance you can see sergeants waving their arms and moving their mouths, yelling at some soldiers; but there is no sound. Their puny voices are so small in the presence of the continuous roar of explosions that they cannot be heard. I am one of the few to make it to the end of the assault field in any semblance of order. Just a handful of us keep up the pace and do not get distracted by the discharge of ordnance. My confidence concerning what it will be under combat conditions has not been enhanced. Clearly, chaos must rule in combat. There can be no effective voice communication in an intense firefight or under bombardment. This is not the way I have seen it in the movies. This is not good.

Saturday afternoon we were given the night off. Sunday was to be a free day, too. We cannot go off post, and we cannot go into restricted areas. This primarily means that no one can go over to the WAC barracks. One guy said that during detail day he was in a truck that drove by their barracks. A lot of the WAC recruits were standing at attention as a female sergeant cussed them out. He said it was far worse language than the sergeants used on us. He repeated some of the language he heard the women sergeants use. It was grossly sexually explicit. None of us ever used language like that no matter what kind of off-color joke we told or how angry we got. The general feeling was that the women recruits took a lot more hell than we did. We felt a degree of sympathy in our ranks for them.

There was a canteen or dance hall of some sort. You could go there on Saturday nights. We heard that WACs would be there. They played records and served 3.2-percent beer. There was nothing else we knew of to do on post on a Saturday night. Everyone went to the dance hall. Army buses came by on a regular basis, picking up guys to go to the dance hall and returning them to the barracks. The last run was at 11:30.

They seemed to enjoy playing records by Smokey Robinson and Aretha Franklin. I had been so immersed in my studies for the last two years that I simply had had no time to listen to the radio. Thus, I was out of touch with the popular music scene. Even the old records were new to me. I enjoyed the music. The behavior of the soldiers and WACs was interesting to watch. They were very awkward with each other. It reminded me of fifth-grade dances held in the gym and chaperoned by local do-gooders. The boys would stand at one end of the gym and the girls at the other. When the music started, the adults would direct both lines of children to walk out to the center of the floor. Whoever ended up opposite you when the lines met was your dance partner. Here, the men stood closer to the bar while the women gathered at the opposite end of the building. The dance floor was between the two groups.

There were always people dancing whenever the music played in the dimly lit hall. However, there were many more people not dancing but staying in their close-knit groups, drinking and talking. There was little mixing of the sexes. Most people seemed to be there to look at the other sex without being too obvious about it. Everyone was overly polite. A lot of the guys were dancing by themselves, moving with the beat of the music. It was pretty frantic. I knew how to slow dance, but I had never mastered the art of rapid body movement in rhythm to a fast beat. The black soldiers were really good at it, as were a lot of the white guys. After a couple of beers, I thought I was catching the knack for it, too.

While I was ordering another beer, a tall WAC near me was jostled just a little bit, causing her to bump my arm as I picked up my plastic glass of beer. It spilled. She apologized and offered to buy me another. I laughed and accepted. As she got hers, I asked her where she was from. That was the safest and most-often-asked question. She said she was from the Pacific Northwest.

"Why did you join the army?" I asked, raising my voice so she could hear me over the music.

"My dad's a career officer, and I have two brothers who are officers. Both of them are in Vietnam," she explained. "I felt that anything I could do to help make things better in the army would help them out. After all, they're risking their lives for America and freedom. It's the least I could do."

"How do you feel about draft dodgers?" I asked, guessing mentally what her answer would be.

"They have to do what they think is right, just as I do," she replied with a smile. "Why are you here?"

"The draft forced me in," I replied. "I'm signed up for OCS."

"Well, I hope you don't miss your wife too much," she said nodding her head at my wedding ring.

"I miss her. They keep us so busy and so tired that I don't get to think about it much. We're going to be together in about three weeks when they give us our three-day pass," I said, smiling.

"That will be nice for both of you," she said, sipping her beer.

The disc jockey had just put on a rare slow-beat record.

"Do you want to dance?" she asked with a smile.

"Okay." I set my beer on the counter and stood up.

We talked as we danced.

"What do you think about women in combat?" she asked.

"I guess it would be okay. You must have an opinion about it," I replied, trying to be as noncommittal as I could.

"I think women are as tough as men. If they want to fight and can go through the training, I think they should be allowed to do it. There are many examples in history of women doing well in combat. Just look at what the Russian women did slowing down the Germans," she rattled off.

It was clear that she had been thinking about the topic for a while.

"Now tell me your *true* opinion," she said with conviction.

"Well, I think women ought to be the only ones allowed to go into combat," I stated, then flashed a grin.

She smiled broadly. The music stopped. Laughing, we thanked each other for the dance and returned to our separate corners.

Overall, the place was a little boring. I liked the music and the beer. I did not want to dance. There was no one I really wanted to talk to except Anna. I ran into a couple of guys who had been in my basic training company, but none that I felt very close to. Catching the ten o'clock bus and getting some catch-up sleep seemed better to me than sitting there getting bloated on 3.2-percent beer.

There were about ten guys and a WAC on the bus. A couple of the guys were sitting together, but mainly everyone was sitting in isolation, as I was. The WAC was sitting alone about halfway back. When the bus pulled up in front of the first barracks complex, it stopped. The doors opened. One guy, sitting alone at the front of the bus, stood up and started to go to the door. He hesitated a second and then turned around. Without saying a word he walked back to the WAC, leaned over her, and kissed her. With her hands in her lap, she kissed him back. He stood straight up, turned, and walked off the bus. No one spoke a word.

The silence continued as the bus pulled out. At the next stop, two soldiers near the front stood up. They both walked back to the WAC. First one kissed her and then the other. Not a word had been spoken. After the kiss, they walked to the front of the bus and departed.

Again there was silence as the bus pulled out. Two more stops and two more kisses. No one spoke. They were never very passionate kisses. Somewhere between a kiss of hello and a kiss of good-bye on a first date with the hope of getting a little more passionate next time.

My barracks came up. Three of us got up to get off the bus. I was sitting about three seats behind the WAC and across the aisle from her. I had no desire to kiss her. The other two dutifully lined up for their kisses as I walked by them.

The night air was brisk. The bus pulled away as the three of us went to our separate barracks. The kissing puzzled me. I felt sad. I felt sad for all of us.

Sleeping in Sunday morning was a treat. It was the first time since joining the army that I slept late. In the afternoon I went to the PX with a couple of the guys. You never knew when you would get a chance to buy supplies. Toothpaste, spare shoelaces, shoe polish, writing paper, postage stamps, and the like were bought and stored in the locked footlocker at the end of our bunks. While at the PX, I ran into my friend Tom from basic training. It was truly good to see him. The last time we had been together was during the basic training proficiency test on the bayonet course. He had been right behind me. When I started to respond to the sergeant's first set of bayonet assault instructions, my mind was focused. I was unaware of what was happening to the men in front of or behind me. After completing the course, I was immediately hustled off to another testing station. I never saw Tom after that. He was on an earlier train to Fort McClellan. The AIT company to which he was assigned was six or seven miles from my barracks. I agreed to walk over that evening and visit him. Of course, that assumed that the army did not have other plans for me.

Tom's barracks was identical to mine. It was just in a different location. All the same, it felt strange walking into a barracks full of men I did not know. Guys were sprawled out on their bunks; others were playing cards, reading, or doing have-to tasks like polishing shoes.

I spotted Tom.

"Hey, Tom, I made it," I said as I approached his bunk. He was leaning against the metal frame with a pillow propped up to soften the press of the iron bars against his back.

After the usual exchange of greetings, we talked.

"How's your AIT company?" he asked.

Strange question, I thought. Basic training and AIT companies are all the same. They are what they are, and you get on with your life.

"It's okay. How's yours?" I responded.

"It's not like our basic training group. These guys are different. Nobody cares what happens to you here. No one helps you. You're on your own with them. There are a couple of real strange guys in this company," he said in a hushed voice, so as not to be overheard.

His comments turned a couple of nearby heads that held blank expressions. You cannot say anything in an army barracks without being overheard by someone. That is just reality.

"Did you see what happened to me on the bayonet proficiency test back at basic?" he asked with a broad grin.

"No, I lost track of you. I seem to remember some commotion or shouting around me, but I didn't know if that had anything to do with you or not," I said as I settled down on the side of his bunk.

"Well," he began, "right after they called you to go and you started to walk up to the first cement platform a sergeant way out in the middle of the second set of dummies shouted at me to get on a cement platform and wait for an assault command. You know how hyped up we were. I was so scared I would mess up. I was really tense. The whole scene was confusing to me. I didn't know for sure where he wanted me to go, so I took a couple of steps forward and stopped. I just didn't know where to go. He screamed at me to get my butt in gear. I didn't think. I just ran. And then, there it was, right in front of me: a cement platform just like the one I saw you go to. I jumped onto it and stood at high port, looking straight ahead at the dummy down range, waiting intensely for the sergeant to call out a bayonet assault order, hoping I wouldn't mess up. My elbows were out from my body and my legs were bent. I was ready to spring as soon as the order was given. I stood there and stood there, but no order was given. My feet were split. I was ready. Still no order. This isn't right, I thought. I let my eyes move around while keeping my body rigid, ready to attack. People were shouting everywhere. I saw a sergeant waving his hands and screaming something, but he was too far away to make out what he was saying. He seemed to be looking at me and started running toward me. Then, off to the left, I saw another sergeant waving his arms and running at me. Two or three more sergeants were coming at me, too. They all got there at about the same time. I was scared to death. I held my position. Nothing they said made sense. No one was shouting out a bayonet assault order. All at once, they were in my face. They were all pointing down. I looked down. My combat boots were buried in wet cement. It was so deep it had covered the tops of them and seeped down inside. I was really hyped up, so I hadn't felt it."

I was roaring with laughter. The idea of Tom standing there like a statue with his feet anchored in wet cement was just too funny. We laughed so hard that tears ran down our cheeks.

Later, we talked about what would happen to us after AIT. He guessed that he would be assigned to a combat unit in Vietnam. If he signed up for any special training, he would have to become RA instead of US. That would mean another year in the army. He wanted out as soon as possible. So, he guessed he would just have to take whatever they gave him. I liked Tom a lot. He was so pleasant and sincere. A very gentle person. Clearly, he was bright. I do not know what kind of a student he was in high school. He could have been an excellent one if that was what he had wanted.

He said that his dad had been in the army during the Second World War. His dad worked with a guy who had been in the same squad with him in Europe. Tom worked with them during his summer vacations. They were house painters. They never talked about their combat experiences. However, at the end of the day, as they were all picking up, one or the other of them would always say, "Well, I guess we had better police the parade ground," and then they would laugh and laugh. Tom said that he had never understood what they were talking about until he got into basic. We were always having to form lines and then walk across the landscape, picking up scraps of paper, cigarette butts, spent chewing gum, and anything else that was not natural to the spot. It was a real drag, particularly when you were dead tired. They called this task "policing the parade ground."

Tom and I agreed that in civilian life we could always say, "High port," to each other and break out laughing while everyone around us would not have a clue as to what we were laughing about. I never saw Tom again. The army had a way of separating you forever.

The next day is detail day. The sergeants have us fall out and line up. The senior sergeant asks for two volunteers. You've got to be kidding me. Everyone knows that no one volunteers for this stuff. Finally, two guys volunteer. There is always that 10 percent who do not get the word.

They are given the day off. Can you believe it? Now they are asking for five volunteers. I raise my hand. Congratulations to me. My four companions and I have KP duty. We get on a truck and ride to a mess hall I have never seen before.

My assignment is to pour fifty pounds of potatoes into a mechanical potato peeler, close the lid, turn on the electric motor, and let it run until all of the potatoes are peeled, check each potato as I remove it for any remaining eyes, and cut them out when found. I have about four hundred pounds of potatoes to peel.

Interesting work up to 150 pounds. After that it became tedious. As I was starting to pour in my fifth bag of potatoes, the head cook came up to me.

"Are you the one with the master's degree in psychology?" he asked in a quiet voice.

"Yes, Sergeant. It's in school psychology," I replied.

"Soldier, come over here and take over from this man," he ordered some guy collected from a different AIT company. "Follow me," he told me as he walked back to the cook's sleeping quarters.

"Go ahead, sit down," he said, motioning me to a chair as he sat in the one opposite it. "Do you want a drink?" he asked as he poured himself one from a whiskey bottle.

"No, thanks. I get a headache if I drink in the morning," I said as I struggled to make sense out of the situation.

"Do you do marriage counseling?" he asked, taking a short sip of whiskey.

The question stunned me. "No, Sergeant. I'm trained to work with children, adolescents, their parents, and teachers," came my soft response.

"Well, that will do," he said with sadness in his voice and body. "My wife and I are arguing a lot. It's getting pretty bad."

"I just did not get into marriage relationships in my training," I said with a degree of strain in my voice. I did *not* want to be there. This was not what I was supposed to be doing. There were potatoes that needed to be peeled. Men were sweating and cursing and working too hard back on the other side of the room. I was supposed to be with them. I felt guilty and off balance.

He was angry. "What the hell, You were trained to deal with people who have problems weren't you?" he shouted. Before I could respond to his question, he went on: "This is the same thing. Don't play games with me. How would you go about counseling someone who was angry with you? What did they teach you to do? Tell me, damn it."

This was bad. I had to respond. "Well, I'd probably use the Rogerian counseling technique."

"Don't give me that education crap. Tell me what you would do," he demanded.

"I'd listen. I'd get the person to talk and listen. To let the person know that I was hearing what he was saying, I'd restate what he had told me, using my own words. If I hadn't heard or understood what he said, he would correct me after I restated what I thought he had said. I would have to be careful not to argue with him over what he said. All I'd be trying to do is let him know that I had heard what he said. I wasn't trying to correct or change what he'd said. I wasn't arguing with him. That's the hard part, not arguing with what people say. You just want to listen and let them know that you heard what they said. Most people who are angry don't feel anyone is listening to them, I think." I spoke in a slow methodical way. I could be in bad trouble if this guy took offense at what I said.

"Yeah, that's it," he said with a smile as he rocked back in his chair. "She's always complaining that I never listen to her. I knew it would be good to talk with you. Show me how to listen."

We spent most of that morning practicing reflective listening techniques. The sergeant was a quick learner. He never took another drink. I think he was just trying to be friendly with me by offering me one. When I declined, he was sort of trapped into having to pour himself a short sip. When he had to leave the room to supervise lunch, he would have it no other way than that I take the rest of the day off. I actually wanted to be with the KP detail. There was no persuading him on that. After lunch he insisted that I return to his room and take a nap. He said he knew how hard they worked us in training. I had to be tired, he stated. He was pulling rank on me. I was ordered to rest. He would wake me in time to catch the truck back to my barracks. It was like the doctor ordering you to take medicine that you were afraid would taste bad but you knew it would be good for you. I slept a full three hours. He shook my hand when I left. On the truck, the guys wanted to know what had happened to me. I told them the cook wanted my advice on a personal problem he was having. They laughed.

The rest of the week was consumed with more weapons training. We started on the M60 machine gun. Before you get to fire it, they teach you how to break down the weapon, clean it, and clear it of jammed rounds. The M60 fires the same caliber bullet as the M14: a 7.62-millimeter slug. Having the same ammunition for several types of weapons makes resupply a lot easier. The big problem with the machine gun is remembering to fire in short bursts. If you keep firing for extended periods of time, the barrel will overheat. An overheated barrel will start to warp. A warped barrel will explode. The machine gun is then out of action and the machine gunner is probably dead, as are the ammunition belt holder and anyone else close by.

A good field of fire is important for the machine gun. You have to establish the weapon's firing zone. It is best to have a long, wide, level field to your front, with no trees or obstacles that advancing troops can hide behind. The tripod the machine gun sits on has bars and levers on it and a little wheel that spins. You can rig the thing so that you do not have to think too much to spray your field of fire. Once rigged, the weapon will only swing so far to the left or the right and will only elevate or depress the muzzle so far. This is particularly helpful for night firing. If the enemy is trying to sneak up on you at night, you do not have to see him. You just spray the whole area with the machine gun. Everything within the field of fire will be killed. Those blank areas not covered by the spray of machine-gun bullets are picked up by other weapons. Rifle fire, grenade launchers, and other automatic weapons are placed at the right spots so that nothing in front of the good guys can get through the field of fire.

Firing the M60 was exhilarating. The M60 is a very accurate weapon. Every fifth round or so is a tracer round. It makes a red dot streak of burning phosphorous through the air so you can see where your bullets were going. They make your fire look like trails of fireworks traveling horizontally above the ground. It is very pretty, particularly at night. The sound of the gun going off and your forced concentration in controlling such power makes everything around you nonexistent. It occupies your complete attention.

Late one afternoon on the firing range, a couple of sergeants carrying a large ammo box full of clipped-together belts of bullets ready to feed into the M60 stopped beside my station. Usually they gave you only thirty or forty rounds to fire at a time. Once you fired those rounds at your designated target, your turn was over. It was always a disappointment to fire so few rounds after waiting such a long time for your turn. They had about twenty machine guns on line. That meant we waited in long lines before we got the chance to shoot our ten seconds worth of bullets. I was particularly pleased with my shot groups and shot bursts on the gun. It just seemed that I had a knack. With those rounds, I could adjust the weapon and fire it so that my initials were carved into the fifty-five-gallon drums we were shooting at. I could feather squeeze the trigger so that only one round fired at a time, as with a repeat-fire M14. That enabled me to control more of the rounds spitting out of the machine gun. I would initial my drum and then redirect my fire on someone else's drum and initial it, too. A lot of the guys just shot off all their rounds in one big burst or had such trouble retargeting their weapons that they never shot off all of their allotted rounds. That produced a surplus of unfired bullets at the end of the day. Those surplus rounds were in the ammo box the sergeants had brought.

"He's the best shot. Let him fire them off," the sergeant standing behind me said as I turned and saw that he was pointing at me.

"Here, burn off these rounds," one of the sergeants said, handing my loader the box of ammo.

Whoa! This is going to be fun, I thought. After the first rounds were placed in the automatic feeder slot, I slammed down the plate on top, which locked the railroad tracks of the ammo belt into the gun.

"Short bursts, short bursts. Remember to fire in short bursts," said the supervising sergeant as he motioned for me to fire down range.

TAT-IT-TAT, TAT-TAT-TAT-TAT-IT-TAT. I was in my own world. Nothing existed but the gun and me. *TAT-IT-TAT, TAT-TAT-IT-TAT-IT-TAT-TAT-TAT.* I was really zeroed in. My target barrel rocked. I was playing tic-tac-toe on it. I squeezed off more rapid firing to draw the horizontal line showing that I had won. More ammo flew into the machine gun. It just kept firing. I spun the little wheel on the horizontal controller that turned the barrel within the wide range of fire. I took on other fifty-five-gallon drums. The bullets kept coming. The ammo belt seemed unending. The stream of tracers burned their way across the open space. I thought it would be neat to see how close I could come to the base of the drums without hitting them. Dust flew up in front of them and arched around their bases, following the natural curve of their placement on the ground. Still the bullets came. I switched to ricocheting the bullets off the ground into the drums and rotating from one drum to another in an X pattern. Damn, it was fun!

PONG, PONG, PONG, PONG went my helmet. Lifting my finger from the trigger and turning my head, I heard nothing except for the screaming of the sergeant. His voice sounded small and puny in contrast to the continuous roar of the machine gun.

"Cease-fire! Cease-fire!" he screamed. "The barrel! You're overheating the barrel!" I looked at it. Smoke rose from its entire length. No doubt about it, it was hot. The shimmering heat waves rising from it, the smell of burning oil, and the rising smoke told you that any flesh that touched it would be instantaneously cooked.

I looked around. Every gun on the line was silent. Every eye was on me. No one was talking. It had been a hell of a show.

"Nice shooting, Son. Just remember the barrel; you don't want to burn it up," the sergeant said under his breath as he motioned for me to leave the weapon.

Friday morning we were told that those of us who passed Saturday morning's inspection without a mistake could go off post Saturday night. It would be an overnight pass. The rest of the company would receive an on-post pass.

As best as I could tell, only four guys got through Saturday morning's inspection without a mistake being found. To my surprise, I was one of them. The guy in the bunk across from mine was the only fellow I personally knew who got one. He had some relatives living near Anniston. They would pick him up at the fort's main entrance that evening. It was a family affair. We both knew it would be inappropriate for him to invite me to go along.

There was no place I knew of to go. I might go downtown and see a movie, but that was it. Without Anna, what was the point of going off post? It would be a waste of money to sleep overnight in a motel just because I could. Besides, I could not go to sleep in a motel. It was not my home. I would feel out of place there. The barracks were my home if I was not with Anna.

My off-post pass began at noon. The first thing I needed to do was go to the PX, get a pocketful of change, and call Anna. We made plans to meet in Atlanta two weekends later. I assumed that I would get a three-day pass as they had promised. If the army changed its mind after Anna bought her plane tickets, we would just be out the money. She would make all of the hotel arrangements. Five of us guys had made plans to drive to Atlanta. They all had relatives or friends there. One guy had someone who would drop off a car for him to pick up in Anniston. We would share the cost of gas. They were kind enough to agree to drive me to the airport. Anna and I would meet there, as we had in Philadelphia. It was great to talk with her for that hour and a half. She was happy about my off-post pass and hoped I would see a good movie in town.

Feeling really good as I left the telephone booth in the PX, I bought a copy of *The Anniston Star*. It did not reveal much. There was one movie house in town. There just did not seem to be much to Anniston— and even less going on there.

Looking up from the paper, my eye fell onto an old acquaintance from basic. Stone had been in a different platoon than mine. Our paths had crossed several times in basic. He was okay. Stone never said much. You could tell from his eyes that he knew what was going on, though. He did not miss much. While he was about as tall as I was, he had me in weight by a good twenty pounds. None of that weight was fat. Stone was solid muscle. You knew just by looking at him that you did not want to mess with this guy. His disposition was pleasant enough. He would smile with his eyes before a slow grin would grow on his straight face. I did not know much about him or his background. The thinning hair and a few permanent wrinkles around his eyes suggested that he was older than I was. Perhaps he had worked on construction jobs outdoors and been aged by the sun. His physical build fit that of a man who made his living with his strength. He was going to Field Artillery OCS. I assumed he was one of the college guys, but I did not know it for a fact. He seemed more mature and somewhat older than the fresh graduates from college. If he was a college graduate, I doubt that he went to an Ivy League school. His accent was definitely Midwestern. If he wanted to tell me about himself, that was fine; and if he did not, that was also okay. Out in the field,

it did not make all that much difference. If you were a pain in the behind, that was the reality. How you got that way did not much matter
to those who had to cope with you. Being a fool or someone you could
depend upon was what you were, not who you were. You could count
on Stone.

"What's up with you?" Stone asked, looking at me with those smiling eyes.

"I got an overnight pass with no place to go and no one to go with,"
I said, laughing and shaking my head.

"Hey, I'll go with you," he said with a smile that matched those eyes.

"Great. What and where?" I responded, pointing at the paper.

"Hell, I don't know. We'll get us a good meal, find a couple of good
bars, and just hang out," he blurted out, grabbing the paper from my
hands.

"I'd thought I might catch a ride downtown and walk around just
to reconnoiter the place. Maybe catch a movie. I don't want to stay overnight in a hotel," I said as we walked out of the PX.

"Sounds like a good start. I'll meet you back here in an hour in my
civvies. Then we can catch a cab to town," he said as he started walking away from me.

"Great! Here in an hour," I shouted as the distance was quickly
growing between us. Things were looking up. This was shaping up into
an all-around good day.

Even though we were in our civilian clothes, anyone seeing us would
know that we were army. Our short GI haircuts were a dead giveaway.
Then our excellent physical condition and the shadows under our eyes
from lack of sleep were the next obvious clues. The fact that our civvies
were somewhat too big was another hint as to our status. The intense
training had our body weight either down or distributed differently in
the natural conversion of loose body fat into lean muscle. But the most
obvious tip to our military status was our shoes. No one in civilian life
wears black, spit-shined military dress shoes. Our civilian dress made us
look more unusual and ultimately military than if we had been in our
army fatigues. We would have felt more comfortable in the fatigues.

I had thought that Anniston was a big city. Judging by the size and
configuration of its downtown district, it was a simple small, southern
town. On the main street were a movie theater, department store, hardware store, country diner, hotel, and small specialty shops. The main-
street stores were all in orange, brick-faced buildings. A few of the side
streets contained similar buildings. That seemed to be it. Residential

homes on streets lined with shade trees seemed to surround the down-town district in all directions. As a kid traveling through various towns in the Midwest, I would judge the size of a town by the number of movie theaters it had. Really small towns had only one movie house. It was not a town without at least one movie theater; it was a village.

Neither Stone nor I knew anything about the movie. That was okay. It was a movie. We had not seen it, so we went. The film was definitely of pulp quality, a mystery designed to play as the second feature at the drive-in. Both of us were bored. If it were not for the fact that we had been denied the opportunity of seeing a movie, we would have left in the middle of it. As it was, we got a few good laughs by making fun of it. We were two of five people watching the late-afternoon flick.

When we left the theater, it was about 5:30 P.M. No one was on the street. No cars were on the road. It was as if the town was deserted. Stone wanted to find a bar. It was okay with me. We walked up and down the street. Everything was closed. There weren't even any closed bars. One small diner was open. It did not have any customers in it. We checked out a few of the side streets without success.

The waitress in the diner was pleasant. She asked us how the army was treating us. That brought a good laugh from both of us. We sat down at a dimly lit corner table near the big picture window fronting the street. Stone told me to go ahead and order for him. He said he was go-ing to go down toward the hotel and play out an idea he had. That was fine with me.

When he got back, the waitress was placing our plates on the table. Meat loaf, mashed potatoes with gravy, green beans, tossed salad, a din-ner roll with a pat of margarine, and coffee. When the waitress left, Stone, displaying his big smile, pulled up his shirt to reveal two whiskey pints stuck in his pants.

"The town's dry. I had to pay $10 for each pint. There are no bars anywhere," he stated with just a hint of mischief in his eyes. "But," he said with emphasis, "there are a few spots where the good ol' boys gather on Saturday nights out in the woods. We can hit them later."

"Let's do it. It's better than going back to the barracks or sipping three-point-two beer," I said as I grabbed my water glass and held it un-der the table in response to Stone's pulling out a whiskey pint and mo-tioning to me for the glass. Hell, this was like being a teenager all over again. I didn't have to worry about where to eat or sleep. The army took care of that. All I had to do for the army was my chores. They did all of the thinking for me. They drove me to school; they made sure I had the right supplies and clothes. When they weren't there to tell me what to do, I could do what I damn well wanted to do. As long as I didn't break too many of the army's rules and didn't get in trouble with the law, I could be as irresponsible as I wanted to be. Since I was so strong and so well trained, I I could handle any of the good ol' boys that wanted to be nasty. Well, I could handle the situation as long as Stone was with me. Anyway, everyone was pretty nice to army recruits. My best opinion on the matter was that most likely no one would mess with us.

I felt the alcohol right away. The whiskey burned my throat going down and flushed my face. I felt invigorated. We laughed louder and longer at stupider and stupider comments we would throw out at each other. This was really enjoyable.

"Time to leave," Stone said. It was dark outside. We left the waitress a large tip. She had stayed behind the lunch counter most of the time we were there. Whenever our water glasses emptied, she would come over and fill them. As we drank more and more, we became sloppy about hiding the pints. She knew we were drinking but was good enough not to comment. We had consumed about half of our little bottles.

Stone said that a taxi driver would know where the action was. We just needed to get a cab. We asked the waitress for the number of a cab company. She volunteered to call one for us.

Ten minutes later, we were entering a cab.

"Where you boys wanna go?" the cabbie asked over his shoulder.

"Just drive us around a little and show us the town," Stone replied.

"You boys new to the area?" he inquired as we pulled away from the curb.

"Yeah, we're out at the Fort. This is my first time in Alabama," I replied, leaning on the back of the front seat so he could hear me better.

"Fuck the army!" the cabbie shouted and laughed. We laughed with him.

"So you've been in," I stated with a big grin.

"Hell, yes! They sucked me in during Korea. If my ass hadn't been frozen 'bout as hard as a rock I'd damn well have gotten it shot off when the Commies sent in all of those Chinese troops."

"Gee, that was a tough one," Stone said, jumping in. "I heard that we almost lost that one when the Chinese came storming down from the north."

"You're damn straight about that, Son. Fortunately, the U.S. Army had two things going for it," he said, looking at us in the rearview mirror.

"What was that?" I dutifully asked.

Grinning from ear to ear, he turned his head to look at us as we sped down the road, "They had me there to kick some butt and the Chinese army was just a little more fucked up than ours was."

We roared with laughter. This guy was all right.

"How're they treating you up there?" he asked, jerking his head in the general direction of the base.

"They keep us out on training exercises late at night. You don't get much sleep. The vines and stickers in the bush are bad," Stone responded.

"This Vietnam thing is getting pretty big. It might get as big as Korea if we're not careful," he said authoritatively. It was pitch dark outside.

Stone said, "We'll have to go back to the base shortly if we can't find a good night spot."

"This place is pretty dead on Saturday nights, alright," the driver agreed.

Stone leaned up close to the guy's ear and said, "You wouldn't know where there was a night spot we could go to that has some beer and music?"

"This is a dry town and county. There just ain't much going on around here," the cabbie said, shaking his head.

"The hell you say," Stone said with a big smile. "There's got to be a gathering place *somewhere* that you could take us to."

The driver said in a lowered voice, "Well, I do know one place, but it's pretty rough."

"I knew it! I knew it," crowed Stone. "Take us to it!"

"Ah, uh, it's pretty rough. It's way out a dirt road deep in the woods. Most cabbies are afraid to drive out there. I could drive you out near it, but I won't drive right up to it. You'd have to walk down a cut-off dirt road another half mile," he said as his eyes darted from Stone to me in the rearview mirror.

"That's it, that's it!" Stone shouted, slapping his knee. "Let's go! Good party time is a wasting."

We drove what seemed to be a long time down a narrow, two-lane road and then turned off onto a dirt road. It was bumpy and dusty. The noise of the road vibrations kept us from having much of a sustained conversation. About fifteen minutes down the dirt road, tall pine trees hemmed us in tightly to the narrow road. The cab began to slow down.

Putting his right arm out on the top ridge of the front seat, the cabbie turned to look us both in the eyes. "Boys, no cab driver will come out here to pick you up late at night. This is just too rough a place."

Bringing the cab to a stop, he pulled out a pencil and paper from the glove compartment and said: "I'm going to give you my name and telephone number. When you're ready to be picked up, you call this number and ask for me. Tell them you're the two army guys I dropped off. I'll know it's you. You wait right here on this road. See where that little dirt road cuts off down there to the right? That's where I'll be looking for you. I won't stop unless I see you there. You be there, or you don't get picked up. Got it?"

"Yeah, thanks a lot," I said. Stone echoed my appreciation.

"We just walk down the cut-off there?" I asked. Stone was already three-quarters of the way out of the cab.

"Yeah. It's about a ten-minute walk down there to that place," he said quietly.

"What do we owe you?" I asked, reaching for my wallet.

"How about just paying for the gas it took to get you here?" he answered.

"Ah, that's awfully nice," I said, handing him two bucks.

Stone stuck his head back in the cab, "It sure is," he agreed.

"Us infantry have to stick together," the cabbie said with a smile and gunned the motor.

A sweeping cloud of dust trailed behind him. Stone and I stood there on the dirt road, hands in our pockets, watching his taillights disappear into the darkness. We looked at each other for a long moment. In unison, we broke the spell by shrugging at each other. We turned and started walking down the middle of the cut-off road. At first we couldn't see anything except tall tree trunks. They were so thick and deep that it was just one dark line on top of other darker black lines. There seemed no break in them. As we progressed down the road, we could hear music. It was Aretha Franklin kind of music. Then a clearing in the trees appeared. The clearing grew. The headlights and taillights of cars backing up or slowly moving into parking spaces illuminated the area. There was a large, windowless cinderblock building in the middle of the open space. It had one of those British-type guardhouse-shaped entrances. You know, like the one you see on television when those guards at the royal palace in London stand there at attention with the big, black beaver hats on and American tourists try to make him smile. He's always standing in front of this little guardhouse. Well, his guardhouse is here, in these woods. You go through it to get into the cinderblock building. People were moving from the cars to the guardhouse. A couple of guys here, a man and a woman holding hands there. All of the people seemed to be moving from the edge of the woods to the center of the clearing and the guardhouse entrance.

A turning car's headlights scanned the moving crowd. We were mov-

ing toward the guardhouse. The light momentarily illuminated everyone. Instantly, Stone and I knew why the cabbie had said this was such
a bad place: The people were all black. Neither one of us had to say anything. This had the potential of being bad. We looked at each other as
we continued our strides toward the door. We were committed. We were
going inside.

I stepped into the guardhouse first. *POW!* Something hit both of my
shoulders at the same time. I was slammed up against the wall. My captor had me pinned against it. His hands were pressing back on my shoulders. Two other large black men were in my face. Quickly looking up, I
could see Stone in the same position, pressed against the opposite wall.
Someone else ran his hands up my pants legs. He felt around my crotch.
Then he ran his hands up both sides of my waist. I felt the half-empty
pint bottle being efficiently removed from its protective spot in front of
my belly button. A hand held it up to my face.

A deep voice from a form standing between the two groups pinning
Stone and me to the walls said, "Five dollars to get in, and five dollars
apiece to bring in the pints."

Multiple hands released me from their grip. I reached for my billfold
in my back pocket. Stone was doing the same. It was very quiet. No one
moved. We were blocking the doorway. A long line of people were waiting outside, anxious to get in.

"What brings you boys here?" the voice in the shadows asked.

Before I could respond, Stone shouted, "Fuck the army!" while displaying the happiest grin I had ever seen on his face.

That brought a spontaneous roar of laughter from our captors and
me. They slapped us on the back in good cheer, took our money, and
opened the inner door. We walked inside.

The place was jumping. On stage were a six- or seven-piece band, a
female vocalist, and two go-go girls bathed in ultraviolet lights shimmering and shaking to the blaring music. The dance floor was crowded
with people twisting and shouting. They were having a good time. Off
to the left, a bartender was serving beer. Ten-cent bags of pretzels and
potato chips hung overhead. In the far corner by the bar was a pinball
machine. The bar was fairly well lit. The dance floor and stage were
dark. A few tables were scattered here and there against the walls of the
dance area. Most people were standing or dancing. There were so many
people in the place it wasn't feasible for anyone to be sitting, as far as I
could tell.

Stone and I immediately went to the bar to get some beer. As we
walked up to it, I noticed that we were being shadowed by two very

large black men. Each of them was capable of picking Stone or me up and tucking one of us under each arm to carry around for display purposes. It was clear to us that we had better not step out of line or we would be squashed in short order. A casual glance around the place made it clear that we were the only white people in attendance. There weren't going to be any white boys joining us.

Holding our bottles of beer, Stone and I returned to the edge of the dancing crowd. Our shadows moved with us. Stone began dancing by himself, moving to the music. I joined him. Any inappropriate behavior on our part would be bad. We had to keep from making anyone mad. One thing was for sure: we had better not look at, talk to, or do anything else to interact with the women. That could provoke a disaster. We stayed absorbed with the music and our dancing. We shouted and applauded with everyone else at the end of the band's various songs. Sipping our beer, dancing, or just standing in our little space listening to the music seemed to be safe enough.

From time to time someone would move around or through our little space. A few of the men would pause and ask, "Why are you here?"

"Fuck the army," was our constant response.

"Oh, yeah. Right on, my man!" or some similar response would come back with a friendly smile as the communicator drifted away.

Whenever Stone or I would return to the bar or go to the bathroom, our shadows would follow us. Dancing most of the night away works up a sweat. Sweating works up a thirst for beer. We drank a lot of beer. I was feeling it. Somehow we had managed to consume all of our whiskey. The bartender took the empty bottles. He never spoke more than a few words at a time to us. "What do you want?" "Another beer?" and "That's two more dollars," seemed to be the limit of what he was willing to say to us.

Our shadows never spoke. They never got close enough to speak to us. Sometimes I wondered if they weren't keeping people away from us more than they were watching to catch us making trouble. I did not think about them too much. I was just aware that they were always watching.

During one of our many trips to the bar, I asked Stone, "When do you have to be back at the barracks?"

"Any time I want," he said, with a sly grin.

His answer did not make sense to me. My weekend pass was pretty specific. I had to return to post by 6 P.M. Sunday. I pressed the issue. "No, Stone, I meant when is your weekend pass over?"

"I don't have a pass. I just decided to give myself a holiday," he said matter-of-factly.

Oh no! I thought. Stone is AWOL (absent without leave). Gee whiz, how do I get myself into these things? Well, nothing has happened so far. All we have to do is get back on post and get Stone to his company. If he gets in trouble with his sergeants, that's his business, I reasoned. The momentary stress left me.

Late into the evening, while Stone and I were at the bar getting another beer, I told Stone: "I'm ready to go back to the barracks. I'm really tired. I've got to get some sleep."

"I want to play some pinball first," he said, walking over to the machine.

"Okay, but I've got to sit down or lie down. I'm beat," I replied.

Putting a quarter into the machine, Stone said: "Fine. Sit down. I'll be done in a little while."

I looked around. There was no place to sit. The bar had no seats. I could see no chairs, period. People were everywhere. The only place there were no people was under the pinball machine. Without hesitation, I crawled between Stone's feet and sat beneath the machine. He was really into the game. He would pound on the sides of the machine in an attempt to assist the pinball in finding the right slot to roll through or bumper light to ricochet off. I was safe under the pinball machine. There was no risk of being stepped on. This was an excellent idea, I thought, as I stretched out on the floor and put my arm under my head for a pillow. I would just catch a few minutes of sleep. No, I was wrong. It was too noisy. The floor was too hard. No matter how I twisted, turned, or positioned my body, I could not find a comfortable position. Finally, I gave up. I crawled out from under the protective border of Stone's two legs and the four legs of the pinball machine.

"C'mon, Stone, it's time to go," I stated matter-of-factly.

"Okay. Let's go call the cabbie," he said as we walked to the end of the bar near the pay phone. We both emptied our pockets of their change onto the top of the bar. Neither of us could find a dime in the mess of coins. We constantly rearranged the pile but failed in our goal. It was frustrating. We laughed at each other as we carefully moved coins from one side of the pile to the other.

A voice from behind us asked, "You boys ready to go back to the barracks?"

We turned in unison and said "Yes!" with surprise and relief in our voices at the insight displayed by the question.

The speaker was one of our shadows.

"All right then, we'll get you back to the fort," he said, motioning for us follow him.

Stone and I up scooped up our coins and looked at him with expectant faces. He motioned to a couple of other men. They came forward and without a word ushered us to a door behind the bar. I had failed to notice it before. The door opened to display a large white stretch limousine. They opened the rear door for us. As I was ducking my head to get in, the voice said, "Once you're on post, tell the driver where your barracks are." With that, the door closed and we were off.

When we drove through the main gate, the driver turned his head to speak through the little hole created in the glass wall separating us by a sliding glass window. "Where are your barracks?"

I did not know. I had no idea how to get to them. I had never entered the fort this way before. Stone was no help. He could not keep himself from chuckling about something. The driver decided to slowly drive throughout the base, hoping we would spot our barracks. After several extremely slow passes by identical buildings in different locations, I finally made mine out. I could tell it by its location in relation to the barracks on the hill that the National Guard guys were in and the location of the company armory. With my barracks as an anchor point, we drove around looking for Stone's barracks. I had never been to his barracks. I had no clue as to where it was. Neither did Stone. It slowly became obvious to me that Stone had been drinking just a bit too much beer to be of help.

The wondering ended when I suggested that Stone spend the night in my barracks. I remembered that the guy in the top bunk across from mine had also gotten a pass. He was the one staying overnight with relatives, I seemed to remember. Stone could sleep in his bunk. The guy was a decent enough sort. He would not mind someone sleeping in his bunk just one night. In the morning light, Stone would be able to find his barracks without too much difficulty, we reasoned.

I was really tired. We thanked the driver. He drove quietly off into the night. After showing Stone the bunk he was to sleep in, I quickly stripped down to my underwear and crawled into bed.

It was close to noon when I woke up. Stone had already left. I smoothed out the sheets he had slept under and went to lunch. When I got back to the barracks, I started preparing my gear for the next day. We were going camping. The sergeants had said that we were going to be sleeping out under the stars for several days playing war games. We needed to put underwear, socks, poncho, toilet gear, and the like into our packs. Our web belts needed to have a full canteen, entrenching tool, and ammo pouches attached to it. Monday morning we would be issued some C rations, pick up our weapons, and be trucked out to our disembarkation point.

As I was sitting on the side of my bunk working on the web belt, the guy from the bunk across the aisle approached me.

"They said you let somebody sleep in my bunk last night," he said with tension in his voice.

"Yes, he was lost; couldn't find his barracks. I didn't know what else to do. I was hoping you wouldn't mind," I said with concern in my voice. He did not appear to be at all happy.

"Well," he began with a sigh, "he crawled between the sheets with his dirty shoes on. My sheets are filthy."

"Oh, that's bad. That's really bad." I was mortified to hear that. "I'm truly sorry. You can use my sheets. They're not that dirty; we can trade," I said, meaning every word.

Damn that Stone. He knew better than that. He must have drunk more than I had figured to do that. We would not be getting clean sheets until we came back from the field. Trading sheets with the guy was the least I could do. I was really sorry.

"Naw, that's okay," he said, standing over me. "I just didn't know if you knew what was up."

"I'm so sorry this happened to you. It's a long story, but the guy badly needed a bunk to sleep in. He—"

"It's okay. I just wanted you to know," he said as he walked briskly away from me.

CHAPTER 12

In the Field

Wherever we were, it had taken us a long time to get there. The trucks took us deep into the woods over mud roads that lacked the benefit of regular traffic. The three-hour truck ride was jolting. We complained and made jokes. For all we knew, the army would make us march out of here rather than provide us with transportation. We were not going to knock the transportation all that much. The thing about the army is that you never know what the next day will bring. No one tells you the long-range plan. You just go from day to day, doing exactly what the sergeants tell you to do.

After the truck ride, we marched with full packs and gear. The load was heavy. Before the first hour of marching had passed, we were all wet with sweat. It was a cold day, but the exertion was causing men to take off their field jackets and roll up their shirtsleeves. By the end of the third hour, the marching was getting old. Someone said he had overheard a sergeant saying that we would reach our base camp area by sunset. I hoped that was the truth. None of us were physically worn down. We were just hot, uncomfortable, and bored with walking deeper and deeper into the woods. Anyone who got separated from the company would never find his way back to the barracks. We were totally isolated and dependent on our leaders. You just trusted that they knew what was going on.

At the top of a large, mostly tree-barren hill, the column halted. This was base camp. We were immediately ordered to stake our claim to sleeping areas by squads. We would be sleeping under the stars. No tents had been issued to us. If it rained, I guess we would simply have gotten wet. If the army didn't want us to get wet, it would order that there be no rain. Life has a way of mellowing out when an organization as powerful as the U.S. Army is handling things. We knew this to be true—except when the army messed up. No one told you about it. Your personal misery factor was the only barometer you could rely upon for knowing when the army messed up.

We unrolled our sleeping bags. Since the base camp was on the top of the hill, it was not possible to have us put our sleeping bags in neat rows. We had to find whatever semblance of level ground we could to sleep on. This task tended to spread us out in a rather haphazard manner. The sergeants said that since the ground was so hard we would not have to dig foxholes to sleep in. If this had been a real combat mission, however, we would have had to dig the foxholes. Thank heaven for simulated warfare. It was obvious that the hill had been used before. There were half-dug foxholes all around the top third of the hill. They had been there for a while because the weather had rounded out their sharp edges. They provided the little bit of level ground that most of us found for sleeping.

As darkness set in, we got out our C-rations. No fires were allowed. We ate the food cold. Many of the guys would not eat all of the foods in a C-ration carton. Some would trade a can of ham and lima beans for a can of reconstituted scrambled eggs or some other item. A lot of guys simply did not want to eat all of their rations and offered what was left to anyone who wanted it. I ate everything. It did not matter if I liked it or not. Little tins of peanut butter and jelly were the items guys gave up most often. I had never liked either of them in civilian life. Here, I ate every one given away.

In the woods, anything could happen. You did not know when the army would remember to resupply you with food. It was easy to get separated and lost from the others. I ate to have calories just in case I needed the extra energy. You could not afford to become weak out there. Physical weakness meant getting hurt or making mental errors, which meant wasted energy. Staying as healthy as possible was important. I surely did not want to go through weeks of marching with another smashed toenail or some other hurting body part. No one would feel sorry for me or give me the day off. You kept going—no matter what.

Fortunately, we were going into a cloudless night with a quarter moon overhead. You could almost see your shadow in the soft light reflecting off the moon. People were moving back and forth. *Clanks* and *clangs* were constant as tin cans, metal canteens, and steel pots bumped into rifles, each other, ammo magazines, and any number of other metal objects. The sergeants called the squad leaders up to the top of the hill to talk to them. We stayed by our sleeping bags and backpacks, smoking and talking. Muffled laughter could be heard throughout the company area. Almost everyone was loose enough. We were making it through training okay.

"The sergeants say that we are tactical now," Bill, our acting squad leader, told us upon returning from the hilltop.

One of our squad guys asked, "What's tactical?"

"We are in the war games now," Bill whispered. "There's another company or two out looking for us. They are the enemy. We have to set up a perimeter guard to defend the hill. If they find us, they could attack, charge up the hill, and mess up our gear and stuff like that. We have to get ready to repel them if they attack tonight."

"So what do we do?" responded another squad member.

"I don't know. The acting squad leaders are supposed to meet back on top of the hill in about fifteen minutes. We'll develop a plan then. When I know something, I'll let you know, okay?"

Of course it was okay. We had no choice in the matter. I began looking around. There were a few scattered clumps of trees here and there down the hillside. Way off toward the bottom of the hill was a dirt road. It looked as if it were about five or six football fields away from where we sat. On the other side of the road was a wall of black. It was nothing but trees as far back into the darkness as you would want to go. Daggone, I thought, there could be an army of men in there right now just waiting for the order to charge and we'd never know it. This was a really exposed spot to be in.

Here they would come out running as hard as they could, screaming at the top of their lungs. Their M14s would be spitting fire. Oh, yeah, they would be firing blanks; but it would not make any difference. We would be in chaos. People would be falling all over the place. They would step into the half-dug foxholes and fall. They would trip over sleeping bags and step on guys trying to fire their rifles from the prone position. We were not prepared to be attacked. Then in the morning, you would have to spend all kinds of time finding your personal gear. It would be strewn all over the place. That was assuming they didn't take you as a prisoner somewhere.

I had heard that they took guys prisoner during these simulated war games. They would tie you up and drag you through the bushes. After they roughed you up some, they would torture you. I doubted that they would draw blood. The army would not allow that. They would just pull you up by the ropes on your arms and put you under a lot of muscle strain. Stuff like that was what you could expect if you were captured.

In short, the rumor mill felt that it would not be good to be caught. I had no intention of being caught. My mind was pretty set on that point.

The squad leaders went back to the top of the hill. You could see people moving around on the hilltop. There, dark figures seemed to move with purpose. Arms would point off in a direction. Three or four figures would separate themselves from the clump of people and walk off to wherever the arm had pointed. Someone came from the hilltop to our squad.

"You four men," he said, pointing to the four beside me, "come on with me. Bring your rifles."

They got up and followed him over the hilltop and down the other side. We all recognized each other when we got up close. If you did not know the guy's name, you still knew he belonged to the company. You had seen him in the barracks or eaten at a table with him or stood in line with him to get ammo. Things like that brought us together so that we all pretty well knew one another.

Someone else came down to our group and took two more of us off to be on perimeter guard duty. There were just a couple of us left. I decided to go up to the top of the hill and get a better look at what was going on.

At the top, people were moving here and there. You could see the beginning of a circle of men squatting down about a third of the way down the hillside. They must be the perimeter guard. One guy I liked fairly well was giving directions to a couple of other men. I approached him.

"What's up?" I asked.

"Ah, we're trying to make sense out of this," he replied with a degree of frustration in his voice. "They appointed a bunch of us as acting platoon sergeants and told us to set up a defense of the hill for tonight. Nobody can agree on what to do. They finally set up a perimeter defensive line around the hilltop."

"Well, nobody's told me what to do yet. It's a little boring. Tell me what to do to help," I told him.

"Mainly, they're just placing bodies out there to fight if we get attacked." He paused as a group approached us in the darkness.

"Where are you assigned?" a voice from the group asked me as it got close enough to see my face.

"I haven't been yet," I replied.

"Here's one you can use," the voice said to a shadowy figure beside him.

"Okay, we're going down the hill. Come on," the shadowy figure said, motioning me to join the group.

We walked down the side of the hill. He placed men at different spots and told them to stay there until they were relieved.

In a short while, it was just the shadowy man and me walking down the hill. We approached a clump of trees. It was a scraggly stand of three or four trees with a bush or two in the center of the clump.

"You stay here. You're the forward observer," he said.

Looking down at the dirt road that separated the dark woods from my exposed position and seeing that I was just twenty yards or so away from it did not make me comfortable. "What do I do if they're in the woods?" I asked with genuine concern.

"If you hear them in there, just let us know back at the top of the hill. We'll send someone down to relieve you. The sign is 'red' and the countersign is 'wolf.' If someone approaches your position, call out, 'Red.' If he doesn't say, 'Wolf,' he's not one of ours," he said as he withdrew into the darkness toward the top of the hill.

This was not good. I was in a bad position. There was not even a good place to hide in this clump of trees. Open ground was all around me. There was no ground cover between me and the top of the hill. It was just an easy walk through the short grass all the way to the top. The hilltop was so far away that you could not see movement at its crest. I knew there were people moving all over the top of it. They were so far away that they would never hear me yell if the enemy started coming out of the woods. Any fool on the enemy side could guess that this clump of trees had an observer in it. Their whole army could charge out of the woods, cross the road, and cover the twenty yards to my pitiful trees in a flash. If I were to escape them, I would have to hear them moving the brush as they got close to the tree line for their charge. Listening was my only defense.

I sat with the bushes to my back. I faced the road. At least the enemy could not see my profile. I would be partially camouflaged in the dark. Loading my M14 with a magazine of blank shells, I was as ready as I could be. The point was not to move. In the shadows, the enemy could overlook my form from a distance. Only movement would cause his eyes to focus on my position.

If I were in charge of the enemy company, I surely would send out patrols. One of the patrols would be to this clump of trees. I would have them sneak up without making a sound. They would jump the sentry with such quickness and suddenness that he would be knocked out and dragged back as a prisoner. Since this was only a war game, we would not physically knock him out. We would just pin him down and tell him we would kick the shit out of him if he yelled out. Then we would take him back into the trees as a prisoner and interrogate him. Learn about how well the hill is defended. I wished I were the enemy. My plan for them was a lot better than the plan my guys had for me.

It struck me. The thought struck me that if this were a real war, I would get killed here. This was not a defensible position. By the time I knew an attack was about to come out of the woods, it would be too late. I would be shot in the back trying to run up the hill in this open ground. The only warning the guys on the hilltop would get of the attack would be the sound of gunfire killing me. This was not good. I was nervous. There was no concern on my part that I would fall asleep on guard duty.

The night wore on. It was too dark to see my wristwatch. Sounds from the top of the hill decreased to just about nothing. I strained to hear something move in the tree line directly in front of me. I could hear sounds, but they were tiny. They were not the movement of ten, fifty, or two hundred men. Maybe it was just one man sneaking up on me. He would be slowly moving up the hill. Just one leg would move up as he pressed his chest and belly to the ground. He would hold it there, motionless, for thirty or forty seconds and then push off with it and be two feet closer to me. He would wait a little longer and then he would move a foot or two closer in the night. The darkness would cause his form to be just another shadow, a darker spot in the landscape of dark and darker. I would never know the difference unless I actually saw a movement. No shade of darkness was too obscure to be scrutinized by my stare. I was not going to be captured. I was going to get the hell out of there as fast as I could when they came for me.

There was a noise. It was definitely a sound. Someone was walking. He was coming from the left, paralleling the road. Yes, it was real. I could hear muffled voices. It was a patrol. They were coming to capture me. The voices moved closer. I heard muffled laughter. What the hell? They were pretty confident to be approaching me laughing on the way. How could I deal with this many? They could jump me. It would be easy enough to do. One could keep my attention while two of them moved to both sides; then they would all rush me.

"Halt!" I said in a loud voice, lowering the barrel of my M14 so that it pointed in their direction.

They kept talking in their muffled voices as they moved closer to me.

"Red," hissed from my lips.

No countersign came from them. They just kept walking toward me. I could see their forms. There were four of them. Two of them kept muttering as they slowly walked toward me.

Stepping from the bush with my M14 leveled at their faces, I said with the force of my fear and anger for being in this situation: "Damn you to hell! Stop right there. I've rigged this thing to full automatic. These blanks will shoot paper wads into your eye sockets and blow out your brains. You stop, or I'll blow you away. You know these paper wads can kill you if they hit you just right. I've got you."

They froze. Nobody moved. No one talked. What was I going to do now? They could rush on a moment's notice, and I could not stop them.

"Drop to the ground, facedown! Move fast, you bastards! I'm pissed now. Drop!" I commanded. The bastards were not going to drag this dude off without knowing they had been in a real fight.

Almost instantly they hit the ground. The guy in the lead began going down and the others followed. He was a little chunky. That's strange, I thought. How did a chunky guy make it this far into infantry training and stay chunky? This is still a bad situation, was the message in my mind. They have to be disarmed. I had not seen their M14s. Their weapons had to be collected. They could swing the muzzles up and—*POW!*—they had me right where I thought I had them.

"Spread your legs and arms, spread eagle. *Now, you assholes!*" I demanded with the force of a desperate man about to be sucked into a whirlpool of mud and filth.

Immediately they complied. As I walked forward to pick up their weapons, I realized that I would have to walk between their legs and arms. One of them could scissors his legs around mine while rolling over. That would bring me down in a flash. I needed to be quick and careful. No rifles. They have no rifles. Something is very wrong here. Maybe they are a special unit and only carry side arms, is the thought that springs into my mind as I lean over and pat down the sides of the chunky one. No, No, No! This can't be! He's got a major's gold leaf on his shoulders—or is it the silver leaf of a lieutenant colonel? I cannot make out the color in the weak moonlight. It does not make any difference. This guy is a big-time officer. I am patting down a major or a lieutenant colonel. No side arms on him. They must be here inspecting the troops. Well, he is going along with it. I'm only doing my job. The man next to him is a captain. The other two are lieutenants. If the major had decided not to go along with it, the other three would be on my case. No one has a weapon. As these thoughts raced through my mind, I patted them all down just to be sure. What am I to do now? I've got to carry this out as if I don't know who they are.

"Okay, boys," I said in a low but firm voice. "Now we are going to low crawl up to the top of the hill. No talking between you. I've come this far without your tricking me. I'm not about to let you hatch any plans now. Remember, this rifle is on full automatic. It'll sting the hell out of your butts. Let's go, start crawling."

They did; they started low crawling up the hill. It was a long way. They had to have been depressed. I was behind them. After ten yards I began to slow down. They could not tell that I was not keeping up. The distance grew between us. After twenty yards I stopped. They just kept steadily crawling up the hill without speaking a word. Finally, I lost sight of them in the darkness. I would have loved being at the top of the hill when all of that brass came into view, low crawling up the side of it. When they discovered that nobody was behind them would have been a fun moment, too.

Good sense told me to stay away. If they got mad, it would not be hard to find me. Mine was the only clump of trees around. I would have a hard time convincing anyone that the incident had happened at another stand of trees.

More time passed. I began to worry. With your body trapped in a single spot and your mind unoccupied by activity, the mind tends to work on your worrisome thoughts. It invents a host of options that are predominantly dire in nature. Lost in these thoughts, time passes unnoticed.

Contemplating a life in military prison, I found myself overreacting to the crunch of footsteps rapidly approaching from the rear. Someone was coming directly toward my sanctuary from the hilltop.

I turned from facing the road to confront my assailant. "Halt!" I shouted into the darkness. "Red."

"Wolf," came the reply as the figure materialized. It was one of our guys. "I've been sent to relieve you. You can go up and get some sleep."

Relief flooded over me as I lowered my rifle. "Did you see any officers come by on your way down?" I asked as casually as I could under the circumstances.

"Naw," he replied. "But that don't mean nothin'. I've been dozing in the sack the last couple of hours."

Up at the top of the hill, I decided to look for someone I knew to ask about the officers. I soon found my friend, the acting platoon sergeant.

"Did any officers come up here a couple of hours ago?" I asked.

"Why yes, a major and some others. They were all sweated up and dirty looking. They told one of the sergeants that we had good sentries. Why, did they talk to you?" he asked innocently enough.

"No, no one talked to me," I said, thinking that, in a way, I was telling the truth. They never said a word to me. I thought it best not to mention the encounter. I could still be in big trouble. Then again, I might just get by with this if I kept quiet.

The morning brought more marching. We spent about two hours getting to where we were going. It was a training site with bleachers, posters, a chalkboard, and pointers. We started to learn about explosives. Setting up claymore mines was the first lesson. The word was out that some sergeant had accidentally turned the convex side of the mine toward the bleachers holding the trainees. When he pushed the detonator button, it wiped out about a third of the guys in the first three or four rows. Rumor said that it had happened just a couple of weeks ago. Who knew for sure if the rumor was true? In any event, we never got to see a live demonstration of how the thing looked when it exploded.

During one of the smoke breaks, I was walking with a couple of buddies to the honey bun truck when a black sergeant hollered out, "You, Soldier, come over here."

I pointed at myself and asked, "Me?"

"Yes, you. Your friends can go on," he said with an unreadable expression on his face.

Approaching where he sat on a log, I asked, "What do you want, Sergeant?"

"You were one of the two white guys at Grundy's last Saturday night, weren't you," he said in a nice enough tone.

"Yes, that's right," I replied, not knowing if I was in trouble or not.

"Sit down here." He motioned to a place on the log beside him. "That took a lot of courage for you to be there."

"Naw, we were just having fun," I said, grinning.

"You saw how everyone treated you with respect. No one hassled you, did they?"

"You're right. Everyone just let us enjoy ourselves. It was a nice break," I said with respect.

"Well, that wouldn't happen to a black man going into a white place like that. They really treat blacks bad here. You saw that we don't treat whites like that. We can get along. People don't have to be so mean. The whites have their country clubs and their private get-togethers, but there's nothing for us blacks. Everything here is for whites only. We can't get anything they have," he related with great sincerity.

"I'm sorry they're making it so bad for you here. It's just not fair. How do you deal with it?" I asked.

"We have no choice. We just stay away. Mainly, we and our wives stay on post or go to Grundy's. That's about the only place we have where we won't be harassed." He said with great sadness in his face. "You're alright. We all know who you are. If you need any help, let us know. We'll back you up," he said as he stood up and held out his hand to me. We shook hands and nodded as we looked into each other's eyes. Then I went to the honey bun truck. I never told anyone about the conversation. Nobody knew about my adventure at Grundy's. I would tell Stone if I ever saw him again. So far, our paths had not crossed.

After a full day of training, we marched for the mandatory two-hour trip back to base camp. After chow they marched us off again. It was dark when we reached a dirt road with trucks waiting for us. We drove through the backwoods for another hour or so before they stopped. It was another training site. Bleachers, posters, chalkboards, and pointers greeted us again. This time we were to experience live fire at night. There must have been several other companies present. Trainees were there when we arrived, and more trucks kept arriving to off-load additional troops.

The way they explained the exercise made the whole process simple enough. You lay in a prone position with your head centered over the top of your weapon. Then you pointed the weapon in the direction your head was looking and fired. It was too dark to aim any better than that. Standard white paper targets were about a hundred yards down range. You could just make them out in the darkness. We loaded up a magazine with live ammo. Every seventh round was a tracer round.

There were more sergeants there than I had encountered in one place before. I think they were afraid that we would end up shooting each other. We lined up about twenty men deep behind each firing pit. The order to commence firing was given to the fifty or so men on the firing line. The flashes of muzzles and the arcing lines of tracer rounds were just plain pretty. The tracer rounds' glow seemed to leave a continuous red/white streak from their point of origin until they hit something or skipped off the ground in unpredictable patterns in their ricocheting attempts to stay alive.

My turn came. The sergeant lay on the ground right beside me.

"Stay calm, keep your weapon pointed down range, Son," came his soothing voice into my ear. "When you squeeze off the first round, hold off firing the next for just a second or two to get reoriented."

What was he talking about? There was nothing to get reoriented *to*. I had fired the weapon so many times. I was even a darn good shot. Well, you had to tolerate being treated like a fool often enough in the army. This guy was not going to get my goat.

"Ready on the left?" came the cry from somewhere behind me.

"Ready on the left!" came the answer from a voice out of the darkness.

"Ready on the right?" the same questioning voice blared.

"Ready on the right!" a responding voice shouted.

"All ready on the firing line. Commence firing," was the order.

CRACK! my weapon spat. The bright fire blast of the burning gunpowder from the rifle's muzzle blinded me. Everything was stone black. I simply could not see. If a herd of elephants wearing sneakers had charged my position, I would have been trampled to death before I knew what had stepped on me. Geez, the enemy would have me. I could not see anything. I could not hear anything because the blast of the rifle with my head hanging over the top of the firing chamber had my ears ringing.

In the confusion of my mind a sound started coming through. At first I did not know what it was. "Calm . . . refocus . . . When you're . . . Fire again," came the sergeant's voice.

I squeezed the trigger. Another blinding flash. The shadowy movements I had begun to notice disappeared into solid blackness. Night blindness in a real firefight would be a very bad thing. Before I could fully understand what I was doing, my seventh round, the tracer, arced from my barrel. I could see it flying across the field toward the target that should be somewhere near the spot where the disappearing round landed. That was satisfying. At least I knew where I had shot that one. The next thought was depressing. Someone sitting out in a tree line looking my way could follow that tracer streak right back to my head perched above the rifle's stock. Night fighting could be very risky business. Then my magazine was empty. They retrieved the paper target. I had hit it four times. It was a miracle.

We waited almost forever while every soldier they had trucked out to the range went through his night-fire exercise. When it was over, we clambered back onto the trucks. The one-hour-plus ride and the hour-or-so march back to base camp left few hours for sleeping before dawn.

Quickly, the overwhelming feeling of being in the field was fatigue. Whenever we took a ten-minute break, whether it was on a march or during training, we would close our eyes to catch a few Zs. Guys began falling asleep in the bleachers during classes and falling on the men in front of them. I was always tired, but I was not about to fall asleep. It was hard to understand how someone could "fall" asleep. You had to make the decision to sleep and then you slept. That was how it was for me. I had never "fallen" asleep in my memory. It just was not in my behavior pattern.

At last we were in the trucks going back to the barracks and a three-day pass. I was going to be with Anna in Atlanta. The ride from Fort McClellan to Atlanta seemed to take forever. The guys let me off at the airport. This time Anna recognized me right off. She had us booked into a first-class hotel in the heart of downtown Atlanta on Peachtree Street. It was so good to be with her. We did not leave our room very much. We went out to eat, talked some, and I slept a lot. That consumed my three-day pass. Once again our parting was hard. Her plane left before I was to rendezvous with the guys at our predetermined time and pickup point. We were all on time. Good, tight, dependable, secure, comforting military time.

CHAPTER 13

The Ambush

The first thing Monday morning we were trucked out into the field with full gear. It was camping time again, army camping time, that is. This time the sergeants were not concerned about base camp attacks. There did not seem to be much order to where we unrolled our sleeping bags. The company just had this area in the woods we occupied. Some of it was clear of trees and brush, and some of it was not. Very little of the ground was level. A dirt road ran through the center of our area. It ran between two low-lying hills that were the center of where we had our sleeping gear spread out. My squad ended up on the side of the left-hand hill near the top. We could not see the road from there, but we could hear the occasional vehicle drive by. It seemed that everywhere you looked were sleeping bags and army gear. The area had been used before. There were half-dug foxholes with edges weathered away, just as in the previous week's base camp area. By the time we had all settled in, it was getting dark.

Most of the sergeants walking around were new to our group. They were training cadre. That is, they were not affiliated with the noncoms that gave our company orders back in the barracks area. The sergeants we knew stayed in the civilized area our trucks left. As far as I could tell, the woods sergeants were employed by the army to meet us in the woods and provide us with a new experience. But then, what did I know? The army did not consult with me about much of anything. They did not give you a future. You only knew about the present moment or the next most immediate assignment they were presenting you. Of course, we were constantly reminded of the long-range future by the instructing sergeant's repeated phrase, "This will save your life in Vietnam."

Just as my squad was policing its empty C-ration tins, a staff sergeant came up to us. "Who's acting squad leader?" he inquired.

"We don't have one appointed," said someone close to where he was standing.

"Okay, *you're* acting squad leader," he told the respondent. "At nineteen hundred hours have the squad ready to spend the evening in the field. Make sure everyone has full canteens and gas masks. They can leave the rest of their gear here. Have them stack their rifles over there," he said, pointing to a somewhat level piece of ground we had claimed as our sleeping area not far from the partially dug foxholes.

"What will we be doing tonight, Sergeant?" another guy asked.

"We're going out orienteering through the woods tonight, men," he said. "Now get yourselves ready. You have little more than forty minutes before we move out."

More compass work in the dark. Wouldn't you know they'd have us take our gas masks along? We had heard stories about the Chemical Warfare School people gassing us infantry trainees. No doubt about it, they got a lot of laughs out of making our lives miserable.

I put on a fresh pair of socks. Having dry feet was a comfort. My old socks had gotten sweated up when we marched from the trucks to the campsite. They had a water trailer some jeep deposited near the road. We filled up our canteens. While we waited in the growing darkness, we cleaned our rifles, smoked, and joked. During such moments you always got to know the guys around you. Many of them were college graduates who had chosen not to go to OCS. I had discovered in this way a guy in the company with a master's degree in clinical psychology. He said that he just wanted to serve his two years and get out. He was going to go to a new doctoral program in clinical psychology that was opening up at the University of North Carolina in Greensboro when he got out. His major professor, who was going to be the head of the program, had assured him that he would be admitted into the program as soon as he got out of the army. The soldier wanted to get on with his civilian life just as soon as he could, even if it meant going to Vietnam. He said an army doctor had talked to him about a direct commission in the Medical Service Corps. Since it meant more time in the army, he turned it down. His story confirmed to me that I was eligible for the same direct commission. I asked the guy who the doctor was. He said the physician was back at Fort Campbell, Kentucky, where he had gone for basic training. I was determined to talk to someone in the Medical Service Corps as soon as we got out of the woods.

"Okay, men," the sergeant said. "We're going to travel about ten miles by compass tonight."

We groaned in unison.

He laughed and said: "It's not that bad. We're not going to be sighting off each other. We're going to use large landmarks that stand out in the darkness."

He was a pleasant teacher. We learned to sight our compasses from one hilltop to a key landmark on the next hilltop. He showed us how to keep checking ourselves by having a reference point behind us. We could keep checking that we were on the right compass heading by keeping both landmarks perfectly aligned. As we trekked through the woods, he told us about his tour of duty in Vietnam the year before. We all stayed bunched up close to him so we could hear what it was like. Where he was stationed, there had not been much shooting. Mainly they had helped train villagers in military skills, such as how to use firearms and how to follow a compass. It hadn't been much different than what he was doing with us, he said. He had been fired upon. It was hard to see who was shooting at you. That was why we needed to pay attention during the training on how to spot camouflaged soldiers. The sergeant was quite cordial to us. We appreciated him. When the acting squad leader decided to walk in a straight line down a really steep slope, the sergeant pointed out a better way. He was not going to let us foolishly waste our energy. We got back to our sleeping bags at about 3:30 in the morning. I did not mind the lack of sleep so much this time. I had learned a lot that would help me.

Walking for long periods of time just did not bother us all that much. We were in good shape. Our problem was the lack of sleep. The day always started at sunrise and was filled with training activities. At night they would give us more tasks to accomplish. We rarely got more than three or four hours' sleep a night in the field.

Setting up ambushes and getting ambushed became a major focus of our training. We would be moving through the woods as a squad or a platoon looking for the enemy when we got ambushed. Either we or the enemy wore black armbands. Sometimes the enemy was a squad or platoon from our company; at other times they came from a different company. We were never issued any tear gas to toss, but somebody was because several times the cry of "Gas!" would ring out. We were so conditioned to avoid breathing in the burning tear gas that both the good guys and the bad guys would stop whatever it was they were doing to put on their masks. Getting your gas mask on was critical to your immediate well-being. All firing stopped while people put on their gas masks. Then the everyday tasks of shooting at each other, charging positions, getting the hell out of there, and the like resumed.

Moving through the woods is far more difficult than moving down the dirt road. On a dirt road you travel in two columns, one on each side of the road. You do not want to get bunched up. People who get too close to one another are usually the first ones to get shot. It is a lot easier to shoot into a group of four or five men all clumped together than it is to shoot at one guy at a time. The enemy will usually take the easy kill first. That was what they told us, so it is highly probable that their sergeants taught them the same lessons. Bunch up and get killed seemed to be the sergeants' motto on the trail. The problem was that everyone liked to talk when you were out in the field. It helped to pass the time. Since you did not want to talk in a loud voice and let the enemy know you were there, the tendency to bunch up was strong. The worst time to bunch up was when the column stopped.

Everyone wanted to smoke and joke when we stopped our march. The C rations kept us amply supplied with cigarettes. We never ran out. Someone always had extra ones to lend you if your personal supply ran low. I stayed with my pipe, so my supply of cigarettes went into the loaning pool. Whenever we stopped, we tended to bunch up. The sergeants would spread us out when they were with us, but usually they were not with us. They would tell us to go from one point to another or to set up an ambush at such and such a spot. Then, when the enemy came by, we were to open up on them with our blank-adapter-equipped weapons. They would hunker down and fire back at us. Someone would tell them to move out after we all were about out of ammunition. We would go back to wherever we were supposed to go and get another assignment.

The hardest part about marching in two columns down the road was keeping flank security. Two or three guys would be assigned to walk in the woods along both sides of the road, just about out of sight from the guys on the road. Theoretically, the guys on flank security would see the enemy hiding in the woods waiting to ambush us. Their warning would enable us to escape the killing zone. That was what they called the spot where all of the ambushers' weapons were pointing. When we entered the killing zone, they would open fire and kill us all. Since we were just playing war, no one got killed. All the same, you did not even like to *pretend* that you had been caught in a killing zone. If it happened in play, it could happen for real later on. The flankers had to walk faster and harder than the guys on the road. They did not have a nice flat surface to walk on. The trees, wait-a-minute vines, and underbrush kept slowing the flankers down. If they did not walk fast enough, they fell behind, which negated their purpose for being out there. It did not take much time for the flankers to lose sight of the column and get lost. Getting lost

On patrol with an M14 rifle.

On an ambush with a rifleman, M60 machine gunner, and ammo bearer.

Flank security.

out in woods that you knew nothing about or losing the way back to base camp was to be avoided at all costs. Our group never lost anyone. We were lucky. Stories circulated about guys being lost for several hours. Fortunately, there were so many trainees marching and ambushing each other that you would eventually find some group of guys to join. More often than not they would be from a different company. You could spend many sleepless hours finding someone who knew where your group and sleeping gear were.

For additional security against being ambushed, the column would have a point man and someone trailing behind the rear. The point man always walked well ahead of the column, looking for signs of the enemy, hoping to see them before the main column arrived. He could run back and halt the column. Then whoever was in charge could decide on whether to surprise the ambushers by charging them or going around them without a fight. The rear guard stayed back from the main column, protecting it from any enemy trying to sneak up on it from behind.

Keeping up with the column was not as hard for the flankers when we were all moving through the woods without the aid of a road bed. They could keep up with the column more easily because everyone was dodging trees and being held back by wait-a-minute vines. Unfortunately, the flankers also had a much easier time getting lost from the main column. They did not have the roadbed as a constant reference point. As a result, the flankers usually stayed fairly close to the main column. That reduced security, but it minimized the chances of getting lost.

The point man was the key position for moving the column through the woods. If he could not find the path of least resistance through the tangle of underbrush, everybody suffered. I seemed to have a knack for finding the easiest route through the woods. More often than not, I was the point man. Sometimes we would get someone who definitely did *not* have the knack. After a while, the guys would ask me to take on the task as a favor. I liked the role. I imagined that this must have been the way Daniel Boone moved through the backwoods of Kentucky.

I liked being in the woods. The downside was being so tired. Guys kept falling asleep whenever we stopped to take a break. You always had to check your buddy when the order was given to move out. He could be sitting on a log sound asleep. If someone did not wake him up, he would sleep there for several hours. He would never find the column when he woke up. I just could not understand how they fell asleep like that, but it was a fact. They did.

Very quickly, flank security became a thing of the past. We were always in a hurry to get somewhere. The flankers slowed everything down. We traded security for speed.

Being ambushed or ambushing a column was pretty routine. The fun was in the surprise. If you were the ambusher, finding a good spot in which to conceal yourself while still having a good field of fire was the key to a successful operation. The next important point was making sure that everyone had the discipline to hold their fire until the target was between your first and last riflemen so that you had the enemy clearly trapped. No one could escape the killing zone and double back on you from the front or charge up the side of your firing line from the rear. A real problem for the acting leader of the ambushers was determining if the enemy patrol was too big to ambush. A squad of seven or eight men springing an ambush on a column of five thousand men probably would not fare very well. It was hard to know how many men were in an approaching column unless you had a clear view of the whole area. Since the ambushers were hidden in the trees, their overall field of vision was limited. It was always risky business.

A big disappointment was to lie out all night alongside some trail waiting for the enemy to wander into your trap, only to have him never arrive. This meant that you did not get to go back to your nice, warm sleeping bag. In fact, you did not get any sleep at all unless you accidentally fell asleep. Falling asleep on ambush duty is dangerous for obvious combat reasons. The war-game reason we did not want to fall asleep was more basic: You would disappoint your buddies. If the ambush were sprung, you wanted all the rifle-fire noise you could make. This gives the enemy the impression that there are a whole lot more of you than is actually the case. A lot of noise from your rifles and machine guns tends to discourage adventurism. If enemy soldiers think they can overpower your position by charging through the woods to capture you, they will do it. Convincing them that they would have been killed in an ambush if it had been a real firefight was always difficult. The fact that they were alive with two or three of them holding you to the ground was proof to them that they had survived. You were a prisoner. Surprise and firepower were important elements for a successful ambush during training.

Being ambushed is not all that much fun. First come the shock of surprise and the sinking feeling that in the real world you would be dead right about then. As soon as the enemy opens up on you, you duck for cover while trying to fire back. There is a period of total confusion. Usually your first move to take cover proves to be inadequate. The little ditch you are in is not deep enough because your butt is sticking out, the

little sapling you are trying to hide behind is only wide enough to protect your nose, or you are hiding directly in front of a guy who is firing
his rifle at you. While both sides are hunkered down firing at each other,
almost everyone is trying to figure out how to get out of this mess.

The best feeling occurs when you discover that you are about to be
ambushed and you ambush the ambushers. At least that was what the
sergeants told us. Our group never got that lucky. In fact, I never heard
of any patrol pulling that off. We just took the sergeants' word for it and
imagined it to be true.

Friday night came. We were all dead tired. It was a relief to march in column down a dirt road because you could close your eyes for a few steps.
Those blind steps eased the tiredness. The word was that trucks would
take us back to the barracks in the morning. We would then get Saturday afternoon and Sunday off. Everyone I knew planned to sleep the
whole time. The next week would be our last week of AIT. There would
be no more camping trips, or so the rumor mill said. We would have
daytime training exercises but be in the barracks every night. Then it
was back to Kentucky for me. I had two and a half weeks of leave over
the Christmas holidays to be with Anna. Then I would go to Fort Benning, Georgia, for six months of Infantry Officer Candidate School.

That Friday night, a full moon was just starting to wane. You could
see fairly well in the moonlight. We had been fortunate during our two
weeks in the field. There were no clouds of consequence to blot out the
moon. It had produced a lot of light. The light created deep shadows. If
you were on patrol, the landscape was easy to move through. A downside was the dark shadows. The shadows from the trees made it easy to
conceal yourself if you were an ambusher. Troops could get fairly close
to the trail or roadbed without being seen as long as they stayed motionless. Ambushers had the advantage. Of course, the ambushed were
less likely to run blindly into trees as they sought cover.

None of us had a bath throughout the week. Our lack of sleep, foul-
smelling bodies, and filthy clothing combined into one deep weariness.
Walking up the hill to our bedrolls was a relief. It was almost midnight.
This was the earliest by far that we had gotten back to our sleeping bags.
The other nights it was usually three or 3:30 in the morning. We were
beat but happy. Our platoon had been out on one more patrol. We had
started about two in the afternoon, 1400 hours military time. We had
eaten supper on the trail. No one had ambushed us. We had found no
bushwhackers.

Earlier that night, some cadre sergeants had pulled out our squad to march down a trail that circled back to our base camp. We suspected that we were being set up as someone's lost patrol to walk into a pre-determined ambush spot. Tom had been designated the acting squad leader for the patrol. He was cautious by nature. We moved slowly down the trail hoping to catch the ambushers before they caught us. I was a little frustrated with Tom. He was too cautious in my opinion. Finally, he agreed that we did not need flankers. That made our time on the dirt road pass faster. Faster is a relative term. We were faster than we had been, but we were pretty slow compared to a walk in the park, talking to your girl. It had been a long, tedious walk, but it was over. No one had ambushed us. If there was a prepared ambush, the poor guys had set it up at the wrong spot or at the wrong time. They would probably have to stay up all night waiting for the lost patrol to show up while we were catching z's in our nice, warm sacks.

We sank down beside our makeshift foxholes with tired relief. I propped my back against a tree with my legs stretched straight out in front of me. It felt so good. None of us felt much like talking. We just sat there feeling relieved that it was over. All we had to do now was crawl into the sack, sleep, eat, march to the trucks, and ride back to the barracks. Life was good. Apparently we were the first ones in our company to get back. The hill was quiet.

Our moment of bliss was disturbed by the sound of a pair of combat boots coming up the hill toward our position. In the moonlight we finally made out one of the cadre sergeants who had been with us on and off during the week.

"You men," he said as he approached, "there's one more ambush for you to pull off."

We groaned in unison. Tom, still playing the role of acting squad leader, used his rifle as a stick to help his tired bones line up into a standing position.

"Sergeant, we are through for the night," he stated matter-of-factly.

The sergeant laughed. "It's still a little early to call it a night. *After* you pull off the ambush, you can come back and sleep."

By this time we were all getting up. We surrounded the sergeant to get our orders without much comment.

"The ambush site isn't far down the road," he explained, pointing to the left. "About a mile down the road there's a fork. A platoon will be coming down it in thirty or forty minutes. They'll take the right fork. You set up your ambush along that fork. When they come by you, open up on them. After you spring the ambush you can come back up here and go to bed. The whole thing will be over in an hour, two at the most."

Tom quietly asked, "Isn't a platoon a little big for a squad to take on?"

"Go over to that group of sergeants standing over there," the sergeant said, motioning to five or six sergeants semihuddled together, smoking and laughing, their murmured conversations reaching us from forty yards or so away. They were on the same elevation of the hill we were on. "They'll rig one of your M14s to fire on full automatic and mount a brace on the front so you can use it as an automatic weapon firing from the prone position. That will give you the firepower you need. Be sure to get some extra ammo magazines for it."

We all nodded. Collecting our gear and strapping on our web belts, as a group of one sluggish mind we began wearily moving to the stand of sergeants. Our instructing sergeant walked with us.

"I'll be here on the hill tonight," he said. "When you've sprung your ambush, come on back here and let me know. Then you can crawl into the sack. Okay?"

"Okay," a couple of us replied, somewhat in unison but without much enthusiasm.

As we approached the collection of sergeants, ours spoke to them, "This squad is doing the ambush at the fork. Tim, rig one of their M14s for automatic firing and give them plenty of ammo so they can make enough noise to keep people off their backs." He spoke in a hushed tone that matched theirs.

The eight of us collected our ammo and began walking down the hill in a semi-spread-out fashion, but close enough to each other to talk.

"What do you think?" Tom asked me.

"It ought to be an easy ambush if there are trees close to the road. The ground is level. In this light, the shadows should conceal us. It's not a far walk. I think the sergeant may just be giving us a break," came my tired reply. "Tom, let's get this one over quickly. We're all tired. Let's get it done and get back to camp in short order."

"Okay. Help me pick out a good ambush site," he replied.

We walked down the road in double file with our rifles at high port. No one else was on the road. It was quiet and beautiful. The dark shadows of the trees stretched across the road like black charcoal lines on coarse gray paper. The night was crisp. We needed the field jackets we were wearing. They made us feel warm and secure. We were going back to the barracks in the morning. An ambush was routine work for us after a solid week of them. We were confident we knew what we were doing and that we were doing it well. We felt good.

"Here's the fork," Tom announced as he started to go to the left branch.

"No, hold up, Tom," one of the guys said. "The sergeant said he wanted us to set up the ambush on the right fork."

"That's right, Tom," I said in support of the statement.

"Oh, uh, yeah. Sorry about that. It happens when you get tired," Tom replied, half-chuckling to himself.

The fork was wide and on level ground. There was a ditch on both sides of the road going to the right. It looked like a bulldozer had recently cleared it out. A few downed tree trunks had been pushed into small piles every fifty yards or so along the road. The center of the dirt road was just slightly higher than the ground on its tree-lined sides. They must have cleared out the underbrush when they were making the ditches on both sides of the road.

"Tom, let's not go too far down this fork. Anywhere along the far side of this fork will be a good ambush site. Look at how the tree shadows will conceal our positions," I said, pointing into the tree line. The trees were mostly pine. They were tall and straight without branches coming out of the trunk until they were twelve or so feet off the ground. As far as you looked into the forest there were tall pines with just enough hardwoods mixed in to provide the ground with a soft cover of fallen leaves and dry pine needles. The patchy mix of muted ground cover paired with the slashing shadows of the trees crisscrossing the ground made concealing yourself easy as long as you did not move.

"Okay, let's form a firing line just inside the first row of trees," he said, pointing into the woods. We were about fifty yards down the road's right fork.

In my opinion, we should have spread out a little more. About eight feet separated each of us from the next man. Tom had placed the M14 set to fire on automatic in the third position from where the road split. His thinking was that if the platoon was not completely into our killing zone when something triggered the ambush, the automatic weapon could swing and fire at the rear of the column. It would cut down those guys if they were not caught in the first volley of shots. I thought it was a good plan with the exception that we should have been spread out more.

After we were all set and lying in our prone positions, I told Tom that I wanted to walk down the road and try to see if I could spot our guys in the shadows. Tom agreed. As long as our guys stayed motionless, you could not see them from the road. I knew pretty much where everybody was. Yet, I had to strain to see them in the shadows despite knowing that they were there and despite their relative closeness to the road. This was looking good. Their low profile lying in the prone position was perfect. We were set.

I reassumed my position in the firing line. The dry leaves and pine needles kept the moisture in the ground from reaching us. Lying prone, with my head propped in my hands and my elbows planted in the ground, was so relaxing. It would be easy to drift off to sleep. In the shadows I could see that some of the guys had their heads resting on the ground. If we had to wait any time at all for the platoon to show up, we could be in trouble. No one wanted to go to sleep. This was the last ambush. We did not want to mess it up. So far, we had done alright in training. We did not want to blow it now.

You could hear them coming. The unmistakable sounds of canteens bumping into metal clips and gear inside backpacks hitting other gear reached our ears. These guys were really sloppy. The clanging was pronounced. Maybe they were National Guard guys. You would think that some sergeant would have shaped them up. As they got closer, the clanging, bumping, and banging of dangling equipment grew louder. Then the muttering of their voices and the crunching of lots of boots in the graveled dirt road grew in volume. This was the noisiest, most undisciplined group of soldiers we had heard for the full two weeks we had been in the field. These guys were pathetic. I just could not believe it. Looking into the darkness, I could see our guys perking up on both sides of me. We locked and loaded. You could hear them approach the fork. Tom and I nodded to each other, smiling. We were going to get to go to bed early tonight.

Oh, no! They were taking the wrong fork! They were taking the left fork instead of the one we're on. You could hear them plain as day in the darkness. They were laughing quietly as they began moving away. Tom got up. I got up. We all got up.

Huddling in the center of the road, I said to everyone: "They've taken the wrong fork. Can you believe that? The fools can't keep quiet and they can't read a map."

Tom said in desperation, "We'll have to lay out here in the woods all night. We can't go back until we've sprung the ambush. Hell, this isn't fair. It's just not fair."

"I'm going to bring them back," I said. I was mad. Just because of some fools, we might have to spend the whole night out here. It just wasn't right.

"How are you going to do that?" Tom asked.

"I'll just run up between the two columns and tell them they took the wrong fork. I'll tell them they have to turn around and take the right fork," I said with indignation in my voice.

"They'll see that you're not one of them," someone behind me said. "You don't have a black armband on."

"In the confusion and the weak light, nobody will notice. If I'm spotted, I'll break into the woods. No one wants to chase me in the woods," I blurted out, without pausing to think too much.

"Okay," said Tom, "we'll go back in the woods and wait for you."

"Good," I said over my shoulder as I began my jogging run to catch the receding column on the other fork. As always, my M14 was held at high port.

It did not take more than a minute or two to catch up to the rear of the column. I was not even breathing hard. Jogging farther up the middle of the road, passing the troops on either side, I did not give them much more than a glance. None of them seemed to be raising their heads to look at me. In the darkness, I could not tell how much farther the column extended. There seemed to be a lot of men in this platoon.

Still jogging I shouted out, "Who's in charge here? Who's in charge?" Without a doubt this was the most disorganized group of trainees I had ever encountered. The whole mess just made me mad. "Who the hell is in charge here?" I demanded.

From the darkness in front emerged a panting figure running toward me. As if ready to repel an assault, I halted in the middle of the dirt road with my legs spread and my weapon at high port. I was angry and frustrated.

"Here, here, I am," the panting figure puffed as his form took shape before my eyes. He was definitely overweight. Something was wrong with this picture.

Coming to a halt directly in front of me and whipping out a salute so sharp that his elbow almost hit me in the face, the figure said, "I'm in—cough-cough—charge." He sucked in his breath, still frozen with that salute. I looked in fear at the clear silver insignia attached to his field jacket. Oh, oh, oh. I had a lieutenant colonel huffing and puffing in my face, thinking I was an officer and saluting me. I would be going to jail. I was going to jail for the rest of my life for impersonating an officer during wartime. Oh, help me, help me, somebody please help me. Those thoughts raced through my mind as the colonel stood in my face with his fixed salute. I had to do something. I had to do something *now*. I had to salute an officer when he saluted me.

Snapping a brisk salute, I began speaking as he lowered his arm.

"You've taken the wrong fork," I stated authoritatively. "We'll be here all night. Reverse this column and take the other fork. *Now,* Sir!"

He immediately turned and barked out the order, "Column . . . Halt!" They stopped. Every one of them stopped and stood there in silence. "About . . . face!" he ordered. Up and down the sides of the road combat boots turned on the packed, hard ground and crunched as every soldier obeyed the order. "Forward . . . march!" came his next command. Again his order was obeyed without comment.

The colonel saluted me again. I returned it and he trotted to the head of the column. I stayed in my position in the center of the road, walking between the two rows of men and staying in step with them. I looked straight ahead so as to avoid eye contact with anyone. They might recognize me as a stranger or spot my fear.

Hell, I thought, this just might work out okay. If anyone nabs me, I can plead ignorance. I thought this was the platoon we were supposed to ambush. When they took the wrong fork in the road, I just went out to get them back. All I wanted to do was ambush somebody and go to bed. How was I supposed to know that some lieutenant colonel was out here leading a group of recruits out on some special activity? What was a lieutenant colonel doing in the field with a bunch of recruits anyway? Something was really wrong here.

As the column began turning the corner to take the correct fork in the road, the movement brought me closer to the men marching on the left. Oh no, *oh no!* I'm in real trouble. The man closest to me is wearing captain's bars and the next one has on a major's oak leaves. Two more sets of captain's bars flash in the moonlight. They're *all* officers. This is a whole column of officers. *That's* why a lieutenant colonel is leading them: they're all officers. They must be a training group of chemical warfare officers out on night field maneuvers. How do I get myself into these things? I'm going to jail. Oh, this is bad. This is very, very bad, I say to myself. What can I do to get out of this mess?

Looking to the right in my panic, I can see Tom's face in the tree line. There is Tom's face—and those of a couple of the other guys. Tom's face is raised above his rifle. It is pale white and his eyes are big and white, as are those of the others. They can see the flashing bars and leaves on the officers' shoulders. They know that these are officers and they won't open up. *The hell I say!* In one quick, smooth motion, I level my M14. *BLAMM! BLAMM! BLAMM!* the M14 barks as I shout as loud as I can: "Ambush! *Ambush!* Take cover! AMBUSH!"

The guys in my squad immediately open up. *CAARACK! RATATA-*

TAT! CAARACK! RATATATAT RAT! speak the rifles and automatic weapon as they spit fire toward the road. All hell is breaking loose. The officers on both sides of the road scurry for cover. Some are prone in the ditch. Some have huddled behind downed tree trunks. Everything and everyone is moving fast. Suddenly I am the only one left standing in the road. I had managed to empty my magazine into the woods. Everyone will know I don't belong if I stay here in the middle of the road. I've got to seek cover, too. Move you fool, *move!* is the dominant thought flooding my mind.

Hunching over, I move quickly toward a log immediately to my right front. Two captains are squatting down behind it.

As I approached them, one of them looked me straight in the eye and spat out, "What the hell, we weren't supposed to get ambushed tonight. What the hell's going on?"

"You're right," I instinctively responded. "There's been some kind of foul up." I got closer to them. I had to fit in. Don't stand out and you'll be safe, raced through my mind.

"Hey, who are you?" the captain asked with surprise in his eyes. Turning his head to the other captain, he reached for my jacket and shouted: "He's not one of us! He's not one of us!"

I started to pull away, but it was too late. He had a firm grasp on my collar. "Colonel! Colonel! He's not one of us!" the captain screamed as I strained to pull free of his grip.

He did not let go. The strength of my legs backing away from him was dragging both of us into the center of the roadbed. He kept shouting, but my panic kept me from hearing as the other captain began to understand the situation. He was reaching for me with clawing hands, clutching at air.

Panic time for the kid. "GAS! GAS! GAS! GAS!" I screamed in total terror.

Instantaneously, the captain let go of me. He grabbed for his gas mask and frantically began putting it on, as did his fellow officer. I backed into the center of the road, unsnapped my own gas mask and, as I unthinkingly ran toward the front of the column, pulled it over my face. Just as it was securely covering my face, the puffing colonel came running toward me with his mask's eye lenses already fogging over.

The mask's filters had a muffling effect, but I was able to hear him say, "What is it? What's going on?"

"Get these men out of here," I screamed, pumping my right arm up and down, signaling for him to double time. "Get them out *now!*"

Without hesitation he turned and repeated the double-time signal, shouting as best he could, "Double time! Double time! Get these men out of here, double time!" His muffled shouts continued as he disappeared into the darkness, the entire column matching his pace.

Slowly, the guys in the woods stood up. They walked toward me as I stood in the middle of the road, watching in amazement as the dust kicked up by the running officers started to disappear.

"Those were officers," Tom said in a stunned voice.

"Yeah, I discovered that too late," I said with a slight smile.

"We're in a world of shit," somebody else added.

"Not necessarily," I chimed in. "Look, we were out here to spring an ambush. We didn't know that a platoon or so of officers would be coming by. When they took the wrong fork, I thought they were trainees making a mistake. It's my fault. You didn't know who they were. I was the one who went out and brought them back into our field of fire. If anybody gets in trouble, it will be me, okay?"

"Okay, okay," said Tom impatiently, "but we don't want you to get into trouble."

"Well, maybe I won't. This one needs to play itself out," I commented.

"What should we tell the sergeant?" another asked.

"We'll just walk up to him, tell him we sprang the ambush, and we're going to hit the sack," I stated. "It's the truth. We don't need to tell him or anybody else anything unless they ask us for more."

"Okay. That's what we'll do," Tom said.

"Just don't talk about it," I pleaded. "Don't tell anybody and maybe nothing will happen to me. We'll all be gone in a week. If we can keep it quiet that long, I'll be safe. You know, I could go to jail for this. Please don't bring it up. If anybody asks anything, we'll tell the truth. You aren't to blame for anything. I was the one that brought them to you. You couldn't help it. Just please don't bring it up unless you have to."

We were all in agreement. Tom and I took the lead as the squad climbed the hill to where the sergeants were. The other guys hung back a ways.

The sergeant who had sent us out on the ambush recognized Tom as the two of us approached him. "What happened?" he asked.

"We sprang the ambush, Sergeant," replied Tom. "Can we hit the sack now?"

"Sure. How did it go?" he asked as we turned to leave.

I looked back over my shoulder and said, "About like all the others, Sergeant."

"Fine," he said. "You men go on and get some sleep now."

"Okay, thanks, Sergeant," Tom replied as we retreated into the darkness.

No one said much of anything as we took off our boots, slipped our rifles into our sleeping bags to protect them from prowling sergeants, and then followed the M14s into the comfort of our homes.

As I was drifting off to sleep, I noticed several men come running up the hill to speak to the huddle of sergeants. I could not make out what was being said. The two newcomers were waving their arms as they talked. They were excited about something. A spontaneous roar of laughter erupted from the group of sergeants as one of them pointed over to us. They thought our adventure was funny, I reasoned. They were not mad. We would be protected was my thought as I drifted into sleep.

Morning came earlier than I was ready to greet it, as usual. Our time was filled with breaking camp, packing, and forming up for the long march to the trucks. Later, when we were bunched up with all of the other guys waiting for the order to board, I overheard a group of trainees talking.

"Did you hear that jeep driving up and down the road late last night?" a guy asked.

"Yeah," said another, "it had a loud speaker on it, but I couldn't make out what it was saying."

"Me either," piped in somebody else. "All I could make out was something about an ambush and the Chemical Warfare School."

"They wanted information about a soldier. They were looking for someone who could tell them about a soldier who had done something to the Chemical Warfare School I thought they said," a voice from the group added.

Tom and I looked at each other. Neither of us said a word. I smiled as I reached down from the back of the deuce and a half and pulled him up. He patted me on the back. No one ever spoke to me about the incident.

CHAPTER 14

Odds and Ends

SUNDAY MORNING. Six more days and a wake up. That is, just six more days of advanced infantry training and then waking up the next day and leaving Fort McClellan. Anna and Danville, Kentucky, here I come. It just so happened that Anna's high-school Christmas holiday and my vacation from the army matched fairly well. My leave and her school's Christmas vacation started at the same time. She got two weeks off and I had three and a half weeks of vacation. The first full week in January she would be teaching school while I was home. Then I would be off to Infantry Officer Candidate School. We were very happy about being able to have this time together. The army was paying for my train fare to Danville. It was also paying for my trip to Fort Benning, Georgia. I was to report there on January 11, 1967. What a way to start a new year, I thought. Basic training and AIT had seemed like marking time. Entering OCS was the beginning of the end.

One more trip to the PX on a Sunday seemed to be my purposeless goal for that day. There might be a magazine or a newspaper to read. Lord, I had not read a newspaper since Stone and I were in the Anniston restaurant. It seemed like a lifetime ago.

Reading the *Anniston Times* under a tree in the courtyard fronting the PX was truly a luxury. President Johnson was determined to keep the communists from thwarting democracy in South Vietnam, the paper said. Thousands more troops were going to Vietnam to free up South Vietnamese army soldiers for combat. My friends attending AIT with me would be among those thousands. Some of them would be hit. I wondered which ones it would be. No one ever talked about getting killed. It was just something that you did not mention. The sergeants always said that we should listen to them and learn such-and-such a lesson because it would "save your life in Vietnam." They said it so often and about so many training activities that it became a standard joke. "Police up this area because it could save your life in Vietnam. Peel these potatoes because it could save your life in Vietnam. Keep your rifle barrel shiny because—" Well, there was no need to repeat it. The sergeants did that often enough.

Another story in the *Times* was about troops in 'Nam using the new M16 rifle. It said they were reporting having trouble with the weapon jamming. The army brass flat-out denied it, the paper said. Army sources said that the M16 did not jam any more than the M14 did. In fact, they said, it was a weapon far superior to the M14. It was lighter, had more firepower, and was the weapon of choice for jungle warfare situations like Vietnam.

The story was not reassuring. The rumor mill said that the M16 jammed a hell of a lot. If you filled a magazine up with the twenty rounds it was supposed to hold, it would probably jam. The word was to put in only sixteen rounds. One guy had a brother in the marines in the northern part of South Vietnam. He said his brother had written him the M16 was jamming up real bad. His brother said that he had been in a relief column for an overrun marine position. They had come up on several foxholes where dead marines were huddled over their M16s. From the positions of the bodies it was clear that they had been shot to death while trying to unjam their weapons. As far as we "grunts" were concerned, we were putting sixteen rounds into our magazines until we were sure. We did not care what the army's official position was. In the event of our death, the army would not miss us as badly as we would miss ourselves.

"Jerry? My gosh, it's you! How are you?" asked someone who was rushing over to me. His form was camouflaged by the speckled light of the sun bouncing through the bare tree branches.

I could not make out who it was. Looking up at the figure while in the process of standing up did not prepare me for the bear hug that crashed into me. "Its me, Jim—from basic training!" The enthusiastic voice roared into my ears as my arms were pinned to my sides.

Pulling my head back as far as my trapped torso would allow, I finally saw the guy's face. It was Jim from basic training. The Jim who could never keep up on the long marches or morning jogs, the guy I had hit and pushed down on the ground for a hundred or so men to trample. He was clearly pleased to see me. The guilt I had felt after pushing him to the ground while Hawk and the others pulled on him to keep him in the running formation was still with me.

I'd had no idea what had happened to him. There had been so much confusion at the end of basic, with everyone's orders being changed and people shipping out at all hours of the day and night. Who knew who got what orders or how they had affected their lives? Like so many others, Jim was just one of the many who had disappeared. You had no time to think about what happened to them. It was all you could do to try to take care of yourself while doing whatever it was the army told you to do within the short time frame they gave you.

"We just got to McClellan a few days ago. I didn't know you had been sent here. I got recycled. They didn't let me graduate from basic. The doctors looked at my feet. They couldn't believe I had made it as far in basic as I did. My feet were so badly deformed. At least they understood the pain I had been in. They operated on them and now they're fine. I can run all day and all night. Isn't that great? I can get through the training without any problems. Isn't that great?"

"Yeah, you look good. You've lost weight, too," I said patting him on the back as he freed me from his embrace. He was strong.

"That's because I lost all my baby fat. Now that I can run, I love it," came his joyous response.

He was only getting a couple of days off at Christmastime. His training unit started its cycle the next morning. He was not going to try to get back to New Jersey. It was good to spend that afternoon with him. A part of me kept reflecting on the irony of the situation. If the army had left his feet alone, he would not have had to go to Vietnam and risk his life. The army did not leave his feet alone. He was going to 'Nam. He was so happy about it. I was not so sure he had gotten the best end of the deal. I was not going to tell him that. I just shared in his joy. It was humbling to realize that my knocking him down back then was only an issue with me and not with him. He was a good man. I wished him well.

The assembled company let out a collective moan on Monday morning when we learned that we would undergo a full week of hard training. Up before dawn, hours of marching into the woods to whatever training site we were to go to, and then marching back to the barracks in the dark for chow and sleep.

The word was that the National Guard guys in the barracks next to ours had a thief in their ranks. He had broken into several of his barracks mates' footlockers and stolen a few wallets. They were pretty sure it was one of their own since our company was in the field throughout the previous week, as were the others in our training brigade. So far they had not caught the guy. We had gotten the word to watch out for each other in our barracks.

Just what was the National Guard company doing by not going into the field like the rest of us? They were getting credit for AIT like we were. It was bad enough that they would be going home to "sister Sue" ("Jody's got your girl and gone" went the marching chant) safe from the fear of getting sent to Vietnam. They had been smart enough to join before the draft got them, or they had political connections that pulled strings for them. Now we learn that they do not even have to grunt out the training like the rest of us. On top of having their lives protected, we learn that they steal from one another. Maybe it is better that they will not be in the foxholes next to ours in combat. They would probably get us killed while they were getting themselves whacked, went the reasoning.

Wednesday had been a long one. We had been out at the rifle range. They let us load our M14s with tracer rounds. Every seventh round was a tracer. Watching the burning trail of the tracers always kept us fascinated. The beauty of the fiery trail of the round to its target and then the crisscrossing of ricocheting rounds as multiple weapons fired down range was undeniable—although the meaning of the beauty was sad.

We made the long march back to the barracks. When you are tired, the march back ought to be a lot harder. It never was, because we were going home, home to our barracks. Our hearts were extra light. It was just two more days and a wake up. Before we left the rifle range, we went through the familiar "no brass, no ammo" drill. It had become as routine as tying your shoes. We held our weapons at high port with the bolts open. The sergeants whizzed by, quickly glancing into the receiver as each of us yelled out the slogan. They walked by at such a quick pace that the chant, "no brass, no ammo," blended into a continuous, unending chorus. It was musical, much like a well-conducted rendition of "Row, Row, Row Your Boat" as the various sergeants passed through the multiple rows of men calling out their chant. Later, as we marched back, we told jokes in the ranks. The sergeants did not try to keep us quiet.

On this exercise, the National Guard company had gone with us. The sergeants were careful to keep our two groups apart. Even on the firing range, we were segregated. We came together to get our weapons at the armory in the morning and then to return them in the evening. This pattern at the armory had been repeated several times over the last seven and one-half weeks. It was another old drill. We all accepted it as part of the day's chores. The mill-around time outside the armory was the only opportunity we had to interact with the National Guard guys.

There was not much to the interaction. They were all from Alabama and we were from the North. We did not know any of them personally and they did not know any of us. It was polite enough. We just did not deal with one another.

It was really dark by the time we got back to the barracks. We were hungry. The drill was we had to turn in our weapons before we could go to chow. The four to five hundred or so of us crowded around the front of the armory. We wanted to check our weapons in as soon as possible. The first ones into the building were the first ones to go eat. This time the keeper of the armory keys was late. We stood there pushing each other to get the best position we could for an early entrance into the building. There was a lot of smoking and joking going on. The press of people around the entrance was such that you had to have your rifle barrel pointing into the air or down to the ground. Usually we carried them any which way while we waited to get into the armory. Nobody minded how you carried your weapon as long as you did not point it at anyone. It did not make any difference that the weapon was not loaded. If you pointed it at someone it was because you intended to kill him. There was no other reason to level it at a person. I had never seen anyone lower his weapon at another soldier, and I was an old-timer. At least, we all felt like old-timers. We were not intimidated about being in the army any longer.

Goodwill was strong among us. We were fit, tough, and ready to go. Besides, we only had two more days and a wake up. It did not make much difference that we had to wait. Rushing to get somewhere so you could stand in line and wait was a way of life. We were experts at smoking and joking while we waited. This was a good time for that.

CRACK! went the rifle. The round was from a rifle within our tightly packed group waiting to get into the armory. All talking instantaneously stopped. Heads jerked toward the sound and as the beautiful tracer raced to the stars. We watched until the white phosphorous burned itself out. Death rode the night sky. Death had spared each of us. It was chance. A slight murmur of voices came from the gathering. There were no more jokes. The man with the keys arrived. We quietly put our rifles in their numbered slots and left. Later that evening the word was that the round had come from one of the guardsmen's rifles.

Two more days and a wake up. Today we get to see and fire an M16. The instructors say that it does not jam. It is a fine weapon. We will really like it. After we get issued one in 'Nam we will get so used to it we will wonder why we liked the M14 so much, they say. It feels like a plastic toy. Someone asked if it might shatter if you butt-stroked someone in the head. Once again, we are assured that the weapon will do the job.

At the rifle range, they give us our instructions. The drill is to walk toward a silhouetted target while rapidly firing our M14s from the hip. After we cease fire, the target will be brought to us. We can count the number of hits. Again the advice is to aim low. If you hit the ground in front of it, ricocheting rocks and dirt will fly up, tearing through the target. That will bring a man down. Even if he isn't killed, his wounds will disable him. Besides, a wounded man takes at least two other men out of combat just to take care of him. You get three for one and that's a good deal, the sergeants say.

For comparison purposes, we repeat the drill with an M16. I reasoned that if it is such a good deal to aim low during a marching assault, it must be a better deal to aim at the ground in front of the target. That way all of the bullets will spray up rocks and dirt. When the time comes to count the number of hits in the targets, some of the guys say they had as many as seven or eight holes in their targets, including the rock holes. The sergeants ask if anyone has gotten as many as ten hits on his target. One guy shouts out that he has nine, but no one reports ten hits with either the M14 or the M16. I am embarrassed to tell anyone my score. Each weapon I fired produced more than thirty rock holes in each of my targets. I wondered if it would really be better to spray an enemy with rock splinters than to try to put a bullet into him. Before I decided that one, I would want to talk to a combat veteran. It probably would not be wise to experiment with the idea during an actual firefight.

One more day and a wake up. At breakfast, the word spread fast: Those National Guard guys have done it again. The regular army sergeants hit them with a surprise inspection. It seems that several of the guardsmen are collectors. The sergeants found one live mortar round with gunpowder packets attached to its fins in a footlocker. In one of our many training sessions, we had learned that the gunpowder packets, called "charges," are attached to a mortar round's fins just before it is dropped into the firing tube. The charges ignite when the round hits the bottom of the tube, propelling it on its way to the target—where it explodes on contact. Just about anything that creates a spark near the gunpowder charges could accidentally set the round off. Whoever the traveling friends of the collecting guardsman were, they needed to thank the sergeant who found it for keeping them alive.

The searchers also found several live hand grenades hidden in their personal effects along with a lot of rifle ammunition. It was incomprehensible to us that these guys could be so reckless. If we had been told that our sergeants were pulling a surprise inspection of our wall and footlockers, we would have been worried: Our contraband cookies and candy were stored there. That would be what the sergeants were trying to find. It was just beyond imagining that they would pull a surprise inspection to look for live ammo. The National Guard guys were scary people.

At last the wake up arrived. Joy is being in my baby's arms. I did not have to report to Fort Benning until January 11.

Spending Christmas vacation with Anna was wonderful. She met me at the Cincinnati airport. We drove back to the garage apartment she had been renting since late August in Danville, Kentucky. I hardly remembered what it looked like. Moving her into it and then immediately going to the Cincinnati airport to fly to Fort Dix, New Jersey, had been so hectic. Then the intensity of my concentration on adjusting to the army way during the last ten weeks had just about removed all detailed memory of it. The four-hour drive seemed to fly by in seconds as we shared our adventures, laughed, kissed, and beamed in the presence of each other.

She told me of the holiday visits we would be making, noting that they would be brief. All we really wanted to do was to be solely with each other. Our time together was so precious. I did not know if we would be allowed to have any time together during the six months of training at Fort Benning. Nor did I know if I would have any time to spend with her after OCS before I was sent to Vietnam—assuming that I was unable to get a branch transfer to the Medical Service Corps. I dreaded the thought of that possibility, but it was growing as reality in my mind.

The inside of the apartment was like a postcard picture of the holiday celebration. Anna had decorated it with such a beautiful touch for color coordination. She had a true artist's eye. Our dog of a year and a half, Rusty, greeted Anna excitedly but seemed to keep her distance from me. Rusty, with gleeful excitement, jumped up on the bed that dominated the little apartment. When I followed her example, Rusty growled at me and showed her teeth. I swung my arm at her with knee-jerk quickness, flinging her off the bed and onto the floor in the blink of an eye. My violent reaction surprised me. Why had I been so aggressive? That was *not* my way. Immediately, I went to Rusty and began petting her, telling her how sorry I was. I told her I knew she was just trying to protect Anna. The dog responded to my gentleness. All was right with the world.

Anna and I did everything together. During our first two Christmases as husband and wife we had established the tradition of sending gifts to all our relatives. Because of our limited income, the gifts had to be tokens. This Christmas was no different. We loved shopping together, even though our time to do so was extremely rushed. The joy was in doing it together. We purchased every gift with care. Yet time was our enemy: Christmas came upon us and we still had not wrapped them for mailing. We decided we would just have to mail them late.

We chose to spend Christmas Day by ourselves in the little apartment. Anna worked hard and with great joy to prepare our Christmas dinner. The special treat of the meal was the plum pudding we made together from scratch. It was a tradition we had started our first Christmas together in Oxford, Ohio. Our life there seemed like decades ago. Perhaps it *was* that long ago from an emotional perspective.

We never did finish the task of wrapping and mailing the Christmas gifts. The time was gone before we were ready. The spring semester at Anna's school started at about the same time I needed to leave for Fort Benning. She had a few days of teaching to do before she took me to the airport. Those mornings when she went off to teach and I stayed alone at the apartment were hard. We both fought back tears as we drove to the Cincinnati airport. Leaving Anna is never easy.

Once on the plane, I began to speculate on what was about to happen. I had a sense of adventure about OCS. A part of me was apprehensive, but it was a small part. I had no doubt about my ability to complete the program. It was a relief finally to be starting OCS. The other training had simply delayed me in getting to this point. At last I was starting to make progress that would be a means to ending my military obligation.

CHAPTER 15

Are There Any Questions?

T HE BARRACKS were three stories high. They were rectangular blocks regularly spaced for about as far as the eye could see. The landscape seemed denuded of trees. It was mainly one of gently rolling hills with the many identical buildings towering over everything in evenly spaced rows and columns. Roads passed through them in precisely mapped patterns. Each building had an asphalt area behind it that served as a miniature parade ground for the men living in their respective buildings. Neatly trimmed grass grew in the open spaces not occupied by cement, asphalt, or buildings. Everywhere you looked, uniformed men were quickly moving as if they were ants with unfathomable missions that differed from those of all the other ants indistinguishable from them.

A few brief questions and a lot of walking got me to the right building in the maze. The 63d Infantry OCS Company building loomed in front of me. Toting my life's accumulation of military gear in my duffel bag, I entered.

"Name: last name first, first name, middle initial," the company first sergeant snapped at me.

I responded.

"Fifth platoon. Next!" he said, looking at the man behind me.

The higher your platoon number was, the more flights of stairs you had to climb. Multiple flights of stairs make for a hard climb when you are carrying a stuffed duffel bag on your shoulder. Everyone traveling up or down the stairwell seemed pleasant enough even though all of the men were moving with a purpose. The exception was the three or four second lieutenants in the area. From the glare in their eyes, you knew not to ask them much. When you did, they responded with as few words as possible. Right off, you understood that it was best to avoid them.

A large latrine and shower area was located to the right of the stairwell from which I entered the hallway. The 5th Platoon was to the right, past another stairwell and latrine/shower area farther down the corridor. The 6th Platoon was to the left. I turned right and headed for the double doors at the end of hall. I could see into the platoon bay through the glass in the doors. Chin-high partitions created cubicles on both sides of the long red-and-brown tiled floor all the way back to the end of the building. The wall at the far end held a huge exhaust fan with shutters that partially blocked out the sunlight from the open sky beyond. The fan had to be at least five feet across. A metal grill protected the blades from paper and other objects that might get sucked into it.

As I entered the 5th Platoon's bay, it was full of activity. Men were claiming their bunks and unpacking. Each cubicle seemed to be identical. One set of bunk beds and one single bed per cubicle appeared to be the norm. Three men were to live in each of the little spaces created by the chin-high wall dividers for the next six months. The bunk beds had been set up on the far side of each cubicle in relation to the double doors leading into the hallway. Chests of drawers were pushed together and backed up to the divider that created the boundary between the room and the center aisle. The opening in the divider served as the entrance to the cubicle. Three wall lockers were wedged between the end of the bunk beds and the back wall. Every other cubicle or so had a window. Compactly grouped against the back wall were desks. Underneath the beds were footlockers. It was a standard military arrangement. One bunk, one wall locker, and one footlocker for each man in the cubicle.

About two-thirds of the way back on the left I found a cubicle with just one guy in it. "Mind if I move in?" I asked with a grin.

The black guy stood up from making the lower bunk bed and held out his hand. "No. C'mon in," he said as we shook hands. "Nathaniel Monroe. They call me Nat."

After our introductions, I began to unpack and settle in. I chose the top bunk. Not many people choose the top bunk as a place to sit. It is easier to prepare for inspections. If people do not sit on your bunk after you have made it up, it stays ready for the morning inspection.

It was not long before the bay was full of men. All thirty-four members of 5th Platoon had arrived. We were a beehive. All of us pretty well understood the army drill. You hung your dress uniform in the wall locker and placed your dress shoes and extra pair of combat boots on the bottom. Personal items such as magazines, pictures, money, black shoe polish, spare shoelaces, noninspection-quality combat boots, and contraband items went into the footlocker. Your padlock secured it.

By midafternoon we were in the swing of things. Everyone was asking everyone else what the OCS way was for storing things in the chests of drawers, study desks, and wall and footlockers. Whatever way that was, we knew that it would be the same for every man. The only storage area that received total agreement was the top drawer of each man's dresser. That was where your toilet gear went.

"Attention!" shouted someone near the double doors at the end of the bay. Immediately, silence reigned except for the hushed sound of the hallway doors swinging to a slow stop. Those standing froze. The others sprang to their feet to stand at attention. With the final slight swing of the double doors, the silence became absolute. Officer Candidate School had begun.

"As you were. Everyone assemble on me. *Now!*" demanded a deep base voice with a noticeable edge.

Converging to the front of the bay with haste, we saw the second lieutenant. He was solid as a rock. If someone had said he was a Division I college fullback, all of us would have believed him. His eyes were cold and expressionless. They matched the deep black color of his skin. The slight smile on his lips was incongruent with the menace in his eyes. His demeanor seemed to express a mixture of contempt and amusement.

"Brown, James," barked the lieutenant. We flinched at his words.

"Here, Sir," a tall, lanky fellow spoke up.

"You're acting platoon leader," the lieutenant stated while looking at the clipboard cradled in the crook of his left arm.

"Yes, Sir," Brown replied.

Continuing in his cryptic way, the lieutenant appointed acting squad leaders and assigned each of us to one of four squads. My place was in the 2d Squad.

When he finished assigning us to squads, I was astounded to hear him bark out my name.

"Here, Sir," I shouted, wondering what kind of trouble I was in.

"You're the one with the master's degree in psychology," he said, more as a challenge than as a statement.

"Yes, Sir!" was my immediate reply. Damn. I had hoped to put that fact behind me. I just wanted to get through OCS with as little hassle as possible and get my branch transfer.

"You're the platoon morale officer," he said with a hard grin on his face. He turned to the acting platoon leader. "There will be a meeting in my office exactly thirty minutes from now," he said, glancing at his watch. "Bring the squad leaders. Don't be late." With that, he did a sharp about-face and left.

Second Lieutenant James White was 5th Platoon's tactical officer. We had already picked up on the fact that the tactical officer was referred to as the Tac. Our Tac was going to be with us almost all of the time. Rumor had it that the tactical officer was the one who made your life miserable or enabled you to tolerate it. He was the one you had to please. Lieutenant White did not appear to be the kind of man who would be pleased easily.

When the platoon leader and squad leaders returned, we got the word. There would be a company formation at 1600 hours. Captain Clifford Greene, the company commander, would officially welcome us. We were to be in proper uniform at the 0800 inspection in the morning. That meant wearing brass OCS insignia on our fatigue collars, OCS helmet liners, highly polished boots, and so forth.

The leaders relayed additional information. The platoon bays would be inspected at 0800 hours the next morning. All personal gear was to be appropriately stored, the latrines cleaned, the platoon bay cleaned, and our personal appearance up to military standards. We would eat supper at 1800 hours and breakfast at 0700 hours. Lights were to be out at 2200 hours. I still had to think to translate military time to real civilian time. We were all to be in our bunks at 10 P.M. with all lights out. The officer of the day would make spot inspections to see to it that this rule was followed. No lights except the ones in the latrine and the stairwell would be turned on before 0600 hours. This rule would be rigorously enforced.

Other rules we were to follow included never having furniture polish or floor wax. We were not to use these items in maintaining cleanliness. In addition, no floors were to be spit-shined. Candidates were not to waste their time or money on these items. No food of any kind was to be received by mail, and no food was to be stored in our footlockers or anywhere else in the barracks. We were to eat only what the army gave us, where the army gave it to us, and when the army gave it. If we bought food at the PX or from a honey-bun truck, we were to eat it immediately. No food was to be taken into the barracks. Slush funds were absolutely prohibited. Operating a slush fund was grounds for dismissal from OCS. That probably meant being sent immediately to Vietnam as a rifleman.

All of our clothing had to be marked in the proper military fashion. T-shirts had to have our last names stenciled on them. Boots and shoes had to have our serial numbers in them where they could be easily read. Fatigues and other clothing items also had to be marked. Baggy fatigues would not pass inspection. If necessary, shirts and pants were to be tailored at the waist, along the arms and legs, and elsewhere to make sure they fit neatly. It was always necessary.

We were allowed to keep our footlockers locked. They would be randomly inspected. Contraband found inside it could be grounds for dismissal. Our wall lockers were to be unlocked and open for all inspections.

All meals would be eaten "on the square." That was a new one to most of us. We needed to have it explained. The explanation seemed to come from a B movie. I had seen old movies in which rich kids were sent to military-type boarding schools in England. They ate on the square. I knew it could be done. I just didn't know that I would have to do it myself one day. The procedure was to sit at attention at the dining table with your back perfectly straight and your eyes staring straight ahead. You never looked to the right or left, and you never, ever, looked down at your food. All hand and arm movements were either straight up or down or at rigid ninety-degree angles. Thus, once your fork had food on it, you would raise it straight up until it was at the same height as your mouth. You then would pull the fork back at a perfect ninety-degree angle until it was about to strike your mouth. Just prior to hitting your mouth, you opened up and deposited the food inside. Once over it, you would drop your arm and fork in a straight line back from your face until it was directly over your plate. You then dropped your hand with the fork in it in a straight line down to the plate to obtain another bite of food. Of course, you maintained your straight-ahead stare throughout the maneuver. This process would be repeated until you were full or the tactical officers determined that the company had expended all of the time allotted for that meal.

Several of the guys thought this was a joke. The army could not be serious about having us eat this way. It was not possible to feed yourself in such a manner.

Most of us were recent college graduates. A few of the candidates were former sergeants. Still fewer were recent high school graduates who had been to various army schools before coming to OCS. In OCS, everyone loses whatever rank he held. The program was intended primarily for bright enlisted men who had achieved distinction as noncommissioned officers but lacked a college education. The army sent them to OCS to become officers. As soon as they reported, they lost their stripes.

The remaining candidates were college graduates who wanted to become officers but had not taken ROTC in college. The college graduates who came into the army because of the draft and wanted to become officers were like me. They had gone through basic training and AIT. Most of us were promoted to the rank of private first class, pay grade E-3, upon graduation. When we arrived at OCS they began giving us E-5 pay.

Buck sergeants are in pay grade E-5. That's three stripes on your sleeve. We did not get to wear the stripes, of course, because we had to give them up to enter OCS. The only time you wore any rank in OCS was when you were in an acting leadership position.

We were supposed to wear brass pin-on insignia that said "O.C.S." attached to our collars to identify us as candidates. Unfortunately, they had not issued us any. We would have to buy them at the PX. Even more unfortunate for us was the fact that we were going to be inspected at 0800 hours the next morning and we were expected to have the proper insignia on our uniforms. None of us had purchased said items. In fact, no one seemed to know exactly where the nearest PX was. Someone said he thought it was about five miles from our barracks, but he was not sure. Others said they were pretty sure it was somewhere east of the barracks. A sense of uneasiness was settling in the air.

Another series of rules was passed out concerning how our clothes were to be stored in our chest of drawers, where our training manuals were to be kept when classes began, what study hours were to be, and the like. It was just too much to absorb at one sitting. What we knew to do to prepare for the inspection would require a whole lot more time than we had before the inspection was to take place. Besides, this was our first afternoon here. They would understand that. We needed some time to settle in. Just to be on the safe side, most of us increased our ant-like behaviors.

"Fall out! Fall out!" came the cry. We rushed to the stairwell and raced down them as fast as our legs would go. When we hit the second-floor landing we encountered members of the 3d Platoon pouring through the hallway door. You dared not slow down. All of us had seen the consequences of that in basic, and that was with noncommitted inductees. We were committed. We all wanted to do the right thing because we did not want to suffer the consequences of doing something wrong. Regrettably, we had yet to learn to identify what was right and what was wrong. That is a critical step in learning the army way.

Standing before our assembled group was a captain, a first lieutenant, and the company first sergeant. They were dressed in fatigues. Their tightly tailored uniforms displayed the athletic wiriness of their bodies. Sharp, starched creases in the pants legs and on the sleeves of their uniforms accentuated their fitness. They had the lean look of a distance runner. The tactical officers mirrored that look with one exception: the 4th Platoon Tac was just a little pudgy around the middle. His loud shouting had already distinguished him as a bear. Definitely someone to stay away from. The poor guys in 4th Platoon were going to suffer.

The captain's uniform told us a lot. He was airborne qualified and had been in combat. He wore the blue-and-silver Combat Infantryman's Badge (CIB) and a pair of silver jump wings over his left-breast pocket. This guy could teach us something important.

"I want to welcome you to Sixty-Third Company, Infantry OCS," the captain began. "It is our intention to provide you with the best training possible to make you fully qualified infantry second lieutenants. Your platoon tactical officers and the senior tactical officer, First Lieutenant Best, will provide you with the direction you need. If you have any questions, they will answer them. That is all."

We were assembled on the asphalt by platoons at the rear of the barracks. First and 2d Platoon stood opposite 5th and 6th Platoon. The mess hall was attached to the east end of the barracks behind 1st and 2d platoon. The 3d and 4th Platoons were at the west end so that together the six platoons formed a square U-shaped formation. Being in 2d Squad, 5th Platoon, I stood in the middle of the second rank with the barracks on my right and 6th Platoon on my left. One's sense of place in the army is important. The tactical officers stood in front of their respective platoons.

"Companeeee," screamed Captain Greene.

"Platoon," echoed each of the six tactical officers.

"Atten—*shun!*" Greene commanded.

The response was the sharp slap of the leather from 213 combat boots slamming in unison into the sides of an equal number of boots. These were eager feet. They wanted to do what was right. The minds controlling them were confused as to what was right, but there was no questioning the desire. In the silence Captain Greene performed a sharp about-face maneuver and disappeared into the barracks.

"Puh-rade," Lieutenant Best shouted.

"Puh-rade," echoed the six Tacs.

"*Rest!*" screamed Best.

Again we moved as one. Right feet crisply moved eighteen inches to the right as arms snapped behind backs, making a perfect ninety-degree angle at each elbow, allowing every forearm to be perfectly parallel to each soldier's belt line, the back of every right hand nestled in the palm of every left one, the thumbs interlocked.

"One third of you are quitters. Don't waste our time. Leave—*now!*" demanded Best.

Silence met his demand.

"You look like pond scum," Best hissed. "You are a miserable excuse for soldiering. You'd better get with the program or your ass is grass. The mess hall will be open from 1700 hours to 1730 hours."

The senior tactical officer slowly pivoted his neck from one end of the formation to the other, his eyes glowering. Returning his gaze to the front he shouted, "Companeeee!"

"Platoon," the six tactical officers responded in unison.

"Atten—*shun!*" screamed Best.

Our combat boots again made that crisp, smack-of-leather sound.

"Tactical Officers," shouted Best, "take charge of your platoons." He then duplicated Captain Greene's sharp about-face maneuver and disappeared into the barracks.

As soon as the senior tactical officer was out of sight the Tacs individually shouted, "Dismissed!"

In a surge of bodies, we bolted into the barracks and up the stairs. It had started. We had to get with the program. We were going to be in a world of hurt until we got things figured out. Others had completed it; so could I. The only unknowns were how to do it and how much pain I would have to endure while doing it.

CHAPTER 16

Chowing Down

"**W**HAT DO YOU THINK?" Nat asked as we folded T-shirts and placed them in our respective chests of drawers the only way they could be placed, the army way.

"It's going to be hectic for a few days. The hell with them if they can't take a joke," I said with a smile. He gave me a big grin.

A tall guy in the cubicle behind ours looked over the dividing partition and said, "We'll have fun eating 'on the square'," as he pushed his wire-rimmed glasses back up the bridge of his nose. All three of us rolled our eyes and laughed.

"Chow hall opens in five minutes," someone shouted.

Collectively, we stopped our various tasks and moved to the stairwell. The bay was strewn with T-shirts, fatigues, footlockers and a thousand other items that were in the process of being properly stored but had yet to be placed where they belonged. It was a lot like spring housecleaning. Everything had to be pulled out to get the deep cleaning done. In our case, we were just trying to figure out where to put what—when we still did not know what was what. In short, we were in a state of controlled, hyperactive hysteria. We knew that no matter what we did, it would not be good enough for the morning inspection. It just had to be good enough that your little island did not look worse than the rest. If it did, you would self-select to be the goat. The Tacs would use you as an example. Everyone else would see why they wanted to do better. No one would want to inflict on themselves what they observed the goats experiencing.

Outside, the long line of new candidates snaked into the mess hall. We stood in loose collections of guys talking to each other. We were careful not to seriously disrupt the line's overall quality. This was the last time we would enter the mess hall with such casualness for a long time. Rigid parade rest with no eyeballing would be the only way to stand in line.

"I just got out of the army's language school," the wire-rimmed glasses guy told Nat and me. "I'm Scottie," he added, holding out his hand.

Shaking it, I asked him what language they had sent him to learn.

"North Vietnamese," he said with a sheepish grin.

I rolled my eyes. The army had plans for this guy and he seemed unaware of it. He was tall—about six foot three—and thin, but lean rather than skinny. His back was slightly hunched. It was as if the only muscles he had bulked up were his upper back muscles. You see that in guys who backpack a lot. I liked him right off. The panicky look in so many of the guys' eyes was not present in his. He was together.

As we closed in on the doorway, the talking in line all but ceased. What little there was came across in whispers. The usual muttering of many voices into a blending of continuous sound I had heard in other army mess halls was missing. All was silent except for muffled shouts of anger and command followed by the sounds of isolated running feet and repeated number counting. The strain in the voices of the number counters could mean only one thing: lots of people were dropping and knocking out push-ups. Hell awaited us inside. I stood obediently in line waiting for my turn to enter. When I reached the door I could see tactical officers racing up and down the rows of tables looking for victims.

"You were eyeballing, Candidate!" screamed the chunky Tac. "I saw you, I saw you! You eyeballed that lieutenant when he walked by." He paused for a moment and the candidate mumbled something I could not hear. "Don't try to con me, you scum," the Tac continued. "Drop the fork. Damn it, I didn't say put the fork down. Pick it up. Now drop the damn thing. Drop it! Drop it! Don't you know what 'drop it' means? You drop and knock out fifty."

The guy fell out of his chair into the prone position like frozen wastewater from an overhead jet. "One, Sir; two, Sir; three, Sir," and on he shouted as he did his push-ups.

Another lieutenant was jogging beside a candidate, screaming in his ear that he better not spill a drop of milk from the three glasses of milk on the tray he held over his head as he ran around the tables. Other Tacs were engaged in similar yet equally bizarre acts of harassment.

No one needed to tell us to stand at attention and stare straight ahead at nothing as we went through the cafeteria line or marched to one of the many four-seat tables.

Nat, Scottie, and I landed at a table with just one occupant. Without moving his head, he looked up at me as I sat down. I saw the glance with my peripheral vision and smiled slightly. Before my butt hit the chair, a booming voice jarred my ears.

"You eyeballed, you scum! Get out! Get out! Get out of my dining hall," a red-faced lieutenant screamed into the guy's ear.

He bolted from the chair, and just as quickly as the candidate moved, the lieutenant shouted, "The tray, stupid, the tray! Take the tray!"

As the wide-eyed candidate turned in midstride, the lieutenant swept the tray and its contents of untouched food onto the floor.

"Look at what your stupidity has done. Drop, knock out thirty," he demanded. "Not there," he roared, with his face bent into the guy's face as he held himself in the prone push-up position. "Move your face over so it hits the food you want to look at so bad. Get a good look. Get a good look so you won't need to keep looking at it in the future."

"Sir, yes, Sir!" the candidate shouted as he positioned himself and began rhythmically placing his face in the scrambled food beneath him. "One, Sir; two, Sir," and on it went as the lieutenant shifted his gaze to the three of us.

We were sitting at attention staring straight ahead. I had not eyeballed. Basic and AIT had conditioned me to use my peripheral vision to take things in just before I slept with my eyes open in class. That glassy stare was on me then.

"If you men aren't hungry," the lieutenant barked with his face hovering over the center of the table, equally distant from each of the three of us, "then get the hell out of here so real soldiers can eat."

In a crisp, military move, I reached to where my fork should be. It leapt into my hand. I poked at the center of the plate while staring straight ahead into nothingness. Feeling a mass on the fork, I raised it straight up. At mouth level, my arm bent and the fork entered my mouth. There was no telling what I was eating. I didn't care. Calories were all that mattered. The lieutenant twirled and moved toward the table behind him, shouting, "I saw you eyeballing, Candidate!"

We had escaped the first encounter. My peripheral vision told me that Nat and Scottie were pushing food into their mouths as fast as the military process would allow. We were all dropping food back onto our plates, our trays, our laps, and onto the floor. Some food was getting into our mouths.

"You've been here too long," came the abrupt voice hovering over us. "Get out! Get out!"

The three of us shot straight out of our seats. In a crisp, military fashion we turned and began marching toward the door.

"Run! Get your asses out of my dining hall!" the Tac shouted as we bolted for the exit.

Outside, it was peaceful. We looked at each other. I strained but I was finally able to break wind. The spontaneous laughter was great.

In the platoon bay, the ants were at it. Someone had learned where we could take our fatigues to be tailored. Another guy knew the procedure for getting them to the laundry so they could be starched with the heavy creases displayed in the crisp, body-hugging style of the Tacs. A couple of other guys were setting up a stenciling operation so we could all have our names on our T-shirts. I volunteered for the latrine cleaning detail. The skills I had developed had created a degree of pride within me.

When the announcement came that we had fifteen minutes until lights-out, I was glad. Several of the guys intended to sneak around with flashlights, completing little tasks for the morning inspection. I needed the sleep. When the lights went out, I was gone.

CHAPTER 17

Make Way

"Five days in a row is too much," said Mel Wolfe. The tall, lanky native of Washington state was speaking for the whole group. "We are the only platoon that has yet to pass a morning inspection."

"That's right," Tom Ketch agreed. "All of the other platoons have slush funds. They're buying liquid floor wax, good latrine cleaning supplies, and things to spiff up their bays. We're the only ones not doing it, and we're the only ones failing inspections." Ketch spoke in a quiet voice. I really respected him. He was the only true NCO in our platoon, a real sergeant who had spent time in this man's army. He was the old man of the platoon and had a wife and two kids.

"Go ahead and do it," said Eric Feedler. "We all trust you." Eric was probably the strongest man in our group. The Tacs had already selected him to be the company guidon bearer.

We had tried everything we knew to clean up the bay, but no matter what we did or how long we worked after lights-out, it just was not good enough. Every lieutenant in the company had been in to inspect us except our own tactical officer. They had just ripped us apart. The floors were dingy; the showerheads did not shine enough; the mirrors failed to sparkle; dresser tops were not polished to a high enough gloss, and on and on.

"The captain said slush funds were absolutely not allowed," I reminded them.

"Every platoon has one," Ketch insisted. "They couldn't pass their inspections without it."

I let out a sigh and said, "Okay, I'll run the slush fund. You guys have to protect me."

"Don't worry. We've got you covered," Jim Miller said in an ironic tone. Then he rolled his eyes as if to say my ass was grass. We all laughed. He was a good man.

"I want to be very careful with this," I explained. "We have to keep track of the money. None of us has any to spare. I'll open a separate checking account. When we collectively decide to buy something, we all have to share in paying for it. I don't want to be holding a lot of somebody else's money in the account, so we'll have our agents buy the items and then reimburse him. I'll assess everyone an equal share, collect the money, deposit it in the account and then write him a check for the exact amount. That way I'll always have a record of what money came in and where it went.

"Okay," said Scottie, "but what happens if we need to get a big ticket item? I mean, what if nobody can afford to pay for it up front?"

"Good thought," I responded. "If we agree we need to get some expensive stuff, we can always collect the money first. Then we can pay for it straight out of the checking account."

It was agreed that this was how we would operate.

"One other thing," I said, interrupting the general murmurings of agreement. "We don't want a lot of people spending the slush fund money. That's sure to result in confusion. Let's designate just a couple of guys who can buy things for the rest of us."

Scottie and Gary volunteered to be our designated purchasing agents. Others would serve as backups if either of them were unable to go to the PX or wherever. At the present rate, we were never going to pass an inspection, so no one would ever get to go beyond the first PX anyway.

Fortunately, there was a branch bank at the PX as well as such conveniences as a barbershop and stamp dispenser. The downside was that it was five miles away. No one had car privileges. For that matter, we had fewer privileges than any of the other platoons because of our failure to pass an inspection. During those first few days we spent our free time getting our uniforms tailored and laundered; buying our OCS insignia; spray painting our helmet liners gloss black, which identified us as beginning candidates; stenciling our names on our T-shirts, underwear, and on anything else that was loose; obtaining basic clothing supplies and field gear; and on and on.

The post office was in the opposite direction from the PX. It served a lot of OCS companies, probably the whole battalion and then some. We were each given a post office box. Everyone had his own box. It was nice and private. The only trouble was that they never gave you time to get your mail. There was never a point at which they said, "Okay, guys, you have half an hour to go check your mail." Every minute was taken

Typical cubicle occupied by officer candidates.

A tactical officer wearing a familiar expression.

The first sergeant relaying information.

up with getting ready for the next inspection. Any time spent going to the post office, PX, or getting a haircut was time lost.

We spent the bulk of the workday going to classes or taking our rifles to the firing range to get ready to qualify with them. No one was willing to spend any time helping you zero your weapon. When the time came to qualify, you had to qualify. If you failed, they would pull you out and make you do it again. There was no time to do it over. You would lose the time you had to polish your shoes, shine your belt buckle, polish your OCS brass, get a haircut, and so forth.

Since you did not have time to do all of this stuff in the first place, having to take the time to go back and go through the qualification course again would not be good. As it was, if you went to the PX or somewhere else, it usually meant someone in the platoon would have to do a chore to help you out. Thus, volunteering to go to the PX to buy window cleaner for use on the shower-room mirrors and platoon bay windows meant that someone else would have to polish your shoes for you or put your OCS brass on in the exact army way, and on and on. Few of us had mastered the exact army way of pinning the OCS brass on our collars. All of us had been dropped repeatedly to knock out fifty because the little OCS pins were an imperceptible fraction of an inch off from the army way. A couple of the guys were getting the knack of it. They spent a lot of time helping the others.

Already we were set to take our first written test on the classes we were attending. The last hour and a half before lights-out was designated for study time. The Tacs would spring into the platoon bays, trying to catch someone doing something other than studying. My most immediate pain came from fingerprints on my belt buckle, my dress shoes not being spit-shined to a high enough gloss, or my cubicle floor not reflecting the Tacs' face brightly enough. I was not stupid. The army clearly wanted those things more than they wanted me to max the test on how to lay a World War II minefield.

My strategy for getting details done during mandatory study time was elaborate. I put the shoes I was going to work on that night in the bottom desk drawer along with my little cotton balls, small container of water, and black shoe polish. I then covered the desktop with notes from class and the applicable army manuals. By placing a pencil in the crease, I could quickly open them to pages that would match my notes. As soon as I heard the bay doors open, I would drop the shoe I was working on into the open drawer, quickly push it shut—being careful not to slam it—and turn my torso so that my head, hands, and arms were over the book or notes by the time the Tac had made it within eyeballing range. The whole maneuver required split-second coordination. By doing my personal details for the morning inspection during study time, I was able to crawl in bed at lights-out. Many of the guys took flashlights under their covers after lights-out to complete various tasks. I never did that. I needed my sleep too badly to miss it.

Lost sleep was always a problem. From the very beginning, the Tacs would patrol up and down the aisles of the large lecture halls we sat in for most of our classes. Hardly an hour would go by when a Tac did not spring into a row of candidates to grab one who had fallen asleep during the lecture. The hapless fellow would be dragged out of the row, falling and tripping while knocking books off the continuous desktop for that row. In contrast to the droning of the instructor on the stage below, the commotion and crashing sounds were startling. The desks were arranged in amphitheater fashion with chairs bolted to the floor. Their backs were like the slats in a picket fence. The victim's body bouncing off of them made an almost rhythmic sound. It must have been standard operating procedure (SOP) for the instructors, as they never seemed to interrupt the monotone flow of their words or their use of charts, pointers, and overhead-projector slides while the still-drowsy fellow was dragged out of the classroom.

A couple of the guys really took the classes seriously. Gary Queen's dad was rumored to be a police chief in California. He wanted to become an MP. He figured that the only way it could happen was for him to get the best grades in the company. That might give him a chance to get transferred out of infantry and into the MPs. Another guy was studying pretty hard, but I did not know why. Maybe he just liked to study. He had a master's degree in English, they said. The word was that he wanted to be a diplomat when he got out of the army. As for me, I just wanted to get through it all. They were not laying many World War II–type minefields in Vietnam. Learning information like that did not seem like something I wanted to invest a lot of valuable time in. I needed to pass the test, but I sure did not need to max it. I needed to keep the Tacs off my back. The only way to do that was by spit-shining shoes and floors; polishing belt buckles, OCS brass, and chest-of-drawers tops; and so forth. When they started teaching us stuff like how to call in artillery fire, well, that was different. Several guys had told me that no one was getting branch transfers out of the infantry. I would try my best to learn those things that were going to keep me alive. For now, reducing my pain during morning inspections was my highest priority.

The word was that guys with B profiles would be given priority for

A typical classroom scene.

Candidates at work on an in-class assignment.

getting branch transfers out of infantry. Up to 10 percent of the company could be considered for branch transfers. Thirty percent of the company had B profiles. A B profile meant that something was not perfect with your body. I had an A profile. All of my body parts seemed to function within the army's normal range. My chances of a branch transfer to the Medical Service Corps were looking bleaker than ever.

The morning after buying liquid floor wax, furniture polish, Windex, extrastrength Bab-O, and other cleaning supplies, we passed our first inspection. The army has a way of teaching you about important things.

"Make way!" a loud, strong voice demanded from one of the cubicles near the doors to the platoon bay. "Make way! Senior candidate in the hallway!"

We sprang to attention. It did not make any difference that some of us were half-dressed or engaged in multiple activities. Up to this point, we had escaped harassment from senior candidates—those who were in the final phase of OCS and close to graduation. They had hit several of the other platoons, but not ours. The robin's-egg blue helmet liners perched cockily on their heads distinguished them from us underlings. No one dared move. Anything that drew attention to you meant harassment.

Swiftly, five of them swooped into the platoon bay. Two of them immediately focused on a candidate in his underwear. "Why are you out of uniform?" screamed one of them into the man's lowered face.

Just as quickly, the second senior candidate positioned himself so his mouth was next to the underling's right ear and shouted: "You don't have your dog tags on! You don't have your dog tags on! If this building collapses, how will I know whose mama to call? She'll want to know her baby's dead. Don't you love your mama, Candidate? Don't you love your mama? Answer me, you ungrateful child."

"Sir, yes, Sir," the red-faced candidate shouted back.

In a mocking, singsong manner, the senior candidate repeated, "Sir, yes, Sir, *what?* Do you or don't you love your mother?"

The bugged-eyed wretch shouted out as loudly as his oxygen-depleted lungs would allow, "Sir, yes, Sir! I love my mama, Sir!"

While this little drama was unfolding, the other three senior candidates moved down the aisle, shouting at various junior candidates as they went.

Nat had the misfortune of being just outside our cubicle when the blue-capped birds swooped in. His back was braced against the partition. I stood as rigidly still as possible in the little passageway, looking down the aisle and directly into the side of his head. Just one of them made it down the passageway far enough to confront Nat.

"You're smiling, Candidate," a short, stocky senior candidate blared into Nat's face. Nat's little grin grew into a fully blossomed smile. Poor Nat was in for it now.

Shouts and countershots from other candidates filled the air, but they receded into the background during the time-frozen seconds that we focused on Nat's apparent undoing. The violence of the words elsewhere bounced off Nat, me, and those nearby.

"You're mocking me and the whole U.S. Army!" the beet-red face roared.

Scottie rushed up to the senior candidate and screamed into the side of his red, spider-veined face, "Sir, Officer Candidate Newsome requests

Senior candidates corner a new officer candidate.

A new candidate braces at attention while being instructed by a senior candidate.

permission to speak, Sir!" before Nat had a chance to reply, although his smile had disappeared.

The senior candidate turned his head to look at Scottie standing at attention with confrontation gleaming from his eyes. I sprang from my position, pushed up against the senior candidate, and exclaimed, "Sir,

Officer Candidate Morton requests permission to speak, Sir!" My last words were drowned out by the same demand being made of the senior candidate by five or six others from the platoon. We had him surrounded. Our continuously repeated demands, made as loudly as we could into his face, drowned out his response. We had him trapped. He was surrounded. I looked up to see what the other blue-hats were going to do. To my amazement, none of them were in the bay. They had left and this guy was trapped, alone, without any support.

"Ha, ha, ha," he began laughing. It was a genuine laugh. That was what stunned us into silence.

"Good job, good job," he declared. "Way to come to the aid of your own. Excellent. At ease," he said to Nat.

Looking over his shoulder, the blue-hat saw Junior for the first time —as did the rest of us. Standing on the top bunk in his cubicle, Junior had his shoulders pressed against the ceiling beam. His arms were grasping the beam, which he was pressing into the wedge of his back. The massive muscles of those arms were strained to maximum expansion. He had huge biceps.

"Get down from there," ordered the senior candidate.

"I can't, Sir. I'm holding up the ceiling. If I let go, the whole building will collapse, Sir. We'll all be killed, including the highly regarded senior candidate, Sir.

"It's true, Sir!" shouted his cube mate, Mike, in support. "I heard them cracking just before he jumped up there and saved us all."

We all roared with laughter. This was just too good to be true.

The senior candidate joined in. He was truly tickled.

"You guys are all right," he said. "You know how to stick together. It will help some of you make it. You know that at least a third of you will drop out."

"Sir, no, Sir," shouted Scottie. The rest of us picked up his cry of protest.

"Okay, okay, okay," the blue one laughed, raising his hand for silence.

As we quieted down, he continued: "The only way you'll make it is to help each other. It's remarkable that you've come together this quickly. Maybe you're right; maybe you'll all make it. I don't believe it, but you can hope. You've come this far, and you don't even have a tactical officer."

That was news to us. We had not seen Lieutenant White for several days. No one had thought anything about it. Lieutenants from the other platoons had been in and out of the bay. The other lieutenants had not ignored us during inspections or in the dining hall. It was the way things were. We knew no other way. As far as we were concerned, different Tacs shouting at you was SOP.

"What happened to our tactical officer?" someone asked.

"He was reassigned is all I know. You're supposed to get a new one in about a week. I've got to go now. You guys take care. I'll try to come back in a day or two to see how you're doing. Maybe I can help some of you make it. Hell, maybe I can help you all make it," he said with a grin and a wave.

CHAPTER 18

Lenny's Reign

"Your days of coasting are over," said 2d Lt. Jeffrey Leonard, our newly assigned tactical officer. "I'm here to give you direction." He tried to glare at our assembled group in the front of the platoon bay. His scowl was out of place with his physical presence. One would guess that he was seventeen years old. He had to be older than that. They say the army does not commission anyone under eighteen years of age. Like the rest of us, he had the lean, hungry look of someone who could and would jog all day if he had to. The shadows under his eyes were incongruent with his pale white skin. Red freckles on his face emphasized the paleness of his complexion. They fit with the short, sandy-red hair that crowned his head in a standard military haircut. The final straw that destroyed his military image of a lean, mean, fighting machine was the slightest of hints at the corners of his mouth that he was about to smile. At any second, you expected him to burst into laughter at the ridiculousness of the mess we were all in. "Since I am perfectly clear, you have no questions. Dismissed," he stated. Abruptly, he left.

Everyone was abuzz. My opinion was that not a whole lot more could happen to us to make us more stressed than we were. We continued to fail more inspections than the other platoons. That kept us fairly limited in privileges. The shine on the floor was our most recent downfall. It just was not shiny enough. I had left the latrine detail to be on the floor detail. The candidates taking care of the floor were the ones who needed the extra help. We would wax and buff just before evening study hall. After that, walking around on it was held to a minimum. We rigged up a way for people to walk on bunks, towels, chairs, and the like so that their feet would not touch the floor. In the morning, as everyone was rushing out to the first formation of the day, a crew of us would buff our way out of the bay. They were virgin floors for the officers to trample on as they continued to tear apart loose bedding, throwing incorrectly hung dress uniforms from the wall lockers onto the floor, and stir up improperly folded underwear in the chests of drawers. If it was not perfect, it was not right. An officer followed orders to the letter or he was not an officer. Obviously, we were not officers.

Lenny, as we called him amongst ourselves, kept showing up in the platoon bay. Rather than yell at our failings, he scowled at us as best he could manage. His smile kept bursting through at the wrong times. He would start out expressing shock at something in as earnest a manner as one could hope for only to have the sparkle in his eyes spread to the corners of his mouth and then burst into a big smile. Grinning, he would slip into a sarcastic comment: "I see your barber has a drinking problem, Candidate. Drop and knock out twenty for the poor judgment of letting him get too close to your head. . . . How often have you missed the urinal and hit your shoes since their last shine, Candidate? Drop and knock out fifty. . . . Tell me your senile grandmother pinned those OCS insignia on, and I'll feel better about you, Candidate. Drop and knock out twenty-five."

It seemed that wherever we went, Lenny was there. His crisp observations always seemed to end with "Drop and knock out. . . ." It could be in the hallway of the lecture hall, on the rifle range, or in the OCS area around which you were double-timing. Lenny was there, and someone was doing push-ups. The pressure was intense. We started passing inspections.

Paying someone $5 for a new pair of shoestrings to put into my dress shoes in the hope that it would help me pass my cubicle inspection was nothing. Perfection was the only thing acceptable. The tips of the shoes had to be perfectly aligned with the display combat boots with no fingerprints on the looking-glass shine. Lord help me if I ever had to open my footlocker during an inspection. The inspecting officer would get to see the combat boots I wore when we were out in the boonies. It would be obvious that I wore them and not my display boots. We had been told repeatedly that we were not to spend extra money on "show" equipment. Everything on display was to be what we routinely used. The army would not tolerate wasted money on show. Well, any fool would have known that I could not maintain a mirrorlike shine on the tips of my combat boots if I had to wear them all day. The hours required to achieve a shine like that simply were not available. Hell, you resented the fact that you had to take time to go to the bathroom. It stole valuable time from performing another task that might help you pass the next inspection.

Not a second was to be wasted. If it was, you would be gone. You would not make it.

"Pig privileges! Pig privileges! You've got pig privileges, you scum," 2d Lt. Randall McCook's slightly chubby cheeks puffed and spit the words at us as we began eating our lunch on the square. First Platoon's Tac, 2d Lt. Theodore Hughes echoed the cry.

"Push it in your mouth. Use both hands. Shove, shove. Stuff your mouth. Pig privileges! Then get the hell out and onto the trucks. Move! Move! Get your asses out of here!"

I shoved in bread, a meat patty, and green beans. The mixture fell from my mouth as I chewed. This was great. Gulping milk—with it spilling out the sides of my mouth—helped me to bolt the food down. What a treat! This was the first time I had filled my mouth since I had been here.

"Get out, get out! Move, move!" the Tacs screamed as they ran around the tables and confronted candidates who appeared to be attempting to chew their food or who looked like they were a little relaxed about the whole process.

More food filled my cheeks. More milk flowed down my chest. Jumping out of my chair, I rammed half a meat patty into my pocket and grabbed another handful of green beans. Lieutenant McCook turned to face me. "Exit left," my brain ordered. My body obeyed. Bolting for the outside door, my leg kicked an empty chair. I could hear it bouncing off the floor as I hurtled through the doorway. This was wonderful. My stomach was full.

It was off to the firing range. We had to qualify. Hell, I still had not zeroed my weapon. The distant pop-up targets would be hard to hit without a zeroed weapon. Insecurity sat beside me. I hate that feeling. The final score said I had barely passed. Damn. I was a good shot. Why couldn't I zero my weapon? It did not make sense.

"If you don't screw up, the company will get a weekend pass in two weeks," Lieutenant Best told our assembled group. What astounding news. I wrote Anna about it in that day's letter. Some of the guys said they were going to drive to Atlanta. I told her I could meet her at the airport. Of course, the risk was that they would say we had screwed up at the last minute. In that case she would be there and I would be here. We decided it was worth the risk. The arrangements were made. We would be together.

Anna did not cry when she saw me. It was good to be with her. We stayed in our Peachtree Street hotel room except to eat. One maitre d'

Candidates do punishment push-ups after being caught having a late-night "pogey party."

was ungracious to us. We did look extremely young and the prices were very high. He put us at a table that seemed to be in more of a hallway than the dining room. It took him a long time to bring us the menus. When he did, he walked away without saying a word. Anna had brought along civilian clothes for me to wear. My clothing did not hide the fact that I was military. The leanness, the haircut, the straight posture, and the rigidly held back to keep my body at attention as I sat at the table were a quick giveaway. Maybe the guy realized that we were not of the social class that frequented his restaurant. Then again, he could have had a thing about the army and the war. I did not know what was going on, but something was. Some civilians are like that. We left without ordering. No one acted as if they noticed.

"One, Sir; two, Sir; three, Sir—" came the united counts of the 4th Platoon through the night air into our bay windows. We all left our bunks as quietly as possible to stare out the windows. They were in their underwear in the prone position out on the asphalt formation area behind the building. Lieutenant McCook circled around their straining bodies as he screamed at them.

"Lower! Lower! I want to see your faces smash into the sauce. You wanted them so bad, now wallow in it," he demanded with his mouth beside the ear of a candidate who was about to lower himself from the top of a push-up into the pizza directly below his face.

They had smuggled several pizzas into the barracks. They were having a pizza party after lights-out. It did not make sense. The rules were clear: In bed after lights-out; no food in the barracks. Hell, I had thought you would be sent to Vietnam for such a flagrant violation of the rules. Well, my logic went, they were not going to send a whole platoon to

Vietnam. Lieutenant McCook seemed to be enjoying it as they shouted out their push-up count. I decided to go back to bed. I needed my sleep. It came moments after my head hit the pillow.

The next day, word ran through the platoon. Lenny said we were wimps. All of the other platoons had been caught throwing pizza parties, ice cream parties, or other outrageous things after lights-out and we had not attempted a damn thing. Several of the guys came to me and said we needed to do something. They pointed out that I was the morale officer, so I had to pull something off.

"Okay, let's have a platoon meeting and see what the guys want," I responded.

"We could have a pizza party like Fourth Platoon," one of them offered.

"Yeah, but leave out the getting caught part," I retorted. That brought laughter.

"It's not original," another candidate shot back.

"Well, what can we do that the others haven't already done?" I questioned. There was silence.

"No one's shown a skin flick," one of the guys offered.

"Yeah, that's a great idea," another chimed in.

I cringed. This was not something I wanted to do. This was not like getting a pizza. The army might really get pissed. No, this was not good.

"My wife could smuggle in an eight-millimeter film projector for us," big Eric volunteered.

"Hey, that's it!" "Yeah, way to go." "This is great!" The spontaneous supportive comments were unanimous.

"I don't know how to order skin flicks," I said as a weak protest to the venture.

"Here's a skin magazine," one of the guys said as he poked a copy of *Male* magazine into my face. "It's got a lot of ads in the back that you can send off to."

"It'll take a lot of planning," I countered.

"We can do it," came the reply. Everyone was into it.

"Okay. We have to plan out every detail, with backup plans for the mess-ups," I said, resigning myself to the inevitable.

We worked hard on the plan. No one seemed interested in what skin flick we got. They just wanted it as soon as possible. The selection was up to me. Damn, I had never ordered a skin flick in my life. I had no idea how to go about selecting one. There were three ads that said they would deliver within three weeks of receiving the order. All three of them said that the eight-millimeter film would arrive in a plain, brown-wrapped package with no outside identification as to its contents. That was good, I thought, under the circumstances. The cheapest of the three was selected. There was not enough money in the slush fund to pay for it. I had to make a collection from the platoon. It was not all that much per man. The order was sent. I paid for it from my own pocket and then reimbursed myself from the slush fund after depositing the guys' money. My rules for the slush fund had to be rigidly followed. It did not make any difference that I was making the purchase. The whole platoon had to agree on the item and its probable cost before a purchase was made. Everyone would then be assessed his fair share. A bank record of the deposit and of the withdrawal would be available for anyone in the platoon to see.

When the film arrived in my post office box, I would bring it into the bay and lock it in my footlocker. We would need to show it as soon after that as possible. If we had a surprise footlocker inspection, it might be all over for me. I would have to unlock it and show the contents to an officer. Of all the various contraband items not to get caught with, this had to be the one. We had to show the film as quickly as possible and then get rid of it.

On the designated night, Eric's wife would park in a secluded part of one of the many parking lots in the area. He and a couple of the other guys would sneak out and get the projector, an extension cord, and screen from her. Since this was all after lights-out, we would have to make it look as if they were in their beds in case the officer of the day came in for a bed check. Once inside the bay, we would have to set up guards to watch the stairwell in case the officer of the day started to come up. If he showed up, we would all have to jump back into our beds while at the same time hiding the equipment. This was definitely a risky venture. Everyone had an assigned task. I mailed out the order.

"Have you heard? Have you heard what happened?" one of the guys asked me, with real strain in his voice.

"Not anything that would bend you out of shape. What's happening?" I shot back with an edge to my voice reflecting the tension sent by the messenger.

"A senior candidate just got caught with a skin flick. It arrived at our post office this morning. The brigade commander and his company commander ordered him to open the package in front of them. It was in a plain-brown wrapper. Someone at the post office must have alerted them. Anyway, when he opened it, the brigade commander told him he was dismissed from the program. He already has orders to 'Nam."

Until that moment, I was unaware of the rapidity with which depression could consume one's thoughts. I was going to get kicked out of the program. I was going to be sent to Vietnam as a rifleman. I would not be able to be with Anna for a whole year. This was terrible. I would be humiliated. Depression, despair, agitation, and hope were all mixed up within me. The flick should arrive within the week. Maybe the brigade commander would not notice it had arrived. Maybe no one would notice. Maybe the magazine would send it to the wrong address.

The guys were sympathetic. They knew I was worried. When I made my daily trip to the post office, they would do little things for me. When I got back to the platoon bay I would find that one of the guys had Brasso'ed my spare belt buckle, polished the top of my chest of drawers, or done some other helpful personal task. Their kindnesses were appreciated but did little to relieve my fear.

A package was in my post office box. I could see it through the little window. Quickly, I glanced around to who was looking at me. Would they come running from behind the boxes to catch me with it in my hand? Act calm. Don't draw attention to yourself, were the words in my mind as my fingers fumbled to pull the object from the box.

It was wrapped in plain brown paper. The paper could have been cut from a grocery store bag. The box was just the right size for one of those reels for a reel-to-reel tape recorder. As casually as the act can be done, I unbuttoned two buttons of my fatigue shirt and stuck the flick inside. Just as rapidly, I rebuttoned them. In the process, I dropped Anna's daily letter. Bending down to pick it up, I stabbed myself between the ribs with a corner of the damned box. My quick pace back to the barracks did not draw attention to me. Every OCS candidate walked with a quick, brisk pace wherever he went. You could not get through the program with a casual step.

Bounding up the three flights of stairs, I went straight to my footlocker. Without comment, I unlocked it, dropped the flick in, and relocked it. My single-mindedness had communicated the arrival of the film to the guys in the platoon bay. Several converged on my cubicle.

"Now, all I have to worry about is a footlocker inspection," I said, rolling my eyes.

Speaking in a hushed tone, Scottie stated the obvious: "Well, we've got to get moving on this. I'll find out when Eric's wife can get the projector here. Mel, you take care of setting up the guards. They won't be able to see the flick unless we can figure out some way to relieve them so they'll be able to see some of it."

"Let me know what the final plans are," I said. "I want to make sure everything is covered. Remember, I'm the one holding the bag— er, ah, I mean the film." I flashed a grin that prompted smiles from my coconspirators.

The planning was good. This could not be a sloppy pizza party. The stakes were too high. Part of me just wanted it to be over. Another part of me was excited. It would be great if we pulled it off. Never having seen a skin flick, I was also curious about what it would be like.

That evening, we all pretended that everything was normal. Eric had smuggled in the projector. He had a couple of the guys help him get various parts of it and the extension cord into the bay. They had the pieces hidden behind footlockers, in dirty clothes bags, and behind dress uniforms hanging in wall lockers. We completed our chores and were in the cubicles pretending to be studying when the 3d Platoon tactical officer, 2d Lt. William George, burst through the bay doors.

"Ah ha!" he cried out, standing in front of the swinging doors. The swishing of the doors closing was the sound that answered him. During study time, we did not have to spring to attention when an officer entered the bay. Every back tensed. We knew he was there. He seemed to take a special delight in harassing us. The other Tacs would visit us, but Lieutenant George was the most frequent. He always brought grief with him. Quietly, I placed my Brasso-covered belt buckle in the bottom desk drawer beside my open can of Brasso. Quickly dropping the polishing cloth over both, I pushed the drawer shut with a steady pressure from my foot. At the last second I pulled back on the pressure. Slamming the drawer shut would be a certain giveaway. It would bring Lieutenant George to me as surely as failing to have your name stenciled on your T-shirt would get you fifty push-ups. I had practiced this maneuver many, many times to be prepared for this very moment.

Turning a page of the training manual from the day's classes that I had preopened and carefully propped up on the desktop, I heard Lieutenant George say with anger and satisfaction mixed into his voice, "That's shoe polish on your hands, Candidate. You've been polishing your shoes instead of studying, haven't you?"

Immediately, the three candidates in the next cubicle sprang from their chairs and stood at attention as Lieutenant George entered their space. "Open the bottom drawer," he demanded. Tom did as he was ordered. "What's this? What's this?" demanded Lieutenant George.

"Sir, it's a shoe-polishing rag, Sir," responded Tom in a voice practically choked off from the force of his braced chin being drawn into his chest as he stood at rigid attention.

"I've caught you. I've caught you, haven't I, Candidate?" the lieutenant demanded.

Tom, knowing that a candidate or officer never lies, responded with a sharp, "Sir, yes, Sir."

"I want a three-page military letter on my desk no later than forty-eight hours from now. It will be typed single-spaced, without error, and it will explain the importance of studying during study hall."

"Sir, yes, Sir!" Tom shouted back.

Lieutenant George's steps began again only to stop at our cubicle entrance. I could feel his glare. With deliberate slowness, I turned the page of the training manual on my desk. The standoff continued. I wrote a note. The silence prevailed. At last the feet turned and moved on. There was a commotion at the end of the hallway. It was too muffled to make out. Someone was catching Lieutenant George's ire. Just one more routine encounter. Nothing was out of sync. Everything was in order. Lieutenant George did not suspect what was about to happen.

"Lights-out!" came the cry.

We all crawled into our bunks. To my amazement, someone was shaking my arm. "Wake up," Nat whispered in my ear, "it's twenty-three hundred hours. Let's go."

I could not believe it. I had actually fallen asleep. Already, the bay was alive with shadowy movement. Everyone was up. A guard was posted in the top bunk nearest the double doors, straining to see a corner of the stairwell. He would sound the alarm if the officer of the day was approaching. From this point on, we were all in danger. I was no longer the only one with the flick.

Eric and his crew moved with precision. The film screen was set up in one cubicle. The projector was propped up on a footlocker sitting on top of a chest of drawers in the opposite cubicle. I threaded the film into the projector. I knew eight-millimeter film projectors well. My college courses in education had made sure that I master the many teaching aids for classroom use. I chuckled at the thought of telling Professor Ullrich how I was applying his teachings.

There we all were. Some wore T-shirts to match their white, army-issue boxer shorts and others did not. Thirty-four men, minus the relay of posted guards, placed themselves in various positions around the furnishings to view the magic of the screen.

The clicking sound of the projector matched the white and dark flashes on the screen. An obviously middle-aged woman who might have been attractive in her youth stood before us in a conservative blouse and full-length skirt. She had an unconvincing smile that was focused straight ahead at no one as she mechanically unbuttoned the blouse to reveal a large black brassiere. It covered all of her fleshy breasts and most of her upper chest. A quick movement to the side zipper on her skirt allowed the skirt to drop below her knees. You could not tell exactly where it fell, as her feet and the floor were not shown. Her black panties covered slightly less flesh than our boxer shorts did. My eyes kept shooting to the bay doors. If the OD came in now, we would never get everyone back into their bunks and the projector hidden in time. Fate ruled our destiny.

Slowly the woman on screen turned. We got a back shot of her moderately overweight hips and of the slight roll of loose flesh at her sides. This was really bad. There was nothing sexy about this film.

Facing us, the lady reached up to her left bra strap. She let it fall while holding the covering to her breast. There was definitely some cleavage exposed. Crossing her arms, she used her left hand to drop the strap from her right shoulder. Before that breast could be fully exposed, she caught the cup and held it in place. More cleavage, but no more than you would see on a crowded Cincinnati street near Fountain Square in the summertime.

Murmurs were coming from the men. Abruptly, the scene changed. For $20 you could order a film titled "Monique Undresses," the message on the screen said. As it told us how to order the next film, Monique removed a nylon stocking from an extended leg peeking out from a floor-length skirt with a long slit in it. Then the film was over. We moaned, muttered, and laughed at our foolishness as we sprang into motion. The screen was folded, the projector dismantled, and the film returned to my footlocker within seconds.

In the morning I was faced with a stark fact: I did not know how to get the film out of there. For the moment it was safe, but only until we got hit with a surprise footlocker inspection. Eric said he could not risk passing it on to his wife with the pieces of the projector. I understood that. In turn, I could not just toss it in the dumpster. They were always having candidates crawl into it and wallow around in the kitchen garbage for breaking some dining-hall rule like eyeballing, talking while at the table, or failing to do something right as the designated server at the officers' table in the front of the dining hall. No, it would be discovered in the trash. Since our fatigue shirts were tailored to be skin tight, I could not walk far with the film tucked under it. Someone was certain to notice the bulge. I had a real problem. If I got caught with it, they would not give me push-ups; they would give me the boot. Fortunately, we had yet to have a footlocker inspection. Maybe we would not have one. I was safe for a while.

We were feeling pretty cocky about ourselves. We had really pulled it off. This was no kids' pizza party; this was a real act of risky derring-do. We had pulled it off and no one knew. It added spring to our step. The only nagging problem was that damned reel of film in my footlocker. A week passed and none of the Tacs indicated any knowledge of our skin-flick party. With each passing day, my sense of urgency about getting rid of the film diminished. Finally, it was just a little dull toothache pain that never quite went away. It was something that had to be dealt with, but not today.

We knew immediately that something was wrong. The deuce-and-a-half trucks had brought us back from the day's training exercise a little earlier than usual. As we began jumping out, there were lieutenants everywhere. This was highly unusual. They were screaming at us. Candidates were frantically running even as they were shouted at.

"Move! Move! Get up there and bring your footlocker down to the company formation. Move! Get there and get back down here. Move! Move!"

Already guys were running out of the barracks with their footlockers on their shoulders. Others had placed them in front of their spot in the company formation and stood at attention as lone sentinels. The sparsely scattered figures at rigid attention stood out amidst the chaos of screaming lieutenants and running candidates.

Along with everyone else, I ran as fast as I could into the barracks. Lieutenants were even in the hallways and on the stairwells, shouting as loud as they could. Men dodged each other as those loaded down with footlockers on their shoulders, in their arms, or on top of their heads hurled themselves down the stairwell, passing those scampering up for there own burdens of sin.

Fear was in my heart even as my feet moved as fast as they could up the stairs. This was it. I would be found out. What was I going to do? Oh, God, help me. Grabbing my footlocker from under the bunk and hoisting it onto my shoulder caused me to bump into a desk, knocking the training manuals stacked on it to the floor. No time to stop and pick them up. An officer stood at the bay doors shouting incomprehensible words, which could only mean we were to move faster. As I ran toward the double doors carrying my load, I scanned the mess. All of the cubicles were out of order. The bay was a total mess. Papers and training manuals scattered on the floor, chairs overturned, bunk beds pushed out of alignment. Where had all of the lieutenants come from? I figured that they must be from the other training companies. Rushing down the steps faster than I ever imagined was possible with the heavy load on my shoulder, I reflected on this fact. These Tacs would really come down hard on contraband in your footlocker. There would be no mercy for a skin flick. If it had not all been moving so fast, I would have paused to cry. This was the end. I was undone.

About half of our platoon had formed up by the time I arrived. My spot was waiting for me. Second Squad was the second row. I was in the middle of the row. There were three men to my right, the side closest to the barracks. I knew my spot by heart. Some of the other platoons were better formed. They had been the first to get off the trucks. Already, the officers were having them open their footlockers. You could see the officers reaching into them and pulling out forbidden objects. Candy bars, cookies, floor wax, and furniture polish were all thrown into the air, which was full of Tacs' screams of rage at these flagrant rules violations. The officers would kick over entire footlockers so that their contents were sent flying in every direction. Candidates were being dropped to knock out untold numbers of push-ups, their voices mingling together in the counting.

Cries of "one, Sir; two, Sir; three, Sir," blended in with "thirty-eight, Sir; thirty-nine, Sir," and "Fifty-five, Sir," followed by "One, Sir, two, Sir," as a newly assaulted candidate began his punitive count. The blending of the count with the shouts of the officers amidst the cries of "Sir, yes, Sir" made a scene of madness that escalated my fear.

Two officers started on our platoon. They came from where the 6th Platoon was forming. The end men were spilling out the contents of their footlockers and then dropping for push-ups. An officer came over from 4th Platoon and began dropping guys just to my right front. I was about to be next.

Without thinking, I dropped to the ground. "One, Sir; two, Sir; three, Sir," I screamed loudly as I could as I rapidly counted out my perfectly formed push-ups beside my still-locked footlocker. An officer's boots walked past my straining face. They stopped in front of the man next to me as the order was given for him to open his footlocker.

"Seventeen, Sir; eighteen, Sir," continued my count as my comrade spilled the contents of his footlocker onto the asphalt. A shoe brush rolled under my chest. It did not stop my rhythm. I simply lowered my chest onto it and endured the pain. The officer's shouts were partially drowned out by all of the other shouts despite the fact that he was so near. Chaos was everywhere.

"One, Sir; two, Sir; three, Sir," my squad mate called out, counting each push-up.

"Fifty, Sir," I screamed in triumph. I sprang to my feet and stood at rigid attention. Staring straight ahead with no eyeballing, I shouted as loudly as I have ever shouted, "Sir, yes, Sir!"

Still with eyes fixed straight ahead, I bent down, picked up my locked footlocker and smartly placed it on my shoulder. Then, without a sideward glance, I ran toward the barracks as fast as my load would allow. Taking two steps at a time, I wove through the maze of terrified men, unintelligible shouts from officers, and into the platoon bay. Once inside, I rushed to my cubicle. After placing the footlocker in its proper spot, I returned just as quickly downstairs and reassumed my place in the formation. I remained at rigid attention until all of the other men in the platoon had regained their position in the ranks upon completion of their personal ordeals. As soon as the entire platoon was back in formation without footlockers, we were dismissed.

Later, as we were restoring the platoon bay to its pre-footlocker-inspection state, several of the guys asked me what had happened about the film. When I told them the story, we laughed. God had heard my prayer. Now, if only He could help me get rid of the flick. The core problem was still with me.

Two Sunday mornings later, the word spread like ants converging on a discarded candy bar. Lenny had been relieved of command for conduct unbecoming an officer. We were once again without a tactical officer. He was going to a holding company and then to 'Nam. A holding company was for trainee dropouts who had quit the program or were kicked out, as well as other people sent there for a variety of administrative reasons. The men there were all awaiting orders. Until they came, the men reportedly just hung out.

It was said that Lenny had been arrested for disturbing the peace late Saturday night or early that morning. His wife had locked him out of their trailer and he stood outside banging repeatedly on the door and shouting at her while doing so. People in the trailer park had called the police. Further complicating the matter was the fact that Lenny was not wearing any clothes. Who knows if the story was totally or partially true? All we knew was that that was the word and that Lenny was nowhere to be found.

We had gone weeks without an assigned tactical officer before and we could do it again. Besides, we knew the army would eventually assign us another one and that he would harass us like all the rest. In the meantime, Lieutenant George, Lieutenant McCook, and the other tactical officers seemed capable of picking up the slack. They were. Right off we began failing morning inspections again. At this stage, that meant we got no Saturday or Sunday afternoons to go out of the barracks area. We could not go to the post theater, the PX, or out for a haircut. Without neatly cut hair you could be personally restricted to the barracks, even if the platoon had post privileges. There were other infractions an individual could commit that would result in personal barracks restrictions, but they were too numerous to mention.

In preparation for a Saturday personal inspection, Bill, one of my cubicle mates, asked me to give him a haircut. I told him there was no way I would agree to cut his hair. My mother used to cut my and my two brothers' hair with hand clippers. It was hell. As soon as the clippers got dull, which was right away, they would pull your hair—and that hurt. Your natural response was to pull away. Unfortunately, doing that caused her to cut a big wad of hair out, which made your head look as if it had multiple dips in it.

"Ah, come on," Bill pleaded. "You can do it. Nobody else will. Look, I've got electric clippers in my footlocker. They're a lot easier to use than those handheld ones. Please. If you don't do it, I'll never pass tomorrow's inspection. I haven't been off barracks restriction for weeks. This is my only chance. I won't be mad if you mess up. I've got nothing to lose, please."

"Okay," I reluctantly agreed, "but it won't come out right. I'm only agreeing because I know you won't get post privileges anyway."

It was terrible. I could not get his hair even anywhere. There were huge gaps all over his head. With it being military short to begin with, you would think it would be impossible to make much of a mess. Well, you would be wrong. Finally, I just stopped. No matter how hard I tried, it just got worse and worse.

"What are we going to do?" Bill asked. I felt sick. He really looked bad.

"Well, maybe the lieutenant will just walk by in a quickie inspection of our cubicle and not look closely at you. I don't know." There was nothing else to say.

The three of us stood at attention in our cubicle. We were standing in a neat row in front of the bunk beds. Our shoes were shined, bedding taut, floor shined, and the other details attended to in the hopes of passing Saturday morning inspection. All was ready—except for that hair.

Lieutenant George entered the cubicle, his hands clasped behind his back. His lack of comment as he ran his gaze carefully over the contents of our chests of drawers meant that our razors, soap, toothpaste, and toothbrushes were all in their proper places. Our T-shirts, boxer shorts, fatigues, and socks were correctly folded and placed in their exact spots as required. Pushing past the three of us, he peered into our open wall lockers. The dress uniforms were neatly hung. Each wall locker was identical in content and in the way those contents were stored. Without a sound, he moved back to the center of our cubicle. He was leaving. We had made it. In mid-stride, he stopped. Turning, he placed himself directly in front of the butchered one.

"Who did this to you?" he asked, a hint of pity in his measured, whispery voice.

"Sir, I don't know what you mean, Sir," my protective friend replied.

Iron was in Lieutenant George's next words, "Who did this to you?"

"Sir, he did, Sir," Bill replied, with a slight nod of his head toward his companion, me.

Positioning his nose to within half an inch of mine, the lieutenant said, "Candidate, you're restricted to the platoon area for the weekend." Turning to my companion, he added, "You have post privileges so you can get a haircut."

Quietly, calmly, Lieutenant George left the cubicle.

"Lieutenant Leonard has gotten his orders. He ships out to 'Nam next week. He's going to come by Sunday and say good-bye." Well, I thought, that's nice of him. He was okay. I never saw him go out of his way to give anyone grief. He just did his job of staying on our case like all of the others did. I hoped things worked out for him.

"Hey, morale officer," one of the guys said to me, "let's give him a going-away present."

"Yes," piped in the other guys, "let's give him a present."

"Okay," I agreed, "Let me think about it and make a recommendation."

It did not take me long and the guys agreed. We would give Lieutenant Leonard our skin flick. Some of the guys went to the PX and got wrapping paper and a bow. We covered for them while they were shopping.

Lieutenant Leonard stood before us in front of the bay's swinging doors.

"I just want you guys to know that I really appreciated the laughs we had together," he said. "I think you're a good bunch of men." His voice was tinged with sadness, but that old hint of a grin at the corners of his mouth was still there.

Walking forward from the crowd toward Lenny, I said, "Sir, we know that your leadership will save lives in Vietnam. We all appreciate the time you were able to spend with us to help us learn the OCS way. In appreciation, we would like to give you a gift."

Pulling my right arm from behind my back, I revealed the package we had gift wrapped for him. It was in the same box in which it had arrived. I thought the bow was a particularly nice touch.

Immediately, he broke into a big grin. "I know I'll enjoy it for its entertainment value," he said as he took it from me. Tucking it under his arm, he braced at attention and saluted us. We saluted back. He turned and left.

The 5th
Platoon's
motto and
roster.

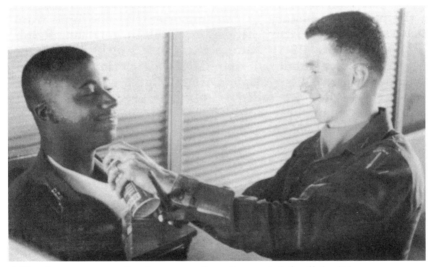

A Tac demonstrates what happens when the cap is left off the lid.

Buffing the floor of the platoon bay.

An OCS platoon on the march.

Assembling for a formation behind the barracks.

Candidates stand at attention in formation.

No "eyeballing" allowed!

Candidates low crawl toward a Tac.

CHAPTER 19

0800

"Candidate, you're not studying," said a soft voice coming from the entrance to my cubicle.

My stomach touched the roof of my mouth. How had the Tac gotten here? I had not heard the bay doors open. How could I have been so careless? I had slipped up big time. Jumping out of my chair and knocking the shoe-polish can to the floor, I braced to attention.

"Sir, yes, Sir." I responded. The shoe-polish can continued to roll across the floor.

"I want a single-spaced, typed, two-page military letter on my desk by zero-eight-hundred hours. It will address the importance of studying during the designated time. Do you understand?"

"Sir, yes, Sir."

He quietly moved on down the bay with more than a hint of smugness in his swagger. At least my loud responses had alerted the others to his presence.

Hell, I've gone and done it to myself, I thought. What is a military letter? A few of the guys had been assigned them, but none from within my immediate circle of friends. Not only was I in the dark about the nature of a military letter, I was also clueless as to how I could get a typewriter. Nobody had a typewriter. Hell, one would never fit in a footlocker. I would have known if someone had one of them. It would have been obvious and completely unmilitary. A guy would have had to dump it his first day here. There were no typewriters.

Even if I had access to a typewriter, there was no time to get a military letter done before lights-out or after lights-on in the morning. We had slightly more than just an hour before lights-out as it was. All of that time was needed to get ready for the morning inspection. In the morning, you barely had time to dress, shave, pee, and make it to the chow line before morning formation. After that we marched, ran, or were trucked off for a full day's worth of training. There simply was no time to write, let alone type, a military letter. On top of that, the Tac's first-floor office was locked at night. The door was not opened until 0800. The whole thing was impossible. I was stressed. The others had done it. There had to be a way. The last two thoughts kept me from losing my cool.

As soon as study time was over, several of the guys converged on my cubicle. I blurted out my brief story and told them about the impossible task I had been given.

"Not to worry," Mel said. "A couple of guys in the front cubicles have become experts at pulling this off."

He went on to explain that they had acquired a key to that Tac's office. After lights-out, they would sneak down, open his office, get the typewriter off his desk, and bring it up here. After I had the letter typed, they would smuggle the typewriter and my letter back to his office, lock the door, and everyone would be happy. They would even explain how to compose a military letter since they had already acquired the skill.

"Being the ones closest to the bay doors, they learned how to do this fairly early in the program," he said, laughing.

Nat volunteered to hold a flashlight for me while I typed. He was a good cubicle mate. Our other cubicle partner would keep his eyes glued on the sentinels posted near the bay doors. If they signaled that the OD was coming, he would relay the message instantly. Theoretically, the three of us would have enough time to douse the light, hide the typewriter under the bottom bunk, and get back into our racks before the OD made it to our cubicle. It seemed like a workable plan. It was the only plan.

I was amazed at how quickly they had developed a solution to the problem. It was obvious that I had been ignorant of a lot that had been going on around me. These guys were resourceful.

"Lights-out," came the cry. We jumped into bed as darkness fell with the flip of a switch. The streetlights outside provided just enough illumination for us to move around without bumping into things. Of course, the stairwell light and the latrine lights shining through the bay doors made it relatively bright for the first few cubicles. After a short hour of silence, I heard the bay doors squeak open and swish shut. It had begun. Someone was sneaking down to the first floor. He or they would unlock the Tac's door and whisk the typewriter up here. God, I hoped they did not get caught. I would feel terrible if that happened.

Fifteen minutes later the bay doors squeaked again. A shadowy figure scurried hunch-backed down the aisle. His white T-shirt and boxer shorts stood out in the darkness.

"Here you are. Let me know when you're ready for us to take it back," he said, setting the typewriter on the bottom bunk, Nat's bunk. He had also swiped some typing paper and correction fluid. These guys were really good.

"Thanks," I whispered, "you've saved my life in Vietnam."

He chuckled, slapped me on the back, and disappeared into the darkness.

Nat held the flashlight as I wrote my draft in pencil. We moved as one to the typewriter. I had taken typing in seventh grade. That was a long time ago. It was painful for me to type. I kept making errors. Both of my cubicle mates proofed the document. It took several tries before I achieved perfection. By definition, a military letter has no mistakes.

At last it was done. The hour had gone quickly. I sneaked the typewriter and letter up to the front of the bay. The lookouts saw me coming. We spoke in hushed voices. They said they would handle it from there. I started to thank them, but they motioned that there was no time. As they headed for the stairs, I returned to my bunk. Sleep came quickly.

In the morning, the lookouts said all had gone well. The Tac never said a word to me about the letter, so I guess all did go well. There was a nagging problem, however, which caused me to keep thinking about the whole process. The Tac knew that it was impossible for me to get the letter on his desk without breaking a hell of a lot of rules. Why did they force us to be dishonest? It did not make sense. They had drilled into us that officers never tell lies. Why were they forcing us into dishonest behavior? Apparently this had been going on for some time. Another question was how those guys had gotten hold of the Tac officer's keys. They had to be part of a pretty elaborate underground group that went beyond just our platoon. How did this group do all of the work that I was doing to pass inspection *and* have the extra time to play these games? Things just did not make sense to me. Something was wrong with this picture. Following the rules did not get you into the inner circle, and it was clear that there *was* an inner circle.

I was glad to be outside of the loop. All I wanted was to get through. Hope was still in my heart that I could get into the Medical Service Corps. All I needed to do was let them know I was here. That was my heart doing the thinking, not my head. It was pretty clear that the spirit of the bayonet would prevail. None of us were getting out of infantry.

CHAPTER 20

Troubles

I LIKED the army's meals. The food tasted good to me. Feeding so many men was a difficult task. I never complained about the food. The fact that we never got all we wanted had nothing to do with the food's quality. It was the continual harassment that kept the quantity down. After a while, the food's taste did not really matter. What mattered was getting enough calories. Our stomachs must have shrunk. By the time they started easing up on the mealtime harassment and forcing us to eat all of our meals on the square, we could not put much food into our stomachs. They seemed to fill up on the first helping. When you were outside the mess hall, you were so involved in the everyday task of trying to get more done than could be accomplished that it did not occur to you to think about eating.

The trucks had just off-loaded us for the day. Like everyone else, I was headed for the barracks to change out of my sweat-soaked fatigues. The Tacs would jump on us hard if we were in anything but freshly creased, clean, and unwrinkled fatigues. You just did not knowingly bring pain on yourself.

"Hey," one of the guys from 3d Platoon said as he approached me, "our Tac wants to see you in his office on the double."

"Thanks," I replied, feeling that old dread creep into me. You know the kind I mean. Remember the dreams you had in which you had to take a test that you had forgotten to study for? I knocked on his door. Lieutenants McCook and George greeted me.

"Come inside, Candidate," Lieutenant McCook said while making a mocking bow.

I stepped into the open doorway and saluted. "Sir, yes, Sir. Candidate Morton reporting as ordered, Sir."

They returned my salute. "Candidate, this package came for you in the mail today," Lieutenant George sneered as he held a paper-wrapped shoebox in front of my face.

I knew not to reach for it unless so directed. Being stiffly braced at attention was my only defense. My sweet wife's handwriting on the outside was unmistakable. Immediately, I knew what was inside. This was going to be another world of hurt. I had told her not to send me any food. She loved sending me things to eat. Obviously, she had forgotten.

"Open the box," Lieutenant George ordered, his voice dripping with meanness.

Taking it out of his hands, I tore it open. It was crammed full of her wonderful chocolate-chip cookies. Her daily letter sat on top of the congealed mass.

"Put the letter in your pocket," ordered Lieutenant McCook.

I obeyed.

"Now put a cookie in your mouth, Candidate," hissed Lieutenant George, who had picked up the box and was holding it in front of my face.

Picking one up, I bit into its side.

"I said, 'Put a cookie in your mouth,' not take a nibble, Candidate!" Lieutenant George screamed, his mouth up close to my right ear.

Reflexively, my hand pushed the whole thing inside.

"Another one now, quickly!" Lieutenant McCook screamed into my left ear.

I immediately crammed in a second one, which pushed the first cookie deep into my throat.

"Another one!" screamed Lieutenant George. His demand was instantly followed by Lieutenant McCook's echoing order.

I stuffed cookies into my mouth as fast as my hands could move. It was "pig privileges" all over again. I bolted a few swallows down to keep from strangling. The mass of cookies in my oral cavity had filled every possible space between my cheeks and gums. Even the cracks between my teeth were stuffed with cookie matter. I was unable to close my mouth and still they demanded that I pack in more. Finally it was clear that there was no room at the inn. A wet, sticky mass of partially chewed cookie dough fell to the floor.

"Stop, you pig! You're messing up the floor," Lieutenant McCook demanded as he pulled the box away from me.

"Do you want any more cookies, Candidate?" Lieutenant George inquired in the sarcastic manner he had perfected so well.

"No, Sir," came my muffled response as a few more cookie crumbs fell from my partially open mouth. I continued to move the mass with my tongue, trying to make it moist enough to swallow.

"You really enjoyed the cookies, didn't you, Candidate?" Lieutenant McCook seemed to demand more than ask.

I vigorously nodded my head up and down.

"Have you had enough of your cookies or would you like some more?" the lieutenant asked.

"Sir, I'm full, Sir," I said with a little clearer articulation, having just bolted another chunk down my throat.

Lieutenant George tossed the three-fourths-full box into the trash-can beside the desk.

"You'll write your sweet wife that you loved her cookies, won't you?" Lieutenant George ordered.

I nodded. This whole process was starting to look like a prank upper-classmen would pull during fraternity hell week. It was silly and it was funny. I wanted to laugh but had enough sense to suppress the urge.

"Be sure to remind her not to send any more, though," he said with a tender smile beaming from his face. "Now get out of here!"

"Sir, yes, Sir," I said, saluting.

They immediately returned my salute. I made a smart about-face and exited the room.

By the time I got to third floor, I was openly chuckling. The guys wanted to know what was up. We all had a good laugh. The gamesman-ship was becoming apparent.

My name was on the duty roster. I had been selected to be the officer's mess table orderly for the evening meal. This was the one detail every-one seemed to dread the most. The guys who had pulled the duty had reported terrible harassment. The task seemed simple enough.

The officers ate their meal at a long table that stretched across the front of the dining area. It gave the tactical officers a full view of all of the candidates as they ate. The orderly simply had to fulfill the Tacs' de-mands as they made them.

Naturally, you were to serve them in a military manner. That meant standing at attention or parade rest until called upon. When an officer spoke to you, you marched over to him with precision. Slouching while you walked, failing to make a sharp ninety-degree turn at a corner, drop-ping food on your shirtfront, having sweat visible in your armpits or dirt under your fingernails, not speaking clearly enough, spilling water while filling a glass, or putting too many spears of broccoli on the officer's plate were just a few of the miscues that could cause misforturne to visit you.

My four years of waiting tables, bussing them, and performing other dining-hall tasks during my college years were at last paying off. Almost all of the officers had finished eating and left. None of the ones who were left seemed to be paying me any specific attention. When one of them signaled that his water glass needed refilling, I moved from where I stood at parade rest against the back wall and filled it. I bumped into no one; not a drop of water was spilled. I bussed all the dishes from the same side of every officer. I ensured the butter dish was always full of butter patties. I was especially careful to keep out of the way of the Tacs when they jumped out of their chairs to harass candidates seated at the tables in front of them. Just fifteen more minutes and I'm done, I thought. It had not been such bad duty after all. I began to feel just a little cocky.

Lieutenant George raised his index finger. I marched to his left side. "Sir, yes, Sir," I responded smartly.

"Please get me a glass of milk, Candidate."

"Sir, yes, Sir," came my quick reply. I performed a stellar about-face and crisply marched back to the milk dispenser. It was on the other side of the wall I had been standing against. That wall separated the dining room from the cafeteria-style serving line. Racks of empty glasses were stacked beside the milk dispenser. This late in the meal, there were not many racks left. They would be running the used glasses through the dishwashing machines shortly. I reached for a glass and filled it. Not too full, I reminded myself. Lieutenant George would be likely to jump me for allowing milk to run down the side of the glass, which would cause his hand to be soiled.

Promptly returning to the officers' table, I placed the full glass of milk to the left front of his plate. Having completed the task, I returned to attention just behind him and hesitated. He might have another request.

"Candidate, I said to bring me a glass of milk. Now take this back and get me a glass of milk," Lieutenant George said with that edge to his voice.

Immediately, I picked up the glass as I responded, "Sir, yes, Sir."

Rushing back to the milk dispenser, I tried to figure out what I had done wrong. Nothing came to mind. Quickly, I grabbed another glass out of the rack, filled it, and returned. My military demeanor must not have pleased him. I was even snappier in my moves. The glass was before him.

"You drink the damn thing now," he hissed, "then you go back and get me a glass of milk."

"Sir, yes, Sir," I said and emptied the glass in one continuous swallow.

Rushing back to the dispenser with all the speed I could muster, I could not figure out what I was doing wrong. I returned to his side and set the glass down.

"Drink it right now, then get me a glass of milk!" shouted Lieutenant George.

I did, and I did.

"Drink it. Now get me a glass of milk."

I swallowed it whole. By now my stomach was hurting, but I pushed on.

"Drink it. Now go get me a glass of milk."

I did.

"Drink it, and get me a glass of milk."

I did.

"Drink it, and get me a glass of milk."

I did. I was going to vomit. No, I had to hold it in. This was deep shit. I was in trouble and could not get out. A soldier in the kitchen was setting a newly washed rack of glasses on top of the ones already there. Most of the glasses in it were different from those in the bottom racks from which I had been getting glasses. That was it. All of a sudden I knew. How stupid of me. He had asked for a *glass* of milk. He wanted a *glass* glass. I had been putting his milk in *plastic* glasses. I quickly filled the glass glass and brought it to the table. I set it to the left of his plate.

"At last, you followed my orders," he said, glaring at me.

"Sir, request permission to go out. I'm going to—" I cupped one hand over my mouth and turned as he shouted, "Get out of here!"

His command came too late; I had bolted for the door. Milk was already spurting from between the tightly clenched fingers pressed against my mouth. I had just made it out the door and begun flying down the steps when a projectile of vomit shot several feet out in front of me. It was a fascinating white stream that kept a tight arc form until it struck the asphalt beside the dumpster. The force of the impact caused it to splatter in a wide circle. Some of the candidates arriving late for chow deftly dodged it and entered the mess hall. I was not enough of an unusual sight to draw more than a passing glance.

Lieutenant George had said to get out of there. I had complied with his order. There was no need to go back. I had completed my tour of duty. Lieutenant George never referred to the incident. I told a couple of the guys about it in case they had to pull mess-hall orderly duty. Too many other things were going on to dwell on a trivial incident like this.

We had just come up short on another inspection. This called for a platoon meeting. Several of the guys were sent to the other platoons in an effort to try to figure out what they were doing right and we were doing wrong. It just did not make sense. The best we could come up with was that our bathroom walls were dingy. All of the other platoons' bathrooms seemed to have a fresh coat of paint on them. Our paint looked faded. We decided to buy some paint from the PX and repaint the latrine. I cautioned the guys that it would cost some real money and that we did not have much in the slush fund. As a matter of fact, we actually had a deficit. The week before, a couple of guys had bought some stuff for the group. They had not turned in their receipts to me. The items had cost more than the reserve currently held in the savings account. They apologized for the delay, but they could not find the receipts right off. They said one more search of their footlockers was all they needed. We agreed that if they could not find the receipts we would reimburse them on the basis of their estimates. Since we did not know the cost of the paint and painting supplies, we would have to wait until they had bought the items before I determined how much each of us should pay into the slush fund. It was agreed. The next Saturday afternoon, Scottie and Mel would buy the paint supplies. We would hide them overnight and paint on Sunday.

That Thursday, trucks brought us back to the barracks from training in the midafternoon. This was an unexpected treat. No one was there to harass us. We could get on with getting on. Now was my chance. A couple of the guys agreed to cover for me if something came up. I was going to sneak out and go to the base hospital. This time, I was going to talk to someone in authority about a transfer to the Medical Service Corps.

I had a general idea where the hospital was located. It could not be more than five to eight miles from the barracks—an hour's jog at the most. I put on clean fatigues. The airborne shuffle would not wrinkle my elbows or the backs of my knees too badly. I hoped I would not sweat up my armpits all that much. I even put on my display combat boots and polished my black OCS helmet liner again. A good military image would not hurt me, even if it did not help my cause.

The hospital was a maze through which everyone moved with a purpose. They knew where they were going. I seemed to be the only one out of place. Someone directed me to the office of the colonel in charge of personnel or something like that. It was almost four o'clock by the time I found his office. The white-clad receptionist was preparing to leave when I entered the office complex.

"Yes?" she inquired pleasantly enough.

"Ma'am, I'd like to speak to the colonel," I replied politely, holding my shiny helmet liner in the crook of my arm.

"May I inquire as to the subject matter?" she asked in a professional tone.

"I have a master's degree in psychology and need to know if that qualifies me for a direct commission in the Medical Service Corps."

"Please be seated. I'll speak to the colonel." Her request was followed with a most pleasant smile.

I felt foolish but determined. This matter needed to be resolved.

"The colonel will see you now," she said, holding the door open and motioning for me to enter his office.

Entering the office with a brisk step, I approached his desk, stopped, stood at attention, saluted crisply, and stated, "Sir, Officer Candidate Morton."

He seemed amused. With a slight wave of his hand toward his head that continued until it was a finger pointing to a chair, he casually said, "Please be seated." ·

Dropping my salute, I said, "Thank you, Sir," and sat down.

"You have a master's degree in psychology do you?" He seemed to be asking more than reflecting my words.

"Yes, Sir, a master's in school psychology from Miami University of Ohio. A couple of days after receiving it, I was in basic training at Fort Dix. There I heard that I might be eligible for a direct commission as a first lieutenant in the Medical Service Corps. Up to this point, I have not been able to speak with anyone who knows if this is true or not."

"I can see that you're enrolled in Infantry Officer Candidate School," he said with a slight smile.

"Yes, Sir," I responded.

"Well, you are correct. You are eligible, but we feel that Infantry OCS is good training for our officers. As soon as you are commissioned you may apply for a branch transfer. We will consider your request then," he said with a pleasant grin.

I understood. It was too late. I was in the infantry. They were not going to try to get me out. Either this guy was a fool and thought the army was going to let me out of the infantry after I got commissioned, or he just did not want to take away all of my hope. I think he just did not understand; but I was just an officer candidate, and he was a bird colonel.

"Yes, Sir. Thank you for your time, Sir," I said, standing to attention. I saluted. He kind of waved his hand around his head and smiled. OCS helmet liner in hand, I left at a brisk pace. There was a long way to go to get back to the barracks. I had scuffs on my display combat boots that would take hours to work out. There was no time to waste.

"Something's wrong," Scottie said. He and Mel had just returned empty-handed from their Saturday mission of getting the paint.

What could go wrong with a simple paint purchase? The seriousness of their expressions told me to pay attention.

"We'd gotten a lot of paint and stuff," Scottie continued. "Our arms were full and we were scooting stuff on the floor to keep our place in the checkout line when this old man in civilian clothes standing behind us in the line asked us what we were painting. I figured he was just a civilian, but still it's better to be careful. Anyway, we just said some stuff and turned away from him. He asked us if we were in OCS. Of course, we had to say yes. I mean, we were in uniform with our OCS brass on and the helmet liners and all. So then he says: 'You don't have anything to paint; you're in training. Why are you buying all that paint?' So I say, 'We don't have to talk to you about this; you're a civilian.' He pulls out his wallet and shows us his military ID. He's a full colonel. He wants to know what OCS company we're in, our names, our serial numbers; and he writes it all down. Then he ordered us to return all of the paint."

Yes, this is not good.

"I think we're going to hear some more about this," Mel chimed in.

Yes, I think he is right. I sighed and said: "Well, we'll just have to let it play out. You told the truth. I don't see where you've done anything wrong. Maybe it won't go any farther than that. We'll just have to wait and see."

This was not good at all. A heavy gloom seemed to hover over me the rest of that day and into Sunday morning.

"Lieutenant George wants you in his office on the double," said a messenger who came over to my cubicle.

I rushed down and knocked on the Tac's open door.

Lieutenant George ushered me in. Several tactical officers were there, including First Lieutenant Best, the company executive officer. They were all grim faced.

"Are you operating a slush fund?" Lieutenant George spat into my face.

"Sir, yes, Sir," I instantly shot back.

"Weren't you told that there were to be no slush funds?" He glared at me as he spoke.

"Sir, yes, Sir."

"Did any of the Tacs order you to create a slush fund?"

"Sir, no, Sir."

"Then why did you disobey orders?"

"Sir, the platoon was failing inspections. We decided we needed to get additional things for the platoon and that we all needed to share in the costs. We thought all of the other platoons had slush funds. That was why they were passing inspections and we weren't. The guys asked me to run it. I agreed."

The questioning went on. I explained how I operated the fund, pointing out how careful I was to keep all of the records so everyone would know what money was collected and where it went. I had all of the records. They could have them.

An impromptu conference erupted among the lieutenants. They seemed to be assuring themselves that the colonel would not think that they had ordered me to do this. There was an undercurrent of concern for *their* welfare. They seemed to be more concerned about *their* problem than the trouble *I* was in. It did not make sense to me.

Abruptly, First Lieutenant Best left the group and approached me. "The battalion commander, Lieutenant Colonel Stavros, has ordered that you return all of the money in the slush fund to the men immediately. No exceptions will be tolerated. Do you understand?"

"Sir, yes, Sir," I stated. This *was* serious. A lieutenant colonel, the OCS battalion commander, had given a direct order for *me*. "But Sir, there isn't any real money in the account. Some of the guys still have to turn in money to cover their share of what has already been spent. I'm sure it's more than what I have in the account. I'll have to collect some money from the guys to pay them back. Until then, the account is technically overdrawn."

"You are ordered to return all of the money owed to the men *now*. Got that, Candidate?"

"Sir, yes, Sir."

"You are to be outside my office at thirteen hundred hours tomorrow," Best continued. "I will escort you to Lieutenant Colonel Stavros's office. You will report directly to Colonel Stavros and explain the slush fund to him. Do you understand?"

"Sir, yes, Sir."

"That is all. Dismissed."

I had to return the money. There was no money to return. I have been ordered to return the money. I have to return the money. What money? There is no money. The colonel wants the men to have their money back, but a couple of the guys are out several dollars and I don't have the money to pay them back. Surely the colonel wants them to be paid back, too. He doesn't want *me* to be out any money and he doesn't want *them* to be out any money, but he also doesn't want me collecting money to square the account in order to pay the guys the money that is due them. He just wants me to return to the men all of the money that they are owed.

How am I going to get out of this mess? I am going to be kicked out.

This is it. All I can do is tell the truth. This is a train on a one-way rail-road track. I don't know where it's going, but it's on the track going full steam ahead. It's going to go where it's going. All I can do is tell the truth. This is the end. I am depressed with weariness. It is all too much. The cards have been dealt. I have to go through the motions, but this one is beyond my control. All I can do is tell the truth.

Back in the platoon bay, I explained the situation. As I talked, Scottie and Mel were called down to see the lieutenants. They were told to report to the colonel with me. They said they told the truth, just as I had done. That is all any of us can do, I advise them. We have to stick with the truth. I just hope we get the opportunity to tell the truth. If everyone starts shouting and carrying on, there is no telling how this thing will get screwed up.

"What are you going to do about returning the money?" Scottie asked.

"I have to return some money to every man," I replied. "It's a direct order. I have to be able to tell the colonel I followed his instructions."

"But you'll be disobeying his order if you give people money that's not theirs and that you don't have," said Scottie. "Just explain it to him when he talks to you."

"No, it's too risky. If I don't get a chance to explain or if he doesn't understand my explanation, he'll say I disobeyed his order. What I'll do is I'll go to each man and explain that I've been ordered to return all of the money in the slush fund, but since we know we owe more money than we have in it, I don't know what to do. To be on the safe side, I will return one cent to each man. That way I'll be able to say that I have re-turned money to each man. As I return the penny, I'll ask each man to lend it back to me. That way I will have returned a penny to each man but it will be the same penny. Since the last man I return it to will lend it back to me, I will have the penny I started out with. Every man will have gotten money back and no one is further in debt. I'll explain it to the colonel if I get the chance. If I don't, then maybe you'll get the chance. Remember, the truth is all we have."

"You're taking this thing to the extreme," Mel said. "You don't have to go to all that trouble."

"I think I do," I replied. "I'm the one who's really in trouble. You guys were just my agents. Just tell the truth. We know what it is."

That night I told my story to each man. I gave each one a penny. Then I asked him to lend it back to me. Each man held the penny in his hand before I took it back.

At breakfast, the guys told me that the word was out about Lieutenant White, our first tactical officer. He had been the one who appointed me to serve as the platoon morale officer on our first day of OCS and then disappeared before the end of the week. We went without a Tac for a couple of weeks, until Lieutenant Leonard arrived and took over. Rumor had it that Lieutenant White had been extorting money from the candidates in the class before ours. He would order someone to write a military letter and then accept money from the guy in lieu of the letter. He supposedly did a lot of stuff like that. The other tactical officers were afraid that Lieutenant Colonel Stavros would think they had been trying to get money out of us through our slush fund. Of course, they had done no such thing. If the matter comes up, I told Mel and Scottie, we can let the colonel know the truth on that score.

The three of us stood at attention together with our backs pressed against the wall outside the colonel's office. Several of the 63d Company tactical officers were standing off from us near the opposite wall, talking in muffled voices. All of their faces were grim. They kept looking over at us as they mumbled to each other.

A lieutenant I had never seen before came out of the colonel's office. He looked at me for a moment and then said, "The colonel will see you now, Candidate."

I entered his office. It was spacious. He sat at a large wooden desk with his hands folded. Walking up to the front of it, I saluted and said, "Sir, Candidate Morton reports, Sir."

He quickly returned my salute. I dropped my hand and remained motionless, staring straight ahead at the wall over his head.

"Stand at ease," he said in a soft voice. "Look at me."

I did. He was a physically fit man. There was a lot of gray mixed in with his close-cropped brown hair. It was almost totally gray on the sides. He was remarkably calm. There was not the slightest hint of a smile on his face or in his eyes.

"Why were you operating a slush fund?"

I told him.

"Weren't you told that it is against regulations to maintain a slush fund?"

"Yes, Sir. We were told that on the first day of OCS, Sir."

"Then why did you disobey orders?" he asked in a calm voice while he stared directly at me. His unblinking eyes held me motionless.

"It was a platoon decision, Sir. Since I was the appointed morale officer, the guys thought I should be the one to run it. I agreed. I kept careful books, Sir. No purchases were made unless the whole platoon agreed to it and to the amount each man was assessed. I kept careful records of all of the money that came in and all that went out."

"Did you return all of the money to the men as I ordered?"

"Yes, Sir, but it wasn't much. Actually, Sir, there were some outstanding debts, and they were more than what was in the account."

"Did you return money to each man?"

"Sir, yes, Sir."

"That's all, Candidate. Dismissed."

I came to attention and saluted. He returned it. I did an about-face and went back to my place against the outside wall.

The colonel called out, "Send the other two in."

They entered. The door was closed.

A few brief glances came my way from the group of lieutenants. I thought things had gone fairly well with the colonel. He seemed to be a kind man trying to get to the bottom of the story.

"I think things are going to work out," I said in a hushed tone.

Lieutenant George rushed over to me. He was angry. He put his face within inches of mine. Through clenched teeth he hissed at me: "We don't need you to tell us things are fine, Candidate. We're in control here. We know things are fine. Got it?"

Startled at his anger and his near assault, I straightened my head, looked straight ahead and replied, "Sir, yes, Sir," in a hushed but brisk tone.

After ten minutes or so, Scottie and Mel came out of the colonel's office and rejoined me. A moment later we were told to go back to our barracks. The tactical officers stayed.

As we walked back, the three of us shared our encounters with the colonel. He had asked them a lot of the same questions he asked me. When he asked them if I had returned any money to the men, they told him I had returned money to every man, but that it was not much. He then asked them how much I had given each man. They told him that I had given each man a penny and then borrowed it back. I asked what his reaction was to that. They said he just looked at them for a couple of seconds without saying a word and then asked them some other unrelated questions.

A week passed. None of the officers mentioned the event. It was as if it had never happened. I had straightened out the details of the slush fund and closed it out. Thank God, I was through with it.

A group of four or five guys approached me one evening shortly after that. "We've got to get the slush fund going again. There're some things we just have to get. The guys in the platoon want you to set it up again."

I was stunned. "No way," I replied. "Not only will I *not* run a slush fund, I will not contribute to it. I don't want to know anything about it. Hell, if I had anything to do with it and it was discovered, they might send me to jail instead of Vietnam. I can't do it. It's just too risky for me."

No one ever mentioned the slush fund to me again.

CHAPTER 21

Second Lieutenant Ken Strauss

His eyes were what you noticed first. They were steady. They did not look at you and dart away. When he looked at you, they revealed nothing of the thoughts behind them. The guy could have been an officer in the Prussian army of old. Leanness, ramrod-straight posture, short black hair shadowing his skull, finely chiseled facial structure, and earnestness constantly in his expression created a no-nonsense air about him. A black leather brace worn over his left thumb with an accompanying black leather strap wrapped around his wrist provided the final touch to his superb military image. Our tactical officer had arrived.

Immediately, we began passing inspections. He quietly and efficiently told us what improvements to make. They worked. The other Tacs significantly decreased their surprise visits to our area. Their spontaneous harassment of us in the mess hall, on the parade ground, and during training also diminished.

Lieutenant Strauss established a weekly teaching/training session. He set aside one midafternoon in the middle of each week for that purpose. A candidate was selected to instruct the whole platoon on some military issue. The lieutenant explained that we would constantly be training the troops assigned to us. We needed to get comfortable doing it.

My turn to instruct the platoon came. I had a week to prepare. Strauss took notes during the presentations. Apparently, he used them to help him form an overall evaluation of each of us. I was not concerned about a grade. It was important to me that he thought well of me. In the end, I knew it did not make any difference. As long as I got passing grades in the classes I took and did not break any major rules, I was going to graduate. I was ultimately going to be an infantry platoon leader in Vietnam. Knowing that, it still mattered to me that Lieutenant Strauss respected me. There are men like that. There is just something about them that you know is good. It becomes important to you that they value you. Lieutenant Strauss was one of those men.

Most of the instruction presented by the other candidates had been poor. In my opinion, their greatest sin was boredom. Close on the heels of that was their lack of humor. They all knew the material they taught. Obviously, they had memorized some military task, lesson, or whatever from one of the military manuals that had been issued to us. When they made their presentations in the aisle between our cubicles, the biggest task was staying awake. Since the guys were all platoon mates, you did not want to embarrass them. You stayed awake. You asked meaningful questions at the end you were sure they could answer. Then it was over.

Hell, I was going to have some fun with the task. I had done a semester of high school student teaching to obtain my Kentucky teacher's certificate. Then I spent two years in graduate school teaching undergraduate classes for my major professor during his absences and teaching study skills to the university football team. I had also taught a summer at a junior college. On top of that, my master's degree was, after all, in school psychology. I was trained to assist teachers and to utilize good educational strategies. There was no question in my military mind that I was a good teacher. My task was not to prove that point; my task was to have fun with the guys and get a few ideas across that might help them. That helping part was not as important to me as the having fun part was.

"How to Be Stealthy on a Combat Patrol" was my topic. There were no military manuals that directly addressed the topic I selected. We had gotten bits and pieces of it from our training in basic and AIT. You would have thought the army could have been more helpful on this topic since rumor had it that going out on patrol was a major part of the infantryman's job in 'Nam. I got Nat to agree to help me. He would slip into the cubicle next to the largest collection of the men in the aisle. Once there, he would hide behind a partition. On my cue, he would yell, "Hootie hoo! Hootie hoo!" His cue would be my saying something about strange sounds in the night.

The presentation was to be about a half-hour or so long with a question-and-answer period after it. All told, the performance was to last about an hour.

The time had arrived. Lieutenant Strauss stood at the back of the assembled group. Nat was in his hiding spot. I had to be subtle in my switch from straight military instruction to humor on the side. If it appeared to Strauss that I was ridiculing the whole OCS training program, I just might be in trouble.

The presentation started straight enough. I greeted the men in the identical manner used by the vast majority of military instructors who had addressed us from the present OCS classes on back to basic. Standing before the group at rigid parade rest with eyes fixed on nothingness, I said in a deep, commanding voice: "Greetings, men. Today, we are going to learn how to be stealthy on combat patrol. You will learn the proper nomenclature, the proper strategies to use, and how to implement them. Are there any questions?"

Without pausing for any questions to be asked, as we had been taught to do by example, I launched into a monotone presentation of old facts we all knew. This part of the presentation was important to set the stage for the finale. Silence, blending in with your surroundings, and surprise were the key elements of stealth, I emphasized. Every successful operation is a success because of preplanning and prepared troops, I said, echoing dozens of past instructors. Then I addressed the need for taping down metal objects such as canteens, ammo clips, the buckles on backpacks, backpack contents such as metal C-ration cans, compasses, rifle slings, and the like. Giving silent commands and using hand-and-arm signals was discussed next.

These pieces of information consumed about twenty minutes. The men's eyes had that glassy stare. They were looking straight ahead into nowhere. Clearly, they were mesmerized by my stereotypical military presentation. So far, I had been successful. It was now time to move beyond the realm of reality.

"Now, men, imagine that you are in country," I intoned. "This is it. Tomorrow, in the predawn hours, you will lead your men into the dangers of the jungle. Make sure they are well fed. Bring in a couple of cases of the pork and beans that you got on sale from the honey-bun truck. Make sure every man eats his fill. Your thoughtfulness will promote loyalty from the troops. Pass out rolls of duct tape for them to use to secure their web gear. Wrap some of the tape around your mouth and approach the men with a finger to your covered lips. They will know what you mean and appreciate the reminder.

"Naturally, you can't sleep. This is your first combat patrol. You don't want to make the men nervous. They have to feel confident in your leadership. You feign sleep. The silence is broken only by the muffled breaking of wind you and the troops experience. The music of the moment grabs you. It is beautiful in the jungle. Things just never seem real without background music. Now that music is in your ears. The offense to your nostrils is of no concern. Charlie likes that smell. He will relax his guard. It might be the very edge that makes the difference in a combat moment.

"You gather your men around you at the debarkation point. When you leave the safety of the wired compound, you know this is for real. You and your men are on your own in the darkness. A last-minute check makes sure all is in order. You pass out cigarettes from the hoard you collected out of C-ration packs to the men who forgot theirs. When you stop to rest on the trail, the men can light up. It will calm their nerves. The smell of cigarette smoke in the middle of the jungle is reassuring to troops surrounded by the unfamiliar scents coming from the jungle floor. Rumor has it that Charlie loves the smell, too. Lulling the enemy into a false sense of security is a tactical advantage."

I issue my instructions in a hushed tone as I pace back and forth in front of my platoon mates. With hunched back, I continue in a conspiratorial manner. The men have lost their glazed OCS classroom stare. They are with me. Big grins are showing up. Lieutenant Strauss has stopped looking at the ceiling. He is hard to read, but it is clear he is not openly angry. I have his attention.

"Now you're on the trail," I continue. "The predawn light has yet to come. It's hard to see the ground. You hope the frequent snapping of twigs being stomped on by you and the others sounds like the chirping of jungle tree frogs. The loud crackling of the radio on the back of the platoon radioman is the only thing that keeps you calm. There is comfort in the familiar. Suddenly, a horrible cry comes from the trees above you. You freeze. The jungle sounds are all strange, new, unexplainable things that might be the harbinger of danger. Again that nerve-wracking cry: Could it be a jungle bird?"

"Hootie hoo! Hootie hoo!" Nat screamed from behind the cubicle wall.

Instantly, Lieutenant Strauss spun in the direction of the cry and roared with laughter. It triggered everyone else. Pandemonium broke out.

Nat responded with an even louder, "Hootie hoot!"

"Men, men," I shout above the laughter and twisting of bodies as guys try to catch a glimpse of Nat in his hiding place. "Men, don't let the unexpected control you. Be prepared for the unusual. Your men are looking to you for leadership. Freeze in your tracks and think. A bird in the jungle isn't worth a revealing sound on the trail. That's what you must remember about being stealthy on the trail. Are there any questions?"

That last comment prompted even more laughter. There were no questions. The guys were having too good a time commenting to each other over the shenanigans of the moment. I dismissed them.

Not long after my tour of duty as a military instructor, Lieutenant Strauss caught me with a can of furniture polish firmly clutched in my hand during evening study hall.

Braced at attention with the contraband in my hand, I did not know what to expect as he circled me. He had the slightest hint of a compressed smile on his lips. My cubicle mates stood at attention trying to avoid eyeballing either of us. These kinds of scenes were tense.

Lieutenant Strauss leaned toward my ear and whispered, "I want a military poem on my desk by 0800 hours tomorrow morning. Got that?"

"Sir, yes, Sir," came my loud reply.

Calmly and quietly, Lieutenant Strauss eased out of our cubicle and continued his inspection of the platoon bay.

We instituted the tried-and-true system. After lights-out we posted guards and lifted the typewriter. I wrote the impromptu poem while someone held the flashlight. As I composed it, another candidate typed it for me. After I finished, the typewriter was returned. The military poem was left on Lieutenant Strauss's desk for his reading at 0800.

The poem, which alluded to the necessity of picking a few soldiers to cover a retreat, read as follows:

> Rat-a-tat-tat, rat-a-tat-tat,
> Too many to stop, too many to save.
> Rat-a-tat-tat, rat-a-tat-tat,
> A few to remain so many can live.
> Rat-a-tat-tat, rat-a-tat-tat,
> Who to select, who to remain?
> Rat-a-tat-tat, rat-a-tat-tat
> To leave the best, to leave a friend
> Rat-a-tat-tat, rat-a-tat-tat
> So others can live, so others can die
> Rat-a-tat-tat, rat-a-tat-tat
> You have to decide, who lives and who dies.
> Rat-a-tat-tat, rat-a-tat-tat
> It echoes as long as you live,
> Rat-a-tat-tat.

Lieutenant Strauss never said a word to me about the poem. A few days later, it was posted on the platoon bulletin board.

Weeks went by. I was informed that I was to be the acting platoon leader. Every week, one of the candidates was selected to be acting platoon leader. The platoon leader got to appoint acting squad leaders for that week. The team then carried out the routines expected of them. The acting platoon leader reported to Lieutenant Strauss every morning to receive the day's orders.

A lot of the guys changed when they became platoon leader. They began lording it over the rest of us. A few of the guys held it together pretty well. They were clearly in the minority. At the end of the week, everyone in the platoon evaluated the platoon leader. Somehow, those evaluations played a part in the overall process of determining whether or not a candidate graduated and received his commission. It was important to do as well as you could.

Most of my week as platoon leader was spent in the field practicing ambushes. We were trucked out fairly far into the woods and got back late at night. There was no significant drilling.

I was feeling pretty good about the week. From my perspective, there was never a legitimate reason to scream and shout at people to get them to do what they were supposed to do. Everyone in the platoon was highly motivated to do the best job they could. If they messed up, there was a reason. They needed assistance instead of orders to do more push-ups.

Tuesday and Wednesday were long days in the field. We marched and played war games, practicing setting up an ambush and then rushing off to another location. As we hurried through the woods (we were always in a hurry), I was impressed with their beauty. We entered marshy flat ground nestled between the wooded hills. Shallow streams crisscrossed the level ground. Between them were large stretches of bright green moss. The leaves on the trees had yet to come forth, which allowed the sun to shine directly on the moss. I wished I had had the time to stay and look at it. Instead, we sank ankle deep into the wet moss, leaving ugly mud puddles in the empty holes. Our combat boots were caked with mud. Toes became wrinkled because we wore water-soaked socks all day. We tracked mud into the barracks, badly marring our highly shined floors. The gear we wore was in no better shape. Splotches of dried mud covered our web belts, packs, and canteen covers. By Wednesday night we had lost our shining edge. I was not concerned. The guys knew what to do to get everything back into military shape for the Saturday morning inspection. We would get it done and get our off-post weekend pass. It was becoming a fairly regular routine.

Actually, I preferred my week as platoon leader to be in the field. They did not harass us as much in the field as they did when we were back on post. They called being on post "garrison duty." Besides, when you were in the field, the platoon leader was less likely to have to call out all of those fancy marching commands. You know: "column right, march"; "two steps to the rear, march"; "prepare to stack arms, stack arms"; and all of that old manual of arms stuff. I had not had a chance to practice giving those orders. I was afraid I would mess up and make a fool of myself. Being in the field was just fine with me.

First thing Thursday morning, Lieutenant Strauss informed me that he was going to conduct a major inspection at 1600 hours that afternoon. We would have classes in the morning. Lunch would be in the dining hall. We would get back from our afternoon classes at about 1500 hours. He said he expected us to be back up to our regular inspection standards by 1600 hours. All of our gear was to be clean. There was a lot to do and almost no time to do it in. I called the squad leaders together. We had our marching orders. They got with their guys. The rush was on.

"Atten—*shun!*" someone shouted in a cubicle near the bay doors. Lieutenant Strauss stood there, his swagger stick impatiently slapping the sides of his perfectly creased fatigue pants. The starch in them was so thick that he must have forced his legs into the trousers. They had opened just enough to allow the contour of his legs to push a hole into them that ultimately made a perfect curve around his thin runner's legs. The tightly tailored remains stayed stuck together, accentuating the crease into a rigid knife blade preceding the rest of his body. The man looked *sharp*.

Rapidly, I marched to the front of the bay and smartly saluted. "Sir, Fifth Platoon is ready for inspection, Sir."

Without a word he returned my salute. He walked into the first cubicle. All three of the candidates living there stood at rigid attention in front of their bunks. It was the usual drill. Lieutenant Strauss went straight to their wall lockers. I followed slightly behind. He motioned for me to look inside the first one. As I leaned forward to see, he pointed his swagger stick at the pack stuffed into a corner at the bottom of it. I could see mud on the shoulder straps. A stiff brush would have removed it with just a few strokes. Obviously, those strokes had not been applied. The lieutenant shook his head. He gave me the briefest look of dismay. Damn! I thought. There's no excuse for that. Hell, everyone was busy; but this slip was so obvious. Why had the guy let something so simple go undone?

We moved to the next wall locker. He picked up a pair of combat boots. There were tiny traces of mud in the crack where the sole is attached to the leather. He held the offending shoes up to my face for me to get a good view and shook his head in silent disgust. The slam of the shoes hitting the floor of the wall locker seemed to echo throughout the bay.

In the next cubicle he found caked mud under one of the bunks. Someone had kicked it to the far end of the bunk, up against the cubicle divider. He motioned for me to get down on my hands and knees to look at it with him. The swagger stick whisked it out into the center of the cubicle. Picking it up with his black-leather-wrapped hand, he ground the dry mud into dust and let it slowly fall to the floor. The clenching of his jaw told me how irritated he was.

The third cubicle was no better. The green wool blanket on the bottom bunk was covered with multicolored splotches of dried mud that told the story of a last-minute attempt to smear it away. It was a pitiful attempt that just made matters worse. The streaks were clearly visible.

"What's that shuffling sound back there?" the lieutenant demanded as he rushed to a cubicle in back. I had heard it, too. We both knew full well what the sound was: Someone had attempted to do some last-second cleaning instead of standing at attention.

Entering the offending cubicle in quick, long strides, he glared at the men standing there. They looked straight ahead. Only Gene's eyes broke the military brace. They were wide. The whites totally rimmed his pupils. The lieutenant knew what it meant. He just did not know the why of it.

"Which one is your wall locker?" he sternly whispered into Gene's face.

"Sir, the second one, Sir."

Taking his time, as if he knew that his prey had been caught in a trap with no possibility of escape, the lieutenant walked to the wall locker. He moved the door wider open with his swagger stick.

"I am not believing this!" he screamed. We all started at the abrupt change in the loudness of his voice. This was out of character. This was bad.

Lieutenant Strauss reached down into the locker, threw out a backpack, and then came up with a pair of mud-caked combat boots. As he brought them out, large chunks of mud fell off them onto the floor. He wheeled to confront me with the boots.

Holding them to my nose momentarily before he smashed them to the floor, he glared at me and hissed, "Candidate, I want to talk to you in the stairwell." With that, he wheeled and stomped down the aisle with me in pursuit.

The swinging doors continued to swing as we stood on the landing. He turned to me with those Strauss eyes burning and said: "Do you think this is a game? Do you think I'm playing with you? You get these men into shape. Do you hear me? I will inspect this place at 0900 hours Saturday morning. You had better get this place clean."

Before I could respond, he twisted away from me and bolted down the steps. My shouted, "Sir, yes, Sir!" bounced off his back as he disappeared from view on the second floor landing.

Slamming the platoon-bay doors, I shouted, "Squad leaders to the front!"

I was angry. They had embarrassed me before the lieutenant. They had known what had to be done. Just because I was a nice, easy-going guy, they had thought they did not need to do what was right. I could not believe it. They had let down on my watch. They had humiliated me because I was easy-going. I was pissed.

The four squad leaders walked to the front. We stood at a distance from the rest of the men, but I kept my voice low so they would not overhear our discussion. "By God, you had better get these men in shape," I said. "The lieutenant is coming back at oh-nine-hundred Saturday to reinspect. We're going to pass that inspection. I don't give a damn if we have to stay up all night Friday. This place is going to be spotless, do you understand? Do you know how angry I am?" I demanded.

"It's okay, Jerry, we'll get it done," Mel said, trying to calm me.

"Hell, it's not okay!" I shot back. "I can't believe Gene didn't even try to knock the mud off his damn boots. He probably did it on purpose to make me look bad for messing up one of his details a week or two ago."

"Oh, no, Jerry, you're wrong," Scottie said, shaking his head with a worried look. "Listen, we'll take care of this. You just stay out of it. We'll see that we pass the inspection. Don't talk to any of the other guys. We'll give you updates on how we're doing. Let us handle this, okay?"

"Yeah, you're right. I'll stay out of it, but you all keep me posted on how they're doing." I felt somewhat chastened by Scottie's levelheaded response.

It was all I could do not to comment or tell someone what to do. Basically, I just looked around. I could not suppress my angry eyes, but I did manage to keep my mouth shut. They worked hard. Everyone scrubbed and cleaned as fast as they could. Finally, I just stayed in my cubicle working on my own gear. Scottie and Mel stated the obvious: There had not been enough time for anyone to get ready for Lieutenant Strauss's inspection Thursday afternoon. We could not have passed it. I knew they were right, but my stuff would have passed. I had gotten myself ready for the inspection. If I had done it the first time, they could have, too. It just did not add up. If I could do it, everyone else could do it. They just failed to work hard enough the first time. I thought everyone maintained the standards I did. It was the only way to survive this place, went my reasoning. Apparently I was wrong.

"Atten—*hut!*" came the cry at 0900 sharp that Saturday.

Smartly saluting, I stated, "Sir, Fifth Platoon is ready for inspection, Sir."

Lieutenant Strauss returned my salute without comment. He entered the first cubicle. He carefully looked each man up and down and observed every wall locker with equal care. He moved items around with his swagger stick. No words were spoken. Cubicle after cubicle, the pattern was the same. After he had inspected all of the cubicles, he walked to the front of the bay. I followed a respectful pace behind him.

At the bay doors, he turned to face me. Expressionlessly he stated: "The platoon has passed inspection. They have off-post privileges."

Bracing to attention, I saluted sharply, saying, "Sir, yes, Sir."

He returned the salute and left. No other words were exchanged.

I was relieved but not happy. I knew that I had lost it on Thursday afternoon. I had lost my emotional composure. I had been an asshole to the guys.

Sunday afternoon, Scottie, Mel, and I went to the post theater. Before the movie started, we went through the mandatory standing at attention and saluting the flag on the screen during the national anthem. It seemed so redundant to do it. It was as if our intelligence and loyalty were being questioned every time we went to see a movie. Nonetheless, we did it. It was the army way. After the film, I apologized to Scottie and Mel for losing it. They were pretty good about it. Yes, I had lost it; but it was the first time. Everyone else had lost it a lot more times than that. But everyone else did not matter to me. I had been a foolish ass. Now I had to live with it. I appreciated their words of comfort, but the truth was as it was.

CHAPTER 22

Tactics

"Now, draw on your map how you would have your platoon maneuver across the terrain to get from point A to your objective," the tactics instructor directed. "When you have drawn your route on the map, bring it to me for review."

The terrain map in front of me was pretty clear: There were steep hills between me and the objective I was supposed to reach with my platoon. The most obvious way to get there was through the narrow valley that ran between the ridgelines on both sides. It was so obvious that the enemy was sure to expect you to come that way. Every other possible route required you to go over steep hills, then down into other valleys, and then over more steep hills before finally going back down to the objective. No question about it. If I were trying to defend the objective, I would set up ambushes along that valley trail. Anyone coming down that trail had one hope of staying alive: they had to hope the enemy was not there. If he was, some or all of your men were going to get hit unless you could discover the ambush and ambush the ambushers. Risky business, no doubt about it.

Obviously, you would not lead your men into an ambush. Surprise the enemy. Approach him from the unexpected position. Hannibal led his men over the Alps and conquered the Roman legions. Alexander the Great avoided certain defeat by staying away from a mountain pass. His men found a goat trail over the mountains. They surprised the waiting enemy force and routed it. I was not a great student of history, but the point here was obvious.

The map's contour lines indicated that the top third of the hills on the left were quite steep. My men would go over the big hill on the right, down the ridge, and then slant up a climbing ridgeline on the next hill so they would not wear themselves out making a steep climb. Besides, it looked as if there was a slight dip to that ridgeline that would make it easier walking if the underbrush was not too thick. The map did not tell you what kind of vegetation existed on the hillsides.

We would be tired after going over the two hills. Approaching our objective from the rear was worth it. If the enemy were there we would have them by surprise. Best of all, it was not likely that we would be ambushed along the way.

I was pleased with my solution. After I waited in line for a few minutes, my turn came to have my choice of routes graded. The solution was well marked on my map.

Leaning over it as he sat at the grading table, the instructor said: "No, you want to go right down the valley. Your solution would take too long. It could be done your way, but it'd take too long."

He scribbled "75%" on it and said rather loudly, "Next."

No one told me time was a factor in this problem. Well, if that was what they wanted, that was what I would put down for future solutions. Take the quickest route. Forget about avoiding likely ambush sites.

"When ambushed, charge," said the instructor. "Some of you will get hit; but if all of you stay in the killing zone, everyone is dead. Charge through the killing zone and counterattack."

Damn, that was a hell of a way to stay alive. We talked among ourselves. None of us was certain what we would actually do. It would depend upon the situation. Logic said that routinely running through the enemy's line of fire, straight into his blazing guns, was not always the best way to stay alive.

The bleachers we were sitting in had been placed high on the ridge. Rolling hills stretched in every direction beneath us. This was so we could see where the mortar rounds we called for fell.

"Someone guess how far it is from here to that tree over there," the sergeant said, pointing at a lone tree standing on a low hill to our left front. No one spoke. Several of the guys were studiously avoiding making eye contact with the sergeant.

We had spent the first two hours that morning being lectured to as we huddled in the bleachers. The early morning air was cold. Clouds blocked out the sun. A heavy mist was in the air. We had been allowed to put on our ponchos. We sunk our faces into the neck of it. With the hood covering as much of your head and face as you could manage, the warm air of your breath was captured. It felt good. As all of us had learned way back in basic, surrounded as you were by the warmth, it was easy to fall asleep. Many candidates did. Sometimes they would fall from their perch on the bleachers into the backs of those in front of them. If that guy was also dozing, it could have a domino effect. Occasionally, four or five guys would go down at a time.

My poncho was pulled up over my nose, but I was determined not to fall asleep. The one thing you had to be able to do in 'Nam was call in accurate artillery fire. I had heard too many of the sergeants talking about artillery shells landing on the troops who had called in the strike. You just had to know exactly where you were, where the artillery was located, and where the enemy troops were. If they were attacking your position, calling for fire would blow them away. Your lives would be saved. Make a mistake, and the shells landed on you or they landed on some harmless spot. The enemy then overran your position and everyone was dead. Accuracy was important.

They had formulas for plotting your position, the artillery's position, and the enemy's position. Once you had figured it all out on your grid map, you called in the coordinates and gave the order to fire. Grid numbers, distance to the target, and compass headings were important bits of information. It was a complicated business. The price of a mistake was high. I asked a lot of questions. This was not like learning to lay a World War II–type minefield in Germany. This was something I *had* to know.

"You, yes, you," the sergeant said, pointing to me. "Tell me how far it is from here to that tree."

"Sergeant, I really have no way of knowing. Please ask someone else."

"No, I'm asking you. Go ahead, Son, take a guess," he said as he motioned for me to come over to where he was standing with a PRC-25 radio. "The mortars are behind that hill," he said, pointing behind us. "They've got *all* the information they need except the distance to the target. Give me a figure."

The hill we were on dropped steeply away right in front of us. Then, a long way down, it turned into a gentle slope leading up to the small hill on which the tree stood. I imagined I had a football field in front of me. I tried to picture it as it had looked in my high school playing days. Our football field was a hundred yards long and continued on for an extra twenty yards before you got to the wall at the other end. I stretched that imaginary 120-yard football field straight in the air from my feet toward the tree, but it fell far short. Fixing the point where the imaginary football field ended in my mind's eye, I extended the whole field out from that point. Following this procedure, I was able to estimate that the tree was 575 yards from our location. All of the mental calibrations had taken place within the span of a natural pause in a normal conversation.

"I'd say it's about five hundred and seventy-five yards from here, Sergeant—but that's only a guess."

"Good! Call it in," he said, handing me the PRC-25's telephone receiver.

"Now, Sergeant, it was just a guess," I said, handing the phone back to him.

He refused to take it. There was steel in his eyes. The smile had left his face. "Call it in," he ordered.

I did. "Target five hundred seventy-five yards, fire one round." Then I handed the phone back to him.

"Watch the tree! There's a round coming in," he announced so that the groups of candidates scattered around would all watch.

Behind us we heard the *whumph* sound of a mortar round leaving its tube. Several seconds later, *blammmm!* The round exploded in the top of the tree. I had hit the thing. I could not believe it.

The sergeant said under his breath, "Nice call."

At the end of the week, we took our written exam for calling in artillery fire. I scored a ninety-eight. It was my highest score since starting OCS and it seemed to be the highest score of anyone in the company. Usually the MP hopeful or the English major got the top scores in the company. They wanted them and studied for them rather than interact with the guys in their platoons. I was surprised that I had beaten them on the test. Deep down, I still felt shaky about how to call for artillery support. When I got to 'Nam, I would have to get someone to help me. I sure did not want to get anyone killed because of my stupidity.

We were out on patrol during one of the many field exercises they put us through. Nothing much doing but pushing through the underbrush. As usual, I was on point. I would rather be the point man, using my eyes to find the easiest way through the brush, than walking the hard way. The hard way is pushing through the thickest brush, with all its thorns and scratching branches, when you can see an easier way off to the side. Seeing a better path but not being able to take it is truly frustrating. Why the point man doesn't see it is the question. I had an eye for finding the best trail. I liked that task, and the guys often asked me to do it. It worked out all the way around.

I could see a clearing up ahead. We were about to break out of the heavy brush. The clearing had tall grass and clumps of bushes here and there with a few trees sprinkled in for good measure.

When we broke into it, I pulled up, waiting for the acting platoon leader to determine how he wanted us to move across the open space.

He decided he wanted us to form a wide line and walk through it to the tree line on the other side. We all expected to be ambushed on this patrol. Sometimes you were the pigeon. We sensed that this was a setup. We were to make somebody else's day. They had been told we would be coming toward them. We were going to give them the experience of pulling off a successful ambush at our expense. The most likely spot for an ambush was the tree line. If they opened up, we would be in a good position to return fire.

The ground under the tall grass was rougher than usual. It seemed to rise up when you were not expecting it. There were clumps in it. They caught the toe of your combat boots. Thus the line was not straight. Hell, the line was never straight.

Pow, pow, pow. Ratta-tat-tat, ratta-tat-tat. Powpowpow. Rifle and automatic weapons fire came from everywhere and out of the ground.

"Run, run, run!" someone shouted over the noise. People were yelling all over the place.

I ran. Immediately, on my left one of the guys from another platoon in the company came shoulder high out of the ground. He was firing his M14. As it fired, he swung the muzzle toward me. My forward momentum carried me across the trench in which he stood. I swung the barrel of my own M14 down and opened up as I was making the leap.

"You're dead, Jerry! Fall down! I got you before you fired," he shouted.

"The hell you say!" I cried back as I continued running. Damn, they were well camouflaged. I never would have seen them. Hell, I probably would have fallen into one of their trenches if the guy had not popped up.

I don't know, I thought, maybe he really did kill me. Maybe I was dead. Even if I was, there was no point in lying on the ground playing dead. I still had to stay with my platoon. If this had been Vietnam and real bullets were flying around, I most likely *would* be dead. A sobering thought. Anyway, now I understood what the sergeant meant about running through an ambush. When you know you are dead if you do not go through, you just go on through.

"C'mon, Jerry, nobody'll know," said Lane. "This whole business is stupid. How many times have we been on a compass course?" He was right, of course. There was no need to do another one. I had found every stake and was always one of the very first guys to complete the daylong stretch through the woods correctly, following the compass headings they gave us.

Lane wanted me to duck out with him. We would slip off into the woods, take a long nap, have a couple of smokes, relax for the day. When the time was right, we would come out at the other end of the course as though we had just completed it. We would take the day off. I felt guilty about doing it, but Lane was awfully persuasive. Finally, I agreed. It was nice to catch up on lost sleep. The day was not too cold. The sun was warm. There was no wind. It was just about perfect for napping. I could not shake the feeling of guilt, though. It ruined the day for me.

Nat said he was quitting. He was dropping out of OCS. I could not believe it. He would not tell me why. I offered to help him with any problems he might be having. I wanted him to stay. He was a good man. It did not make sense. He told Lieutenant Strauss the next morning. When we got back from the day's training, all of his gear was gone. I never saw him again.

A week later, Jim and one of his cube mates said they were dropping out. Jim was one of the really cool guys. He was the one who played Atlas, holding up the building by standing on the top bunk with his back pressed against a ceiling beam when the senior candidates came around to harass us. He said that he had come to realize that he did not want to be responsible for other men's lives. As an infantry lieutenant, that was just what he would be. I had never thought of it quite that way. He was right. I understood his reluctance. He did not want the responsibility. I was willing to accept it.

Before we became senior candidates, around 35 percent of the guys in our platoon dropped out. That was about average for the company. As far as I could tell, all of them could have completed the program. They were good men. I had a hard time understanding it. There just was no time to ponder the situation. We had too many things to do to dwell on this phenomenon.

We had another tactical maneuver for the day. In the predawn hours they trucked us out to the middle of nowhere. Lots of troops in the field. I was assigned to a squad made up of guys from a mixture of the other platoons. This was not unusual. They were constantly stirring us up. It was a rare treat to be in a squad or platoon with someone from your own platoon when out on maneuvers. In general in the field, you had only a nodding acquaintance with the soldiers assigned to your group. You really never got a chance to get to know them as good friends. I guess that was why we did not care that much if the leaders messed up. You did not feel close enough to any of them to make the effort to tell them they were making a mistake. Who needs someone mad at him? The tactical officers made our lives miserable enough. You did not knowingly need to add stress to your life.

Our group got its orders. We were to rendezvous at a point on the map by 1600 hours. It was a large clearing. Helicopters would be there to pick us up and fly us back to main post. It would be a real treat. If we did not get to the site—they called it the pickup zone (PZ)—on time or we got lost, they would take off without us. This time I cared that the platoon leader read the map right.

He had the map and the compass headings. I did not. He chose not to share the information with the rest of us. After taking his first sighting, we took off. By midday, we all knew we were lost.

Finally, I got a chance to look at the map. Since our leader could not identify our starting point, it was rather academic as to where we were now. This made getting to where we were supposed to be at 1600 hours problematic.

We had an interesting debate as we tried to read the topographical map. Attempting to match what we saw around us to the map's terrain features and then guess where we were at that moment was a stress-inducing experience. Eventually, we reached a consensus. In approximately an hour's march, if our speculations were right, we would cross a fairly large streambed.

We were wrong. Clearly, we were badly lost. The platoon leader had a little trouble recognizing that fact. The rest of us did not. His failure to admit the obvious must have been the result of the weight of leadership. We finally decided just to keep moving north. The platoon leader did not like our solution, but he agreed to it rather than continue the patrol on his own. By following a northerly heading, we would eventually come to a gravel road. We would wait there until an army vehicle came by. That was better than running around in the boonies for a couple of days without food or iodine tablets for water purification.

At 1500 hours one of the guys said he could hear chopper engines. We stopped and listened. It sure sounded like it, but we could not be quite sure. We changed course and started moving toward the sound. It got stronger. At 1530 hours we broke out of a tree line into a large clearing. There were the helicopters. The captain in charge of loading up the troops congratulated us on making such good time. We graciously accepted his praise.

Inspections seemed to be an important part of being tactical. A combat unit needs all of its equipment and that equipment needs to be in good working order. We were to have a full field-gear inspection. A lieutenant colonel or full colonel would be coming through all the platoon bays to inspect. This inspection is important, the Tacs told us. We had better do well. Of course, we would first have to un-spit-shine our floors for the inspection. It was only the Tacs who wanted the floors spit-shined. The senior brass did not want us to spend our time doing it. When they inspected, the floors could not be spit-shined.

There was a special problem to be overcome for this inspection. None of the platoons had been issued all of its field gear. Most of us lacked entrenching tools. Each man was to have one-half of a pup tent. We had zero halves. The list of missing items seemed endless. No matter, the word from Captain Greene was that we had to pass the inspection.

One of the guys in 1st or 2d Platoon had a couple of friends in an OCS company several barracks away that had successfully completed a similar inspection. They had done it by borrowing their missing equipment from a lot of other OCS companies. Their tactical officers did not seem to know that the equipment they displayed for their inspection was primarily borrowed equipment. At least, no one openly told them about it—and they never asked. The point was to pass the inspection, so they did.

There was a lot of after-hours smuggling. We finally completed the acquisition phase two days before the inspection. The hard part was trying to determine where to lay each piece out on your bunk. The word we got on how to do it kept changing. The entrenching tool seemed to be a favorite. At first, it was to be at the top of the bunk with the handle down. Then, the handle was up. Next, it was to be sideways in the middle of the bunk with the folded tent-half directly above it. There were several more location changes after that.

Since everything was to be the same for the entire company, the minutest change in the placement of any item meant a monumental effort had to be mounted to get the word out to every candidate. Right off, half the company would get the wrong message. Then, when the corrected message came, many of those who had gotten it right the first time thought it was a new change, so some of them changed their layout while others did not. Further attempts to get it right inevitably caused other guys to get the wrong message, making them think they were wrong when they really had it right.

It got so bad that we finally had just one person get the word out. That person went to each bunk to see that whatever it was was placed right. We were still making changes as the inspecting major—not a colonel after all—walked in.

The company passed. We had managed to obtain all of our field gear. It made me wonder if stateside combat units in the real army went through a similar charade to pass their combat-readiness inspections. Were they really ready to engage the enemy, or was all of their equipment on temporary loan from other units? I guess it was okay if only one of the units was called up on twenty-four hours' notice for combat. I would hate to be about to go into combat if three or four of the units had to be called up. We might find out what was really meant by the phrase "a paper army."

I liked firing the .50-caliber machine gun the best. You could squeeze off just one round at a time or pop off a whole string by firmly pressing on the butterfly trigger. A sergeant told us that some guys in 'Nam were so good with it that they could hit a VC two miles away. They would have a .50-caliber set up to guard a base camp. The gunners generally could spot a VC two miles away if he were standing on some open ground. You could see the guy get hit. He would fly off his feet. He was so far away that the sound of the gun firing would not reach where his body lay until long after the bullet arrived.

They had us fire the .50-caliber machine gun from the top of a cliff. Some old armored personnel carriers (APCs) were sitting on the low ground about a mile away. The task was to hit an APC. We were firing rounds capable of piercing the armor. If the APC were full of troops, the bullet would ricochet inside the APC. A lot of men would be hit. If I were in an APC and heard a .50-caliber going off, I would start sweating.

Later, sitting inside a tank gave me a new level of respect for tankers. There are so many easy ways to get hurt inside one. When the gun turret moved to sight in a target, the loader could accidentally have his arm on the large, gearlike track. Zap, his arm is off. When the cannon fires, if anyone is directly behind it, he is peanut butter on the wall. The recoil from the gun would do an eye-blinkingly quick job on him. When the shell casing pops out of the breech, it flies out. Put your head in its way and your head is gone. Let a live cannon shell get loose and roll around on the floor, and you would be thankful if you got off with only a broken leg. The round could go off. Naturally, tanks are usually moving when they are in a firefight. They bounce around a lot—hard. Any crewmember could bounce his teeth off a metal wall or crack his head on a protruding piece of something. In addition, the smoke from the main gun firing is blinding, suffocating, and toxic. Anyone with a touch of claustrophobia would be in trouble inside a tank. Heaven to a tanker must be the sweet smell of fuel rising in the cabin while a cigarette dangles from his lips. It is okay to smoke because he is already dead. No thanks. I would rather be in the infantry.

A candidate sights down the barrel of a tripod-mounted M2 .50-caliber machine gun.

A sergeant instructor shows candidates how to prepare the M2 .50-caliber machine gun for firing.

A candidate
carries a belt
of .50-caliber
machine-gun
ammunition to
the firing line.

Candidates get a ride atop an M48 medium tank.

Candidates get a look at an M48 medium tank, the army's main battle tank
during the Vietnam War.

An M113 armored personnel carrier, with trim vane deployed, prepares to demonstrate the APC's "swimming" ability.

CHAPTER 23

Camping Out

They had built us up for this. We were to be tactical twenty-four hours a day for the entire time in the field. That meant almost a full two weeks of playing war games. At no time were you safe from ambush or attack. Other OCS companies were participating in this maneuver as well. Our company had been divided up. The platoons were mixed up so that just a few of us 5th Platoon guys were together. Some of them would be the enemy. We would be issued C rations and ammo. If our food got captured, we would have to go hungry unless we captured some other unit's food.

The field cadre would be trucking in supplies. We could capture trucks, jeeps, or whatever. You had to stop a vehicle in order to capture it. They did not want us getting run over trying to capture a moving truck. Whatever was in any truck we captured was ours. Of course, the same thing could happen to our supplies. We would have to provide security for our supply vehicles when they were stopped.

At any time, one or all of us could be captured and held prisoner for an unspecified period. The enemy could interrogate us for information about patrols, base-camp location, supply drops, and so forth. Our mission was to seek out and destroy the enemy. We were to put into practice all of the tactical knowledge we had learned. Failure to perform successfully could jeopardize one's chances of graduating. This was serious business.

Our trucks seemed to travel forever through a maze of dirt roads and unending woods. As we rolled along, some of the trucks would split off from the main group. Finally, we were down to four trucks carrying two platoons. The hundred or so of us in the four trucks would stay together for the whole exercise. Any other units we encountered were the enemy. As soon as our trucks stopped, we were tactical and subject to attack at any time. Conceivably, the trucks could stop in the middle of an ambush site.

Abruptly, the trucks stopped. According to plan, we immediately jumped out of the backs of them and formed a 360-degree perimeter defense in anticipation of being attacked on the spot. We moved without a word; all commands were to be given silently using hand-and-arm signals. No one was to make unnecessary noises that might attract the enemy's attention. Once we had secured the area, the designated unit leader would signal for us to withdraw from defending the trucks and head for our rendezvous point. He had a map and had pinpointed its location about five miles deeper in the woods.

The rendezvous point was where we would form our base camp. From there we would operate our patrols, receive our ammo and food supplies, and maintain security. It was home, our safe haven. Its location had to be concealed from the enemy while we searched out and destroyed the base camps of the multiple enemy forces in the area.

Staring into the woods from a prone position with my M14 pressed against my shoulder and my finger on the trigger was a rush. Quickly, my eyes scanned the nearby trees and those at a distance. There was no movement. The quietness of the woods was a stark contrast to the idling truck engines behind me. The trucks would stay in our protective circle until we moved out. Then they would go wherever empty army trucks went until they returned to take us back to the barracks.

I was in the middle of the protective circle on the left-hand side of the truck column. Men were in identical prone positions all along that side of the trucks, as they no doubt were on the other side of the trucks. Now all we had to do was wait for the silent signal from on my left or right.

The afternoon sun felt good on my back. It took the chill off the cold spring air. Actually, it was pleasant just to rest on the roadside. A guy could easily drift off to sleep. As the minutes dragged on into five- and ten-minute clumps, I began to feel more and more comfortable. Heck, I had not been given any responsibilities on this leg of our exercise. I just needed to do what I was told. No one asked me to look at the maps and figure out where to go. I did not have to walk flank security, point, or bring up the rear. The radioman was with the unit leader. All I had to do was walk along in the middle of the column. Just keep my place in line and I would get a paycheck at the end of the month. Not bad, not bad at all, I was still lying there thinking when someone grabbed my foot. I twisted around with a start, ready to fight.

"Jerry! Something's wrong. I'm going on the other side of the trucks. We've been lying here for more than thirty minutes. That's too long," the guy holding my foot whispered in concern.

"Okay," came my muted response as I began sensing another foul-up. Damn, I thought, nothing ever seems to go right in this man's army.

I turned around at the sound of running footsteps behind me. The guy who had gone to check things out raced around from the back of the last truck.

"Shit, they're all gone. The other side of the trucks is deserted. There's nobody there. Someone screwed up. Somebody didn't pass the word to move out," he said with real strain in his voice.

Hell, we were lost before we even got started. This was an all-time first for me. On top of that, none of us had seen the map or had a clue as to where the base camp was. The unit leader had not included any of us in his inner circle. Half of his outfit was lost in the woods and he did not even know it. The lost half had no clue as to where the other half was headed. This was just the berries!

One of the guys wandered over to our group of bemoaners. He said there was a clear trail heading off into the woods on the unguarded side of the trucks. They must have taken that trail, he speculated. If they had gone any other way, they would have had to go through thick under-brush. We would have heard more than fifty men crashing through it. But none of us had. Besides, there were no broken branches, kicked up dirt, or any of the other signs you would expect to find in the aftermath of that many men using brute force to push their way through such dense brush. They had to have taken the trail. It was the most logical conclusion. One thing was certain: we could not stay there with the trucks for the whole exercise.

The decision was made. We would take off down the trail, walking as fast as we could. Quickly, we appointed someone to bring up the rear. There would be no flank security. We needed to move too fast for that. Everyone was to keep the man ahead of him and behind him within sight at all times. If anyone lost visual contact, the whole column was to stop immediately. We were not going to lose anybody else. No one wanted to be lost out here. There would be no food after we ate the one C-ration meal we had been issued. You could wander out here for a long time. None of us had the slightest clue as to where we were, where anyone else was, or how to get out of this wilderness. Yes sir, we were not going to lose anyone else.

It did not take long to break into a sweat. We were pushing ourselves hard. There was no complaining. One hour, then two, and still no contact with the fools who had left us. This was not good.

At last the word came back: we had caught up with the rear of the column. Great. What a relief! I passed the good news to the man behind me. Our pace slowed to a normal march. After another hour of group marching, the whole column took a break. I asked a couple of the guys who had been ahead of me if the unit leader was a little relieved to know he had gotten his unit back together.

"No, he never knew we were lost. Nobody knew we were lost. The point man said when he caught up with the last man in their column and told him that he was glad he had finally found him, the guy thought he was joking. He thought we had been there behind him ever since they left the trucks."

Now, isn't that wonderful, I thought. Gives me a lot of confidence in our ability to screw up. The next two weeks in the field might not be as much fun as I had anticipated.

That night I pulled the first four hours of guard duty. My partner and I both stayed awake in our make-believe foxhole. Theoretically, one of us would sleep for the first two hours and then pull guard duty for the rest of the shift. However, we were too hyped up. There was too much going on. Already, night patrols were being sent out into the darkness. We were given a secret sign and countersign to use to challenge anyone passing through our lines. The enemy could be anywhere. Our patrols were seeking him out, just as his patrols were looking for us. We had to protect the camp. In order to do that we had to know where the enemy was without letting him know where we were. All in all, it was a complicated business.

Sleep finally came. We were all tired. The march into base camp had lasted well into the hours of darkness. Once we reached the rendezvous point, confusion was total. Guys kept being moved around because our leaders were unable to define the camp's boundaries. We ate our cold C rations when we could. Sleeping bags and air mattresses were unrolled whenever you were assigned a spot—only to be gathered up and relocated because someone had changed his mind. A lot of personal equipment never to be found again after those fumbling moves in the darkness. The site will no doubt make some young archeologist's career a thousand years from now.

The night shadows held a lot of unhappiness. A cold front came through, forcing all those not moving around to get into their sleeping bags for warmth. Each personal misery was thought to be owned by that person and the few squad members with whom the darkness allowed him to communicate. No opportunity for organized discontent existed. The joint misery of the moment created a simple unity.

At 0400 hours everyone was awakened to be ready to repel a predawn attack. The enemy loved to attack during the predawn hours. That was the time when their foe, in this case us, was sleeping or the least alert. A surprise attack would catch us off guard. It seemed to me that there was a fundamental flaw with this assumption. Since we knew this was a strategy of the enemy's, we were ready when we should not be. If the army always did this, then the enemy would be catching on that we were always alert during the predawn hours and would never attack at that time. I would have gladly expressed this opinion to those in command if someone had sought it. They never did. One thing was certain: preparations to repel a predawn attack made you dog-tired for the rest of the day.

One more patrol. At first I had been pretty excited about going out on patrol. After two days of constantly moving on the trail, pulling guard duty at night, and then practicing predawn alerts, fatigue dominated my consciousness.

"Take ten. Smoke 'em if you got 'em," came the word down the line. I sat on a log, wrapped my arms around the barrel of my M14, and let my helmeted head rest in the impromptu cradle I had created with this tripod.

"Wake up! Wake up! The squad is moving out," Duke said, shaking me violently.

"Jeez, thanks," I replied, startled. I was shaken. I had never "fallen" asleep like this before. This was the first time in my life that I had "fallen" asleep. It was scary. I had heard neither the order to move out nor the noise of the men getting up and walking away. Hell, I could have awakened with everyone gone. If it had not been for Duke, that is what would have happened. This was not good. No doubt about it, you cannot close your eyes out here unless you intend to go to sleep.

Two of us are assigned to man a forward guard post. We are positioned about a thousand meters out from the base camp in a clump of bushes halfway down a sloping hill. There is some brush on it, but, comparatively speaking, it is open terrain. Five hundred yards or so farther down the hill is the start of a large tree-and-brush line that has obviously grown up on both sides of a creek. Our orders are to hold this position until relieved. It is unclear, however, just when we will be relieved. If we are attacked, we are to open fire with our rifles. Our firing will alert the guys back in the base camp. They will send us reinforcements.

My partner and I quickly decide that the OCS candidate who thought up those orders had not yet had the opportunity to serve a tour of duty in a forward guard post. We will haul ass the minute we see troops breaking from the tree line. Sure, we will fire our weapons; but that will simply be to make noise. If we waited for someone back in base camp to decide to rescue us from the stirred-up chaos an attack would produce, we would be hamburger in a cannibal's sandwich before they arrived. We would definitely be captured. We were not going to be captured.

The cold was numbing. I decided to build a Dakota fire. Fires were strictly forbidden. The smoke would give away your location. In Boy Scouts I had seen pictures of Dakota fires. They were supposed to be smokeless, I explained to my partner. He agreed to the plan. Neither of us had been warm for more than two days. Using my entrenching tool, I dug two small holes about a foot deep with three inches of dirt separating them. Each was a little more than six inches in circumference. At the bottom, I dug a tunnel connecting the two. Theoretically, one hole held the fire. The other provided a draft to feed the fire with oxygen. Since the fire got plenty of oxygen, it would not smoke. A pretty clever scheme. We could cover both holes if anyone came from base camp before they got to our post. Overall, a foolproof plan. The guys back in the base camp would probably forget we were even out here. They were so screwed up back there that it was pathetic. The disorganization was unbelievable. Every time they put a new candidate in charge, it just got worse. On top of that, the idiots would not listen to anyone's suggestions. Once appointed to command, an instant Napoleon was on hand.

After gathering some small dead twigs from nearby trees, I had my kindling. You could not use wood lying on the ground. It was soaked from the cold rain that fell at night. A few larger twigs on top of the kindling would make the fire last long enough to warm our hands quite comfortably.

At last, it was time to strike the match. The activity had given me new life. I was in control. Things were definitely on the upswing. "Goodbye misery, hello happiness," I think the Everly Brothers' song went. The match was struck. The twigs began to burn immediately.

A column of smoke quickly rose from the hole. Shit! Damn it to hell! It was rising to the sky. The smell of overly smoked fish seemed to surround us. Oh, God, we were going to be discovered. Actually, I had never built a Dakota fire before. It had worked so well in the camping magazine article I had read years ago. No time to debate the issue. We quickly poured out our canteens over the smoking mess. A brief burst of smoke and then it was out.

What was that sound? My partner heard it, too. Guys were talking. Several of them were talking. You could hear them moving on the other side of the creek bed. Judging by the sound of the moving brush, a lot of men were traveling parallel to the creek. Nobody told us about any patrols moving out or coming back through our sector. Maybe they were the enemy. So far, we had failed to find the enemy and the enemy had failed to find us.

Our orders were clear. We were to hold our position if attacked. This could be a bad situation. Fortunately, they kept on walking. You could hear the muted voices and the sound of brush against fatigues getting fainter and fainter until they were gone. A few hours later, we were relieved. Our relief knew nothing about past troop movements in our sector. We told them about the voices. They were not concerned. Back in base camp, our attempts to tell someone in charge about the troops moving to our front failed to get a response. We gave up, opened some C rations, ate, and crawled into the sack.

One of my 5th Platoon mates is assigned to be my squad leader. It is reassuring to be with someone I know. We have been assigned to go out on another patrol. Together we study the map. It is a real confidence builder to know where we are going and how to get back. There is comfort in that.

About two hours out, we hear the grinding of a truck engine. As we continue, it gets louder. Clearly, it is a stuck vehicle. The squad leader wants to stay clear of it. Heck, it could be a supply vehicle. Our rules of engagement say that we can capture it if it is not moving. The supplies would then be ours. What a coup that would be! To my amazement, he does not even want to take a look. Damn, I argue vigorously, we're *supposed* to capture the enemy and his supplies. What's the point of being out here if we continuously pass up opportunities?

"Okay, okay," the squad leader reluctantly conceded. "We'll sneak up to the creek bank and take a look-see."

Eight sets of eyes look at the vehicle stuck in the middle of the creek. Two enlisted men ankle-deep in mud and water are pushing on the back of it as the driver guns the engine, trying to rock it forward one more time. No use; it is badly stuck. My guess is they will have to unload the cases and cases of C rations before they will ever get it out.

"Let's go capture it," I volunteered gleefully.

"No, it could be a trap," the squad leader cautioned.

"Are you crazy? It's obvious they're cadre. They messed up and got stuck. They are no trap. This is a piece of cake," I shot back in exasperation.

"No, we could get in trouble. Besides, we can't carry all those cases back to base camp," he put forth as a lame excuse to do nothing.

"Well, let's go down there and offer to help push it out for two cases of C rations per man," I shot back.

"Look, I'm the squad leader, you're not. It's too risky. We're leaving it alone. Got me?" came his angry reply.

"Okay, I think you're wrong. You're squad leader, okay," I said, and that was that.

We withdrew from the creek bank and continued walking. The grinding of the truck's engine could still be heard as we moved a few hundred yards down the trail. I was on point.

Moving through the brush, what, to my surprise, lay before me but a sleeping soldier with his M14 at his side. Silently, I motioned for the others to be quiet and come forward. Curled up before us was Gene. Good-old-muddy-boots-in-the-wall-locker Gene. He must have been on guard duty expecting someone to come from the opposite direction of our arrival. It really did not make any difference. He was sound asleep. You got him from any direction you wanted to get him.

I poked him with the barrel of my rifle. He awoke with a start.

"Wh—what? Who? What?" he sputtered in surprise.

"Shhhh," I whispered, "any noise and I'll hit you with a butt stroke."

"Damn, Jerry," he said, sitting up and wiping the sleep from his eyes. "Take it easy. I'll be quiet. Shit, I'm in trouble now."

"You sure are. You're our prisoner now," I said as one of the guys picked up his rifle. "Where are the rest of your guys?"

"They must have left me here. I was the last guy in the patrol. We stopped to rest and I fell asleep. Don't take me prisoner. I'll be in a lot of trouble. I've got a map of where we were going. You can take that. It'll show you about where our base camp is. That ought to be enough," he said, raising his voice to a high-pitched whine.

"Look around the area," I said to the other guys. "He might be lying."

"Yes," echoed the squad leader, "that's a good idea."

As the guys spread out and poked the bushes, I asked the squad leader, "Well, what do you want to do?"

"Let's tie him up and get the hell out of here," came his quick reply.

Just as quickly, I shot back: "Look, he can't be here alone. His people have to be around. Let's make a sweeping search and see what's going on."

"No, we've accomplished enough on this patrol."

Damn, this guy was just lacking in a sense of adventure. We could really be on to something.

In anger I stated, "What's with you?"

"Listen, you're not running this squad. I am. You're going to do what you're told," he ordered, with fire in his eyes.

Our prisoner broke the deadlock. "Come on you guys, you've got everything from me you can get. Let me go."

"No, you're coming with us," the squad leader shot back.

I jumped in: "Hey, man, he's right. He's a good guy. Let's not make his life any more miserable than it is going to be. Leave him here."

"Okay, Jerry, but we'll tie him up. That way he can't run back and get some guys to attack us before we get out of here," the squad leader stated.

"Alright," I responded, "but tie him up so that he'll be able to get loose after a while." I did not want him to accidentally starve to death out there.

"Okay," the squad leader agreed as some of the guys went to work tying him up.

"Gee, thanks guys. I'll help you out sometime," Gene said with true conviction in his voice.

We left him there and started back to base camp. As we passed the creek on our return trip, the truck was still grinding away. The mud had not released it.

Back in the base camp, we presented the map, radio codes, and other documents to the unit leader. The 1st Platoon's Tac happened to be in base camp when we reported.

"It's about time somebody did something," the lieutenant snorted. "Everyone on this operation has been a bunch of pansies. You guys had better start being aggressive or we'll leave you out here another ten days."

The whole base camp is on the move. The word is that we have been in one spot too long. The enemy is bound to find us through a process of elimination. That logic makes sense, but no one had let me in on the big picture. As far as I can tell, the whole operation is one big mess. From the buildup the cadre had given us, I thought we would be in firefights almost every day. Either there are not very many candidates in the field, or none of us can find the others. Maybe there just is not supposed to be much contact between units on these field exercises. I just do not know. One thing *is* certain: you are lucky to get three or four hours of sleep a day. Everybody is making a hell of a lot of stupid mistakes. Before you move out from a rest stop, you have to make sure your buddies have not fallen asleep. The real enemy here is fatigue. Maybe that is the lesson the army wants us to learn.

POW! CRACK! POW, POW! RAT-TAT-TAT, TAT! POW! CRACK, CRACK! POW! We are being ambushed. Everyone drops, returns fire, and then starts crawling toward better cover. Damn! They are firing at us from a line of fallen trees more than a quarter of a mile away. You cannot even tell if you know any of them at this distance. Hell, they have botched the ambush. In a real situation, they would have hit only a few of us at best. Given our field of fire, we would have gotten that many or more of them. If I had been in charge of the ambush, I would have tracked our movement and sent men ahead to set up in a better location. I think they would have been better off never opening up on us at that far range. It was a botched ambush. Stimulating nonetheless, at least now we are all awake and alert. Our step has more spring as we pull away.

Another long night march to set up an ambush site. They say the tactical officers told the new platoon leader where and when one of the enemy patrols would be passing down a trail. I do not know the platoon leader at all. It does not make any difference. They all seem to be first-class screwups.

This is a long march to wherever we were going. The cold rain makes it miserable. Our rifles slung over our shoulders, barrels down, pokes the poncho up so that our feet and legs get soaked with the cold rain. Tonight they made me the automatic rifleman. The weight of the extra magazines of ammo seems to push the mud up higher on my boots. It really does not matter. The misery factor could not be much greater. Everything except my rifle and the ammo magazines is soaked. The butt of my M14 is just awkward enough to keep the poncho hood from fitting around my neck. Cold rain drips down my chest.

High on the side of a ridge, the column stops. This is it. I just cannot believe it. We are being ordered to go down the bank. We are going to ambush the enemy from the base of the bank. Sliding down the bank, I have to hang onto tree trunks to keep from falling. It is really steep.

About twenty yards from the dirt road cut into the side of the ridge, we stop. We are to lie prone on the hillside, in the mud, in the rain, and wait for the enemy.

There is no way to keep from sliding down the hillside unless you locked an arm around something. Hooking an arm around a sapling finally stops my slide. Hanging onto the little tree and trying to set up the bipod for my automatic M14 is awkward and difficult. The movements cover me with mud. Anything on me that had a hope of staying dry is history. At last the bipod is set and a magazine is inserted. My motions have removed what little leaf cover was on the bank. The slipperiness of the underlying ground would have brought pleasure to any mud-sliding otter. The slightest adjustment of my arm around the sapling causes me to slide in the mud as if I were a pendulum on a grandfather clock. From the little I could see, the men on either side of me are in the same difficulty. Without relaxing my hold on the tree, I try to loosen my extra magazines so I can pull them out and reload quickly.

Once the M14 opens up, it empties magazines within a couple of eye blinks. To pull off the ambush, they will need the firepower of the automatic weapon. Well, in this case, the *noise* of an automatic weapon.

There is no way in hell I would hit anyone in a real firefight from this position. Only if the enemy stretches his head up over the bank would I even see him. All he has to do is stand against the back edge of the road and I would never know he is there. He is in a better position to pick off me and the other guys than we are to hit him. Why, he would not even have to expose himself to our bullets. He could just roll hand grenades down the hillside. I simply cannot believe someone leading us could be as stupid as this guy is. If I knew who it was, I would exert the extra energy to go and tell him how bad an idea this is.

Since I do not know the guy, I just huddle up the best I can with my poncho and my weapon. Pulling the poncho completely over my head and bunching it around my face traps my breath. It feels nice and warm. This is a comfort. I close my eyes.

BAM! POW, POW! BAM, BAM! POW! POW! I wake up in the middle of it. Pushing my poncho back from my head and off the automatic rifle, I open up. *RAT-TAT-TacT! RATac-TacTa-TAT! TacTac*—Silence. It has jammed! My automatic weapon has jammed. Pulling the breech to my face as fast as I can, I see the problem. A round has failed to seat in the chamber properly. Immediately, I pull back on the bolt without loosening my grip on the sapling. The shell springs out. Then the bolt slams forward and chambers a round. It is ready. Returning to the firing position, I empty the magazine. There is no one to shoot at. I hear noises and shouts from above and the sound of return fire off to my right. There is nothing to see, no muzzle flashes, no bodies, no one stupid enough to stick his head over the edge of the road to see me firing at him. In short, if I had live rounds, I would be shooting the branches off trees. Maybe one of the falling branches would knock out one of the enemy. That is the best I could hope to accomplish.

"Cease fire! Cease fire!" comes the cry up and down the line. We had sprung the ambush. Now it was hours of marching in the dark and rain before we got back to base camp.

At last, we were able to crawl into our sleeping bags. Some poor guys were selected to pull perimeter guard. I was lucky that night. I could sleep. It would not be long before everyone would be awakened for the predawn alert. I struggled to get my boots off. They were soaked, as was everything else. I always used them as my pillow. That way I could guard them. In case of an emergency, they were immediately available to put on. No one wanted to be running blindly through the underbrush without his combat boots on.

My sleeping bag was nestled between a few fallen branches from the large tree I had propped my pack against. I placed my poncho over it as a rain cover. Removing my wet fatigues and bunching them under the bedding, I crawled into the sleeping bag and then pulled my weapon in with me. I was ready for a long winter's nap. My weapon would stay dry. No one would snatch it. All was secure. I pulled my head into the bag until my entire body was covered. The rhythm and heat of my breath quickly lulled me to sleep.

POW! POW, POW! CRACK, CRACK! POW! POW, POW! RAT-A-Tac-TacTa-TacTac! POW! met my ears amidst a barrage of shouts, hollers, and curses. We were under attack. The cloudy dawn light was just bright enough for me to make out people running everywhere as I peeked out from my sleeping bag. There was no way of telling the good guys from the bad guys. Weapons were firing in all directions. Everywhere I looked I saw muzzle flashes. The enemy was running through the camp whooping and hollering. They were clearly pleased with themselves. Lots of our guys were up and adding to the confusion. There did not appear to be a clear reason for me to give up the comfort of my sleeping bag. Rolling over, I pulled the top of the sleeping bag over my head just as a running fool stepped on me. He probably did not even bother to look down at what he had stepped on. My place between the fallen branches appeared to be well camouflaged. I fell asleep.

Around 1100 hours I awoke. What a treat it was to sleep in. The base camp was still in chaos. I felt great. Some of the guys had chased after the enemy into the woods. Many of them got lost. Guys were drifting in from all directions. No one seemed to be aware of or to care about my activities during this great morning. Seeing no need to tell anyone about my luxurious sleep, I did not.

Being one of the few not overwhelmed by sleep deprivation, I observed the lack of clear thinking displayed by my comrades. It was bad.

A candidate carrying an M60 machine gun poses in full camouflage.

Infantry officer candidates on maneuvers with full field gear.

Each decision and subsequent order seemed to be worse than the one before. Our field trip had started at a low point; it had just gotten worse
and worse. Fortunately, it was easy to outmaneuver the sleepwalking
student commanders. My last two days in the field were the least stressful of the whole operation.

Back in the barracks we learned that three guys from the 3d Platoon—
"Third Herd," as they called themselves—had gotten lost during the
two weeks in the field. They were still lost. It took several days to find
them. Helicopters and search teams were dispatched to look for them.
Thinking that they were still supposed to be tactical even though they
were lost and without food, they hid from the choppers and search teams.
    We also found out that at the time my squad captured Gene, he was
the leader of a platoon set up in an ambush site. We had been right in
the middle of all of them. While we stood there debating whether or not
we were going to take Gene prisoner or just tie him up and leave him,
his entire platoon was sound asleep in camouflaged positions all around
us. We never saw them. They never woke up while we were there.
    In just a week we would get an off-post weekend pass. Anna was fly-
ing into Columbus, Georgia. A month or so after that—during the last
part of May—we would become senior candidates.
    Once you made senior candidate, they stopped harassing you. The
basic and intermediate candidates had to salute you and obey your orders. You could harass them as you had been harassed earlier.
    You repainted your helmet liner from black to baby blue. Light blue
was the color of the infantry. You wore a neck scarf matching the soft
blue of the helmet liner. It was quite distinctive.
    There would be a big party on the Friday we turned into senior can-
didates. We were encouraged to bring our wives or girlfriends. A live
band was scheduled to play for us. Then we would get another off-post
weekend pass. Life would be good as a senior candidate.

The weekend I spent in Columbus with Anna was great. Several of the
guys came by the motel to meet her. She has such a beautiful smile. We
became resolved to the fact that I was not going to get out of infantry.
We decided to have a baby. I explained to her the army's dream sheet.
The army lets you request any assignment or training course you want.
That does not mean you will get it, it just means you can officially request it. Since we knew where infantry officers were going, there was no
point in asking for another assignment. I could, however, ask for more
training. Anna and I decided that I would put in for the Psychological

Warfare School at Fort Bragg, North Carolina. I thought I it might as well try to learn how the army attempted to use the principles of psychology.

Since the Kentucky high school Anna was teaching at would be in the middle of finals at the time of the senior candidate party, we agreed that she would not fly down that weekend. She was going to come to Fort Benning a week later to live off post. That was another benefit of being a senior candidate: you could live off post with your wife until graduation, although you still had to make all the formations.

CHAPTER 24

The Chipmunk

As we approached senior-candidate status, a lot of the guys started dropping out. Gene, of the dirty boots and the sleeping patrol, quit. I felt guilty about that. My anger over the dirty boots for that inspection had been out of line. Nor did my capturing him in the field help his case. Things were happening so fast you just did not have time to digest them. Fifth Platoon had done such a good job of staying together. We knew guys from the other platoons were dropping out. Our brag was that we were all going to graduate. It was a shock to see so many leaving in such a short time. We had come so far together. After Nat, Jim, and his cube mate left, we had stabilized. Now, in short order, we had lost more than 30 percent of our guys. It was unnerving. One day we were together and the next day we lost a lot of people. You did not get a chance to ask why or say good-bye. They were just gone.

Lieutenant McCook's 4th Platoon had given him a rabbit. The rabbit was dyed pink. He was very proud of that rabbit. As he stalked between the dining-hall tables, he would shout out about his pink rabbit. He boasted that the rabbit was not dyed pink. It was uniquely and naturally pink. When he sat at the officers' dining table, we could hear his booming voice telling all of the other tactical officers how much his platoon loved him. None of them had been so blessed, he pointed out. Lieutenant McCook seemed to lean the most heavily on Lieutenant Strauss, our tactical officer.

It was my misfortune to be walking past the officers' table after an evening meal when Lieutenant McCook was riding Lieutenant Strauss particularly hard.

"And my children love that pink rabbit," Lieutenant McCook bellowed to Lieutenant Strauss. "My Fourth Platoon men are the most thoughtful and considerate group of men in this man's army. They have balls. They can do anything, including smuggling a pink rabbit on post."

Out of the corner of my eye, I could see Lieutenant Strauss staring at me. I picked up my pace and began moving faster than my table-mates. They fell a step or two behind me, which caused me to stand out even more.

Lieutenant Strauss stood as he shouted at me, "I want my platoon morale officer, now!"

His command stopped me in midstride. I turned. With a brisk military march that included squaring all corners. I approached the officers' dining table. Whipping a crisp salute, I stopped in front of Lieutenant Strauss and said, "Sir, Candidate Morton reports, Sir!"

Returning my salute with irritation, Lieutenant Strauss spoke: "I want a chipmunk, Candidate. I want a live chipmunk presented to me at the senior-status party."

"They can't do it!" Lieutenant McCook shouted. "They'll come up with some stupid substitute. The whole bunch of them are wimps."

"I do *not* want some stuffed toy monkey with wood chips glued to its shoulders. I want a real, *live* chipmunk. Do—you—understand?" Lieutenant Strauss said, his voice rising and face reddening.

"Sir, yes, Sir!" I briskly replied.

"They'll botch it up for sure," Lieutenant McCook shouted, rocking back in his chair. "You'll see, Strauss. They'll wind up giving you some cheap substitute."

"Morton," Lieutenant Strauss said sharply, his eyes squinting at me in a piercing stare, "if you don't present me a *live* chipmunk at the party, all weekend passes for the platoon will be canceled."

Lieutenant McCook shouted out, "They'll get you a mouse and paint stripes on it!" He roared with laughter at his own imagery.

Lieutenant Strauss's face was red. "Get me my chipmunk."

"Sir, yes, Sir," I shot back.

"That's all," he said, dismissing me.

I saluted sharply. He returned the salute. As I walked out of the building, I noticed that talking in the mess hall had ceased. All eyes seemed to be on me as I marched out. Walking down the steps outside the mess hall, I could hear Lieutenant McCook's voice berating Lieutenant Strauss and telling him he had just better be prepared to cancel the passes because we could not do it.

Actually, I was thinking along the same lines as Lieutenant McCook. How were we going to come up with a live chipmunk? I had no idea where or how to capture one. The party was just three weeks off. Maybe chipmunks lived on post. If they did, they had stayed well hidden. I could not recall seeing one during my stay at Fort Benning. Heck, 4th Platoon had someone go to a pet shop and get a rabbit that had been dyed pink. We would just get someone to pick up a chipmunk at a pet store. This was a piece of cake. I felt good walking into the platoon bay.

As I walked into the bay, it was clear that everyone had gotten the word.

"What are you going to do, Jerry?" I was asked immediately.

"We'll get one from a pet shop," came my confident retort.

"That's right," interjected one of the guys. "My wife works at a big pet store in Atlanta. She can get us one and bring it to the party. You can present it there to Strauss, right in front of McCook."

"Good. Give her a call and set it up," I said, clapping him on the back. We were all in good spirits. This was an easy task. We would have fun presenting it in some dramatic manner. It would be great sport watching McCook eat his words.

Our daily routine of inspections, rushing to the mess hall, getting on trucks, attending classes in the buildings and in the field, coming back to the barracks, eating, studying, getting ready for the morning inspection, and lights-out continued uninterrupted.

About twelve days or so before the big party, the guy with the pet-store wife approached me. "We've got trouble, Jerry," he said grimly. "No pet store in America has a chipmunk. My wife has called pet stores all over the country trying to find one and have it shipped to her store. She's talked to pet stores in California, New York, New Orleans, everywhere. This is not the right time of year for chipmunks to be available."

Whoops! I had not expected this to be a problem. Guys were having their wives and girlfriends coming in from all over the country. They were heavily planning on an off-post weekend pass. This had the makings of a disaster.

We called a platoon meeting. It was tense. Ideas were flowing.

"Let's just get something that *looks* like a chipmunk," one fellow threw out.

"Hey, that's it!" another enthusiastically responded. "We'll get something that looks like one and dye it or change it to be a perfect match."

"My wife said a gerbil looks just like a chipmunk," the guy with the pet-store wife said. "It just doesn't have any stripes on its back."

"No, we can't put paint on anything," I shot back. "McCook already thought of that and cut us off. When he challenged Lieutenant Strauss, he said we would probably paint stripes on some mouse or something. Putting paint on some animal won't work."

"It worked for McCook's rabbit," came someone's quick reply.

"Yeah, but he won't admit that," another countered.

"We'll just have to capture our own chipmunk," another chimed in. "That's it. That's what we'll have to do."

This was getting out of hand. "Wait a minute. Does anyone know how to capture a chipmunk or where they live?" I asked.

Answers to my question came in from all sides.

"They live in trees."

"No, they don't, they live in holes in the ground in the woods."

"They live on golf courses."

That last one was too much. Laughing, I asked, "How do you know they live on golf courses?"

"I used to caddy at a golf course and they were a problem. They dug these little holes everywhere. I heard that the groundskeeper caught them by getting a long string and making a noose with it. He'd place the noose around the hole and then play out the string for ten yards or so. Lying on his stomach, he would patiently wait. When the chipmunk stuck his head up out of the hole, he'd jerk the string. The little sucker was caught."

"Well," I said with a sigh, "Does anyone know if there's a golf course on post?"

"I'm sure there is," said Scottie, "but they'd spot right off that you were in OCS and ask what you were doing there instead of out training."

"You're right," I replied, thinking of the slush-fund disaster. "We'll have to look for the chipmunk in the trees or the woods or somewhere else. Who should we get to go out and catch it?"

That question was met with silence.

Breaking the spell, Scottie spoke up: "It'll have to be you. We'll cover for you. You just take a day off and go catch one. Take a day when we're scheduled to be in classrooms all day. We'll cover for you. That way, you'll have all day to catch one."

It was agreed. Two days passed before we were slated for a full day of classroom instruction. I ducked out as the guys were loading onto the trucks.

Three or four miles from our barracks was a large stand of trees. I briskly walked to them. It was important to walk briskly. A candidate with a brisk walk was on a mission. Anyone seeing me would assume that I knew exactly where I was going and why. The probability was low that someone would stop me to ask why I was not with my unit. My pace would tell them I was on a mission that needed to be completed as quickly as possible so that I could rejoin my unit. As I walked, I pondered my mission. There was doubt in my mind as to where chipmunks really lived. Sure, I knew what one looked like; but I could not recall ever actually seeing one in the wild. It was ironic. I prided myself on knowing all about the woods. I had been a Boy Scout camp counselor for two summers outside Kenosha, Wisconsin. Furthermore, my recreational time had been spent hiking in the woods outside of Racine, Wisconsin, during junior high school. I was a camper. Yet, I did not know where a chipmunk lived—let alone how to capture one. This situation was pathetic. There was little chance I would succeed on this mission. It was a waste of time. I wanted to give up. Well, I had to try. All of the guys were depending on me. I had to do what I knew to do, even if it did not work.

In the woods, I looked for chipmunk signs, squirrel signs, any kind of signs. All I saw were a few sparrows. I looked for squirrel nests in the trees. Maybe chipmunks had nests in trees. It seemed logical that they would, although that did not fit with the golf course story. One tree had a hollow knothole in it about thirty feet off the ground. A chipmunk could be curled up sleeping in it at that very moment. No, that was a stupid thought. Nevertheless, I decided to climb up and see. If there was no chipmunk, I would at least be able to tell the guys that I had tried everything I could think of to do.

The tree was difficult to climb. I had to hug it and inch my way up. Right off, I could feel my highly polished brass belt buckle scraping against the bark. Damn! It would take hours and hours of polishing to get it back to inspection level. Looking down at my combat boots, I could see deep scrapes appearing on the toes and sides. My neatly starched fatigue pants and shirt were stained and wrinkled from the pushing and scraping up the tree trunk.

At last I was there. Regrettably, I could not see far enough into the knothole to tell if anything was in it. There was only one thing to do: I had to push with my hand down into it. I hoped I would grab onto something alive and jerk it out. Fat chance, I thought. It was more probable I would get my fingers bitten off. Then I would jerk my bleeding, mangled hand out so fast that I would lose my grip and fall out of the tree. This was just too stupid. I could not do it. But the guys were counting on me. If there was a chipmunk in this knothole and I let it get away, I could not live with myself. I was not going to let the guys down simply because of being bitten by some little unknown creature that probably did not exist in the first place.

Carefully, I slipped my hand into the hole. My fingers were spread to grab whatever brushed against them. Nothing, nothing but filth at the bottom of the hole. What a waste of time. What a waste of hours polishing my boots and belt buckle.

Finally, reaching the ground, I took a good look at myself. My uniform was a disaster. If a tactical officer stopped me now, I would be in a world of hurt. No OCS candidate would be allowed to walk around post looking as filthy as I did. He would attract immediate attention. Someone would want to know what was going on. I had to stay away from people.

For the rest of the day, I wandered through the grassy areas looking for chipmunk holes, nuts, nutshells—anything that might give me a hint that a chipmunk was near. There was no water to be had. Food was out of the question. The day was a disaster. Instead of the senior-status party being a time of celebration, it was going to be a disaster. I felt sorry for the guys and their wives, sweethearts, and dates and sorry for everything else.

I had to come up with something. If we could not get a live chipmunk to give to Lieutenant Strauss, we had to give him something he would accept. The gerbil would have to do. We could not paint it. He would know it was not a chipmunk. How could we make him *think* it was a chipmunk?

As I was hiding in the bushes near the barracks waiting for the trucks to bring the company back from classes, it came to me. This just might work. Crowd control was the key. Everyone would have to be amused and surprised at the same time. The high of the moment would have to carry Lieutenant Strauss into accepting my story. It would work if I could surprise everyone. I knew it could work. I hoped it would work. No, I was pretty sure it would work if I got the crowd with me. It might not. This was our best shot, so it just damn well *would* work. My mind was set. We would do it.

While the guys were off-loading from the trucks, I slipped in with them. We rushed up the stairwell together. Fifth Platoon knew from my appearance that I had tried. I explained that it was not possible to find a chipmunk. There were no arguments with me on that point.

"Are you sure a gerbil looks just like a chipmunk except that it has no stripes?" I asked the pet-store contact. "I've never seen one."

"Yes, I'm sure. It's the same size. The tail is short like a chipmunk's and it has the same short, brown fur," he reassured me.

"Then we'll use it. We'll say it's a chipmunk," I declared.

"That won't work," one of the guys interjected. "They'll know it's not a chipmunk unless you paint it or something."

"No," I said flatly. "We can't paint it. I'll present it as it is with a story. It will work. I've thought it all out. You guys just have to back me up. It's risky, but it's the best I can do with so little time." Turning back to the guy with the pet-store wife, I asked, "Can your wife have it here in a cage to present at the party?"

"Sure, that won't be a problem," he said confidently.

"Okay," I said, turning to Scottie. "You get me a kid's stuffed monkey with wood chips glued on its shoulders."

"Strauss said he wouldn't accept that," came Scottie's quick reply.

"I know. The stuffed monkey is just to set Strauss and the others up. They'll protest; then we'll bring in the gerbil with my story. Strauss will take the gerbil as a chipmunk."

"What's the whole setup, Jerry?" Scottie asked.

"I have to keep it a secret. The key to pulling this off is everybody's spontaneous reaction to the story. If they react the way I think they will, we've got us a live chipmunk. That's all I can say, okay?"

"Okay," said Scottie and several of the guys. Others nodded their heads in approval.

Everything was set for that evening. The gerbil had arrived. Scottie and crew had a stuffed monkey with a large wood chip glued on each shoulder. It looked a little as if it had lieutenant's bars on. I briefed the two crews. No one would mention the chipmunk at the party. At some point, Lieutenant Strauss or Lieutenant McCook would not be able to stand it any longer. One of them would call out for the chipmunk. The 5th Platoon guys and their dates would form a circle around them. That would bring everyone else into the circle to see what was going on. I would make my way to Lieutenant Strauss. After making a short speech, I would call for the chipmunk. Scottie and his crew would be hiding with the stuffed monkey so no one would see it beforehand. They would rush through the crowd and give it to me. I would present it to Strauss. He would say that it was unacceptable. I would tell him that I knew it was and that we had a live chipmunk to give him but I needed to tell him about it first. I would tell a long, involved story about it and then announce its presence. At that point, the other crew would come out of hiding and rush forward with the gerbil in its cage. They would give it to me and I would give it to the lieutenant. The rest was up to the crowd and Lieutenant Strauss. The key to pulling it off was not allowing anyone to see the stuffed monkey or the gerbil until I called for them. We were all agreed on the plan of action.

We were all in our green dress uniforms. The women were beautiful. We were all happy. The tactical officers were decked out in their dress-blue uniforms. They looked like cavalry officers in an old western movie. Every officer had a lovely woman with him—either his wife or a date. I did not know if any of them were married except for Lieutenant McCook. Captain Greene, our company commander, looked particularly sharp. He had a lot of medals. What a relief it was to finally be senior candidates!

The band was a slight disappointment. They looked as if they were all junior high school kids. Maybe they were in high school, but it was doubtful. Their parents had come with them. The accompanying adults sat in the background, but interacted with various band members frequently. For young people, they played fairly well. It really did not make any difference. We were all too happy to let bad music ruin the night.

I missed Anna. However, if she had been there, I would not have enjoyed her very much. I was having second thoughts about my plan, but I was determined not to show it. Its success depended upon the crowd's reaction. I had to have 5th Platoon feeling confident that the event was going to work wonderfully well. From all appearances, they were pumped.

The evening was wearing on. Clumps had formed throughout the room. Some couples were still dancing, but you knew the end was near. The officers and their ladies were in the far right corner of the hall. They sat together around a large table. Lieutenant Strauss and his lady were with Lieutenant McCook and his wife. They were talking.

Suddenly, Lieutenant Strauss shouted out, "Senior Candidate Morton, I want my chipmunk!"

On cue, the 5th Platoon guys and their ladies began converging on the officers' table. The other candidates in the company and their dates automatically converged on the same point. I had my stage.

Maneuvering through the crowd, I approached Lieutenant Strauss. "Sir, Fifth Platoon has been honored to receive your request. It gives all of us a great sense of responsibility to know that our very own tactical officer believes in his OCS candidates enough to make a special request of them. As future infantry officers, we saw your request as a test of our mettle under the most horrendous of conditions: live training to become second lieutenants."

The crowd laughed at that. A good sign, I thought, pausing for effect.

Lieutenant McCook shouted out: "He doesn't have one. I knew they couldn't do it, I knew—"

Cutting him off, I continued, "And in partial fulfillment of your noble request here is your *chip—munk!*" With a wave of my hand, I turned to face the crowd as Scottie and Mel made their way to me, holding the stuffed monkey high in the air for all to see.

A roar of laughter came from the crowd as Lieutenant Strauss shouted out: "I *told* you no stuffed monkey. I *told* you that wouldn't do."

Even as he was speaking, Lieutenant McCook's voice rose above the laughter. "I knew it!" he said. "They were never going to do it. I told you, Ken. Didn't I tell you?"

I held up my hand for silence and spoke in a loud, commanding voice. "Yes, we *knew* that a stuffed monkey with chips on its shoulders would be unacceptable." A hush came over the crowd as I continued. "We just wanted you to know that less-honorable candidates would try to pull such a cruel and trite hoax on you. The men of Fifth Platoon are men of honor. Only a very special chipmunk would do for the tactical officer of the finest of the men who carry the spirit of the bayonet in their hearts. Sir, we have a heroic chipmunk to present to you. Because you are so committed to helping us become the best infantry officers that we could possibly be, you may have missed the newspaper stories about our chipmunk. Being an American chipmunk, he volunteered to join the U.S. Army on one condition—that he be sent to Vietnam."

The crowd cheered good-naturedly at that line. They were with me.

I went on with greater enthusiasm. I was into it. Without thinking, I moved into a slight crouch as I spoke. "He went to Vietnam as a private first class, a P-F-C, thanks to his dedication, good training, and the army's early promotion policy."

A roar of laughter came from the crowd. Lieutenant Strauss was beaming with joy. Even Lieutenant McCook was smiling.

"Quickly, the leadership qualities of your chipmunk showed themselves. He became a buck sergeant, leading his squad into numerous firefights. In the heat of one particularly ferocious battle, your chipmunk became inadvertently separated from his unit. Being a good soldier, he remained tactical."

Another burst of laughter erupted with the guys from 3d Platoon leading it.

In a soft, hushed voice that caused the audience to lean forward to hear, I said: "Your chipmunk found himself on a lonely trail deep in the jungle. He felt the ground begin to vibrate—faintly at first, then more

Candidates and their ladies dance at the party honoring their promotion to senior-candidate status.

Members of the 5th Platoon who achieved senior-candidate status. The author is first on the left in the second row.

and more violently. He feared for his life but stood his ground, an infantryman through and through. To his amazement, a long line of elephants burst around a bend in the trail. They were carrying supplies for the Vietcong down the Ho Chi Minh Trail. Your chipmunk knew those supplies could not be allowed to reach the enemy. Single-pawedly he stood his ground. When the elephants saw this courageous soul defiantly standing in front of them, they panicked. They broke and ran every which way. He had routed the elephants."

The crowd roared in a spontaneous cheer.

I held my hands up for silence. "I know you were just too busy training us to see him honored in the New York ticker-tape parade our grateful country gave this true hero. President Lyndon B. Johnson had him brought to the White House to receive the Medal of Honor. President Johnson told him that our grateful nation wished to give him anything he wanted for displaying such courage in the face of the enemy. Your heroic but humble chipmunk stood at attention, looked President Johnson straight in the eye, and said, "There is just one thing I want to do for my country. I want to give up my sergeant's stripes and attend Infantry Officer Candidate School with Lieutenant Strauss as my tactical officer, Mr. President." Lieutenant Strauss, allow me to present this heroic chipmunk to you," I concluded, raising my hands and motioning to the guys in back of the crowd as they uncontrollably cheered, laughed, and hollered.

The guys rushed the cage with the gerbil forward and placed it on the table directly in front of Lieutenant Strauss. The crowd was in pandemonium. The cheering and laughter went on and on.

With a huge grin on his face and looking down at the gerbil, Lieutenant Strauss sprang to his feet and grandly declared: "It *is* a chipmunk! A heroic chipmunk. Gentlemen, I accept this chipmunk in the spirit in which it arrived."

Another wave of cheers rose above the ongoing cheers and laughter. Hardly noticeable in the noise was Lieutenant McCook bellowing, "It's not a chipmunk! It's *not!*"

The weekend pass was ours.

CHAPTER 25

Experienced Soldiers

THE SENIOR-STATUS party had been a real success. I stayed in the barracks that weekend. No one harassed us. It was pleasant.

Sunday afternoon, I learned that Lieutenant Strauss had not taken the gerbil home.

"He told me to take care of it," the candidate with the pet-store wife said. "What should we do with it?"

"Give it back to your wife," I quickly replied.

"She's already gone back to Atlanta."

"Well, let's keep it in the crawl space under the barracks until we can figure out something."

"Okay," he agreed.

The week started with the same routine. We had to get ready for morning inspection, put on our clean, starched fatigues with the OCS brass positioned just right. No smudges on our gleaming belt buckles or spit-shined boots. It was all routine. We did those chores without thinking.

What was new was that nobody was on our case. None of the tactical officers shouted. No one was dropped for push-ups. Junior candidates eyeballed us with clear apprehension and traces of fear. Our training schedule was not as rigorous. We were getting back earlier.

During breakfast late in the first week of our senior candidacy, the gerbil's keeper approached me in a state of agitation. Spitting out his words, he said: "When Lieutenant Strauss unlocked his office door this morning, he found our gerbil. It was dead. Someone had put a hangman's noose around its neck and hung it from the ceiling light."

Damn! I thought. I should have anticipated something like this. I should have known not to stay with the temporary solution for housing the animal as long as we did.

He went on, "The word is that some guys from Fourth Platoon did it."

"That figures," I commented. "McCook was bent way out of shape that we had succeeded."

"What do you think we ought to do about it?"

"We'd better just let it go."

"Yeah, I guess you're right," he said.

Anna drove down from Kentucky. One of the guy's wives had helped us find a little place to rent. It was not far from post. We had just a few more weeks until graduation. She arrived on a weekend. By Sunday afternoon, we were settled in. There was not much unpacking to do. She left a lot of our belongings up there. We knew that I would get orders to go somewhere else. Whether she could come with me to my new assignment or not was an unknown. We were just grabbing what moments we could to be together.

I still had to maintain my cubicle space in the barracks as if I lived there. All of the inspections, formations, and so forth had to be met. I could go to be with her only at night and on the weekends.

Actually, going home to her meant lost sleep. Normally, when they called for lights-out, I would just crawl into my bunk. Now, I would drive to our little house. We would talk about the day, and then I would go to bed. I had to get up a lot earlier in the morning to be at the barracks to do my share of the work for the morning inspections before the company went to breakfast. I lost a lot of sleep. I was glad to do it.

Scottie approached me at my cubicle desk in an excited state. "Hey, some new OCS candidates have just arrived in one of the barracks about a mile away. A bunch of the guys are going down to let them know what senior candidates are all about. Come on. Let's go."

"No, I don't want to do that," I said with a slight smile.

"Ah, come on. It will be fun," he said enthusiastically. "We won't be too hard on them."

Calmly I smiled and shrugged. "No, I don't want to do that."

"Okay, but we'll tell you all about it, " he said, running down the hallway.

We got off the trucks near the rifle range. Our weapons had been obtained from the armory. The army was going to have us practice our marksmanship this morning. Shouldering arms, the company marched toward the range in picture-book style. There was no eyeballing. Everyone was in perfect step. Our feet were in perfect timing. They made a soft, strong drumbeat on the pavement and gravel. Each step was the same measured length; our arms swung up the same number of inches in perfect unison with one another. No one concentrated on creating this perfection. It was habit. We did it naturally. It would have been unnatural if we had done anything else. A quiet pride was in us. When the command came to halt, all six platoons stopped as if we were one body.

"Ri-ight—*face!*" came the command.

Two hundred men pivoted in unison and stood at silent attention. We changed from being a column of marching men to a long line, a long line that was four rows deep. We were lean. We were sharp in the skin-hugging, tailored fatigues with the heavily starched creases.

"Or-der—*arms!*" Like a machine, two hundred rifles moved to their positions, snugly pressed against the length of each man's right leg while the man remained standing at rigid attention looking straight ahead into nothingness.

Silence fell over the company as we awaited the next order. It would be to stack arms. In those brief seconds of anticipation, a new sound approached the silent company. A column of about fifty men was approaching the company of two hundred. They were marching; rather, they were walking and talking in a loose formation on the gravel road directly in front of the silent two hundred. Their path would take them into the exact spot where the first row of senior candidates would set their tripods of stacked rifles.

As the group came closer, the discord of their feet and the sound of their muted voices greeted our ears. They were trying to march in a formation. You could tell that because the group had a front and a rear with four mixed-up columns within the semisquare mass of moving men.

"Halt!" commanded the first lieutenant walking beside the formation. The group was directly in front of me.

Instead of coming to a halt, the column kind of slowed to a milling of movement in place as the individuals continued to talk among themselves. Several were reacting from either bumping into the man in front of them or being bumped by the ones behind them.

"Ah, come on you guys, stop," pleaded the lieutenant.

Some movement did diminish. Since they were directly in front of me, I could see that they were all officers. Second lieutenants, first lieutenants, and a few captains made up their ranks. They all looked very young. Perhaps they were ROTC graduates going on active duty. Another possibility was that they were National Guard officers in for some summer training.

"Ri-ight—*face!*" the lieutenant shouted.

Most of the officers in the platoon made a swinging motion with their bodies to the right. There was little precision or unison in the movement. Several of the young officers were confused as to which way was their right or left. They turned in the opposite direction. Seeing their error, they corrected the turning in various states of partial turns and urgency. After several seconds of confusion, the entire group was facing the rifle range. We looked directly into the rear of their ranks. Talking within that formation never came to a complete halt. This caused a slight but continuous degree of movement within the formation as people leaned to talk to each other and to hear what was being said.

The longer they stood in front of us, the greater grew the number of them engaged in talking. My OCS classmates and I stood at rigid attention in complete silence. The other group's leader spoke to someone at the head of the group. After a minute or two, he turned and faced his group. "Left—*face!*" he ordered.

The platoon of officers displayed more confusion. Fewer of them knew their left side than had known their right side.

"Forward—march," the lieutenant said in a small voice.

Obediently, the group shuffled down the road in the same disorganized manner in which it had arrived.

"Hey, if you're driving off post, would you mind dropping something off at Lieutenant Stanton's house?" a guy from 6th Platoon asked.

"Sure, I'd be glad to," I told him.

Lieutenant Stanton was 6th Platoon's tactical officer. He seemed to be an okay guy. At least, he never bothered the guys in 5th Platoon very much. I did not mind having to deal with him.

When I knocked on his door, an attractive young woman opened it.

"Ma'am, I'm here to deliver some papers to Lieutenant Stanton."

"Come on in, Candidate!" came the lieutenant's booming voice from within the house.

The woman graciously stepped back from the doorway to allow me to enter.

Sitting in an easy chair with a soda in one hand, Lieutenant Stanton smiled as I approached.

Holding out a large folder, I said, "Sir, Candidate Jones asked me to deliver this to you."

Taking the folder, he looked up at me as the woman sat down on the end of the couch near his chair. Opening the folder, he said, "I suppose you and the other men are wondering what the tactical officers think of your OCS class."

Without reflecting, I responded, "No, Sir, it never occurred to me to think about that."

He seemed a little deflated by my response.

"Well, just what do you want out of the army?" he asked, staring me straight in the eye.

"I don't want anything, Sir. I want to serve my time and go back to do my internship in school psychology. I just want to help children." I felt a little sheepish after that last comment.

He thanked me for bringing him the folder. I left.

At last our orders were in. The company first sergeant called us into his office, we walked up to his desk, and he handed them to us. We all were excited. This was it. My orders said I would be staying at Fort Benning for Airborne School and then going to the John F. Kennedy Special Warfare Center, Fort Bragg, North Carolina, to attend the nine-week Psychological Warfare Operations Course.

Jump school would start a week after graduation. I had not put in for airborne, but it was all right. Anna and I could stay at Benning for another three weeks. I did not know if we would be allowed to live together while I was going through airborne training. In any case, they had granted my request to attend Psychological Warfare School. I would get my chance to learn what the army did in that area. Maybe it would help me in my graduate program when I got out.

Scottie and Mel both got orders to jump school, too. We were going to be in the same class. They had put in for Special Forces training and been accepted. They would also be at Fort Bragg. We hoped we would have a chance to get together at the Special Warfare Center. Who knew what the army would or would not let us do?

We had a lot of details to take care of as graduation approached. We had to buy our dress blues and get fitted in time for the uniform to be tailored so we would look perfect at the graduation ceremony. We needed to learn about the government's life insurance policy and decide if we wanted to buy it. Several of the guys bought insurance with the idea of naming each other as the beneficiaries. That way, they joked, they would make money off the other guy.

Less than a week before graduation day—June 26, 1967—I was called to the first sergeant's office. My orders had been changed. The new orders, dated June 21, superseded my previous orders. I was not going to jump school after all. Instead, I was to take fifteen days of annual leave upon graduation and then report to Fort Bragg on July 13. The orders further stated: "Indiv svc to be util by Comdt HQ USA JFK Cen for Sp Warfare Ft Bragg NC prior to beginning of crs." The course, "Psy War Opns (3A-9305)" began on July 16. At least I thought the course number was 3A-9305. Why did the commandant of the JFK Center for Special Warfare want me for temporary duty (TDY) for three days?

I did not know what my orders meant. Scottie and Mel could not make sense of them either. Our best guess was that, since I had not volunteered for jump school, the army had decided to take me out of it and give me some leave time. We guessed that because the class was scheduled to start just three days after my arrival, the army probably would not assign me to do much. Something still did not sound right to me. Well, I did not have much time to speculate on what the orders meant. Other things would keep me busy.

The change in orders meant that Anna and I would have to move immediately. I had thought I had Anna settled in for the duration of jump school. Now we had to readjust quickly. The details of planning the move to Fort Bragg, leaving the house in Columbus, loading the car, arriving at Fort Bragg, finding a place to live, and then unpacking, all within fifteen days, would be difficult. At least we would be together; we were grateful for that. I was surprised to find a degree of regret about not being allowed to attend jump school. All the way back to graduation day in basic training, I had seen that the army could and would change orders on a moment's notice. It did not consult with the recipient of those orders before the individual received them. That was the army way.

The full-bird colonel addressing our graduation class was about to conclude his speech:

> Now, I know that the majority of you came straight out of college into the army and OCS. You completed eight weeks of basic training, eight weeks of advanced infantry training, and now six months of Infantry Officer Candidate School. You have been in the army for ten months and some-odd days. You feel extremely inexperienced. You think that you still haven't even learned what the army is all about, let alone how to lead men in combat. Well, I've got news for you: When you average all of the time in service of every man in the army right now, today, from raw recruit to

colonels like me, the average time a soldier has been in the army is nine months. So you see, you already have more time in service than the average soldier.

Shortly thereafter, I was commissioned as an infantry second lieutenant in the U.S. Army.

Second Lieutenant Jerry
Morton's graduation photo.

Senior officer candidates pass in review during their graduation parade.

Senior officer candidates stand at parade rest during their graduation ceremony.

Epilogue

W HEN I REPORTED to the commandant's office at the JFK Center for Special Warfare at Fort Bragg, North Carolina, I was taken to see a full colonel. The colonel greeted me pleasantly and informed me that the Psychological Warfare School was expanding its program and creating a staff officer's course in psychological warfare. I was being assigned as a psychology instructor at the Psychological Warfare School. I was to create several hours of instruction for the staff officers' course as well as for other courses. The staff officers' course would begin in approximately three weeks. He realized that I had a lot to do in a short period of time, so he would not keep me any longer. The senior command at the Psychological Warfare School wanted to meet with me as soon as I left the colonel's office.

I remained with the Psychological Warfare School for the full two years of my military obligation. The citation for the Army Commendation Medal I was awarded reads, in part: "He was required to review, revise, and in many instances develop and actually present some 1,350 hours of instruction annually." On three occasions during that time, I received orders to go to Vietnam. The Psychological Warfare School was able to get those orders changed so that they could keep me as an instructor. The senior staff officers at the school went out of their way to provide me with relevant information concerning psychological warfare. They taught me a great deal. I gained a better understanding about why people fight in wars, why they change sides, and how important individual belief systems are in determining the way individuals change when under stress.

Working with the school's staff taught me another important lesson: many of the people in the U.S. Army are dedicated professionals with a strong sense of working for the benefit of mankind. This was particularly evident in the stated purpose for creating the Special Forces and articulated well in the book *Shadow Warriors,* by Tom Clancy and re-tired general Carl Stiner.

Ironically, I was one of the instructors for the psychological warfare class I had been assigned to attend after graduating from OCS. Several of my OCS classmates thus were students of mine. Scottie Newsome and Mel Wolfe (pseudonyms) were in the Special Forces officers' class for which I taught classes. We were surprised to see one another in the classroom. Even more astonishing to me was how many old childhood friends from the many public schools I had attended were now in the army taking my courses.

In the second year of my tour of duty, I began to run into a few of my OCS classmates as they returned from their tours in Vietnam. Most of them had been seriously wounded and were in the recovery process. They all had remarkable stories to tell. Sadly, I never knew what happened to the vast majority of them. Rumor had it that almost all of them had been seriously wounded or killed in combat. One had disappeared.

The immediacy of our world and the next assignment was all that occupied our minds. All of the good people I had known in basic training, AIT, Infantry OCS, and at the Special Warfare Center were known in the moment of the experience only. I would like to hear from them. Perhaps a few of them will read this book and we can reconnect. In a sense, their continued adventures are mine as well.

At that time, citizen soldiers had a seven-year military obligation. When you completed your active duty tour, you were transferred to the army reserve. I still had four years of my military obligation left when I completed my active service. My military occupational specialty (MOS) was declared to be a critical one, which meant that I could be called back to active duty on short notice. It also meant that I did not have to join an army reserve unit. I did not have to attend army reserve meetings nor was I ever called back.

Upon leaving the army I became the only school psychologist serving seven all-black schools as they were being integrated. What I had learned in the army about the change process and how people and their institutions react under stress enabled me to help ease some of the tensions for the children, the school staffs, and the community. After two years of the experience, I returned to graduate school for two years to complete my doctorate in school psychology. I was able to complete my degree in record time primarily because of what I had learned from my service in the army. I then continued my professional career as a school psychologist in both the public school systems and the university setting.

Anna and I have been married for thirty-nine years and have two children and one grandchild.

ISBN 1-58544-359-X